Bob Whyte read the ⸻ ⸻ege, Oxford, 1964-67, and ⸻ went to Cuddesdon College, during which time he served as Student President of the Student Christian Movement. Ordained a deacon in the Church of England in 1969, he served his first curacy in Blackheath, until in 1972 he and his wife, Maggi, began running a Community Education Centre of the SCM in Lewisham. It was also in 1972 that they made their first visit to China, and Bob was invited to serve on the China Study Project Committee. This was an ecumenical project sponsored by the Archbishops' China Appeal Fund, members of the Conference for World Mission of the British Council of Churches and the Catholic Institute for International Relations.

Ten years later Mr Whyte accompanied a seven-strong delegation from the recently formed China Christian Council around Britain and Ireland, and in 1983 he was a member of the BCC delegation to China, led by the Archbishop of Canterbury. He has made annual visits to China for several weeks from 1980 onwards.

He and his wife have two daughters, and his interests include natural history, walking and English literature.

UNFINISHED ENCOUNTER

China and Christianity

BOB WHYTE

Foreword by
the Archbishop of Canterbury

Collins
FOUNT PAPERBACKS

First published by Fount Paperbacks, London, in 1988
Copyright © Bob Whyte 1988
Made and printed in Great Britain by
William Collins Sons & Co. Ltd, Glasgow

For
David and Alison Paton

CONTENTS

Foreword: The Archbishop of Canterbury,
  Dr Robert Runcie   13

Preface   15
Notes on Chinese Spelling and Pronunciation   17
Abbreviations   18
Journal References   19
Acknowledgements   20
Introduction   21

I   First Contacts: Seventh to
     Fourteenth Centuries   31
       The First Nestorian Mission   33
       Christianity under the Mongols   40
       The Franciscan Mission   43

II The Jesuit Mission: 1583-1721   49
       Late Ming China   51
       European Background   53
       Matteo Ricci and the Origins
         of the Jesuit Mission   58
       The Growth of the Church   63
       The Early Qing Dynasty   67
       The Confucian/Christian Debate   71

III To Save Souls: 1721-1860   79
       The Catholic Church: Persecution
         and Survival 1723-1839   79
       Theology and Culture   83
       Dynastic Decline and Social Revolt   93

The First Protestants in China   95
The Taiping Heavenly Kingdom   103
Treaty Port Protestants and
    Catholic Counter-Reformation   106

IV   The Opium of the People: 1860-1912   113
The Tongzhi Restoration   114
Catholic Missions 1860-1900   115
Protestant Missions to 1900   117
The Anti-Christian Movement   129
Christian Social Concern   131
The Rise of Nationalism   137

V   Facing The Revolution: 1912-49   142
The Years of Turmoil 1912-27   142
The Protestant Church in Crisis 1921-27   151
Chinese Catholics 1912-27   159
The Nanjing Years 1927-37   164
Chinese Protestants: Evangelists
    and Theologians   174
The Struggle for China 1945-49   184

VI   The Tide of History: 1949-57   194
The Churches in 1949   197
The Challenge of Marxism   201
Communism, Nationalism
    and United Front   205
The End of the Missionary Era   219
The Three Self Patriotic Movement   228
Protestant Church Life   234
The Catholic Church and the
    United Front   245

VII   The Years of Conflict: 1957-69   255
The Socialist High Tide   255

The Protestant Scene 1957-61   262
Theological Reflection Since 1949   272
Chinese Catholics 1957-62   276 —
The Prelude to the Cultural Revolution   282
The Debate on the Nature of Religion   285
The Great Proletarian Cultural Revolution   288
A Sort of Calm   298

VIII A Hidden Seed: 1970-80   305
      The Hopeless Years 1970-76   305 —
      The Rebirth of Christianity   316
      Chinese Politics and Culure 1976-80   322
      The Growth of the Church 1976-80   337 —
      Research into Religion   354

IX   Out of the Shadows: 1981-87   372
     The Political Context 1981-87   375
     Religious Policy   379 —
     The Life of the Protestant Church   394
        Church Organization   394
        Home Meetings   400
        Continuing Problems   406
        Outside Influences   407
        The Case of Lin Xiangao   409
        The Numbers of Christians   410
        Christianity and Folk Religion   411
        The Meaning of Indigenization   415
        Christian Witness in Contemporary
          China   416
        The Amity Foundation   420
        Overseas Relations   422
        A Brief Survey of Protestant Activity
          in China   426
        Leadership Training   431
        Christian Literature   435

The Fourth National Christian
Conference 436
The Catholic Church 1981-87 437
Catholics and the Catholic Patriotic
Association 437
Chinese Catholics and Rome 439
Catholic Life 1981-87 446
Theological Training 450
Fourth National Catholic Conference 451

X Unfinished Encounter 459
Faith and Culture in China 461
The Form of Western Theology 463
Dualism and Materialism 467
A Time of Reckoning 470
Contemporary Chinese Theological
Thought 476

Appendices
1. Time Line 487
2. Major Meetings of the Chinese Communist Party
and National People's Congress 1949-86 494
3. Important National Christian Meetings 1950-86 496
4. Protestant Leaders in 1986 497
5. Chinese Catholic Bishops 499
6. Theological Seminaries in China 501
7. Number of Protestant Christians 503

Bibliography 505
Index 517

MAPS OF CHINA

Modern China
The Silk Road and China in the Tang Dynasty
The Mongol Empire
China in the Time of the Jesuits (Ming Dynasty)

FOREWORD

I have known Bob Whyte for twenty years, since he was at Cuddesdon, where I was at the time Principal, and have followed with great interest his work as Project Officer for the China Study Project. The advice and help given by him and his wife Maggi in preparing and following up my two all-too-brief visits to China were most valuable.

However, it is not only for personal reasons that I commend *Unfinished Encounter*. In a way that is always scholarly but never heavy, the author surveys the various attempts to extend the Christian Church into China, beginning with the Nestorians in the seventh century A.D., and, in one important sense at least, coming to an end in 1949. It is most valuable that he has shown that whether it is Eastern Christians or Western Catholics and Protestants, all have had to deal with the obstacle that foreignness has traditionally presented to the *cultural gap* mind and heart of China.

In the second half of the book he takes the missionary story beyond 1949, and chronicles, mainly from Chinese sources, the joys and sorrows of this "unfinished encounter" as far as the middle of 1987. There is so far as I know no other single book that deals comprehensively but concisely with this often complicated story.

But there is a second reason why I hope this book will be widely read and pondered. Unlike the Muslim, Hindu and Buddhist worlds, China expresses its deepest insights through art and poetry, friendship and feasting, rather than religion. It is in a sense the original secular society. As, in the decades and centuries to come, Chinese Christians explore the questions which their culture raises for faith, we may confidently expect that they will have much to teach us. I find it of great significance that in his last chapter Bob Whyte finds himself drawn to the insights of the early Eastern Fathers and other Christian writers in the mystical tradition, represented in our own history by Julian of Norwich and others.

This book, therefore, is not only an up-to-date account of the history of Christianity in China, but also a contribution to the future. It is the fruit of ten and more years of listening to, and thinking about, what the Chinese have to say to one another and to the rest of the world. I hope that, as we wrestle with the problems of secularization in Europe and North America, we shall pay attention to the Chinese experience. For those with ears to hear, it speaks to our own hopes and dilemmas. I commend this book most warmly.

PREFACE

This book would not have been possible without the co-operation of many people too numerous to name. I am privileged to have been able to serve as the Project Officer of the China Study Project of the British Council of Churches from 1975 to 1986, a post that provided me with the opportunity to follow closely developments in China in a most exciting period. I am deeply indebted to many Chinese friends for the warmth of their friendship and the sharing of their hopes and concerns. I think especially of friends in Beijing, Shanghai, Tianjin, Nanjing and in Fuzhou, Xiamen and Zhangzhou. I would like to think that they will find in this book something of their story. Inevitably, they will find errors both of fact and of judgement, and it was with a sense of my own presumption that I set about the task of writing. My purpose has been to present to British readers the remarkable story of Christianity in China, in the light of what I have understood to be the main lessons to be learnt from the experience of the past forty years. I believe that I have been guided by the insights and reflections of my Chinese colleagues, but I also know that no outsider can faithfully reflect their feelings or portray the range and depth of their experience. In writing the book I have become very much aware of the immense importance of Y.T. Wu and subsequently of Bishop K.H. Ting within the whole story of post-Liberation Protestant Christianity in China. Bishop Ting's wisdom and diplomatic skill has impressed me time and again. Especially in the years after 1978, it is he who has offered guidance and teaching, having seen most clearly the opportunities for Christians and the constraints of time and circumstance. He has done so out of a profound understanding of his own culture and also of Christian history and tradition.

My thanks are also due especially to David Paton, whose

friendship, experience and wisdom have taught me more than I can ever fully acknowledge. I remain amazed at the prophetic insights of his book *Christian Missions and the Judgement of God* published in 1953. In 1987 his detailed advice about each chapter has been an essential stage in the writing of the book. My wife Maggi's careful critique has also been invaluable, not least because for long years we have shared our love for China and her people, and have so many Chinese friends in common.

Two other people to whom I am deeply indebted are Philip Wickeri and George Hood. Both have offered me helpful perspectives over the years, and in their own respective writings have provided essential tools for my task. Edmond Tang of Pro Mundi Vita has helped me to understand something of the Catholic situation in China, although my conclusions are entirely my own. I am also indebted to Deng Zhaoming, the Editor of *Bridge,* and to the staff of the Tao Fong Shan Ecumenical Centre in Hong Kong for the information they have provided over the years. I am indebted to Brynmor Price and Lawrie Breen whose translation work on behalf of the China Study Project I have drawn upon extensively.

I must also express my thanks to the members of the China Study Project Committee and the Sponsoring Bodies of the Project for making it possible for me to spend seven months in writing the book, especially to Ian Holdcroft, Jim Sutton and Donald Elliott. I should like to record my appreciation for grants to the Church Missionary Society, the United Society for the Propagation of the Gospel, the Society of Friends, the Methodist Church Overseas Division, the Barbour Trust for China Mission, the Pollock Trust and the Archbishop of Canterbury, Dr Robert Runcie. My thanks also go to St Paul's Church, Rusthall, Tunbridge Wells for providing us with a place to live while writing. And to Jessica and Imogen for putting up with a strangely preoccupied father!

Finally, I am grateful to my Editor, Sarah Baird-Smith, who in an act of faith commissioned the book, and who patiently allowed it to grow and grow, while offering much helpful advice.

A NOTE ON CHINESE SPELLING

The system for romanizing Chinese characters known as *pinyin* has been employed throughout this book. The system is used exclusively in China, and more and more generally elsewhere. A few place names have not been put into *pinyin*, notably Hong Kong, Macao, Inner Mongolia and Tibet. "Manchuria" is sometimes used for North-east China.

All personal names are in *pinyin*, with the exception of a few known universally in other forms such as Sun Yat-sen and Chiang Kai-shek. In writing about Christian history in China a particular problem arises with a number of Christian leaders who are traditionally known by non-standard romanized names. Usually in these cases I retain the non-standard form, giving the *pinyin* form also in the first instance and in the index. The most notable cases are Y.T. Wu, T.C. Chao and Watchman Nee. I also retain the form K.H. Ting for Bishop Ding Guangxun, out of respect for his personal preference.

The following may cause initial difficulty:

Beijing is Peking
Guangzhou is Canton
Xiamen is Amoy
Shantou is Swatow
Mao Zedong is Mao Tse-tung
and Zhou Enlai is Chou En-lai.

Pronunciation

Pinyin is very logical and should cause little difficulty to an English speaker except for two sounds:

q........ch as in chicken
x........s as in simple

ABBREVIATIONS

CIM	China Inland Mission
CCP	Chinese Communist Party
CCPA	Chinese Catholic Patriotic Association
CPPCC	Chinese People's Political Consultative Conference
NCC	National Council of Churches
NCNA	New China News Agency – in later reports this becomes *Xinhua*
RAB	Religious Affairs Bureau
SDK	Society for the Diffusion of Christian and General Knowledge
SVM	Student Volunteer Movement
TSPM	Three Self Patriotic Movement
UFW	United Front Work Department
WCC	World Council of Churches
WSCF	World Student Christian Federation

JOURNAL REFERENCES

Bridge, 1983 -   Tao Fong Shan Ecumenical Centre,
Hong Kong
BBC SWB FE   British Broadcasting Corporation, Summary of
World Broadcasts: Part III, The Far East
China Bulletin, 1947-62   National Council of the Churches of
Christ, U.S.A.
China and Church Today, 1979-86   Chinese Church
Research Centre, Hong Kong
China Notes, 1963 -   National Council of the Churches of
Christ, U.S.A.
CSP Bulletin, 1976-85   China Study Project, U.K.
CSP Documentation, 1979-85   China Study Project, Religion
in the People's Republic of China: Documentation, U.K.
CSP Journal, 1986 -   China Study Project, U.K.
Chinese Theological Review 1985 -   Nanjing Theological
Seminary
Ching Feng, 1957 -   Tao Fong Shan Ecumenical Centre
Tian Feng, 1948-64   Three Self Patriotic Movement, Shanghai
Tian Feng (New Series), 1980 -   ibid.
Tripod, 1980 -   Holy Spirit Study Centre, Hong Kong
Zhongguo Tianzhujiao, 1980 -   Catholic Patriotic
Association, Beijing

BOOK REFERENCES

The following books are frequently mentioned in the Ref-
erences under the abbreviated titles:
Wickeri, Philip L., *Seeking the Common Ground*
Hood, George, *Mission Accomplished?*
Documents, TSPM
(See Bibliography for full title, publisher, etc)

ACKNOWLEDGEMENTS

The author and publisher gratefully acknowledge permission to reproduce the following copyright materials:

Raymond Fung, *Households of God on China's Soil*, WCC Geneva, for extracts from the stories "With and Without A Cross", "When Jesus Did Not Come Again", and the translation of the hymn "Angels on High Strengthen Me."

Robert Kotewall and Norman Smith for the translation of the poems by Tao Yuanming and Yan Yun, Penguin Books.

Roger Garside for the translation of the poem "Devils howl as we pour out our grief" in *Coming Alive, China After Mao*, Andre Deutsch.

Yu Shao-ling and the *China Quarterly* for the translation of Sun Jingxuan's poem "A Spectre Wanders in the Land of China".

Gladys Yang and the Oxford University Press for permission to use Lu Xun's "A Poem".

David Paton for permission to reproduce extracts from his personal letters and papers.

Philip Wickeri for permission to quote extensively from his book *Seeking the Common Ground*.

INTRODUCTION

The history of Christianity in China from its first introduction in A.D. 635 to 1987 is the theme of this book, which is intended to provide an overview of the development of Chinese Christianity throughout this period in the light of the contemporary situation of the Church in China. It is not therefore a history of Christian missions to China, rather it is an attempt to trace the encounter of Christianity with the world's oldest living civilization. As will soon become clear to the reader, I am of the opinion that this encounter in past times was all too superficial. I am also concerned to show that Chinese Marxism grew out of the political and social circumstances of China in the nineteenth and early twentieth centuries. However unpalatable to Christians, Marxism appealed to many of the best and most altruistic minds of the younger generation of Chinese intellectuals in the first half of this century, and by 1949 it had also won the support of the overwhelming majority of the people. Therefore 1949 was experienced as a genuine "Liberation" by most of the people, and Marxism came upon the Church as a judgement on its long-term associations with Western power and its captivity within the thoughtforms of the Western world.

My primary concern will be the story of Chinese Christianity after 1949 – how it responded to the experiences of Liberation and sought to redefine itself in relation to the new social order. My interpretation of the Protestant Three Self Patriotic Movement differs from the one offered in most of the popular books on Christianity in contemporary China that have appeared in both Britain and North America. I am convinced that, despite serious shortcomings and mistakes, the decision to follow the "patriotic" option rather than to resist the New China was fundamentally the right choice, and that the resurgence of Christianity since 1979 vindicates those who advocated co-operation with the government even though this meant accepting certain restrictions. Unfortunately, the circumstances of the Chinese Roman Catholic Church were such that prior to 1949 there was no background of reflection on the social and political needs of Chinese society. There was therefore little real understanding of the issues facing the Church after Liberation, and the establishment of the Catholic Patriotic Association was very different from that of the Three Self Patriotic Movement.

The origin and growth of the three principles of self-government, self-support and self-propagation are traced, together with the early attempts to create an indigenous Church. I shall seek to show that indigenization is in itself no guarantee that Christianity is addressing the issues found within its context, nor that its theology is developed in an encounter with the surrounding culture. It is for this reason that many theologians like to speak of "contextualization" and "inculturation" – hardly beautiful words but useful in so far as an awareness of the difference between the three processes is vital. So at various stages in the story we shall look at the cultural context and in what ways Christians sought to relate themselves to Chinese culture. Here, we shall find that we must seek beyond the confines of the "religious" if we are truly to understand the spiritual elements in Chinese culture – we must move beyond dogmatics towards a concern with art and the art of friendship – to the contemplation of beauty in which, perhaps, we may find new ways of speaking that will deepen the encounter. I argue, with some trepidation, that this is indeed the direction of Chinese theological thinking itself, and that we can discern signs that the encounter may now be entering into a new and promising stage. It is my opinion that this has only become possible because the Marxist critique has been taken seriously, encountered and transcended.

Speaking personally I have felt the attraction of Marxism, especially in its Chinese guise. I have also become aware, through following the twists and turns of Chinese politics, of the shortcomings of Marxism but I remain convinced that for

China there can be no going back to a pre-Marxist stage. Looking at some of the most recent changes and the discussions amongst Chinese Marxists and others, I still believe that the Chinese genius is capable of adapting Marxism still further, so that the old orthodoxy inherited from Lenin and Stalin in particular can be replaced by a form of Marxism that transcends the historical limitations of the classical Marxist world-view. There is much that Marxism can still teach us about society, and the insights of Liberation Theology owe an immense debt to it. Christian theology itself cannot continue with any integrity if it has not come to terms with Marxism and accepted that in part the Marxist critique of religion has a historical validity. Karl Barth stands as a decisive figure in modern theology, not least because he recognized this.

But theology also needs to move beyond both liberal and conservative theological forms which, like Marxism, were nineteenth-century creations. In the post-modern world nineteenth-century patterns of thinking are too restrictive, and this is so in whatever discipline you care to name. Traditional Chinese insights into the nature of reality are not so out of date as many have thought. In my personal pilgrimage I have felt impelled into an exploration of the theology of the Greek Fathers and of certain aspects of medieval and Orthodox theology, and have discovered in my own life the importance of contemplative prayer. I also am fascinated by the distinctive insights of Chinese tradition, expressed so supremely in poetry and the visual arts. This book is written in the midst of my search, and I find China always challenging, both from its ancient traditions and from its contemporary socialist realities. So I make no apology for drawing on sources as diverse as Irenaeus, the Desert fathers and mothers, Pseudo-Dionysius, the fourteenth-century English mystics, the Anglican divines of the seventeenth century, the spirituality of the Russian icon painters, and modern theologians such as Karl Barth, Hans Urs von Balthasar, Hans Küng and John Robinson. It is the greatness of Balthasar that he offers a theological aesthetics that takes us far beyond aestheticism into a truly contemplative theology of the glory of God, in which the old *analogia entis* is replaced by an analogy of beauty that offers a new way of apprehending all that is true, good and beautiful within the cultures of humankind. The relevance of such an approach for China will, I hope, become apparent by the end of the book.

Turning to more practical matters, there is perforce an abundance of fact, and often facts that are little known to the average Westerner. There are also all too many unfamiliar names, not least in the very first chapter. The maps, the Time Line and appendices are designed to assist the reader, but unfortunately, those unfamiliar with Chinese geography and Chinese names will have to make some real effort at "inculturation"! Let me also warn the reader: seemingly overwhelmed with words and facts, the undiscerning may be forgiven for not realizing how little we really know about China, and in particular about Christianity in China. The gaps are there, all too many of them. Interpretations are made on the basis of what is known, not on what we do not know! New information will alter our perceptions of some things, confirm others. The study of Christianity in China, most particularly in the contemporary period, remains an inexact art. Hopefully, however, the main lines of interpretation will not need to be altered too much, as they do, I think, emerge out of the more precisely known past history. That earlier history has been extensively studied and the results published in a host of academic books, few, however, of which are readily available to the average reader. In part, therefore, this book is designed to pass on the insights and interpretations of others, although this is always a hazardous undertaking. I rely most heavily on such sources for the period up to 1949. After this there exists a mere handful of books, and for the period after the Cultural Revolution no detailed and comprehensive treatment is available. There are many articles, reports, occasional writings to draw on but, while using these where appropriate, I have relied to a great extent on primary sources, both Chinese and foreign.

Without my eleven years of work with the China Study Project (1975-86), which gave me many opportunities for detailed study, I doubt whether I could have written this book. The China Study Project was established in 1972 under the auspices of what was then the Conference of British Missionary Societies. In 1968 David Paton, then Secretary of MECCA (now the Board for Mission and Unity of the Church of England), was asked to head up a China Committee within CBMS. He agreed to do so only if a full-time Secretary could be found. It is a tribute to those who were concerned that China should re-appear on the agenda of the British churches that they responded to this challenge by finding sufficient money to pay Victor Hayward to be Research Secretary from 1972 until his retirement in 1975. It was Victor Hayward who laid the foundations of the work at a time when few direct contacts with Chinese Christians were possible. When I took over the work in 1975 I little thought that within a matter of months the situation in China would change so dramatically. From a brief to disseminate information about general developments in China, I became caught up in an exciting series of events that led to the normalization of relationships with the Protestant Church in China, and an exchange of delegations in 1982 and 1983. When I handed over the work to my successor, Peter Leung, yet another stage began as the China Study Project became an integral part of the British Council of Churches and Peter Leung the BCC's first ever China Secretary.

The story begins not with missionaries from the West, but with the arrival of a Persian bishop, a member of the Nestorian Christian community, in China in A.D. 635. Few Western Christians know of the existence of the "Church of the East" and of the story of Nestorian Christianity in the heartlands of Asia. Our account necessarily begins, therefore, with peoples and places that are unknown to most of us. China itself is all too unfamiliar to the average inhabitant of the North Atlantic nations. We should perhaps heed the words of Pascal:

"But China obscures", you say; and I reply, "China obscures, but there is light to be found. Look for it."

Pensées

Modern China

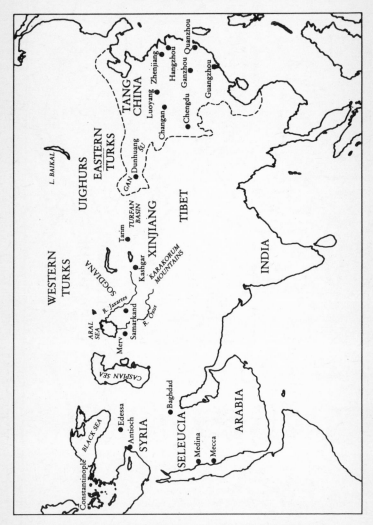

The Silk Road and China in the Tang Dynasty

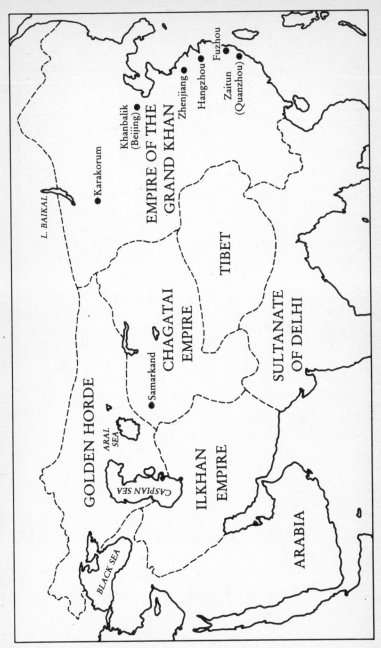

The Mongol Empire

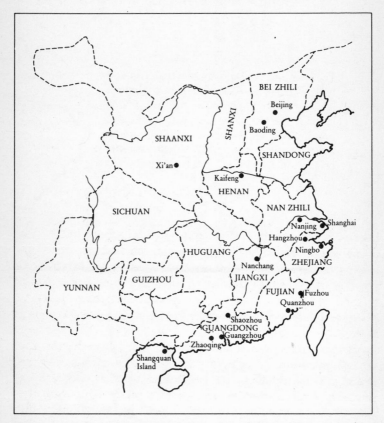

China in the Time of the Jesuits (Ming Dynasty)

I

First Contacts

Seventh to Fourteenth Centuries

> The true and eternal way is wonderful and
> hard to name; its merits and use are manifest
> and splendid, forcing us to call it the
> brilliant teaching. Yet the way without a
> prophet will not flourish; a prophet without
> the way will not be great. When way and
> prophet match and tally all under the sky is
> civilised and enlightened.
>
> From the Nestorian Tablet, Xi'an[1]

Legend has it that St Thomas reached China from India. The
tradition is found in a breviary of the old Malabar rite from
South India in the thirteenth century, and in a Syriac breviary,
possibly of the eighth century or earlier. It would be exciting
to think that these liturgies preserve an authentic tradition,
but in the absence of other evidence, it will have to remain a
legend.

Ancient China was a world unto itself, isolated from the
other high cultures of antiquity by the great natural barriers of
desert and mountain to the north and west. It was also an
agricultural civilization in which man's relationship with the
natural world, including the starry heavens, was of supreme
importance. This relationship was experienced in terms of the
rhythms of agricultural life and the alternations of night and
day. Early Chinese thought was moulded by this basic experience and was expressed in terms of the search for
harmonious, hierarchical relationships. The ideal was to be
found in a balance of opposing forces within an organic
whole that embraced man, the earth and the heavens in an

essential unity. At the same time, just as Heaven (*Tian* in Chinese), is above and man below, so human society reflects a similar pattern: ruler and subject, male and female, father and son. The teaching of Confucius (who lived 551-479 B.C.) was concerned with the development of such harmonious relationships; to find the "Way" (*Dao*). The *Doctrine of the Mean*, one of the *Four Books* of the early Confucian period, sums it up in the words: "If equilibrium and harmony are secured, Heaven and Earth will dwell in it and all things will be nourished by it."

Other schools of thought arose in ancient China, but we need only take note of the great alternative to Confucian thought, Taoism (*Dao*-ism). The crucial difference between the two schools which was to persist down the centuries, was that the Taoists sought the "Way" through an abandonment of a concern with society and a return to nature. The *Dao* is always elusive, to be sought through mystical experience and not social and political activity.

Despite their differences, both schools of thought saw the cosmos as a unity. The dualism of Greek thought, in which the material world is seen as separate from, and inferior to, an immaterial heavenly world, is alien to the indigenous tradition of China. Chinese dualism is not expressed in a contrast between matter and spirit, but in that between man's inner and outer worlds: private life and public life; the family and the State. In the first century after Christ, Buddhism was to introduce into China its own form of dualistic belief. *Nirvana*, the only final Reality for Buddhism, is contrasted to the cosmic world which is ultimately illusory. In its Chinese form (the Greater Vehicle or Mahayana form inherited from the great teachers in Northern India) Buddhism was to be adapted to the genius of China, drawing on the ancient traditions of China to produce forms of Buddhism more in accord with the Chinese spirit. Hui-yuan (334-416), the founder of the Pure Land School, identifies *Nirvana* with *Dao*, the immanent principle of the universe. Buddhism, nevertheless, retained its own distinctiveness and in the Song dynasty of the twelfth century provoked Confucian scholars into developing their own metaphysical basis for the ethical teachings of the earlier tradition. So emerged the great Neo-Confucian synthesis that in the succeeding centuries was to become the prevailing orthodoxy amongst the scholar-officials who formed China's elite.

The First Nestorian Mission

Leaving St Thomas, reluctantly, in India, the first known contact that the Chinese had with Christianity was at the beginning of the Tang Dynasty when "Nestorian" missionaries travelled the Silk Road as part of an unprecedented interchange between China and the lands to the west.

This interchange started in A.D. 635 and lasted until A.D. 845 – covering the greater part of the era of the Tang Dynasty. However, in the chaos at the end of the Tang, Christianity disappeared. It only re-appeared with the conquest of China by Khubilai Khan in 1260, again in a Nestorian form. This second period included the first contact with the Church of Rome when in 1292 or 1293 Friar John of Montecorvino disembarked on Chinese soil. Each of these stories is fascinating, and tantalizing. For contemporary Western students there are a number of huge barriers to understanding. Not only are there enormous gaps in our knowledge, but also few of us begin with any prior knowledge of the people and countries central to the story. Here, therefore, our task must be to attempt to leap over these barriers and present the outlines of each story without too much unnecessary detail. While it is true that these early contacts had little long-term impact on the forms of modern Chinese Christianity, we shall see that the first Nestorian mission is of some significance for our over-all evaluation of the relationship between Christian faith and Chinese culture. The thirteenth-century story is in a way the prelude to the first great European Christian mission to China that began in the late sixteenth century with the arrival of Matteo Ricci in the southern Chinese province of Guangdong.

The Church of the East

The coming to China of the first Christian mission was associated with the tumultuous events in the Persian Empire after the death of Muhammad in A.D. 632. The form of Christianity that had grown up in Persian Mesopotamia was distinct in many ways from that further west. Its minority position in a strong, centralized State which was fiercely loyal to the Zoroastrian religion led, after periods of severe repression, to an eventual accommodation, agreed in 410 at the Council of Seleucia. Christians were recognized as a *melet* or "people", enjoying a certain degree of autonomy in exchange for loyalty to the Shah. It was an arrangement that survived the coming of Islam and continued into the Ottoman Empire after 1301. The "Church of the East", as it called itself, became more and more separated from the Western Church of the Roman Empire where the triumph of Christianity led to a very different relationship between Church and State. The culmination of this process of separation was the espousal by the church in Mesopotamia of the standpoint of the followers of Nestorius, who had fled there from Antioch after Nestorian views on the Virgin Mary as "mother of Christ" but not "Mother of God" were condemned at the Council of Ephesus in 431.[2]

The world of that time is now remote from us, and it requires an act of imagination to visualize how its peoples lived within a very different political geography from our own. The Silk Road linked Antioch to the Chinese city of Chang'an over a distance of five thousand miles, and passed through Persia to the city of Samarkand, most important centre of the twenty-seven city states of Soghdiana. Soghdiana was the area of the great plain of the rivers of Oxus and Jaxartes and it was inhabited by Indo-European peoples who were originally Zoroastrian in religion, but who were increasingly influenced by Christianity. It was a cultured and high civilization, and many of its merchants travelled the Silk Road, bringing horses to China in exchange for silk. The Silk Road then passed through the

Buddhist areas of what is today the predominantly Muslim area of the Xinjiang Autonomous Region of China, arriving at the oasis of Dunhuang in Gansu Province and thence to Chang'an in the province of Shaanxi, the great and thriving capital of China, covering thirty square miles, far more extensive than the modern city of Xi'an. Today, all these areas are arid and threatened by the encroaching desert, but in those days they were much more fertile.

It was in 635 that the Persian missionary Aloben arrived in *[early Tang]* Chang'an, a few years after the Emperor Tai Zong, second son of the founder of the Tang, Gao Zu, had begun the process of reform that laid the foundations of one of China's greatest dynasties. Aloben is said to have come from "Da Jin", a term variously understood to mean Syria, Persia or simply the Mediterranean area. At the time both Syria and Persia were in chaos. Syria had fallen to the Muslim expansion that began after the death of the Prophet, and Persia was shattered by defeat in the war with Constantinople in 622. Dennis Hickley has suggested that Aloben may have been sent as an envoy by the Metropolitan of Merv, on the borders of Persia and Soghdiana.[3] This makes sense as the interests of the princedoms in this area certainly coincided with those of China. In 630 Tai Zong broke the power of the Eastern Turkish empire, and China occupied what is now eastern Xinjiang, meeting little resistance from the Western Turks. As a result of this military consolidation under Tai Zong, the Silk Road was reopened to merchants and also to the flow of ideas and the missionaries of a variety of faiths. However, the Arab armies were advancing from the west and Tai Zong must have been concerned with the threat they posed to the Christian and Zoroastrian areas to the west of the Pamirs. If Aloben did come as an envoy from this area, his reception by high officials would be understandable, as would the promulgation in 638 of an edict of toleration by the Emperor. The edict stated:

The monk Aloben from Persia has come from afar with the Scriptures and the doctrines; we find this religion excellent and separate from the world, and acknowledge that it is quickening for mankind and indispensable. It succours human beings, is beneficial to the human race and is worthy of being spread all over the Celestial Empire. We decree a monastery to be built by the appropriate Board in the quarter of Yi-ning, and twenty-one priests to be appointed there.[4]

Whatever the precise origins of Aloben himself, he certainly came as the representative of the "Church of the East", and China's first contact with Christianity was with this non-Roman form belonging to the world of Late Antiquity rather than to that of the Middle Ages. As Dennis Hickley writes:

The date of its official arrival in China, A.D. 635, places it firmly, though by a narrow margin, in a world in which "Europe" and "Christendom" were not yet thought of as being identical, and in which "Europe" and "Asia" were not thought of as separate worlds.[5]

*Hazy
worldview
of Chinese* [handwritten marginal note]

The Luminous Religion

Tang China was cosmopolitian and tolerant. Its music and dance were much influenced by central Asian forms, and this in turn influenced the development of Chinese poetry – which in Du Fu, Li Bo and Bo Juyi reached its greatest expression. It was also during the Tang that landscape painting entered into its great age. A man such as Wang Wei was able to achieve masterpieces in both poetry and painting. As in similar creative periods in other cultural traditions, new ideas were welcomed, and this contrasted strongly with later times in Chinese history when all foreign influences were regarded with great suspicion. In such a milieu it is not surprising that after Tai Zong's Edict the "Luminous religion from Persia" began to flourish. Unfortunately, little is known about the spread of Christianity at this time, and most information comes from the renowned Xi'an Nestorian Tablet, (set up in 781), almost certainly within the grounds of the original monastery in Chang'an. The monument was only discovered in 1625, and it was the Jesuits and their Chinese associates who first translated its rather obscure text. It seems that under Tai Zong's son, Gao Zong, who succeeded his father in 650, monasteries were established in a number of cities, including Luoyang and Lingwu. However, the claim of the Tablet that "the religion spread throughout the ten provinces . . . monasteries abound in a hundred cities", is generally assumed to be greatly exaggerated.

The tolerant policy of these two emperors came to a temporary end with the seizure of power by the Empress Wu in 690. Earlier in her life she had been forced to become a Buddhist nun, and during her reign she greatly favoured Buddhism. Both Buddhists and Taoists attacked the Nestorian church; but such troubles came to an end in 712 with the accession of the greatest of the Tang rulers, the Emperor Xuan Zong. Under Xuan Zong Christianity enjoyed great favour. Thus the Emperor wrote an inscription to be hung over the entrance gateway of the monastery in the capital. Moreover, he ordered the holding of a Christian service in the Xingqing Palace on the arrival from the West of a bishop (called Ji He in Chinese). Some historians have speculated that such privileges might suggest that some members of the royal family had become Christians, but it should be remembered that the respect shown was no different from that also accorded to Buddhism.

Suppression

Events to the west along the Silk Road were soon to cut the link that sustained the Nestorian church. The An Lushan Rebellion in 755 led to internal chaos and the abdication of Xuan Zong in 756. Although Christianity continued in favour under Xuan Zong's successors, the Tang was losing control of the western Empire to the Tibetans. At the same time the rise of Islam cut the link with Persia, and although Nestorian Christianity was now flourishing amongst Turkic tribes in Central Asia, the contacts became increasingly difficult to sustain as Tang power slipped away. The young church did not have the internal resources to sustain its life without such links: all the available evidence suggests that Christianity remained the religion of foreigners living in the great metropolitian centres. While there does not seem much doubt that there was a significant Chinese following, the community as a whole failed to set down indigenous roots, or to produce native leaders. This cannot have been because of an unwillingness to make the attempt and indeed all the Nestorian texts unearthed at Dunhuang in 1907 were in Chinese and employed Chinese concepts to express theological truths. This is not the place to attempt a survey of this material, which is both complex and difficult to understand, but it is important to be aware of the fact that although some of the documents suggest a degree of syncretism, others reveal a creative use of Taoist and Buddhist terminology to serve Christian ends. The great *Hymn to the Holy Trinity*, written around 800, is the supreme example:

> If the highest heavens with deep reverence adore,
> If the great earth earnestly ponders on general peace and
>   harmony,
> If man's first true nature receives confidence and rest,
> It is due to the merciful Father of the universe.[6]

The limited impact of Christianity at this time may also be related to the religious situation in China itself. Taoism was a powerful force and was being challenged by a Buddhism that had successfully adapted itself to a Chinese context. The supreme achievement of the Indian monk Kumarajiva, and then of the Chinese monk Xuan Zang, in translating Buddhist terms from the Sanskrit into Chinese was not matched by the Nestorian translators. As Latourette has pointed out, Nestorianism arrived at a time when no especial need for a new religion was felt – a great contrast to the situation in the Roman Empire in the early years of the Christian story.[7]

Christianity was, therefore, not in a strong position to survive a sustained attack. In 845 the Emperor Wu Zong, under the influence of Taoist priests, launched an attack on all foreign religions, Buddhist, Manichaean and Christian. He suppressed over 4,600 monasteries and ordered 260,000 monks to return to secular life. Nestorian and other monasteries were

[handwritten marginalia: proto Nestorians just part of ecumenical milieu in Chang'an esp. in the people. But 845 pogrom of religion]

included, and foreign personnel were sent home. Meanwhile in 840 the Tang lost the support of the largely Nestorian and Manichaean Uighur people in the North-west who succumbed to the onslaught of their northern neighbours, the Kirghiz. The Uighurs were forced by hunger to raid Chinese territory, and several hundred Uighur residents of Chang'an were arrested and executed. The political reason for continuing to tolerate the Nestorians and other foreign religions had vanished. It was Buddhism that was the main target but, despite permanent damage, it had the strength to survive.

So ended the first Christian mission to China. It is probable that some Christians remained, and indeed it is known that some of the expelled Christian leaders were able to settle in Guangzhou (Canton). Christians were amongst those in the city put to death in 877 by Chinese rebels. What is certain is that Christianity disappeared from public view, and in 986 the monk Najran, sent by the Nestorian Patriarch to China, reported:

> Christianity is extinct in China; the native Christians have perished in one way or another; the church which they had has been destroyed and there is only one Christian left in the land.[8]

While this is no doubt an over-statement, it is not far from the truth.

The Significance of Tang Christianity

Two aspects of the Nestorian mission are of particular interest to us. First of all, it was free of any association with military and political expansionism. Never again was this to be the case, and such associations were to burden Chinese Christianity up to our own day. Secondly, it had none of that fearfulness expressed by Western forms of Christianity with regard to other cultures and their traditions. As Hickley comments:

> Their instinct was to explain by adaptation to a society with deeply-rooted values of its own, expressed in a

Confucian state "church". In this they were, unconsciously no doubt, following in the footsteps of the Buddhists of an earlier age. The Buddhists managed cultural adaptation and survived; Western Christians, however – at least since the medieval period – appear to be haunted by the vision of a takeover. *The cultural context is not seen as something which has rights of its own.*[9]

The reasons why the first Christian mission to China failed to achieve a lasting position in Chinese society have been much debated, but in the long run circumstances were not as favourable as they might have appeared at first. Later Christians (usually Western Protestants or Roman Catholics), have often implied that the "Nestorian" church could not survive because of its "heretical" basis, and have looked with profound suspicion on its attempts to adapt to a Chinese setting. This is on a par with the almost complete disregard of the "Church of the East" itself which, nevertheless, between the seventh and eleventh centuries was larger and more powerful than any other Christian church. By the year 1000 its adherents probably numbered in millions and it had twenty-five metropolitan provinces and 200-250 bishoprics. The separation between the Syriac-speaking churches and the Western Church was an impoverishment of Christianity with untold consequences. Hickley is surely correct when he suggests that this was the beginning of a process that continued with the split between the Greek East and the Latin West in the eleventh century, and between Mediterranean and Northern Europe at the Reformation. "Thus, step by step, a situation had been produced where the great missionary churches were identified in the closest possible manner with Western Europeanism."[10]

Christianity under the Mongols

The rise of the Mongols under Genghis Khan was unexpected

and devastated the old kingdoms of Asia. As one authority has written of the Mongol impact:

> The political organization of Asia and a large part of Europe was altered; whole peoples were uprooted and dispersed, permanently changing the ethnic character of many regions; the strength and distribution of the principal religions of the world were decisively altered; European access to Asia and the Far East, interrupted for a thousand years, became possible again once the transcontinental routes were dominated by a single authority and travel made safe.[11]

Genghis Khan attacked China in 1212 and in 1215 captured Beijing. However, he then turned his attention elsewhere, and the conquest of China was not completed until 1264 under his grandson Khubilai Khan. It was now that the great flow of peoples and ideas along the Central Asian trade routes restarted. Many foreigners flocked to China, including large contingents of troops from Russia and the West, and whole communities of foreign residents were established in the great cities. The second Nestorian mission to China was part of this over-all movement, and it was also closely tied to the Mongol court and to the destinies of the Yuan (Mongol) dynasty. The Nestorian Church had flourished among the Central Asian tribes such as the Uighurs, Naimans and Onguts, and there were many Mongol Christians. Then in the eleventh century the Keraits, another Central Asian people, converted *en masse*. The importance of this was that the Keraits were closely related to the Mongols through intermarriage. Tuli, the son of Genghis Khan, was married to a Kerait woman, Sorocan, mother of Khubilai. On her death in 1252 Khubilai ordered mass to be said for her soul in the Nestorian monastery in Ganzhou, Gansu Province.

The Mongol capital was established in Beijing and was given the Mongol name of Khanbaliq; as early as 1235 there was a Nestorian church and theological school in the city. A few years later Khanbaliq became a metropolitan see, and in 1289 Khubilai set up a special office (the Zongfu) to take charge of

Nestorian affairs. Obviously, the numbers of Christians must have increased considerably. In 1330 the Archbishop of Soltania wrote that there were more than 30,000 Nestorians in Cathay, that they "are passing rich, with very many handsome and devoutly ordered churches and crosses and images in honour of God and the saints. They hold sundry offices under the . . . Emperor and have great privileges from him." This last point is important and illustrates the fact that these Nestorian Christians were closely linked with the Mongol invaders.

The History of the Yüan records that there were seventy-two Nestorian monasteries in China during the period 1289-1320. The *Topography of Zhenjiang District* (on the Yangzi [Yangtze] River in Jiangsu Province) records that during 1330-32 there were twenty-three Christian families, and a hundred and six individuals, with a hundred and nine slaves. It was here that Mar Sargis, a Christian doctor from Samarkand, was appointed Governor in 1277 by Khubilai. Mar Sargis, after he had been told in a vision to build seven monasteries, did indeed establish six in Zhenjiang and the seventh in Hangzhou. However, two of these were ancient Buddhist temples which in 1290 were restored as Buddhist monasteries – to the delight of the local people. In the *Topography of Zhenjiang* the Christians are classified as "resident aliens" and it is quite clear that very few Chinese adhered to Christianity in this period. The Nestorians remained, therefore, as aliens in the Chinese world, and while some individuals had won great distinction in philosophy and the arts, they were gradually absorbed into the mainstream of Chinese culture. The revolt of the Red Turbans lasting from 1355 to 1367 ended Mongol rule, and on 23 January 1368 the rebel leader Zhu Yuanzhang proclaimed the Ming dynasty. Nestorianism once again disappeared from China, and with the rise of Timur (Tamurlane) who espoused Islam, the Nestorian faith was to be overwhelmed in its central Asian heartland.

The Franciscan Mission   13th cent

One story remains to be told of these early contacts. During World War II the medieval walls of the city of Quanzhou on the south-east coast of Fujian Province were demolished. Amongst the debris were found numerous carved stones and inscriptions including Muslim and Christian gravestones. One has the Latin inscription:

> Hic . . . sepultus
> Andreas Peruginus
> Ordinis . . .
> . . . apostolus
> M . . . XII   MCCCXXXII

"Here lies buried Andrew of Perugia of the order (of Friars Minor) . . ." and the date is probably 1332.[12]

Quanzhou is the city of Zaitun referred to by Marco Polo, a great and thriving port, and the residence of many foreigners. Even today many evidences of its past are preserved, although its status is sadly diminished.

The gravestone is one of the few relics of the first contact between China and Western Christianity. The thirteenth century witnessed the flowering of European medieval culture. Two great religious Orders, the Franciscans and Dominicans, were founded in the early years of the thirteenth century and both showed a deep concern with mission to non-Christian peoples. St Francis himself preached in Egypt, and it was natural that it should be his followers who pioneered the mission to the East. The Crusades had all but ended, but the interest they stimulated in the world beyond Europe marked the beginnings of the story of European expansion. Meanwhile the Mongol threat to Europe was a source of deep concern, and the first Franciscan mission was sent by Pope Innocent IV to the court of the Great Khan, Kuyuk, at Karakoram. It set out in 1245, led by one of St Francis' personal associates, John of Plano Campini. Then, in 1253 William of Rubruck visited the court of the Great Khan Mangu where he

43

was impressed by the Khan's toleration of a variety of religions. Both men wrote accounts of their travels and they are amongst the most fascinating of all travel stories,[13] but neither mission reached China, although the little information they did bring back must have stimulated the curiosity of those who listened to their reports.

The first Europeans to set foot in China were Maffeo and Nicolo Polo who set out in 1260 and returned nine years later with a letter from Khubilai Khan requesting that one hundred teachers of science and religion be sent to China. The reasoning behind this request is uncertain, but it led to the Polos (this time including Nicolo's son, Marco), setting out for China in late 1271 in the company of two Dominicans armed with papal letters to Khubilai. The Dominicans turned back, but the Polos arrived in China, where Marco entered into the service of Khubilai Khan. Rumours reached Europe of the baptism of the Khan, and in 1278 a Franciscan mission prepared to go to China, until news came that the report was false. It was not until 1289 that Pope Nicholas IV finally sent John of Montecorvino to the court of Khubilai, but by the time he arrived in Khanbaliq in 1294 the great Khan was dead. He was, however, well received by the new Emperor Timur.

Friar John found himself in a very cosmopolitan milieu which, of course, included numerous Nestorians from the Turkic and Mongol peoples. There were also the 30,000 Alans in the pay of the Emperor, a people who came from the shores of the Black Sea, and who were not too happy with the Nestorian church. Friar John found a sympathic hearing in such circles, and the Alans converted. In 1338, after the death of John, they sent a mission to Rome asking for help and this led to the last medieval mission that we know of, when John of Marignolli arrived in China in 1342, bringing a great war horse as a gift from the Pope to the Emperor. The Chinese were much impressed with the gift, and it inspired a poem entitled "An Ode to the Supernatural Horse".

John of Montecorvino's most important convert was the Nestorian Prince George (Kerguz), ruler of the Ongut tribe in the great bend of the Yellow River, son in-law of the Emperor, and great-grandson of Alahush, one of the claimants to the title of the legendary Prester John. Prince George was a Confucian scholar and great military commander, and his conversion caused consternation amongst the Nestorian community in Khanbaliq. He became the first Chinese to enter minor orders – an event that provoked the Nestorians to open hostility. Then in 1298 George was treacherously killed by a rebel prince. His brothers reverted to the Nestorian church, although his son was brought up a Roman Catholic. His death removed a major cause of friction, and in 1299 Friar John was able to build his first church in the capital. He also bought forty boys aged between seven and eleven; he baptized them and taught them Latin and how to sing the offices. John of Montecorvino was finally joined by another friar, Brother Arnold of Cologne, in 1303/4, and in 1305 built a second church, this time right before the gate to the Imperial Palace. Without doubt John saw his mission as primarily directed towards the Mongol rulers, and Mass was celebrated in the Tartar (Uighur) language. As John wrote in his second letter dated 1305:

> I have already grown old, and my hair is white from the labours and tribulations rather than years, for I am fifty-eight years old. I have an adequate knowledge of the Tartar language and script . . . and now I have translated into that language and script the whole of the New Testament and the Psalter and have had it written in beautiful characters.[14]

In the same letter John states that he has baptized six thousand people – almost certainly few, if any, Han Chinese were among their number. It was, nevertheless, an impressive achievement, and in 1307 Clement V recognized this when he appointed John as Archbishop of Khanbaliq and Patriarch of the East. He also nominated seven Franciscans as Bishops in China, but only Gerald, Peregrine of Castello and Andrew of Perugia arrived in China, in 1308. For five years the Franciscans lived together in the capital, receiving *alafa* or alms from the Emperor. In his letter of 1326 Andrew of Perugia writes of these imperial grants made to foreigners saying, "the sum of these grants exceeds the income and expenditure of many Western Kings".[15]

It was in 1313 that a wealthy Armenian lady living in Zaitun (Quanzhou) gave money to build a church in that city, and in consequence Friar Gerald went there as Bishop. He died in 1318 and Friar Peregrine succeeded him. The next part of the story can be told in Andrew's words:

> And since for various reasons I was not contented in Cambaliech (Khanbaliq), almost four years before the death of the Bishop (Peregrine) I got leave that the aforesaid *alafa*, or imperial alms, should be paid to me at this city of Zayton which . . . is almost three months' journey from Cambaliech. I travelled there very honourably with a train of eight horses allowed me by the Emperor, and arrived while brother Peregrine was still alive. There is a wood near the city, a quarter of a mile away, and here I caused a fair and fitting church to be built with buildings to house twenty brethren, and with four chambers, any of which is good enough for a bishop.[16]

Peregrine died in 1322 and Andrew succeeded him. It would appear that in Quanzhou the Franciscans did not restrict their activities to the foreign residents. Andrew states, almost certainly with reference to the Chinese themselves: "Of the idolaters, exceedingly many are baptized: but when they are baptized they do not adhere strictly to Christian ways."

Archbishop John died in 1328, and according to *The Book of the Estate of the Great Caan* by John di Cora, "much was he beloved by all, pagans as well as Christians", so that "to his obsequies and burial there came a very great multitude of people".[17] The Franciscan mission remained, with bases also in the cities of Yangzhou and Hangzhou. The Alan embassy of 1338 to Rome reveals that not all was well. The Mongol dynasty was in decline and this had increasingly serious repercussions on both Nestorian and Catholic Christians. Finally, in 1362, the fifth Bishop of Zaitun, Friar James of Florence, was martyred by the Chinese patriots who seized the city on behalf of the Ming. In 1369 all Christians in the capital Khanbaliq were also expelled.

It is impossible not to be impressed by the dedication and faith of these friars. The journey east was fraught with danger and hardship; amongst Europeans fear of the Mongols was intense, and it was an act of supreme courage to set out at all; few could expect ever to return and some would never arrive at their destination. Nevertheless, some questions must be raised about the mission. As we have seen, it was originally concerned with the Mongols and their Turkic allies, and not with native Chinese. While some Chinese involvement seems probable, especially in Quanzhou, the mission was always dependent on the patronage of the Yüan dynasty. It was inevitable that its destiny would be tied to that of a dynasty that was regarded with hatred by the Han population of China. It is mildly ironic that in this the Franciscans were no different from the hated Nestorians. The Franciscan dislike of the Nestorian Christians was not only based on the negative experiences recorded, for example, by William of Rubruck. To the Franciscans, the Nestorians were heretics in schism with the Holy Catholic Church. As we have noted, many of the initial converts were of Nestorian background. There is little doubt that at this stage in its history the Nestorian church was increasingly corrupt, but there is also evidence which suggests that at least some Nestorians were devout – the remarkable story of the pilgrimage to Jerusalem by two Nestorian monks, Mark and Sauma, in 1278, is one illustration of genuine devotion. In the conflict between these rival forms of Christianity in Mongol China we encounter the result of the separation between the Church of the East and Western Christians in the fifth century. In the thirteenth century it was already too late to overcome the barriers that divided the followers of Jesus. For China, such differences were without interest, and the Ming saw the ascendancy of a Sino-centrism that closed the doors on all foreign ideas until they were forced open in the mid-nineteenth century. The Jesuit mission of the Late Ming and early Qing was perhaps an exception, but as we shall see, it failed to alter the fundamental parameters of Confucian orthodoxy.

REFERENCES

1. Translated in Moule, A.C., *Christians in China Before the Year 1550*, S.P.C.K., London 1930, p. 38.
2. Hickley, Dennis, *The First Christians of China: An Outline history and some considerations concerning the Nestorians in China during the Tang dynasty*, China Study Project, London 1980, p. 6.
3. ibid., p. 10
4. Cary-Elwes, Columba, O.S.B., *China and the Cross: Studies in Missionary History*, Longmans, Green and Co., London 1957, p. 24 quoting translation by Archimandrite Palladius, who discovered the decree in the Imperial Library in Beijing.
5. Hickley, op. cit., p. 1.
6. *Hymn to the Great Trinity*, quoted Lee Shiu Keung, *The Cross and The Lotus*, Christian Study Centre, Hong Kong 1971, p. 17.
7. Latourette, Kenneth Scott, *A History of Christian Missions in China*, S.P.C.K., London 1929, p. 58.
8. Lee Shiu Keung, op. cit., p. 13.
9. Hickley, op. cit., p. 32.
10. ibid., p. 33
11. Barraclough, Geoffrey, ed., *The Times Atlas of World History*, Times Books Ltd., London 1979, p. 128: *The Mongol Empire 1206 to 1405*.
12. Dawson, Christopher, ed., *The Mongol Mission: Narratives and Letters of the Franciscan Missionaries in Mongolia and China in the 13th and 14th Centuries*, Sheed & Ward, London 1955.
13. ibid.
14. ibid., p. 224.
15. ibid., p. 235.
16. ibid., p. 236.
17. Quoted in Cary-Elwes, op. cit., p. 65.

II

The Jesuit Mission
1583-1721

With his task done on the cross,
His blood forms itself into a streamlet.
Grace flows from West Heaven in long patience:
  Trials in four courts,
  Long walks at midnight,
Thrice denied by friend before the cock crew twice,
Six-footer hanging at the same height as two thieves.
It is a suffering that moves the whole world and all ranks.
Hearing his seven words makes all souls cry.

The Emperor Kangxi[1]

A Bridge between Two Worlds

1966–78

At some time in the chaos of the Cultural Revolution, most probably in 1966, the young Red Guards destroyed an old tomb outside Beijing's Fucheng Gate in the west of the city. An unknown scholar rescued the gravestone, and in 1980 was able to return it to its rightful place. The tomb was the memorial to Li Matou, or Father Matteo Ricci, and two of his fellow Jesuits, Adam Schall and Ferdinand Verbiest. The tomb was fully restored and walls and flower altars added in 1984. It *new road 1984* was an indication of the more open and relaxed policies towards cultural interchange and religious expression being put into practice in the People's Republic of China under the rule of Deng Xiaoping.[2]

Chinese nationalists in the twentieth century have been heirs to a tradition of anti-Christian sentiment that stretches back to the time of the Jesuit mission. The Chinese Communist Revolution was also a nationalist revolution, and the Chinese

Communist Party, committed to dialectical materialism, has had little good to say of Western missionaries. However, in more recent years, Ricci and his fellow Jesuits have been accorded an honourable place in history, as pioneers of East-West interchange. Thus Lin Jinshui in an article published in *Social Sciences in China* in 1983 has written:

> He was the first to introduce European science and culture to China and, at the same time, he brought to Europe knowledge of life in China. He is known as an astronomer, mathematician, geographer and sinologist. Despite the role he played, Ricci has been little studied in this country. In the past he was subjected to much criticism; it is but recently that the value of his contributions has begun to be affirmed.[3]

This view of Ricci as a bridge between cultures is fine as far as it goes, but it leaves out of consideration the main purpose of the Jesuit presence in China: the conversion of the Chinese people to Christianity. Where this purpose is recognized it is either excused in the light of the cultural interchange it produced or it is dismissed.

Liang Qichao, an influential reformer and opponent of Marxism, wrote in 1926:

> The seed of late Ming and early Qing science came from the hands of the Jesuits . . . The missionaries of that society had a clever way of preaching Christianity; they understood the psychology of the Chinese. They knew that the Chinese did not like religion of extreme superstition so they used science as a lure, since the Chinese lacked science. On the surface evangelism was their side-line and the converts were allowed to worship the Chinese *Tian* (Heaven) and ancestors. Such a method was carried out for years, and both sides were satisfied.[4]

Here it is assumed that the encounter was on the level of a bargain in which the dictum of the nineteenth-century reformer, Zhang Zhidong, would apply: "Chinese learning for the basis; Western learning for the application." No real encounter at the level of belief is presumed to have taken place, it being all a matter of expediency. Liang's viewpoint also presupposes a view of the relationship of science and religion that only emerged in Europe during the eighteenth century, and in China in the late nineteenth century. The encounter between the late Ming world and the world of sixteenth- and seventeenth-century Europe certainly revealed a profound divergence in the understanding of man and the cosmos, but it is quite misleading to interpret it in terms of a conflict between science and religion.

The Jesuit mission must be evaluated in the dual context of Europe and China during the sixteenth and seventeenth centuries. Only by understanding the roots of the mission in the theological and cultural perspectives of the time can we hope to come to a satisfactory evaluation of the whole enterprise and its long-term significance.

Late Ming China

Late Ming China was a curious mixture of ineffective, corrupt rule and intellectual vitality. Under the Zhengde Emperor (1506-21) China entered into another phase of dictatorship by eunuchs and favourites, a phase that only came to an end with the collapse of the Ming and the victory of the Manchus in 1644. The economy steadily deteriorated during the sixteenth century and China was subject to harassment by Japanese pirates and Mongol invasion. Owing to the corrupt taxation system there was wide-scale evasion, and there was extensive land seizure by the powerful resulting in the impoverishment of the peasantry. A successful reform was carried out and this, combined with improvements in agricultural productivity due to new strains of rice and the importation of American food plants, led, in the 1570s, to a period of economic expansion. It was short lived, as Court extravagance and renewed military conflict in the 1590s brought about a catastrophic decline. The war against the

Japanese general Hideyoshi after his invasion of Korea in 1592 could only be paid for by heavy increases in taxation which, in turn, triggered a series of local rebellions. In the early years of his reign the Wanli Emperor (1573-1620) was fortunate in his Chief Grand Secretary, Zhang Juzheng, an able administrator, but the secretary's death in 1582 left a vacuum that was filled by the eunuchs on whom the Emperor came to depend. It was during the reign of the Wanli Emperor, in 1583, that Ricci arrived in China.

In contrast to this somewhat unstable political and economic situation there was a growth in the vitality of intellectual life which freed scholars from the more rigid aspects of the Neo-Confucian orthodoxy that had grown up after the twelfth century around the ideas of the great philosopher Zhu Xi (born 1130). Early in the sixteenth century an outstanding military leader and thinker named Wang Yangming had challenged some of the fundamental tenets of Zhu Xi. Zhu Xi's influence had led to a stress on self-cultivation, frequently at the expense of involvement in public affairs. Wang Yangming urged a unity of knowledge and action ("Knowledge is the beginning of action and action is the completion of knowledge"). He adopted an idealist view of the identity of mind (*xin*) and principle (*li*), and he taught that man has an innate knowledge of what is right and wrong. Such knowledge leads to action out of *ren* (human-heartedness or "love"). He called for a return to the "sagehood" associated with the early thinkers of China, who had successfully combined the cultivation of inner wisdom with an active public life. Wang's influence during the late Ming was considerable, and was responsible for the growth of private academies offering education to men of all classes. These academies became important centres of intellectual ferment and of political opposition to the corruption at court. Attempts at suppression by the court failed and in 1604 the influential Eastern Grove (Donglin) Academy was restored. Its members fought valiantly against corruption, but the rise to power of the notorious eunuch Wei Zhongxian, under the Tianqi Emperor in 1625, resulted in its leading members being thrown into prison and tortured to death or driven to suicide.

The story of the decline and overthrow of the Ming cannot be told in any detail. Suffice it to say that even as the Tianqi Emperor succumbed to the evil influence of Wei Zhongxian, so the Manchu power was growing in the north-east. Although Wei was disposed of by the Chongzhen Emperor (1628-44), who sought to curb factional struggles, it was too late, and internal order continued to disintegrate. Finally, massive peasant rebellions broke out and in 1644 Beijing fell to the rebel leader Li Zicheng. In despair the last emperor of the Ming hanged himself on Coal Hill. It was not long before the rebels in turn succumbed to the invading Manchus.

Before we turn to the story of the Jesuit mission from its beginning in 1583 to its sudden demise under its erstwhile patron, the Emperor Kangxi in 1721, we must take a look at the developments in Europe that led to the sending of missionaries to the East, after a gap of two hundred years.

European Background

Renaissance and the Age of Discovery

In his fascinating study of Ricci, *The Memory Palace of Matteo Ricci*, Jonathan Spence has provided a profound insight into the mind-set of sixteenth-century Europe. Ricci listed three major reasons why Chinese literati flocked to his house in Nanchang in 1596: their conviction that the Jesuits could turn mercury into pure silver; their desire to learn Western mathematics; and their eagerness to master his system for learning by memory. Spence comments:

> The list is completely believable in the context of the European intellectual and religious life of Ricci's time, when memory systems were combined with numerological skills and the arcane semi-scientific world of alchemy to give the adept a power over his fate that

mirrored the power of conventional religion.[5]

The transition from the medieval world to the world of the modern era was a long and complex process. The shift in perception that gave rise to both Renaissance and Reformation can be traced back to the time of the Crusades and the spiritual renewal of the thirteenth century. Scholastic philosophy was the supreme expression of the medieval worldview, but the order it assumed was to break down in the wars, plagues and disasters of the fourteenth century. Meanwhile new economic forces were at work in the cities, giving rise to a class of citizens whose desire for learning marked the beginning of the process of the secularization of knowledge and the growth of a non-clerical humanism. The sixteenth century witnessed the beginnings of the modern secular State and the break-up of the medieval religious synthesis. It is important, however, to keep in mind the many continuities with the past. There was nothing untoward in Ricci's association with alchemy, with all its magical undertones, even if he would have rejected the magic of the "cunning men" who continued to play a major role in the life of both Catholic and Reformed Europe; the origins of science lie very much within this world of arcane learning. This is most clearly seen in the link between astrology and the science of astronomy. Belief in the influence of the stars over man's lives was one of the chief motivations for observing the heavens, and this, significantly, was one area where European and Chinese shared similar viewpoints. It was to prove a vital link for the Jesuit mission to China.

The expansion in the horizons of medieval Europe through the great voyages of discovery was a process which, as we have seen, also had its origins in the thirteenth century. The Age of Discovery really started in 1492 when Christopher Columbus set out on his first voyage. It is easy to assume that the early explorers were impelled by the same motives as their nineteenth-century counterparts, whereas in fact, the quest for new worlds was inspired by far more than a desire for adventure and economic gain. Indeed, both Columbus and

Vasco da Gama, and many other travellers, set out in the belief that it was God who was sending them. Their vision was of the creation of a universal Christian Empire whose advent would usher in the Millennial Kingdom. Political, economic and social circumstances in the sixteenth century seemed to combine to make the fulfilment of this vision possible. It was, however, a medieval dream that informed them, and not the spirit of the European Enlightenment. It was unfortunate that the particular history of the Iberian peninsula, from where these first great sea voyages set out, gave a new twist to the old dream, introducing a deep vein of intolerance which was to become a hallmark of European expansion in later centuries.

The emergence of both Spain and Portugal as great powers during the early sixteenth century was rooted in the triumph of the Iberian peoples over their Muslim overlords, a process that was more or less complete by the end of the previous century. The *reconquista* was also seen as the triumph of Christianity over Islam, and it left a legacy of hatred for foreign religions and a tendency to seek the solution of religious differences through the use of force. Portugal's great voyages of discovery, under Henry the Navigator, had, as one important objective, the encirclement of Islam. Christian kings were the agents of God. Informed by this crusading spirit, Portuguese treatment of native peoples was harsh and insensitive. No wonder that when in 1517 they reached Guangzhou, their reputation as pirates and invaders had preceded them and the Chinese authorities were not inclined to allow such ill-favoured barbarians access to the Middle Kingdom. The Chinese view of Europeans as "barbarians" was shared by sophisticated Muslims and the native peoples of the countries they pillaged – providing a marked contrast to the, generally, civilized behaviour of the Chinese explorers who travelled the same seaways under the command of the great Ming admiral Zheng He in the early fifteenth century. The Portuguese soon discovered, however, that Ming power was too great to be challenged with impunity, and eventually the Portuguese settled peacefully in Macao. Their presence there was a source of Chinese suspicion and hostility for centuries.

The religious motivation behind early European expansion is too easily overlooked or dismissed as a mere excuse for economic greed. It explains why in 1515 Pope Leo X granted to Portugal exclusive privileges over Christian missionaries along the route to the East. So was born the *Padroado*, the protection and patronage of missions. Spain, whose rise followed that of Portugal, went West and was granted similar rights of patronage on this route. From Mexico, Spain conquered the Philippines, which became a base for operations in the Far East, including trading visits to Fujian Province and the arrival of missionaries on the island of Taiwan. Spanish methods were even more savage than those of the Portuguese, and Chinese fears that the Jesuits were agents of these aggressive foreign powers were to surface time and again.

Such fears were not without foundation. Both Spanish and Portuguese adventurers contemplated the conquest of China itself. In June 1583 the Bishop of Manila, Domingo de Salazar, wrote to Philip II of Spain:

> I maintain that you can send an army so strong that the whole power of China will be helpless to injure it, and that this army has the right to enter and traverse the provinces of China; it can impose peace upon those who disturb orders, it can oblige the King and the officials of this realm to allow the Gospel to be preached and to protect its heralds . . .[6]

The fateful alliance of Christian mission with European expansionism was being forged. Nevertheless, such attitudes were not shared by all, and it is notable that those Jesuits who were to play outstanding roles in the mission to China, and who exemplified a very different approach, came from countries where nationalism had not yet developed. Ricci was anxious not to become too closely associated with Portuguese power in Macao or with the Spanish Philippines. In 1603 China sent officials to Manila in pursuit of the rumour that mountains of silver and gold could be found in Luzon. This, combined with the presence of increasing numbers of Chinese traders and artisans in the Philippines, convinced the Spanish that an invasion was planned and resulted in the massacre of up to twenty thousand Chinese. Ricci in Beijing wrote of his concern in early 1605 to a friend in Rome:

> There was much talk at court here about the matter and we were afraid some harm might of come of it, because we had always been careful not to let ourselves be known as friends of [the Spaniards] up to the time of this event.[7]

Reformation and Counter-Reformation

The rise of the new learning amongst educated lay élites; the conflicts within a Church in which the great currents of medieval spirituality had ceased to flow; the rising tide of nationalism; all these forces combined to tear Christendom apart. The humanist values of a Thomas More or an Erasmus could not stand against the mixture of political calculation and passionate religious conviction that led first to the Reformation and then, in reaction, to the Counter-Reformation. Christians on both sides of the divide stressed "purity of Faith" and denounced "heretics" in terms previously reserved for the "infidel". The positive side of the religious upheaval was the re-vitalizing of the faith of the people and we can now see that, for example, Martin Luther's spirituality was not so different from that of St John of the Cross. From the perspective of the time, however, this could neither be seen or accepted, and not surprisingly, spiritual renewal found formal expression in a new dogmatism.

Two important movements of reform emerged within the Catholic Church. The first reform is linked to the Council of Trent that met from 1545 to 1563. In response to the Protestant challenge, abuses in church life were corrected and many Catholic doctrines were clarified and re-stated. At the same time power was centralized under the Pope in a manner that reflected the current centralization of monarchy within Europe. The Catholic Church after the Council was dominated by a view of doctrine that was drawn from medieval scholasticism. Its static, positivistic view of dogma was to curtail, and eventually overwhelm, any truly creative response to the encounter with native cultures and traditions. It was this development that lay behind the controversy over the Confucian rites that dogged the footsteps of the Jesuits.

The second movement saw the restoration of the vitality of the older religious Orders and the creation of new Orders. Foremost among these were the Jesuits, who dedicated themselves:

> to strive especially for the defence and propagation of the faith and for the progress of souls in Christian life and doctrine . . . to go . . . to whatsoever provinces they [the popes] may choose to send us – whether they are pleased to send us among the turks or any other infidels, even those who live in the region called the Indies . . .[8]

Their aim was to recoup the losses in Europe and to conduct mission in the newly discovered lands. The founder of the Jesuits, Ignatius Loyola, shared the vision of the new world order to be achieved through the recovery of the Holy City, Jerusalem, and the conversion of the peoples. Many of the most talented young men in Europe were attracted to the Order, and it was in the forefront of scholarship in many fields. Francis Xavier was one of those who in 1534 joined Loyola in a vow to make the pilgrimage to Jerusalem and to carry the Gospel to the Turks and heathen.

Matteo Ricci and the Origins of the Jesuit Mission

Francis Xavier

The Jesuit approach to China was conditioned by this European background, but it was also deeply influenced by their experience in Asia. The policy of accommodation that became the hallmark of the Jesuit mission to China was the result of wise leadership reacting to the circumstances in which they were placed. It was all the more remarkable in the context of Counter-Reformation theology. Francis Xavier, who never set foot on the Chinese mainland, dying of fever on 3 December 1552, on the offshore island of Shangquan (Sancian), set the tone of the future mission. After a spell in India he spent the years from 1549 to 1551 in Japan, an experience that convinced him that the key to the conversion of the East lay in China. In one of his letters he wrote:

> I hope to go there during this year, 1552, and penetrate even to the Emperor himself. China is that sort of kingdom, that if the seed of the gospel is sown, it may be propagated far and wide. And, moreover, if the Chinese accept the Christian faith, the Japanese would give up the doctrines which the Chinese have taught them . . .[9]

It was also in Japan that he came to understand the need to reach native peoples on their own terms. This meant becoming an integral part of the culture, although without compromise to Christian belief. These fundamental insights were adopted as the policy of the Jesuit mission after the Italian Jesuit Alessandro Valignano became Visitor of the Far Eastern missions in 1574. However, most Jesuits in Macao did not accept this approach, and when Michele Ruggieri was instructed to learn "to read, write and speak" Chinese there was considerable resistance. Only after Valignano had taken decisive action in 1582 did it become possible to embark on the China mission.

Matteo Ricci

Matteo Ricci was born on 16 October 1552 in Macerata, Italy, of a noble family. At the age of seventeen his father sent him to Rome to study law, but Ricci soon applied for admission to the Jesuit Order, into which he was received on the feast of the Assumption, 15 August 1571. He studied philosophy and mathematics under the well-known mathematician Christopher Klau (Clavius), friend of Kepler and Galileo. In 1578 he set out for India, where he was to spend four years before being assigned to the Chinese mission. He arrived in

Macao on 8 August 1582, and began to study Chinese along-side Ruggieri. Ricci was more adept, and within a few years he was able to translate into Latin the *Four Books* (the *Confucian Analects*, the *Book of Mencius*, the *Great Learning*, and the *Doctrine of the Mean*). In 1583 Ruggieri and Ricci established residence in the southern city of Zhaoqing, having shaved off their hair and beards and donned the grey robes of Buddhist monks, assuming on the basis of Xavier's Japanese experience that as such they would be received with respect. It was a mistake that was rectified in 1594, when Ricci received permission from his superiors to don the silk robes of the Chinese literati.

Ricci shared Xavier's belief that the key to success lay in the conversion of the Emperor, but before establishing himself in the capital Ricci had to spend many years in other cities. After Zhaoqing he spent seven years in the city of Shaozhou, also in Guangdong, and here he avidly studied the Chinese classics, achieving a depth of knowledge that impressed the highly educated scholars he met when he established residence in the important city of Nanchang in Jiangxi Province. He moved here in 1595, having found the political climate in the southern capital of Nanjing, in the midst of the war in Korea against the Japanese, uncongenial to foreigners. Nanchang was famous for its scholars, and he was welcomed by the members of the Eastern Grove Academy who were still active there despite imperial disfavour. He achieved a considerable reputation, and was much respected by the literati and upright officials amongst whom he spent much of his time.

He remained determined to obtain a reception at the imperial court, and in 1598 actually made a brief visit to Beijing but was forced to retreat. On his return journey south he once more made it to Nanjing and, with the Korean war having come to an end, found a different mood prevailing. Nanjing was kept by the Ming as a second capital, and all government agencies were duplicated here. Thus there were many eminent scholar-officials in residence, and Ricci forged friendships with some of the most influential, something that stood him in good stead when he did finally get to Beijing. His own studies continued and he issued a revised edition of his world map, the first edition of which had helped him to establish his residence in China, away from the Portuguese enclave of Macao.

Xavier had understood the need to send men of learning to China and Japan, and the presentation of European science and mathematics was to be an essential aspect of the Jesuit mission. However, as Joseph Needham has pointed out in his monumental work *Science and Civilization in China*, the coming of the Jesuits was "by no means an unmixed blessing for Chinese science". The basic reason for this was that, while importing the superior elements in European science, they also "imposed a fundamentally wrong world picture, that of the solid world spheres, on the fundamentally right one which had come down from the Xuan Ye school, of stars floating in infinite empty space". He also points out that in some cases the Jesuits were "really only reminding the Chinese of things which they themselves had developed long before, but which the degenerate science of the Ming had forgotten".[10] One outstanding example of this concerns the making of clocks. European clocks were becoming highly sophisticated and were hugely successful in impressing the Chinese. Yet Chinese clock-making technology had been in advance of the rest of the world until the fall of the Northern Song in 1127.

Ricci prepared very carefully for the embassy to Beijing, selecting gifts designed to convince the Wanli Emperor of the worthiness of the bearers. Eight packhorses and more than thirty porters carried the gifts, arriving in Beijing in January 1601. There were religious paintings, which deeply impressed the Emperor because of the use of perspective, unknown in China; there were clocks with hanging weights, spring-driven desk clocks, prisms and mirrors; the books such as Abraham Ortelius's cartographic masterwork, *Theatrum Orbis Terrarum*; musical instruments such as the harpsichord, that the Emperor commanded four eunuchs to learn to play under the instruction of one of the Fathers. The embassy was a success, and Ricci was at last able to reside in Beijing. For the next nine years, until his death in 1610, he stayed in the city. The sending of such an embassy, and the Chinese response, fits neatly into the traditional framework of relationships between foreigners and Chinese officials. Ricci had the perspicacity to see the importance of acting in this way in order to fulfil his main purpose of evangelization. He was out to impress, and this was very necessary in the context of suspicion of Westerners and their real objectives in coming to China. His sensitivity and wisdom was to be the hallmark of the Jesuit mission over the next hundred and twenty years.

Ricci's world map became an object of great interest to literati, and in 1600 brought Xu Guangqi, one of China's outstanding Confucian scholars, from Shanghai to Nanjing to find Ricci. Xu soon returned to Shanghai, but three years later he was baptized. He was to become a high official at court and China's most famous Roman Catholic. His commitment to Christianity was soon to be shared by a number of other prominent intellectuals of the time, including Li Zhicao and Yang Tingyun. Li first met Ricci in Beijing in 1601, and two years later sought baptism, although in fact he was not received into the Church until 1610 as Ricci insisted that he must give up his concubines before being baptized. Yang was converted in Hangzhou in 1611 by Lazzaro Cattaneo and the newly arrived Nicholas Trigault. The three converts became known as the "Three Pillars of the Early Catholic Church".

Ricci's life in Beijing was hectic by any standards. As many as twenty visiting cards would be left at his residence every day, and on special days such as New Year it could be over a hundred! On some days he had barely time to snatch a meal. His visitors included many eminent officials and also relatives of the imperial family itself. The Governor of Guizhou republished his world map and wrote in the preface: "Ricci has been so long in China that he is no longer a foreigner, but a Chinese."

One small but fascinating incident is worth recording. In 1605 a Chinese Jew, Ai Tian, sought out Ricci, thinking he must be of the same faith. It slowly dawned on Ricci in the course of their conversation that Ai Tian was in fact a Jew. Thus was discovered the small Jewish community in Kaifeng, one of China's ancient capitals sited along the Yellow River.

Slowly, a small Christian community was formed in Beijing and in a few other places such as Baoding, a city in Hebei just south of the capital, where by 1607 there were some hundred and fifty Christians. Ricci reported that Beijing in 1608 had "already more than two thousand Christians, among them many scholars".[11] Ricci's time in this world was now limited, and he died on 11 May 1610. He was entombed on All Saints Day (1 November) 1611 on the plot of land outside the Fucheng Gate granted by the Emperor.

The Growth of the Church

Ricci had chosen Nicolo Longobardo as his successor, despite their very different temperaments and disagreement over the use of ancient Chinese terms for God. Longobardo was in favour of using an invented term (similar to the policy adopted by the Jesuits in Japan), and he continued to advocate his views amongst his fellow Jesuits. It is a tribute to the calibre and integrity of the missionaries that although Longobardo failed to convince his confrères, the debate never became acrimonious. Under his leadership the work began to spread into other parts of the country. By 1622 there were thirteen Jesuits working in China, but the extension of the mission depended heavily on the support of eminent Chinese converts. Up to his death in 1633 Xu Guangqi was active in fostering the growth of the Christian community, especially in his home city of Shanghai. In 1608 he invited Cattaneo to Shanghai, and within two years there were over two hundred converts. While in enforced retirement from 1621 to 1627, during the reign of terror conducted by the eunuch Wei Zhongxian, he built a larger church on his estate at Xujiahui (Ziccawei), so laying the foundations of one of the major centres of Chinese Catholicism down to our own day. By 1650 Bartoli reported that Shanghai "had from eighteen to twenty thousand faithful and is one of the most splendid Christian centres in the empire".[12]

The next generation of missionaries was also arriving from Europe. One such was Giulio Aleni, who arrived in 1613. In 1621 he was invited to the province of Shaanxi, where he spent five months laying the foundations of the Church in that part of China. On his return journey he spent time in Shanxi Province, once again succeeding in establishing the basis of a thriving Christian community. Alfonso Vagnoni took over the work in 1625 with the support of Han Kuang, a sympathetic non-Christian, and during the 1630s the Christian community grew. By Vagnoni's death in April 1640 there were around eight thousand converts in one hundred and two Christian communities.[13] Aleni's great work, however, was to be in Fujian, where he went in April 1625. He was to reside in the province for twenty-five years, until his death in 1649. By the late 1630s there were churches in each of the eight prefectures of Fujian.

Aleni had been preceded in Fujian by both Dominicans and Franciscans from the Philippines, but the two Orders only established an effective presence after 1633, with the arrival of the Dominican Juan Baptista de Morales. It was de Morales who launched the first round in the Rites Controversy that was eventually to destroy the Chinese mission. He attacked the whole principle of accommodation with the Confucian rites, on the grounds that it was a condonation of superstition. For the time being the Jesuits were able to defend their position, but the rigid theological stance of the older Orders, which regarded all non-European cultures as inferior, was more attuned to the prevailing mood in Rome, with the result that the Jesuit position became more precarious as the seventeenth century wore on. In China in 1637 the behaviour of a group of Franciscans in Fujian led to a severe persecution of the Christians in the province. There was little the Jesuits could do except try to pick up the pieces.

The Church in Shaanxi also expanded under the legendary leadership of Etienne le Fèvre, who worked there for most of the time from 1635 until his death in 1657. By then there were some twelve thousand Christians. In 1640 Ludovico Buglio went to Sichuan, and a number of communities came into existence, although the real growth in this province began after 1696 with the arrival of two Lazarist priests and two priests of the recently established Société des Missions Étrangères of Paris. The period of growth here was in the following century, but that belongs to the next phase in our story.

The growth of the Church under the Jesuits was steady and with an increasing geographical spread. The next logical stage would be the training of Chinese clergy. However, the Jesuits in Japan had always opposed the ordination of Japanese, and in 1606 the General of the Society had directed that Chinese should not be ordained. Longobardo opposed this with vigour, and eventually permission was given. Owing to the difficulties of finding suitable candidates and training them it was only in 1664 that Zheng Weixin was ordained as the first Chinese Jesuit priest. In 1688 three more were ordained, including Wu Li, a noted Qing artist and poet.

The Nanjing Persecution

It should not be thought that all this progress happened without opposition. Reference to the persecution in Fujian has already been made. Chinese fears of Westerners were, as we have noted, not without foundation. In 1935 local Chinese in Shaozhou suspected Ricci and his colleagues of being linked to the Portuguese in Macao. They "came from Macao, and have much dealings with foreign countries, contrary to China's laws. They have built here a house with walls, like a castle, where they shelter over forty people who also have come from Macao."[14] The fear and suspicion that Ricci encountered on his first visit to Nanjing in 1595, during the Korean campaign, can be more readily understood when it is realized that the Japanese invading armies included over fifteen thousand Japanese Christians under the convert general Konishi Yukinaga.[15]

The welcome accorded to the Jesuits by many literati was balanced by suspicion of their intentions amongst other scholars. On the popular level, there was curiosity, frequently

65

mixed in with mockery and even overt hostility. In 1592 Ricci and a colleague were wounded in an assault by drunken youths on their house in Shaozhou. Despite such incidents the local governments were generally careful to protect the foreign visitors, and it was not until 1616, some years after Ricci's death, that the first officially organized anti-Christian incident took place. It was to be the first in a series of such incidents, though in itself it amounted to very little.

The Vice-President of the Nanjing Board of Rites (the government Board responsible for the examination system, religious affairs and also dealings with foreigners), a man called Shen Que, wrote a series of memorials to the throne denouncing the Jesuits and calling for their expulsion. It was only on his third attempt in 1617, with the support of the minister of the Beijing Board of Rites, that a reply was received. Meanwhile the two men had already arrested the Jesuits and some Chinese Christians in Nanjing. The edict of 16 January 1617 was mild in tone, but deemed it wise to deport the missionaries. The resulting measures were not severe, except in Nanjing, as most officials contented themselves with the closure of churches and the temporary withdrawal of the Jesuits to other places. In Nanjing, however, Shen Que ensured that the edict was enforced, and after being tortured Alphonse Vagnoni and three other Fathers were sent to Guangzhou for deportation. Vagnoni and Alvaro Semedo returned in early 1618 disguised as newly arrived missionaries. Shen had, in the meantime, been promoted to Beijing, and the persecution came to an end. In 1622 he was forced to retire and he died two years later.

The incident was unpleasant, but limited in its effects. It revealed for the first time the strength of anti-Christian feeling amongst a section of the scholar-officials, especially those sympathetic to Buddhism. It was responsible for the first collection of anti-Christian writings, edited by Xu Changzhi and entitled *An Anthology of Writings Exposing Heterodoxy* (*Poxie ji*). Shen Que was one of the forty contributors, and while their antagonism to Christianity was in part motivated by the fear of foreign aggression, in part by xenophobia, at root the opposition related to the heterodox nature of Christian teachings.

The Early Qing Dynasty

The origins of Qing power lay in Manchuria (North-East China). Here in the early years of the seventeenth century the Jurchen people (commonly known as Manchus), consolidated their tribal power under Nurhachi (1559-1626). In 1616 Nurhachi declared the Later Jin Dynasty, and from 1618 the Manchus fought the Ming. Nurhachi was defeated by China and died soon afterwards of his wounds, the Kingdom passing to his eighth son, Abahai. In 1636 Abahai re-named his dynasty the Qing, and in a series of brilliant campaigns extended Qing power throughout the territory north of the Great Wall. Abahai died in 1643, and the conquest of China became the work of Nurhachi's fourteenth son, Dorgon. It was his forces that wrested power from the rebels of Li Zicheng in the capital and from Ming loyalists elsewhere. Dorgon himself was reluctant to become Emperor, and the five-year-old Fu-lin was proclaimed the Shunzhi Emperor, with Dorgon as one of two regents.

Over the next few years it was Dorgon who established the foundations of Qing government throughout China (except in the South-West). On Dorgon's death aged thirty-eight in 1650, the young Emperor assumed control and soon showed himself a conscientious and deeply religious young man. Unfortunately, the Emperor himself then died, aged twenty-two, and his heir was still a young child. Nevertheless, in 1661, at the age of fifteen, he assumed absolute control, taking the reign title of the Kangxi Emperor. So began one of the greatest reigns in Chinese history.

The Jesuits at the Qing Court

Xu Guangqi and Li Zhicao had worked closely with Ricci in translating outstanding European books on mathematics, geography, hydraulics and astronomy. In 1607 the first such book was published, the initial six chapters of Euclid's *Elements of Geometry*. Xu went on in later life to produce a series of his own works, including a famous work on agriculture. It was, however, in astronomy that the Jesuits made their most apparent contribution to Chinese sciences – despite the inadequacy of their world picture. The importance of the calendar in pre-industrial society must be borne in mind, as well as the enormous political significance of the accurate prediction of dates and cosmic events, in a society in which the Emperor was seen as the mediator between heaven and earth. The Astronomical Bureau under the Ming consisted of two bureaus: the traditional Bureau and the Muslim Bureau established under the Mongols. Both systems were in decline in the Late Ming, and the emperors sought for people able to make an accurate calendar. The Jesuits were able to step into the breach.

Adam Schall von Bell was born in Cologne in 1592 and received an excellent education in the humanities, astronomical science and mathematics. He arrived in China in 1623, spent some years in Xi'an, and then in 1630 he was called to Beijing to take over the work on the reform of the calendar in collaboration with Xu Guangqi. Schall was able to weather the change in dynasty in 1644, and the Regent, Dorgon, asked him to prepare a new calendar. In this way the Jesuits were able to serve the purposes of the Manchus in consolidating their authority. Dorgon had Schall appointed Director of the Astronomical Bureau, and under the Shunzhi Emperor Schall achieved a unique position at Court. On one occasion the Emperor even visited Beijing's Southern Cathedral. But Schall's hopes of converting the Emperor came to naught, and in his last years the Emperor turned to Buddhism.

Schall had achieved his pre-eminence at the expense of the discomforted Muslim astronomers. Opposition to the heterodox religion amongst some scholar-officials remained. In 1659 an orthodox but fiery Confucian named Yang Guangxian memorialized the throne against the Jesuits, especially attacking Schall's calendar. In early 1661 the Shunzhi Emperor died, but despite continued attacks by Yang, Schall remained secure under the Regent Oboi. However, in 1664, Yang accused the Jesuits of selecting an inauspicious date for the burial of the infant son of the Empress in 1658, thus causing the early death of both the Empress and the Emperor. To the Manchus this was a telling accusation, as they were traditionally believers in Shamanism. It resulted in the most serious persecution to date, although the death sentences against Schall and some of his Chinese assistants were commuted. However, five Chinese Christian astronomers were executed, and all Christian churches were closed. All Christian missionaries except the four Jesuits in Beijing were ordered to Macao, where they remained in detention until 1671. Schall died on 15 August 1666, and was posthumously restored to his titles and ranks by the Emperor Kangxi.

The importance of Yang Guangxian lies not in his brief triumph over his Jesuit enemies but in his long-term influence on the Chinese literati in the nineteenth century who led the anti-Christian movement of that time. Yang's work, *I Could Not Do Otherwise (Budeyi)*, was, in fact, far more sophisticated in its attack than most nineteenth-century writings on the subject.

Christianity and the Kangxi Emperor

The last phase of the Jesuit mission began auspiciously with the assumption of supreme power by the Kangxi Emperor in 1668. Kangxi was anxious to adopt a workable calendar, and the Flemish Jesuit Ferdinand Verbiest was able to demonstrate the superiority of the Western system. In 1669 Yang Guangxian was sent into exile, and Verbiest was appointed Director of the Astronomical Bureau. In 1692 the Emperor issued an edict of toleration. So began a period of growth and seeming success. Unfortunately, in Europe the attack on the Jesuit policy of accommodation was being pursued with vigour, and in China the seeds of the destruction of the mission were being sown by the insensitive policies of the other religious Orders.

The attitude of the Emperor towards Christianity was more

complex than has been generally allowed. There is no doubt that he was deeply interested in the science taught by the Jesuits, and he developed an active knowledge of mathematics and astronomy under instruction from Verbiest and other Fathers. He also developed a close friendship with them, and showed himself to be sympathetically interested in their religious beliefs, as his poem cited at the head of this chapter reveals. There seems no reason why the friendly relationships and toleration should not have continued throughout his reign, if the Roman Catholic Church had maintained its previous support for Ricci's original policies.

On 26 March 1693 Charles Maigrot, Vicar-Apostolic in Fujian, promulgated an order forbidding the rites honouring Confucius and ancestors, and prohibiting the use of the terms *Tian* and *Shangdi* for God. In 1700 the Jesuits appealed to the Emperor to support their interpretation that the rites were not idolatrous. Kangxi confirmed their viewpoint. This appeal infuriated the opponents of the Jesuits, and in 1701 Pope Clement XI decided to send a Papal Legate to China to resolve the dispute. On 31 December 1705 Charles de Tournon, the Apostolic Visitor in East Asia, had an audience with Kangxi. The Emperor was now very aware of the differences between the Christians in his Empire, and he expressed his displeasure at what he rightly saw as a denial of the unity that Christians claimed to profess. He made known to de Tournon his expectation that the policies of Ricci would be followed, and he warned: "if in the future, anything is done against the [Confucian] doctrines, it will be very difficult for the Westerners to remain among us."

De Tournon, influenced by men such as Charles Maigrot, then issued his "Decree of Nanjing" dated 7 February 1707. It condemned the rites and ignored the Emperor's personal viewpoint on the matter. From then on Kangxi gradually lost patience, although he never lost his respect for his Jesuit friends. The Papal Bull *Ex Illa die* of 1715, confirming the Decree of Nanjing, still found the Emperor willing to enter into dialogue. Rome was not prepared to listen, and finally, on 21 February 1721, the Emperor issued his famous edict banning Christianity. Not until 1939 was the Vatican to reverse its ruling of 1715. In China Christianity was not to disappear, but for the next hundred or so years it was to become a persecuted minority, out of touch with the mainstream of Chinese life. The great enterprise was over. The intellectual debate between Confucian tradition and Christianity was not to be revived until the twentieth century, and by then Confucianism itself was in retreat before the challenge of another Western ideology – that of Marx's dialectical materialism.

The Confucian/Christian Debate

The story of the Jesuit mission in China would not be complete without a brief discussion of some of the issues that occupied the minds of both the proponents and opponents of Christianity. The debate was conducted within the framework of the scholastic theology of the Council of Trent and the Neo-Confucian philosophy that dominated the thinking of the scholar-officials with whom the Jesuits came in contact. Of course, Buddhist and Taoist thinkers also opposed the Christians, but there was no attempt by the Jesuits to enter into a meaningful debate with these groups. We have seen, however, that late Ming China was a period of vigorous intellectual discussion, and that many felt an acute personal crisis as they sought to wrestle with the relationship between inner wisdom and social concern – the issues raised by Wang Yangming against Neo-Confucian orthodoxy. It will be helpful to begin by looking at the standpoint of converts such as Xu Guangqi. How did they understand their faith in the light of their Confucian upbringing?

Xu Guangqi and the other converts came to see Christianity as the fulfilment of Confucian tradition. Xu was deeply concerned about the relationship of self-cultivation to public life, and he clearly found in Christianity a way out of the dilemmas posed by traditional Confucianism, whether that of Zhu Xi or of Wang Yangming. It is not surprising that he understood his new faith very much in terms of its moral power to foster an active sagehood, but this he interpreted in the light of his understanding of salvation and a universal love that transcended the Confucian differentiation between degrees of love (*ren*, human-heartedness). By adopting the Christian understanding of a personal God Xu went beyond Neo-Confucianism. There is no indication in his writings that he felt a tension between his Confucian morality and his Christian faith, yet it must be said that, however personally fulfilling he may have found this synthesis, it was not to convince the majority of his fellow scholars.

Ever since Xu's death it has been customary for Chinese scholars to draw attention to the fact that he and his colleagues were deeply concerned to spread knowledge of Western science, and little or no acknowledgement of their religious commitment has been made. Yet a careful reading of their writings on Christianity makes it clear that their Christian commitment was not made out of expediency. They fully accepted Ricci's analysis of the relationship of Christianity and the Confucian tradition. What then was this analysis?

Original Confucianism

Ricci in his study of the Confucian classics had become convinced that the Neo-Confucianism of Zhu Xi and his followers was a distortion of the original teaching of Confucius. In his greatest work, *The True Meaning of the Lord of Heaven*, published in its final form in 1604, Ricci sought to show that the ancient Chinese had believed in a creator God. He criticizes both the Taoist concept of *"Wu"* (non-being) and the Buddhist *"Gong"* (Voidness), suggesting that the original Confucian belief in *"Shangdi"*, the Supreme God, is correct. He argues that the Chinese *"Tian"*, *"Heaven"*, is not impersonal, and he opposes this to the Neo-Confucian *"Taiji"* or *"Supreme Ultimate"*. He goes on to argue for the existence of the immortal soul, separate and distinct from the material creation. In this way he denies the "organic", non-dualistic, conceptions of Chinese philosophy, while seeking to show that his views are compatible with the tradition derived from Confucius.

Ricci spoke, therefore, of Christianity "supplementing" original Confucian teachings. It was this belief that enabled the Jesuits to argue that the Confucian ancestor rites were compatible with Christian discipleship. A great deal of Ricci's book is concerned with self-cultivation, drawing on the *Spiritual Exercises* of Ignatius Loyola as well as on Chinese tradition. He seeks to demonstrate that Christianity is concerned with the cultivation of virtue, and he adopts the Confucian concept of the "upright heart and the sincere will". He accepts that human nature is basically good, but argues that the individual is always subject to "passion", showing that our natures have been infected by selfish desires. In order to attain goodness, the individual must have *de* (virtue), and this involves a deliberate choice by the will. Ricci was attempting to deal with the whole question of sin, which, at least as usually understood in the West, is a concept absent from Chinese thought. He attempted to grapple with this issue, and to demonstrate that the rewards and punishments in the afterlife are not incompatible with the Chinese belief that "sincerity" is the result of the natural manifestation of human nature, and has no need of a motivation based on either the promise of reward or the fear of punishment. His arguments attempting to justify the existence of heaven and hell were unsatisfactory, and provoked much opposition. In a perceptive study Sister Goretti Lau has commented:

> Ricci's eschatology . . . reflects a Scholasticism of the later Middle Ages which tended to look upon life as having two distinct phases, the two connected by the moment of death. There is no mention of penetration and transformation of our life in this world by eternal life. Ricci's descriptions of eternity remain on a very physical and material level.[16]

The Chinese critics of Christianity denied the dualism underlying the theology of the Jesuits. Thus Huang Daozhou writes:

> My body and spirit are not fundamentally two distinct

> things . . . Everything under Heaven is but one single thing and comprises no duality. The sun, the moon, the four seasons, the spirits, the gods, Heaven and Earth are but one thing and comprise no duality.[17]

The universe contains within itself its own organizational principle and creative energy, and there is, therefore, no need of a Creator God. The Chinese considered incredible the Christian teaching on the origin of the world as being within the past few thousand years. For them the universe had evolved over vast periods of time – ninety-seven million years according to the eighth-century Buddhist monk Yixing.

The Christian view destroys the unity of human nature and sets up a conflict between soul and body that produces anxiety and a lack of harmony. Related to this is the undermining of the duty of filial piety. At first the willingness of the Jesuits to allow respect to be shown to ancestors muted this criticism, but they were then accused of teaching that the first loyalty was to God and not to one's parents. Nor were the critics convinced by the Christian view of human nature as sinful, and they rejected Ricci's views on self-cultivation, maintaining that there is no opposition between nature and culture: man is a free moral being whose development depends solely on good nurture.

> Ultimately, what the Chinese criticisms of Christian ideas bring into question are the mental categories and types of opposition which have played a fundamental role in Western thought ever since the Greeks: being and becoming, the intelligible and the sensible, the spiritual and the corporeal. Does all this not mean that Chinese thought is quite simply of a different type, with its own particular articulations and its own radical originality?

This is the question posed by Jacques Gernet in his study of the Jesuit impact on China.[18] Without doubt, the theology current in Europe in the sixteenth century was deeply influenced by dualistic categories and was unable to enter into a real dialogue with Chinese thought. It could not have been otherwise, and the long-term impact of Ricci's views within China was minimal. Xu Guangqi was remembered as a scholar but not as a Christian, except by the remnant of Christians that survived after the Emperor Kangxi's proscription of Christianity in 1721. Ricci's understanding of Chinese ideas was limited, and he clearly misunderstood such doctrines as the *"Wu"* of the Taoists, the Buddhist *"Gong"* and the Neo-Confucian *"Taiji"*. His conception of an "original" Confucianism is also to be questioned, although his contention that the ancient Chinese believed in a personal creator deity remains a subject of intense disagreement amongst modern scholars.

Gernet's contention that Chinese thought is radically different from that of the West must be taken seriously, but his generalizations need to be qualified. Ricci took the Taoist *"Wu"* and Buddhist *"Gong"* to mean "nothingness", whereas their meaning is akin to that Christian theology which in both East and West has always refused to give a name to God, who as the ultimate reality must exhaust all human attempts to describe him. The scholastic philosophical assumptions that lay behind the formalism of Counter-Reformation theology precluded the Jesuits from coming to grips with the non-dualistic and organic thought forms of China. Nor were they able to appreciate the dynamic mode of Chinese thought which contrasted strongly with the static assumptions of the Western theology of the time. Ricci failed to appreciate the dynamic of tradition: in China's case the coherence of Confucian tradition over the centuries. Hence his quest for an "original" Confucianism, which even rejected much of the thought of Mencius who lived only a hundred years after Confucius.

It is also true, however, that Ricci's whole discussion is aimed at dialogue with Confucian tradition. He took this tradition seriously, and in this was in advance of the Western missionaries, Catholic and Protestant, of the nineteenth century. His antagonistic attitude towards Buddhism and Taoism were similar to those of the later century, but his reasons were only in part the result of the limitations of his theological perspective, which precluded any positive awareness of the spiritual truths and possibilities for salvation within other religions. He was also influenced by the negative attitudes of the Confucian scholars amongst whom he spent so much of his time.

From today's perspective can we say that Ricci succeeded in his ambitious task of "supplementing" Confucius? As far as it went, it was a great enterprise, and it is with justification that Ricci is remembered with respect by all who seek to continue the dialogue between Christian faith and Chinese culture. The status and importance of Ricci's Chinese converts demonstrate that the reaction to the Jesuit mission by Chinese scholars and officials in the late Ming and early Qing was far more complex than is usually assumed. Of course, Xu and his fellows were a small minority, but others were sympathetic and on many occasions afforded protection to the Jesuits. Neither Xu, Li or Yang were ever penalized because of their espousal of a foreign religion – a testimony to the tolerance of China in comparison with Europe. Yet many writers on the subject have concentrated on the opposition encountered by the Jesuits, and have suggested that it exhibits the well-known xenophobia of the Chinese people. Such an explanation is tendentious and inaccurate. It conveniently bypasses the necessity of taking seriously the Chinese critique of Christianity, at least as it was expressed in the theological positivism of the Counter-Reformation. The Jesuits sought to express Christian faith through Chinese modes of thinking but this did not imply any compromise on Christian doctrine. Xu Guangqi obviously found no difficulty in being a Confucian Christian yet, given the nature of the theology taught by Ricci, he could reach such a synthesis only by a rejection of the Neo-Confucian understanding of the unity of Man, Heaven and Earth. The most powerful writers against the Jesuits saw the irreconcilability of the two systems and, rightly, saw Christianity as a challenge to their fundamental beliefs. Certainly, there was an element of xenophobia in the more outspoken reactions, but the most serious opposition was at a much deeper level. The teachings of the Jesuits challenged the very basis of the Neo-Confucian synthesis that had been the prevailing orthodoxy in China since the Song Dynasty.

Hindsight enables us to see the shortcomings in the Jesuit approach, but it should also enable us to appreciate the courage and the vision that enabled Ricci and his successors to win the respect of many of China's most eminent scholars. In a time of European expansion they exemplified a style of operation that contrasted with that of the other religious Orders and with that of missionaries in later times. They sought to come to terms with Chinese culture, for which they developed a profound respect. It is quite unrealistic to expect them to have transcended the thought forms of their European heritage. Their importance lies in the fact that they attempted an accommodation; their failure to transform the thinking of the Middle Kingdom does not detract from the attempt.

REFERENCES

1. Quoted by Bishop K.H. Ting, *A Rationale for Three-Self*, Neesima Lecture, Doshisha University, Japan, 28 September 1984.
2. See reports by New China News Agency, 21 July 1980 and 3 July 1984, reprinted in CSP Documentation, No. 4, 1981 and No. 15, 1984.
3. *Social Sciences in China* No. 3, 1983.
4. Liang Qichao, *Zhongguo qinsanbainian xueshushi*, pp. 28-9. Quoted in Young, John D., *Confucianism and Christianity: The First Encounter*, Hong Kong University Press, 1983, p. 5.
5. Spence, Jonathan D., *The Memory Palace of Matteo Ricci*, Faber & Faber, London 1984, p. 17.
6. Young, John D., op. cit., p. 142, Note 122 quoting Bernard, Henri, S.J., *Aux Portes de la Chine*, p. 186.
7. Ricci in letter to Maselli in Rome 1605, quoted in Spence, op. cit., p. 216.
8. *The Constitutions of the Society of Jesus*, St Louis, 1970, pp. 65-8.
9. Coleridge, H.J., ed., *The Life and Letters of St Francis Xavier*, Vol. 2, pp. 347-8.
10. Needham, Joseph, *Science and Civilization in China*, Vol. 3, Cambridge University Press 1959, pp. 437f.
11. Ricci in letter to his brother dated 24 August 1608, *Opere Storiche III*, p. 390.
12. Bartoli, Daniello, S.J., *Dell'istoria della Compagnia di Gésù, La Cina. Terza parte dell'Asia*, Vol. III pp. 45f., cited in Dunne, George H., S.J., *Generation of Giants: The First Jesuits in China*, Burns and Oates, London 1962, p. 308.
13. Dunne, op. cit., p. 303-5.
14. Fonti Ricciane, Pasquale M. D'Elia, S.J., ed., *Storia dell'Introduzione del Cristianesimo in Cina*, 3 vols, Rome 1942-49, 1/324, quoted in Spence, op. cit., p. 53.

15. Spence, op. cit., p. 51.
16. Lau, Maria Goretti, *Some Eschatological Thoughts in Matteo Ricci: The True Idea of God*, Tripod, No. 12, 1982, p. 98.
17. Huang Daozhou (1585-1646), quoted in Gernet, Jacques, *China and the Christian Impact*, Cambridge University Press 1985, p. 201.
18. Gernet, op. cit., p. 208.

III

To Save Souls
1721-1860

The need of the non-Christian world is indescribably great. Hundreds of millions are today living in ignorance and darkness, steeped in idolatry, superstition, degradation and corruption. It is our duty to evangelize the world because all men need Christ.

John R. Mott

The Catholic Church: Persecution and Survival
1723-1839

The Emperor Kangxi's impatience with Rome led, as we have seen, to his Edict of 1721 banning Christianity. However, persecution only began after Kangxi's death in 1723. The Yongzheng Emperor was hostile to Christianity and his Edict of 10 January 1724 demanded the closure of all churches, and that Christians renounce their faith. The Beijing Jesuits alone were to keep their positions as advisers on scientific and other matters, and the four churches in the capital were allowed to stay open. Up until the death of the Yongzheng Emperor in 1736 a number of missionaries were able to work outside Beijing, although subject to periodic persecution. Under the Qianlong Emperor (who died in 1796), however, matters became far worse, although again in Beijing worship continued – in 1743 Beijing was said to have forty thousand Christians and a thousand people were being baptized each year. The severe persecution started, as in the past, in Fujian, and in 1747 Petrus Sanz, Vicar Apostolic in the province, was arrested and executed, together with four other Dominicans and many Chinese Christians.

In spite of increasing restrictions, some foreign missionaries continued to enter the country, often with great difficulty, and always at great personal cost. The Jesuit Bishop of Nanjing, Laimbeckhoven, consecrated in 1756, only reached the Nanjing area in 1760. He was to live in poverty, in hiding near Shanghai, for twenty-seven years. In 1784 he made a secret visit to Suzhou where he ordained four Chinese priests. He died in 1787 and is buried in Suzhou.

The Jesuit enterprise in China was to come to a sad end in 1773, when Pope Clement XIV suppressed the Jesuit Order. Those in China submitted, although some stayed on as secular priests. In 1783 the Lazarists (founded in 1625 by Vincent de Paul) formally took over the Jesuits' cultural work in Beijing. A few Jesuits lived on in the capital, the last dying in 1814, but the mission as such died with Laimbeckhoven.

The Church in Sichuan Province

Sichuan is China's most populous province, yet it is also remote and inaccessible. Today it is a five-day trip by ship from the triple city of Wuhan in central China, up the mighty Yangzi River and through the three gorges that cut through high mountains on the way into the heartland of the province, but not so long ago it would take weeks, travelling in boats dragged by trackers through the dangerous rapids and shoals. Land access was even more difficult. "The road to Shu (Sichuan) is hard" wrote Li Bo, one of China's most famous poets, but the journey is well worth it, for Sichuan is also beautiful. The story of the Church in this part of South-west China during these lean years is of great interest, for it shows that in spite of severe difficulties and persecution Christianity not only survived but even added to its numbers, in a modest way. We have already noted how the work began in the province in 1640, and how after 1696 the work was taken over by the Paris-based Société des Missions Étrangères. In fact only a handful of foreign missionaries ever arrived, and in the 1747 persecution the two European priests had to abandon the work to the care of a Chinese priest, Andrew Li. When in 1756 François Pottier finally reached the area, there were only two Chinese priests serving four thousand Christians spread over Sichuan, Yunnan and Guizhou – an area of one million square kilometres, with a population of forty million. Pottier was consecrated Bishop and was appointed as the Vicar Apostolic of Sichuan in 1767. In 1764 a local seminary was established at Luoranggou, and it began to train some of the unmarried catechists for the priesthood. Sadly, despite its location deep in the mountains, it was sought out and burned down in 1814.

A small number of foreign priests managed to make the long journey, but their arrival was sporadic and they were always subject to discovery and persecution. Under these adverse circumstances remarkable qualities were needed to serve in China. The Société des Missions Étrangères insisted on three priorities in mission: the personal sanctification of the missionary, the conversion of pagans and the establishment of the local church. The priests who arrived in Sichuan certainly were remarkable men. They entered a situation in many ways not dissimilar to that of the first two centuries of the Christian era. The Christian community of necessity defined itself in opposition to the society around, and it drew its converts from amongst the poorest sections of that society. Just as in the Roman Empire the attitude of the pagan majority was hostile to the new faith, so it was in China. The most serious charge was that Christians seemed to undermine the foundations of society by their rejection of the ancestor rites. This, it was considered, revealed their lack of filial piety.

Christian attitudes towards women were to be a constant source of scandal down to modern times. The Chinese family was a strict hierarchy and for the most part women were at the bottom of the pile. Child brides, concubinage, footbinding, and in some areas female infanticide; these were all reflections of the inferior status accorded to women: they were also to be among the main targets of missionary attack. In Sichuan not only did women share in public worship but under the leadership of one of the more controversial of the pre nineteenth-century missionaries, Jean-Martin Möye, an Institute of Christian Virgins was established. The women frequently engaged in public speaking and even entered into debates with Confucian literati. Möye was an ascetic figure who expressed in his austere enthusiasm the essence of the Jansenist form of spirituality. He illustrates how French Catholics were still deeply influenced by this Catholic form of Augustinian pessimism with its disregard of the "world". Appropriate enough perhaps under the conditions of the Church in China at the time, but how ultimately inappropriate for the encounter of Christian faith and Chinese culture! Still, one cannot help being sympathetic to Möye's willingness to involve women in the running of church affairs, although such major divergences from traditional Chinese social teachings rendered the Catholics open to the charge of heterodoxy. Thus one priest, Gleyo, was arrested in 1769 on suspicion of being an agent of the millenarian Buddhist sect, the White Lotus, who at this period were also making many converts in the province.

Other aspects of the mission caused opposition: notably the custom of baptizing pagan children in danger of death, which developed during the famine years of 1785-6. Some priests later extended this to other children, baptizing without parental permission. This and the scandal caused by the "Virgins" were to be major topics of discussion at the 1803 Synod convened by Bishop Dufresse, who had succeeded Pottier as Vicar Apostolic. Steady growth and a lack of priests led to irregularities and occasional abuses, and with regard to the problem of the Virgins it was suggested that a Rule of Life might be introduced – an issue that was to take on an enormous significance within the Chinese Catholic Church in the mid-nineteenth century.

The figures relating to the growth of the Church in Sichuan are of some interest:[1]

No. of Baptized Members		Chinese Priests	
1756	4,000	1756	2
1792	25,000	1778	9
1801	40,000	1789	14
1804	45,000	1800	16
1815	60,000	1804	20

persecution

So it was that the Church in Sichuan survived and grew in size. Elsewhere the Church was less fortunate, but many thousands of Christians continued to worship, and organized themselves to survive. The roots of a truly indigenous Church had been put down. There was, however, a price to be paid.

Theology and Culture

We are a company of God's army, and we fight against darkness and superstition, and like the Gordon Highlanders, we suffer defeat only to rally to win.[2]

Our historical survey so far has taken us up to the beginning of the modern period. A key element in the discussion has been the manner and degree of cultural interaction between Christian faith and Chinese culture. The Nestorians of the Tang attempted to use Buddhist terminology in their translations into Chinese from Syriac – but, as we have noted, it was the very strength of Tang Buddhism that helped to contribute to the ultimate failure of the Nestorian mission. The Jesuits of the sixteenth and seventeenth centuries sought to discover within Confucianism a cultural basis for Christianity in a manner that in some ways stands comparison with the fourth-century Christian Platonists of Alexandria, who made creative use of pagan Greek philosophy in an attempt to set forth Christian truth in a way acceptable to the cultured Roman world. Of course, there were many differences in the two situations, but there was a common understanding that Christian faith would only succeed in moving to the centre of the stage if it could win the philosophical argument. It is an insight that must be kept hold of, even when circumstances

not stressed

seem to force Christianity to the margin, if it is not to succumb to the narrowness and fanaticism of the sectarian spirit that has marred so much of Christian history.

The experience of the years of persecution up to 1842 were to mark the consciousness of the Chinese Catholic community in the future. It was to remain a church on the margin of society, suspicious of its neighbours, and, with the return of the missionaries, a church that came to define its understanding of faith within the framework of a European theology of particular inflexibility and dogmatism. The triumph of Ultramontanism at the First Vatican Council (1869-70), with its stress on the centralization of authority and opposition to national or diocesan independence, could only have an adverse effect on the conduct of Catholic missions in China. The subsequent Ultramontanist attack on "modernism" helped to ensure that Catholic theology remained in a positivistic mould far into the twentieth century. In France, while Jansenism was officially proscribed, its influence amongst devout Catholics had been widespread, creating a cold rigorism in which Catholic humanism – with its roots in classical culture and its consequent appreciation of, and delight in, the true, the good and the beautiful – found little favour. Spirituality was to react to Jansenism with the cult of the Sacred Heart and similar affective movements, rather than by a return to a theological aesthetics that went beyond either the objectivism of Jansen or the subjectivism of Romanticism and, later, theological liberalism. The French Revolution and its aftermath in terms of antagonism to the Catholic Church also affected the attitudes of believers, producing a monarchist and conservative majority who "opposed the Republic in the name of an almost theological system of 'counter-revolution'."[3] All these attitudes and values were to be taken to China by the French missionaries who formed the overwhelming majority of Catholic missionaries there in the nineteenth century.

The Evangelical Revival amongst Protestants had shattered the emotionless deism and Erastianism that had dominated during the eighteenth century, but its emotional fervour, so

crucial for the revivifying of the faith, also meant the reassertion, in an over-simplified and cruder form, of Reformation
ideas about the contradiction between nature and grace, the
elect and the reprobate. A person is only rescued from
damnation by the free gift of God's grace accepted in an act of
conversion. That itself leads to moral reform through the work
of sanctification by the Holy Spirit. The logic of this in-
dividualistic theology is that grace supplants nature. Human
art and culture, non-Christian religions, all philosophy – are
overwhelmed by the action of God's grace. In seeking to
safeguard the uniqueness of Christ this type of Protestant
theology denies any analogical relationship between human
forms and the form of Christ. Theology becomes disincarnate.
Hans Urs von Balthasar, in his discussion of Dante's *Inferno*,
writes:

> For Luther and thorough-going Protestantism, as well as
> for Jansenism, the sinful world in its entirety is removed
> from the light of divine Eros and has fallen into a state of
> general damnation – with the exception of those for
> whom Christ died on the Cross. Here then Dante's in-
> fernal confines are generalized; they have become the
> confines of the world itself.[4]

A fully biblical understanding surely demands the recognition
of Christ both as the judge of all human systems and as the one
who fulfils and brings to perfection the inchoative or imper-
fect elements in these systems. It is deeply significant that this
more rounded theological perspective has become an essential element in the thinking of Chinese Protestant theologians
today. Bishop K.H. Ting in 1979 said:

> This world is God's, not Satan's. Christ is not an in-
> truder into the world alien to God, but is the first fruit of
> all creation. He is unique, but also akin to us organically
> because he himself is the perfection of that which all of us
> possess as our birthright as human beings, as sons of
> God.[5]

Chinese Spirituality

Unfortunately, the developments in European theology in the eighteenth century, combined with the unfavourable situation in China, led to the creation of Catholic and Protestant communities that were theoretically uninterested in cultural accommodation and were in any case, in practice, marginalized. Until the latter half of the last century few missionaries were interested in the question of Christianity and Chinese culture.

The essentially hostile reaction to Christianity of Chinese of all classes can be better understood when it is realized that after the Opium Wars in mid-century, conversion meant coming under the protection of the foreign aggressors, since extra-territorial "rights" granted in the treaties were extended to Christian converts. There was a very real sense, therefore, in which a Christian convert ceased to be a part of the Chinese community. The jibe, "one more Christian, one less Chinese", was not such an exaggeration! Here too we face an important question concerning faith and culture. In the Roman Empire the charge laid against the Christians was that of "atheism" – refusal to recognize the customs and rites passed down from time immemorial. Following this example, missionaries demanded that converts distance themselves from Chinese traditions. Thus Hur Mackenzie, an English Presbyterian in the Shantou area of Guangdong, wrote in a report that new converts had "to give up the worship of idols – to refuse to make offerings to the ancestors, to decline contributing to the support of idolatrous 'plays' and rites".[6] The parallel with early Christianity was quite misleading of course. Christianity challenged Classical culture from within, whereas in China it was one aspect of Western cultural aggression. A more appropriate parallel might be with the coming of Christianity to Celtic and Anglo-Saxon Britain.

The role and status of religion in Chinese society continues to be a matter of fierce dispute amongst students of religion. It is almost a commonplace to suggest that China's élite has shown itself indifferent to the claims of religion, whilst the common people have manifested a propensity for magical and superstitious practices bearing little relationship to the concerns of the great ethico-religious systems of the world. Such a viewpoint was common amongst Chinese intellectuals in the twentieth century, both Marxist and non-Marxist, and it was certainly the understanding of most missionaries. It is ironic that at home in Europe, Christianity was being forced on to the defensive in the intellectual debate with the rise of Darwinism and Marxism, and that the missionaries brought to China a scientific learning that was rooted in the rationalism of the Enlightenment. It was a contradiction in their own thinking of which they were unaware, but it helps to explain why it was that the long-term result of missionary education was the production of a generation of intellectuals committed to secular rationalism, often in its Marxist expression.

Our discussion of Ricci's attempt to discover an "original" Confucianism behind the "atheist" Neo-Confucian viewpoint has already suggested that the Neo-Confucian dynamic and organic understanding of the cosmos is not necessarily to be interpreted as non-religious. Of course, if one chooses to define religion as essentially dualistic, then, in that sense, it is not religious. However, if we take a religious response to be a response to life and the universe as *awe*-some (holy in the sense of the *mysterium tremendum et fascinans* of Rudolf Otto), then we will find within Chinese traditional culture a profound sense for the things of the spirit. The Europeans, with their religious understanding moulded first by the struggle with paganism, and then by the struggle with Islam, came to China looking for a religious perspective similar to their own. They found, as they saw it, either indifference or superstition. Their task was, therefore, to save souls and to create Christian communities that separated themselves from the mainstream of Chinese life and culture. Arthur H. Smith, one of the most popular commentators on Chinese life, in his famous book *Chinese Characteristics* published in 1894, concluded one chapter with the words:

Of China it might be said, as Gibbon remarked of Rome,

that to the common people all religions are equally true, to the philosopher all are equally false, and to the magistrate all are equally useful. Of the Emperor of China, as of the Roman Emperor, it might be affirmed that he is "at once a high-priest, an atheist, and a god"! To such a state has Confucianism, mixed with polytheism and pantheism, brought the Empire . . .

Its absolute indifference to the profoundest spiritual truths in the nature of man is the most melancholy characteristic of the Chinese mind, its ready acceptance of a body without a soul, of a soul without a spirit, of a spirit without a life, of a cosmos without a cause, a Universe without a God.[7]

Such was the opinion of the overwhelming majority of foreign missionaries. One notable exception was James Legge, later Professor of Chinese at Oxford, who once on entering the Temple of Heaven in Beijing removed his shoes declaring "This is holy ground" – to the horror of his fellow missionaries. On sailing for China in 1839 Legge had rejoiced to be approaching "the seat where Satan has enthroned his power", but his careful study of the Chinese classics later convinced him that the Chinese word *Shangdi* should be translated "God" – in other words, he maintained that Confucianism was monotheistic. He could therefore affirm of Ricci: "About the terms I entirely agree with his opinion, nor do I altogether differ with him about the ritual practices."[8]

The quest for God in the Chinese classics was understandable in the light of the theological positivism that dominated Catholic and Protestant thought from the sixteenth century. Its conclusions were, however, of dubious validity. The wellspring of Chinese spirituality is not to be found in a monotheist faith, even if the term *Shangdi* does indicate an ancient belief in a supreme being – a question over which scholars still differ. A deeper insight into the Chinese response to being human has been sadly lacking in so much Christian discussion of the Chinese attitude towards the things of the spirit. It is a pity that more have not taken the advice of Bishop

Ronald Hall of Hong Kong, in his *The Art of the Missionary*: "Sell every book you have on the religion of China and buy instead some fragment of her art". He went on to say:

> In our sense of the word they [the Chinese] are not religious – but they are artistic. You cannot talk of the religion of China as you can of the art of the Chinese people; not because their art is their religion, but because their art is their life.[9]

We can argue about the term "religious", but the crucial insight is that it is through art that Chinese civilization has expressed its response to the mystery of being. Speaking of the poetry of Tao Qian (373-427) and the landscape paintings of Mi Fei (1051-1107) and Ni Zan (1301-74), Chang Chung-yuan writes:

> There is something inherent in these works that leads us to the inexpressible ultimate that man shares with the universe. There is in them a dynamic process that interfuses with a higher grade of reality. They draw us into a spontaneous and even unintentional unity which, as the Taoist sees it, refers back to Tao (*Dao*) itself, the primordial source of creativity.[10]

This spirit pervades Chinese culture and is present within the most "secularized" Confucian. It informs Chinese Buddhism, and was in great part responsible for the emergence of the distinctive Chan School of Buddhism, or Zen as it is better known to the West.

Folk Religion and Superstition

It is, therefore, with caution that we approach the matter of Chinese folk religion. The Chinese Marxist analysis has accepted the dichotomy between "religion" and "superstition", and has made this the basis for religious policy. In this they would appear to agree with Western missionaries! The term "superstition" is not neutral – it implies a pejorative view of the phenomena being described. But for the Chinese peasant it was these "superstitions" that gave meaning to life and which were their response to the recognition that human effort alone could not guarantee well-being. More recent Western studies have sought to counter some of the simplistic assumptions of earlier commentators. It used, for example, to be widely held that folk religion was nothing more than an amalgam of the Three Great Traditions (Confucianism, Taoism and Buddhism), whereas it is now recognized that while there are many common elements, there was no one Chinese religion, but rather a series of local cults and traditions.

Folk religion had to do with gods, ghosts and ancestors, but there is an important sense in which the ancestor cult was separate and distinct. Ancestor worship itself had two separate aspects: the family cult, and the lineage cult. This latter, especially as practised in Southern China, was concerned with preserving the lineage and its land. The family cult was concerned with one's immediate ancestors, and it brought benefit to the living and the dead: the dead were ensured a smooth passage through the other world, the living were protected against the "hungry ghosts" – the ancestors whose cult had been neglected. Thus ancestor worship concerned family and kinship relations, whereas the folk religion as such did not necessarily involve a kinship link with the gods. The gods themselves were drawn from many sources, including the Taoist and Buddhist pantheons, but the nature of the worship was very different from the Taoism or Buddhism of the educated monks and literati. Popular understanding was that worship was a contract between a god and the believer, and in return for offerings to the god the worshipper was given protection. Divination, frequently through mediums, was a key element in many temple cults, as was the role of the "chanting fellows" who conducted elaborate funeral ceremonies.[11]

The Jesuits had associated with the cultured and highly educated scholar-official class, but both Catholic and Protestant missionaries in the nineteenth century were working amongst the poor and illiterate. The beliefs they encountered at the grass-roots of Chinese society were very different from those espoused by the gentry. In any case, the Protestants brought with them an iconoclasm that, as we have noted above, reacted with vehemence to the "idols" they discovered in all forms of Chinese religion. There is no doubt that in an important sense the gods and demons of Chinese folk religion enmeshed people in a network of cause and effect that allowed slight scope for personal freedom and fulfilment. One of the perennial appeals of sectarian religion in China was that it offered its adherents a release from the bonds of a society in which social relationships were rigidly defined, and whose religion was a mirror image of the earthly hierarchy. The shadow of the ancestors could be long and dark! Nevertheless, as C.S. Song has argued, "The God of early Christian [Protestant] converts in China and Asia was by and large an exorcist God." He points out that the war between Christianity and Chinese superstition developed into war between Christianity and Chinese culture, and he continues:

> Exorcism carried to excess is one of the root causes of Christianity's having remained an alien religion to the great majority of persons in Asia. It has remained a guest religion. Its God is a guest God. As a guest, God cannot speak *out of* the heart of the people; God always speaks *to* it.[12]

As suggested above, we need only look back to our own history to realize that the Christian conversion of the European peoples was accompanied by the assimilation and sublimation of many aspects of pagan religion. It was, moreover, a process that took centuries. Modern missionaries have sought immediate conversion and a rejection of "superstitions" that have allowed for no period of adjustment and sublimation. In some ways their attitude is explicable, coming from a Europe whose pagan past had in the main disappeared, to a China where the beliefs of the literati seemed to have little in common with those of the ordinary people. The suspicion of ancestor rites by the Franciscan and Dominican opponents of the Jesuits in the early eighteenth century was founded on more than cultural arrogance. The Emperor Kangxi's opinions were one thing, the belief and practice in the villages was another. Once again it was Ronald Hall who expressed a profounder understanding of the matter than most missionaries:

> The nearer you are drawn to God the less will heathenism, idolatry and superstition matter. You will see in them as it were the footprints of the eternal. Even in the most hateful of all heathen practices – the offering of human sacrifice . . . there is an echo as it were of Calvary, of the mystery of death and of that greater love which gives its life for another. The nearer you are drawn to God the more you will feel the mantle of his charity thrown over much that to you is utterly abhorrent. And yet the nearer you are drawn to God the more deeply and more vividly you will feel the horror, the cruelty and the wrong.[13]

There will always be a demand that faith makes to culture, a degree of separation from one's past, but it is a question of balance and sensitivity. The over-all wisdom of Ricci and the early Jesuits is revealed even more clearly when compared to the attitudes of the nineteenth century. Of course, Ricci's approach was out of the question after the death of the Emperor Kangxi in 1723. The later missionaries did not make a deliberate choice to work amongst the poor and uneducated; there was little option after the controversy over Chinese rites had convinced the Chinese that Christianity was to be regarded as alien and heterodox. From now on, amongst officials and gentry, the spirit of Yang Guangxian was to prevail. After 1723 Christianity was to be marginalized, forced into secrecy, and it manifested many of the characteristics of a religious sect. It was only because of the *force majeure* of the European powers that it was able to re-emerge publicly, but it was to remain a heterodox sect on the margin of society throughout the nineteenth century. Ultimately, one is forced to the conclusion that European theology lacked the inner resources necessary to an encounter with the spirit of the ancient culture of China.

Dynastic Decline and Social Revolt

It is significant that in the eighteenth century the growth of the Catholic Church in the South-west took place at the same time as the White Lotus sect began to expand in the region, and the persecutions of 1805 onwards must be seen in the context of the systematic attempt by the government to suppress the White Lotus and other related secret societies. The world of the secret society and sect represented an important facet of Chinese popular culture – one where religious belief was related to social protest, either through providing a means of protection for its members or in open rebellion. The history of late Qing China or of the Chinese Church cannot be understood apart from the rise of sectarian rebellion throughout the late eighteenth and the whole of the nineteenth century.

Qianlong died in 1799. His son, the Jiaqing Emperor, nominal ruler since his father's abdication in 1797, had first of all to get rid of Heshen, the unscrupulous and corrupt minister who had dominated the administration for the last twenty-four years of Qianlong's life. Heshen was permitted to commit suicide, and while some of his appointees remained in office the new Emperor instituted an important reform of the administration. The decline of Qing power was therefore not the result of inefficient administration, but was rather related to the range of unprecedented social problems now facing China. It has been suggested that in some ways China in the early nineteenth century was facing the sort of problems being faced by many developing societies now. A long period of stability and peace had resulted in the increase of the population between the late seventeenth century and 1800 from an estimated 198 million (in 1661) to 300 million. Between 1779 and 1850 it rose to an estimated 430 million. The agricultural revolution that accompanied the importation of new food plants from the Americas had worked itself through by 1800, and further dramatic increases in production were no longer possible. Landless migrants poured into the remoter and less fertile areas, as the pressure of population in the richer areas such as the Yangzi region became acute. Social disruption and conflict was the inevitable concomitant of these migrations. Thus, in 1795 the Miao people along the Hunan-Guizhou border revolted in reaction to the seizure of their land by Han Chinese settlers. In 1806 the Miao were crushed with great brutality, and sporadic revolts continued in later years. Another group of Han migrants, the Hakka or "Guest people", moved into the southern province of Guangxi, and found themselves in competition with the various ethnic groupings who make up the population of that region. This time, it was the Han immigrants who were to be worsted, with consequences that were eventually to leave as many as twenty million dead in the upheavals of the Taiping Rebellion and its eventual suppression.

Migration was one result of the crisis caused by the unequal relationship of population to resources. Other serous problems accompanied this fundamental crisis. The whole system of finances and taxation was in disarray, as was the crucially important grain transport system. The increasing numbers of petty officials and their hangers-on compounded corruption and mal-administration, leading to the disintegration of political control. Socially the result was the rise of the secret society and the re-appearance of older sectarian groupings, often combining semi-criminal activities with anti-Manchu political pretensions. One of the most notorious arose in South China, the brotherhood known as the "Triads", who from the mid-1840s engaged in overt acts of rebellion culminating in the Red Turban revolt of 1854. The Triads later became more purely criminal, but the Chinese secret society has always had the function of providing protection to its members, and it has many similarities to the Mafia.

It was, however, the White Lotus that represented the most important of the heterodox movements during the late eighteenth century. The White Lotus groups are a complex and fascinating phenomenon which have received a lot of attention from scholars in recent years. Unlike the Triads, the White Lotus was not really a "secret society" for it was a religious movement with its origins in Pure Land Buddhism in the eleventh century.[14] To this orthodox Buddhist substratum was

added an amalgam of Taoist, millenarian Buddhist and Manichaean teachings. It believed in the coming of the "future"
Buddha, Maitreya, and of the Manichaean "prince of light"
who would bring about the triumph of light over darkness.
This eschatology inspired its followers to rise against the existing order and in times of crisis it was to have a wide appeal. In
1796 there was a widespread revolt led by the White Lotus,
involving the provinces of Hubei, Sichuan and Shaanxi; it was
put down after a ten-year struggle which destroyed White
Lotus power but also drained the imperial treasury – turning
an accumulated surplus into a deficit: "Thus it was the White
Lotus Rebellion, rather than the Opium War, that demonstrated the irreversible decline of Qing military power."[15]
Moreover White Lotus groups re-emerged all over North and
Central China during the next hundred years. We will be meeting them again before too long.

The First Protestants in China

The early years of the last century were, therefore, not an
auspicious time for foreign missionaries to arrive in China.
The only way to obtain entry was by attachment to the trading
enclave in Guangzhou, through which all business with
China was conducted between 1760 and 1834. It is hard for us
to appreciate just how formidable were the obstacles facing
these early pioneers. The long and hazardous sea voyages
from Europe, perhaps taking up to six months of travel; the
great distances between different parts of China; official and
popular hostility; the increasingly unsettled state of the
countryside; exposure to endemic diseases and unhygienic
living conditions; all took their toll, especially on the children
of missionaries. Service in China was expected to be for life,
and for many life was to be all too short. Unlike the merchants
trading in opium and other less lethal commodities, there
were few material compensations. Whatever our contemporary reservations about the theology and style of the
missionaries of the nineteenth century, it is important not to

forget how much they gave of themselves, how much they lost in terms of worldly security and comfort (even if nineteenth-century Europe had its own share of social deprivation). It was through their labours that the Protestant Church in China was founded, and that in spite of the mistakes and failings of all-too fallible men and women.

The earliest pioneers, like Robert Morrison of the London Missionary Society and his associate William Milne, found themselves isolated in a foreign enclave where they met with scant sympathy from many of the foreign merchants. They also faced the task of learning the Chinese language and of preaching the Gospel in a vast and unknown country. Morrison arrived in 1807, and by the time of his death in 1834 he and his four colleagues had baptized only ten Chinese converts. Morrison had originally secured his presence in Guangzhou as a translator for the East India company, and in 1816 he accompanied Lord Amherst as interpreter on his ill-fated embassy to Beijing. Thus from the beginning Protestant missions were linked with the merchants and governments of their countries of origin. It was to prove a mixed blessing.

Protestant Literature Work

Despite the immense difficulties, the achievement in these first years was considerable, even though it could not be measured in terms of numbers of Christians. The obsession with numbers of conversions was not a characteristic of Morrison and his colleagues, although it was soon to become a hallmark of Protestant missions in China, fired with the vision of carrying the saving gospel to the perishing millions. Morrison and Milne concentrated on the work of translation. The publication of the Bible in Chinese in 1819 was a fine achievement. William Milne in the same year published his tract *Dialogues Between Two Friends*, which was to prove a long-lasting success, with possibly one million or more copies being printed by the beginning of the twentieth century. The tract succeeded in making a competent presentation of Christian doctrine, albeit within a somewhat restricted theological framework. It was, however, its style of presentation that made it remarkable, for in its dialogue between two Chinese friends, one of whom is a Christian, it succeeded in capturing something of the quality of Chinese friendship. In contrast with, for example, Hindu culture, the convivial company of old friends plays a large part in Chinese tradition and finds frequent expression in both painting and poetry. This may be one reason for the tract's outstanding success in comparison with so many later publications of this type. Too few missionaries were concerned to establish lasting friendships with Chinese.

So began one of the most characteristic methods of Protestant evangelizing work. Hundreds of tracts were to be published in later years, many of indifferent quality. Protestant fundamentalism naturally put a high premium on the written word, and in this instance the missionaries' own self-understanding chimed in with the stress on the importance of the written word in China. For Chinese culture, throughout its four-thousand-year-old history, the written language has provided a focus of unity through the use of ideograms in which phonetic elements are incidental. The same written character is used for all Chinese spoken dialects, with the result that people from the North and from the South can write to each other but may not be able to converse![16]

Morrison's version of the Bible was an impressive achievement but it was in need of considerable improvement. In 1850 the so-called Delegates Version of the New Testament was published, after a collaborative effort by a variety of denominations. However, a number of contentious issues had arisen over the translation of certain terms, notably the word for "God". The argument hinged over the choice of *Shen* (lit. spirit) or *Shangdi* (the Supreme God), with the British generally choosing the latter and the Americans the former term. We have noted the significance of the use of the term *Shangdi* for Ricci, Legge and others – amounting to an acknowledgement of the legitimate place of Chinese culture within a Christian perspective. For opposite reasons *Shen* was generally favoured by the more conservative missionaries, as it was considered a more neutral term. The Catholics had, it may be remembered, originally opted for *Shangdi*, but this had been over-ruled later in favour of the term *Tianzhu* (Lord of Heaven). The delegates in the 1840s did not even consider this term, although later a few missionaries, notably of Anglican background, suggested its adoption. In the event the 1850 New Testament was published in two editions, using different terms for God. The plan to publish one text of the Old Testament foundered and two different translations were published, one in 1853, the other in 1862. The failure to agree on terms was to be a source of continuing diversion within the Protestant churches, and even today some Christians prefer *Shen* and others *Shangdi*.

First Converts and Charles Gutzlaff's Chinese Union

The first baptism of a Chinese into the Protestant Church was conducted by Milne on 16 July 1814. It was, however, another Chinese early convert – Liang Fa (known to the West as Liang A-fa) and baptized by Milne in 1816 – who was to become the first ordained Chinese evangelist. Why, one wonders, did Liang and his fellow converts find Christianity attractive? It has been suggested that it was their background that provides the key. They were tradesmen and farmers who had received a few years' formal literary training. Thus they were neither members of the élite of Neo-Confucian scholars nor part of the illiterate masses. Their training had given them a Confucian concern with ethical conduct, but neither Confucian self-cultivation nor the ritualistic salvation offered by folk religion satisfied their search for moral transformation. Christian monotheism provided them with the answer.[17] Liang A-fa is best remembered for his tract *Good Words to Admonish The Age*. Liang remained a Confucian in his morality, and he shared with many late Qing morality books a disgust with the decadence of Buddhist monks, the general immorality in society and the inability of popular religion to offer a morality that could confront these evils. These early Chinese Protestants added to their traditional moral concern teachings on the equality of all and the denunciation of image worship. These were prominent themes in Liang's tract, together with an emphasis on apocalyptic that was to influence deeply the future leader of the Taiping Rebellion.

One man was to be a key figure in enthusing both future missionaries and their home supporters with a vision of the conversion of China's millions. Charles Gutzlaff was impatient with the restrictions being placed on the work of evangelizing. He was born in Prussia in 1803 and, after ordination in 1826, sailed under the auspices of the Netherlands Missionary Society to join Walter Medhurst in Batavia, capital of Dutch Java. Here he was fired by Medhurst with the desire to go to China and he learnt to speak fluent Chinese. Exasperated with the timidity of his society he broke with it, and set off in a Chinese junk in June 1831 to make his first voyage along the Chinese coast. Gutzlaff was in many ways a man of vision but his enthusiasm continually overwhelmed his sense of judgement, and it was constantly to land him in trouble. His adoption of Chinese dress and his willingness to follow a Chinese way of life reveal his genuine commitment to China, but his romantic and idiosyncratic character led to a series of unfortunate incidents. So it was that his next two voyages were in foreign ships, the last an opium trader, and from these he busily distributed tracts. He was a great believer in the efficacy of the Word spread through the distribution of literature, and he showed little interest in follow-up activities or nurture. In 1834 his lack of judgement was to lead him to accept an appointment as a Chinese Secretary in the British Department of Trade and, in consequence, he became directly involved in the First Opium War of 1840. He was unabashed in his use of his political role to foster his missionary activity – most of which concerned the continued distribution of literature.

It was in 1844 that Gutzlaff formed the Chinese Union, an organization which employed Chinese evangelists to work in Guangdong province. Gutzlaff's claims for the Union and his use of Chinese assistants have led some to maintain that the Union was the "germ" of a Chinese church. In fact the Union was nothing of the sort, and Gutzlaff was naïve in the faith he placed in the Chinese agents that he employed. The sober facts behind the Union were that it was led and inspired by Gutzlaff and was in no way a native organization; it failed to make any significant impact, and a fair number of the Chinese he employed were involved in the opium trade. Thus, Rudolf Lechler of the Basel Mission Society determined to try out Gutzlaff's methods of going outside the treaty ports and adopting Chinese dress. He was soon to be disillusioned with the Chinese Union, for he found in the Shantou area of Guangdong scant evidence of the conversions claimed. One of Gutzlaff's Chinese helpers confessed to him:

> If anyone was pleased with our narratives about Mary and Joseph, and so on, we asked him if he would be baptized, whereby his sins could be washed away; and upon his consenting thereto, water was brought. But there was no question about further instruction . . .[18]

Lechler's general conclusion about Gutzlaff's helpers and preachers was that they "could not help for they themselves were unconverted".

In his book *Mission Accomplished? The English Presbyterian Mission in Lingtung, South China*, which is essential to understanding Protestant missions in China, George Hood offers a useful critique of Gutzlaff's approach. Gutzlaff relied on itinerant preaching and Hood comments:

> When the preacher belongs to a self-confident aggressive culture, such a method is unlikely to bear the marks of humility but more likely to convey didactic superiority. It offers little or no opportunity for a genuine meeting of minds and hearts, nor does it provide for the nurture of those who respond to the word preached.[19]

Moreover, his distribution of literature was done in close association with both the opium trade, and the humiliation of the Anglo-Chinese War and the forcible opening of China. Gutzlaff can be credited with the attempt to use Chinese Christians in a native ministry, but the Chinese Union was not a success and the idea of a native ministry had been in the minds of Milne and the other early missionaries from the start. Hood rightly points out that in the eyes of most Chinese those of their fellow countrymen who served foreigners were "Chinese evil-doers". Finally:

He was appealing to the Christians of Europe in ways which fitted all too well into their romantic visions and their self-confident cultural superiority.

Gutzlaff is important because he himself epitomized in his own person and style of mission much that was unacceptable about the Protestant mission in China. At the same time, he manifested a personal courage and dedication that was also a hallmark of many missionaries. His tragedy was that he failed to see the contradictions of his own situation, whereas many lesser men and women would never lose a sense of ambiguity over their role and status. Gutzlaff is also important because of the claims made for him by Hudson Taylor, founder of the China Inland Mission. Taylor acknowledged Gutzlaff as his mentor, and he certainly inspired Taylor with his romantic vision of reaching all China as soon as possible.

Education was to be one of the great contributions of the missionary movement to the development of modern China. Morrison began this work when the Anglo-Chinese College was founded in Malacca in 1818. In 1842 it was moved to Hong Kong. The objective was not only to give Christian instruction, but to introduce the English language and Western culture. The establishment of the Morrison Education Society in 1839 was an important stage in the development of Christian-run schools in China. Medical work was to become a means of contact with the Chinese people, and in 1835 Dr Peter Parker opened a hospital in Guangzhou. Parker helped to found the Medical Missionary Society in 1838, with its aim being the "alleviation of human suffering, and the extension of Christianity".[20] Such a development did not happen without controversy. There were many who felt that the task of the missionary was preaching the Gospel and nothing more. In reply those who defended Parker argued that "the surgeon is himself a preacher and makes his hospital a chapel".[21]

The first American missionaries to arrive in China were David Abeel and Elijah C. Bridgeman, sent by the American Board of Commissioners for Foreign Missions. They arrived in Guangzhou in February 1830. Abeel did not stay long, but Bridgeman was joined in 1833 by Samuel Wells Williams and the two men collaborated in the production of *The Chinese Repository*, which was the first outlet in China for serious Western sinological scholarship. In 1834 they founded a Society for the Diffusion of Useful Knowledge in China – their motivation being the peaceful opening of China through information about the West. Bridgeman's view of China changed from seeing the Chinese as heathen idolaters to a people "advanced as far as any people ever have gone, or can go, without the aids of divine revelation".[22]

The Opium Wars and Unequal Treaties

The plain fact was that in the situation before the First Opium War there was no real prospect of forming a viable Protestant community in China itself. The scandalous trade in opium, pushed by the East India Company with the open connivance of the British Government, was the excuse used for the forcible opening of China to foreign trade during the First Opium War (1839-1842). The results were the British acquisition of Hong Kong and the opening up of Guangzhou, Xiamen (Amoy), Ningbo, and Fuzhou as Treaty Ports. The Americans and French signed similar treaties in 1844. Under the notorious "most favoured nation" clause included in the Supplementary Treaty between Britian and China of October 1843, any later treaties with other powers would equally benefit the British. Naturally, all other powers later claimed the same provision for themselves. So began the series of treaties that the Chinese have always called the "Unequal Treaties", and which were slowly to force China to accept foreign influences, including Christianity. France was able to secure the exemption from punishment of any Chinese whose Christianity was deemed sincere (December 1844 Edict), and in February 1846 the promulgation of the toleration policy

throughout China, together with the concession that all confiscated churches be returned. While these measures were
obviously directed at the Chinese Catholic community they
also greatly benefited Protestants. However, it was the Sino-
French agreements in 1858 and 1860 that really changed the
situation for Christianity. France had assumed the role of pro-
tector of Catholic missions, and it was the execution of a
French missionary, Auguste Chapdelaine, in Guangxi in 1856,
that gave France the excuse to join in the Second Opium War
(the "Arrow" War). In the Sino-French treaty of 1858 (the
Treaty of Tianjin, ratified 1860), France won considerable
rights for Catholic missions. These were further extended in
the Convention of 1860, and the Chinese text went further,
due to the duplicity of a French interpreter. According to this
version, not only was all land and property seized in the past
to be returned, but land could be bought or rented by
missionaries anywhere in China. It also stated that those who
arrested Christians illegally would be punished.

It was, therefore, through force of arms that the way was
cleared for trader and missionary to penetrate China. Perhaps
it is no surprise that in 1922 a survey of the progress of Protestant mission to China was published with the unfortunate
English title, *The Christian Occupation of China*. The Chinese
people as a whole would not forget the way in which Christianity had secured its position there. Popular hostility was to
continue, and many local officials and literati were active in
fostering it. However, fear of the subversive and heterodox
nature of Christian teaching was greatly exacerbated by an
unforeseen result of early Protestant missionary activity – the
rise of the Taiping Heavenly Kingdom.

The Taiping Heavenly Kingdom

Liang A-fa's tract *Good Words to Admonish The Age* first
introduced Christianity to the man who was to rock Chinese
society to its roots in the middle years of the century, Hong

Xiuquan, the Heavenly King, self-styled younger brother of Jesus Christ, and leader of the Taiping Rebellion. One day in 1836, during the imperial examinations in Guangzhou, a copy of Liang's tract was given to Hong Xiuquan. Its effect was not immediate, but it appears that it was the major source through which Hong interpreted his vision of a venerable old man with a golden beard handing him ensigns of royalty and a sword, and telling him to exorcize demons and bring the world back to the true teaching. He became an ardent Christian, albeit with some unorthodox characteristics, and in 1844 he and a friend, Feng Yunshan, began missionary work amongst their native Hakka community in Guangxi. Hong was soon to return to Guangzhou where in 1847 he received instruction from the American Baptist Issachar J. Roberts. On his return to Guangxi in 1847 he found that Feng Yunshan had succeeded in creating a whole network of local congregations who formed the "God-Worshipping Society". The Hakka were the "Guest-people", of the majority Han race but distinct from the original inhabitants. They found it impossible to maintain their position and became increasingly impoverished. The crisis was coming to a head in the 1840s, and Christianity provided the inspiration that was to transform the Hakka into the militant spearhead of the greatest peasant rebellion in world history.

Liang's tract preached Evangelical faith, with its division between the saved and the reprobate. It also, however, was confused in its teaching about the heavenly and earthly kingdoms, and suggests an apocalyptic view of a world crisis that might occur any number of times. It was an explosive mixture and, after various delays, during the famine of 1849-50, the Hakka gathered their forces. United by strict discipline and a fanatical creed, they won military victories against Qing forces and on 11 January 1851 proclaimed the Heavenly Kingdom of Great Peace (*Taiping Tianguo*).

The Taiping's irruption into the central regions of China, and the capture of the rich rice-growing areas around the Yangzi River, was truly spectacular. In March 1853, numbering some two million persons, they took the great and

Hakka
Peasant
Revolt

important city of Nanjing, which was to be the Taiping headquarters until its recapture in 1864. Taiping belief and practice
during these years was strongly influenced by Christian
teachings, but other heterodox elements were incorporated.
The original core of "God-Worshippers" was diluted by the
huge number of new non-Hakka recruits, and it was only in
Nanjing itself that it was possible to apply their teachings with
any rigour. Equality of the sexes, puritanical social mores, a
stress on universal equality, and the call for the abolition of
private land ownership were the hallmarks of their teaching.
Christian teaching on equality of all under God was linked to
ancient Chinese utopian dreams of the "great harmony", and
to anti-Manchu sentiments. They were also heir to earlier
traditions of social protest such as the White Lotus and the
Triads, but what is most striking is the difference from all past
movements. Christianity was not merely an incidental ingredient: it provided the ideological foundation.

The defeat of the Taiping in 1864 by the re-organized Qing
armies, led by the brilliant general Zeng Guofan, with the
crucial assistance of "Chinese Gordon" (Major Charles
Gordon of the Royal Engineers), was ensured by the failure of
Taiping political organization. Absolutism and increasing
corruption and in-fighting amongst the various "kings" undermined the Heavenly Kingdom from within and led to serious
strategic mistakes. However, there was a more important reason
for the Taiping failure, and one related to the origins of the movement in an alien creed. Philip Kuhn suggests that their rejection of traditional values meant that they found it difficult to
extend their control into the rural hinterland around their captured cities, and also that it prevented them making effective
alliances with other groups of more traditional rebels, such as
the Nians who were waging their rebellion during the 1850s in
the area of the Huai River, to the north of the Yangzi Region.[23]

The historical importance of the Taiping is immense. It
marks the watershed between traditional and modern China.
The Qing was able to recover some of its lost power as a result
of the measures of re-organization provoked by the rebellion.
Yet, it was to be a temporary respite for traditional society. It

was no wonder that traditionalists feared Christianity and were suspicious of the foreign missionaries who flocked to China after 1858. Events on the coast accompanying the rise of Western power in China were only one part of the scenario. It should be remembered that even after the collapse of the Taiping and Nian rebellions the 1860s and '70s saw the outbreak of huge Muslim Rebellions in the North-west, engulfing the new territory of Xinjiang and the ancient provinces of Gansu and Shaanxi.

Treaty Port Protestants and Catholic Counter-Reformation

The years between the treaties of 1842 and those of 1858 did not see a great expansion in the work of Protestant missions. Almost all the work was located in the newly opened treaty ports, and while some began to probe the hinterland around the open cities no Protestants attempted to move far inland. It was otherwise with the Catholics, who already had knowledge of Christian communities in many parts of the country, and who could now expect to have former churches restored to the local congregations. So while William Chalmers Burns and James Hudson Taylor in the mid-1850s adopted Chinese dress and ventured outside the treaty ports for the first time, encountering the disapproval of most other Protestant missionaries, Catholic missionaries were arriving in considerable numbers and dispersing throughout the country.

The Catholic Church: Control and Expansion

At first the newly arrived missionaries concentrated on traditional Catholic communities, but new work was begun in some areas. The Dominicans moved back into Fujian and by 1858 had rebuilt thirteen churches. The Lazarist mission was mainly in the north, including the areas north of Beijing. The

Church in Inner Mongolia had been founded in the early eighteenth century by refugees from the persecution, and the village of Xiwanzi had become their centre. A church was built in 1750. In the 1830s Xiwanzi became the centre of the Beijing Diocese and some Lazarists had already returned. In 1840 Mongolia became a Mission Vicariate under Monsignor Mouly C.M., and in 1846 he was made the Apostolic Administrator of the Beijing Diocese. In this way the foundations of a vigorous Catholic community were laid.

The Franciscans returned to Hunan, Hubei, Shanxi, Shaanxi and Shandong, although work in many of these places was to be hampered by persecutions. The Société des Missions Étrangères returned to its old areas, but it was also able to undertake much new work in Manchuria, Guangxi and Guangdong. It was to continue its tradition of training native priests as a priority, in contrast to other Orders. The Xianfeng Emperor who acceded to the throne in 1850 was strongly anti-foreign, and he encouraged the harassment of the Catholic communites. Nevertheless by 1860 the Catholic community in China was growing once more.

The return of the missionaries bringing a degree of protection to the vulnerable and persecuted Catholic communities was not an unmixed blessing. Quite apart from the reinforcement of the image of Christianity as a foreign faith, Chinese Catholics had developed their own patterns of life. Unfortunately for them, these patterns did not necessarily conform to the rigid notions of authority that marked the nineteenth-century Catholic missionaries. There is no doubt that isolation had produced confusion over doctrinal matters in some areas, and the fears of the missionaries were not without foundation. Yet the imposition of European forms on what was now an indigenous church was to inhibit the growth to maturity of the Chinese Catholic Church. One might even say that the present-day divisions and agonies of Chinese Catholics can be traced back to the policies of the missionaries in the middle years of the last century.

It was the Jesuits in the Jiangnan area (Anhui and Jiangsu south of the Yangzi) who, ironically, were most responsible for this process of imposition. Jiangnan was one of the strongholds of Christianity in China tracing its origins back to Ricci's famous convert Xu Guangqi. In the years since Laimbeckhoven, the last Jesuit bishop, had lived in hiding near Shanghai, Jiangnan Catholics had built up a distinctive form of organization. Clan leaders managed church affairs, and Christian women, known as "Virgins", had great influence. Thus from 1800 to 1850 the Nanjing church was led by a widow called He Daguan. These women cared for chapels, often built by the Christians themselves, instructed the children, led prayers at Mass and supported any clergy who visited. In 1842 the Vicar Apostolic, Monsignor Louis-Marie de Besi, invited the Jesuits to return, and local Christians welcomed them, remembering the Jesuits of old. These Jesuits were different. Their clash with de Besi over the control of monies sent from Europe was understandable – in essence the issue was over the control of the Jesuit mission. The Jesuits won this battle when in 1856 the Pope suppressed the diocese of Nanjing and divided it into vicariates apostolic, with the Jesuits taking charge of the area around Shanghai and Nanjing cities.

It was their moves against the native leadership of the Church that were to show how much attitudes had changed since the seventeenth century. After 1856 they ordered all Chinese secular priests to live in Jesuit houses under their discipline. Under the imperial proclamations restoring church property they were able to claim back many churches, thereby bypassing the clan councils who, for want of a role, gradually disappeared. The "Virgins" were another matter. The Jesuits sought to discredit them: they forbade them to exercise leadership in worship and suggested that the only legitimate way of life for such women was as members of religious orders under the triple vow of poverty, chastity and obedience.

To continue this story beyond our present period, in 1869 some French sisters founded a native Chinese congregation, the Association of the Presentation of the Blessed Virgin (Presentadines). The idea was that they would replace the

"Virgins", but in fact the "Virgins" remained, albeit with their power curtailed. At the heart of this confrontation was the issue of local church autonomy over against foreign (in China this meant French) ecclesiastical control. The extension of Jesuit control was facilitated by the Taiping Rebellion. Although the evidence is unclear, it seems that the Taiping eventually turned on Catholics, and that many Catholic villages in Jiangnan were destroyed, with the population fleeing to Shanghai and settling around the Xujiahui Cathedral. If so, then it was probably the result of the Jesuits siding with the Manchus, and Chinese Catholics being seen as allies of the Jesuits.

Thomas Breslin has commented on this whole process:

> By destroying the Chinese form of church organization, the Jesuits in Jiangnan made certain that the Catholic Church in China would be patterned upon the Roman model, which featured the dominance of a numerous clergy and the subordination of the laity . . .[24]

It also meant the destruction of female leadership and the re-assertion of male dominance.

The Jiangnan situation was perhaps unique, but other missionary Orders also imposed European domination on the Chinese Church. The Lazarists forced a second-class status on Chinese priests, and in general it can be said that the whole style of mission was one in which Chinese Christians were subordinate to an increasingly powerful foreign leadership. It is remarkable that even in spite of this many Chinese Catholic communities managed to maintain a measure of communal government whenever a mission station was handed over to the control of Chinese priests. The spiritual strength of the Chinese Catholic Church was to be proved in a later age when once more the foreigners found themselves unwelcome.

In 1860 the Church in China, both Catholic and Protestant, was on the verge of a new stage in its activity. The Taiping Rebellion was soon to come to an end, opening up many areas to travel. The opium wars and subsequent unequal treaties had prepared the way for foreign traders and missionaries to

penetrate throughout the nation. Catholic Orders were sending numerous personnel to China – the Jesuits alone had sent
fifty-eight new missionaries between 1843 and 1857. There
were now just over eighty Protestant missionaries, and by 1860
a number were ready to move out from the treaty ports. It
looked as if an unprecedented opportunity had been given to
Christianity to make a major impact on the Middle Kingdom.

A House Divided

One wonders what attitude the Protestants took to the
Catholic Church and the existence of long-established Catholic communities. Morrison enlisted the assistance of two
Chinese Catholics in order to learn the language, and used a
Catholic translation of the Bible to assist him in his work of
translation. Charles Gutzlaff's attitude towards the Jesuits was
in part admiration, in part criticism. Popery and Romanism
were anathema but he admired the courage, dedication and
intelligence of the Jesuits. Gutzlaff's attitude was perhaps
more generous than many, although Hudson Taylor was to
adopt a similar standpoint, expressing his appreciation of the
courage of Catholic priests in travelling into the interior at the
risk of their lives:

> Entering by stealth, living in concealment . . . ever and
> anon meeting with imprisonment, torture, and death
> itself, they have presented a remarkable instance of
> fidelity to their calling.[25]

Yet admiration for their courage was outweighed by dislike of
Rome. Not untypical was the attitude expressed in Shantou by
the English Presbyterians:

> Alas! China knows far more of Popery than of true
> Christianity, and if we ourselves dread the political in-
> fluence of a religion which has an earthly head in an alien
> country, we can sympathize with the Chinese in their
> fear to some extent.[26]

Nor was the Catholic view of Protestants any more

enlightened. In Catholic eyes Protestants were dangerous heretics who could only impede the spreading of the Gospel. Violent incidents between Catholic and Protestant neighbours were not unknown up to the 1949 Revolution. Moreover, Catholics tended to see Protestantism, in the words of one Catholic scholar in 1934, as "different Protestant sects fighting each other and always at variance".[27] The dogmatic and authoritarian nature of the Tridentine Church was fundamentally anti-ecumenical in spirit, but Protestantism certainly laid itself open to the charge of sectarianism.

In Chinese Roman Catholicism is called the "religion of the Lord of Heaven" *(Tianzhujiao)* whereas Protestantism is called the "religion of Jesus" *(Jidujiao)*. No wonder most Chinese, even today, look upon Catholicism and Protestantism as two distinct religions!

REFERENCES

1. The information on Sichuan is largely based on Jeanne, Pierre, *The Early Church in Sichuan Province: A Study of Conditions Leading to the Synod of 1803, Tripod* No. 15, 1983, pp. 52f.
2. *Women's Evangel*, 17: 186 (1898), quoted Miller, Stuart Creighton, "Ends and Means" in Fairbank, John K., ed., *The Missionary Enterprise in China and America*, Harvard University Press, 1974, p. 273.
3. Droulers, Paul, S.J., in Chapter XVIII, *Religion: The Western Tradition, Catholicism, The History of Mankind, Cultural and Scientific Development, Vol. V, The Nineteenth Century 1775-1905*, George Allen and Unwin Ltd., London 1976.
4. Balthasar, Hans Urs von, *The Glory of the Lord, A Theological Aesthetics, Vol. 3: Studies in Theological Style: Lay Styles*, T. & T. Clark, Edinburgh 1986, p. 91.
5. Ting, K.H., "Religious Policy and Theological Re-orientation in China", Address at Toronto School of Theology, October 1979. Reproduced in *CSP Bulletin* No. 13, July 1980.
6. Hood, George A., *Mission Accomplished?* p. 81. See also Hood, "The Planting of a Mission", *CSP Journal* No. 1, April 1986, p.15.
7. Smith, Arthur H., *Chinese Characteristics*, Fleming H. Revell Co., New York 1894, p. 313.
8. Legge, James, *The Nestorian Monument of Hsi-an Fu in Shen-Hsi, China*, London, 1888, p. 58.
9. Hall, Ronald, *The Art of the Missionary*, pp. 14-15, quoted in Paton, David M., *"R.O.": The Life and Times of Bishop Ronald Hall of Hong Kong*, Diocese of Hong Kong and Macao & the Hong Kong Diocesan Association, Alan Sutton Publishing Ltd., Gloucester 1985.

10. Chang Chung-yuan, *Creativity and Taoism, A Study of Chinese Philosophy, Art and Poetry*, Wildwood House, London 1975, p. 55.
11. For a useful summary see Watson, A.J.L., "The Mind and Senses of China" pp. 307-11 in Hook, Brian, General Editor, *The Cambridge Encyclopedia of China*, Cambridge University Press, 1982.
12. Song, Choen-Seng, *The Compassionate God: An Exercise in the Theology of Transposition*, Chapter 10, "Taiping Christianity", pp. 208-9, SCM Press, London 1982.
13. Hall, Ronald, op. cit., pp. 63-4.
14. For a detailed account of the White Lotus see Overmyer, Daniel L., *Folk Buddhist Religion: Dissenting Sects in Late Traditional China*, Harvard University Press, 1976.
15. Jones, Susan Mann, and Kuhn, Philip A., "Dynastic Decline and the Roots of Rebellion" in Twitchett, Denis, and Fairbank, John K., Gen. Eds., *Cambridge History of China*, Vol. 10, Part 1: "Late Ch'ing 1800-1911", Cambridge University Press, 1978, p. 144.
16. Bays, Daniel H., *Christian Tracts: The Two Friends in Christianity in China, Early Protestant Missionary Writings*, ed., Barnett, Suzanne Wilson, and Fairbank, John K., Harvard University Press, 1985.
17. Bohr, Richard P., "Liang Fa's Quest for Moral Power", ibid., pp. 35f.
18. Hood, op. cit., pp. 48-9.
19. Hood, op. cit.
20. MacGillivray, D., ed., *A Century of Protestant Missions in China (1807-1907), being the Centenary Conference Historical Volume*, Shanghai, American Presbyterian Press, 1907, p. 653.
21. Quoted in Spence, Jonathan, *The China Helpers: Western Advisers in China 1620-1960*, The Bodley Head, London 1969, p. 53.
22. Drake, Fred W., "E.C. Bridgeman's Protrayal of the West", in Barnett and Fairbank, op. cit., p. 92.
23. Kuhn, Philip, "The Taiping Rebellion" in the *Cambridge History of China*, op. cit., pp. 316-17.
24. Breslin, Thomas A., *China, American Catholicism and the Missionary*, Pennsylvania State University Press, 1980, p. 13.
25. Quoted in Broomhall, A.J., *Hudson Taylor and China's Open Century*, Vol. 3: "If I Had a Thousand Lives", Hodder and Stoughton, London 1982, p. 411.
26. Hood, *CSP Journal* No. 1, April 1986, p. 13 quoting United Reformed Church Archive 42/9 No. 23 of 1 August 1870.
27. D'Elia, Paschal M., *The Catholic Mission in China: a short sketch of the history of the Catholic Church in China from the earliest records to our own days*, Shanghai, Commercial Press, 1934, p. 58.

IV

The Opium of the People

1860-1912

> The earlier missionaries survived and were
> so far successful perhaps just because they
> lacked the kind of sensitiveness which
> makes deep friendships with another
> people. Much of their strength and of their
> imagination was absorbed in dealing with
> the practical problems that confront the
> pioneer . . . Living in China will help you
> see how subtle and delicate a matter friend-
> ship is . . .[1]

It is a staggering fact that by 1836 opium was the world's most
valuable single commodity, and almost all of it was imported
into China by British traders. Until 1832 they relied on Chinese
dealers and distribution by gangsters and Triads, but in that
year Dr Jardine sent his heavily armed clippers up the South-
east coast of China: Gutzlaff's third voyage was on one of
these boats. As a result opium addiction rapidly expanded,
and by 1890 it is estimated that ten per cent of the population
were smoking opium, of whom perhaps five per cent or fifteen
million people were addicts.

Gutzlaff's foolhardiness was not shared by other missionaries, many of whom were active in the campaign against
the trade, but all missionaries benefited indirectly from the
opium wars and the various treaties and edicts that followed
China's defeats. This chapter will be concerned to look at the
developments in the Church between the end of the Second
Opium War and the collapse of the Qing dynasty in 1912. A
number of crucial issues for the long-term future of Chinese

Christianity and its relationship to Chinese society came to the fore during these years, and these will form a major part of our discussion. Many details concerning the work of Catholic and Protestant missionaries will have to be omitted. However since our main concern is not with the history of the missionary movement in China but with the story of the Chinese Church and its place within the Chinese world, this should not detract from our purpose.

The Tongzhi Restoration

The collapse of the great rebellions in the 1860s and the defeats in the Second Opium War were to change the internal situation in China as well as her external relations. Under the Tongzhi Emperor (who reigned 1862-74) Qing power was revived, and the dynasty was able to survive for a further fifty years. The real power was in the hands of the Empress Dowager Cixi, although the regency was shared with the Empress Dowager Cian and Prince Gong. After the death of the Tongzhi Emperor, Cixi installed another boy Emperor, Guangxu, on the throne, thereby ensuring the continuation of her own rule. It was a period in which the old order, with its Neo-Confucian orthodoxy, managed to prolong its life with the support of men such as Zeng Guofan, the architect of the Taiping defeat, and Li Hongzhang, the promoter of the Self-strengthening Movement. This movement was a superficial attempt to introduce certain aspects of modernization into China while leaving the traditional system more or less intact. The idea was "to learn the superior barbarian techniques to control the barbarians". It resulted in the establishment of a number of enterprises such as the Jiangnan Arsenal, the Kaiping coal mines, the Shanghai Cotton Mills and the creation of the Beiyang Army. Bureaucracy, nepotism and a lack of understanding of modern economics, joined with the refusal of the Empress Dowager Cixi to allow significant major reforms, led to the failure of the Movement. The Chinese defeat in the Sino-Japanese War of 1894-5 demonstrated this failure in a humiliating way, and paved the way for the demise of China's ancient system of imperial government.

The partial recognition of the superiority of foreign military and technological power was given concrete expression in the establishment in 1861 of the Zongli Yamen to handle foreign relations. The dynasty was compelled to accept that the traditional manner of relating to foreigners could not be sustained. The Western powers themselves adopted more cautious policies and were satisfied with the concessions wrested from China. They were not, however, prepared to treat China as an equal, and the proposals by Rutherford Alcock for a revision of the treaties were rejected in London – to the chagrin of the Zongli Yamen officials. The unequal relationship of the great powers to China put the missionary at the front-line, and anti-foreign feeling usually found expression in attacks on the missionaries and Chinese converts. Such attacks were to become more frequent in the 1870s as the missionaries pushed further inland.

Catholic Missions 1860-1900

We have already seen that after 1842 Catholic missionaries moved back into areas inhabited by Catholics. The number of European missionary groups grew over the years, with the major ecclesiastical territories divided amongst them. There was little co-operation between the various groups, most of whom were nationally based. The French formed the overwhelming majority, and the French protectorate over the Catholic mission in China led to frequent appeals to the "rights" including intervention in legal cases. In 1908 the Vatican tried with comparative success to halt such activities.

The Catholic territories were divided into vicariates apostolic (served by a Vicar Apostolic), prefectures apostolic, independent missions and missions. The missionary Orders had little contact with each other save through their superiors in Rome, and the vicars apostolic, while exercising episcopal authority, were directly under the authority of Rome and were not members of a native hierarchy. As time went on the number of converts grew considerably, although far too many priests were concerned with numbers of baptisms. In 1910 one French priest in Xinfeng Jiangxi consistently intervened in law-suits so that his clients embraced Christianity to gain a favourable settlement. In this way the priest hoped to achieve his goal of twenty thousand conversions![2]

A typical example of growth can be found in the history of the Catholic Church in Inner Mongolia, which was originally under the Lazarists. The work was taken over in late 1865 by the new Belgian Order, *Congregation Immaculati Cordis Mariae* (CICM or the Scheut Fathers). The village of Xiwanzi was the centre of the work but under the leadership of Theofiel Verbiest, founder of CICM, the work expanded over an area two thousand five hundred miles long and seven hundred miles broad which included the Gobi and Ordos deserts. It was an area half the size of Europe with a scattered population of twelve million. By 1884 it had been divided into three dioceses, Central Mongolia (Xiwanzi Diocese), the Southwest, and the better off Diocese of Rehe in the east, which contained the only urban church, in the city of Bagou. The essentially rural nature of Chinese Catholicism could not be better illustrated. By now the number of converts had grown from seven thousand in 1865 to eighteen thousand, served by twelve Chinese priests.[3]

Another aspect of Catholic mission work which received much attention from the Scheut fathers was the so-called "Holy Infancy" movement. Verbiest was the chaplain to the movement in Belgium, and much support for this work in China came from Europe. Abandoned babies, usually girls, were picked up, baptized and cared for in orphanages. It was a work that was misunderstood by many Chinese and which gave rise to many horrific rumours. The mythology was to persist down to our own day, for in 1973, as part of the Cultural Revolution campaign against religion, a children's picture book was published in Shanghai with vivid pictures of nuns beating Chinese children in an orphanage – all somewhat reminiscent of Oliver Twist![4] Opposition to Catholic work in the area was expressed in 1891 in attacks against Catholics by the Zaili sect rebels, and in 1899 in the Boxer Uprising, in which several thousand converts were massacred together with eleven priests and one bishop (see below).

The condition of the Catholic Church in China at the turn of the century seemed healthy on paper. Despite the Boxer massacres the number of converts rose from under 200,000 in 1842 to 742,000. By 1907 it had reached one million. But behind the figures there were serious problems relating to the fundamentalist style of most missionaries, the domination of the Church by foreigners, the second-class status of Chinese priests, and the number of nominal converts. By 1915 the Vatican determined to do something to remedy the situation, but we must leave this phase of the story to the next chapter.

Protestant Missions to 1900

Protestant missionary activity only began in earnest after 1860. The influx of new missionaries from a host of different societies (by 1905 there were sixty-three separate ones), raised problems that had remained in the background in earlier years. Denominational origins had little meaning for the earliest missionaries – united as they were by their biblical fundamentalism and evangelical faith. Nor was the original objective the founding of permanent mission stations. It is remarkable how many of the pioneers saw their roles as intermediaries, whose primary task was the fostering of a Chinese church. Gutzlaff's ill-starred Chinese Union was at least an attempt in this direction.

After 1860, denominational background became of increasing importance, and most societies attempted to establish mission stations in the major cities with a chapel or church, a school and a dispensary or even a small hospital. Each denomination imposed its own idea of appropriate church organization on the area in which they worked, and control was vested in the hands of the foreign missionary. There was very little inter-denominational co-operation except over specific programmes and projects, notably through the Bible Societies, and work in social welfare, medicine and education. Competition between societies was generally avoided through the so-called "comity" arrangements, under which it was agreed that each mission would work within a designated block of territory. These arrangements were only partly successful as some of the smaller denominations ignored them. Another problem was that under these arrangements it was possible for missions of the same denomination but of different national origin to develop separate work. Thus English Anglicans worked in Fujian, Canadian in Henan, American in Shanghai and Nanjing. However, the Anglican Church was one of the first to draw together its disparate parts, and the bishops met together in 1897, 1899, 1903 and 1909, and in 1912 they adopted the constitution of the *Zhong Hua Sheng Gong Hui* or Anglican Church of China.

Successful formation of denominational church structures pointed to another problem for the Protestants in China (as indeed throughout the world): did the Protestants belong to one Church or many "churches"? The principles of church order accepted by Anglicans differed radically from the congregational principle of the local church espoused by many non-conformists, while Presbyterian and Methodist ideas fitted somewhere in the middle. In the long run denominational division seemed unnecessary and somewhat absurd to most Chinese Protestants, but it was to be these different principles which were to persist beyond the dissolution of the "churches" themselves and which today pose a serious and unresolved problem for the Church that has emerged out of the chaos of the Cultural Revolution of 1966-76. Other matters such as different ideas about the sacraments of Holy Communion and baptism (believer's or infant baptism), and the nature of the ordained ministry, were also to affect the Church after the Communist Revolution.

Our survey of the Protestant Church begins with an

evaluation of the China Inland Mission (CIM). It is an appropriate starting point because, despite its apparent newness of approach, it was in many ways the successor to the first Protestant missionaries. It was not for nothing that its founder James Hudson Taylor claimed Charles Gutzlaff as his spiritual father. It is also important to assess the role of the CIM in relationship to the denominational societies and to the emergence of an independent Chinese Church.

Hudson Taylor and the China Inland Mission

The story of James Hudson Taylor, and the origins and growth of the China Inland Mission, has been told many times. Most recently a six-volume biography of Hudson Taylor has told the story in immense detail.[5] Many have been moved by the faith and courage of Taylor and his early colleagues, but most accounts of his life are uncritical, in the sense that they do not attempt a dispassionate evaluation of the work of the CIM. Of Hudson Taylor's greatness there need be no doubt. His vision of a non-denominational mission that embraced the whole of China was realized, and the CIM was to become the largest of all the missionary organizations in China.

Taylor arrived in Shanghai in 1854 while it was partially occupied by Triad armies. He had come to China under the auspices of the China Evangelization Society, whose aim was to push into the interior of China. He soon learnt the language and started to preach in the city, despite the dangers of civil war going on around him. The majority of city missionaries considered his wish to move outside the treaty wall to be misguided, but he found a few kindred souls. In December of the same year he made his first trip by junk into the hinterland, with Jospeh Edkins of the London Missionary Society. It was the beginning of a series of such ventures as Taylor became convinced that it would be possible to establish mission stations outside of the Treaty Ports. These first years were to be fraught with difficulties. Missionary suspicion of this brash newcomer, the failure of his Society to provide proper support, and the obstruction of Chinese officials, were all to test his resolve. In 1857 he resigned from the Society, frustrated with their inefficiency (it was dissolved in 1860). During these early years he worked in Shantou with William Chalmers Burns, with whom he had shared some of the boat trips around Shanghai, and in Ningbo where in 1858 he married Maria Dyer. Never far from his mind was his ever urgent concern to work in the interior and to establish a "native Agency". It seemed, however, as if all his plans were to come to nothing. In 1860 as a result of ill health he and Maria returned to England, where they remained for five years. It was in England however, that he laid the foundations of the CIM, and he began to train his first recruits. In late 1864 the first group left for Ningbo. They arrived in a China very different from that left by the Taylors – for with the recent treaties and the ending of the Taiping Rebellion missionaries were free to travel throughout the country.

The Taylors themselves returned in 1866 with a further group of twenty-two recruits and work got under way in Hangzhou, Nanjing and the city of Huzhou. The next few years were to be fraught with problems: in 1868 Taylor was driven out of Yangzhou by a riot, and there was considerable criticism of the mission in Britain. In 1870 Maria died, and in 1875 he injured his spine. In spite of all, by 1876 the CIM had fifty-two missionaries, almost one-fifth of the Protestant total, together with seventy-five Chinese assistants, two hospitals and ninety-two mission stations. It was a key year for the missions, for the Chefoo (Yantai) Convention made travel in China's interior much safer. By 1890 there were Protestant missionaries resident in all eighteen Chinese provinces, with the exception of Hunan. It was the CIM which led the way in many of these provinces. By 1895 it had 641 missionaries and 462 Chinese assistants with 260 mission stations.

Many of the CIM missionaries had little formal education, and Taylor also recruited many unmarried female missionaries. The CIM did not fit into the usual mould of the missionary society, being more concerned with penetrating into the remotest parts of the Empire than with establishing permanent mission stations. It was, and it remained, committed to the saving of souls as its priority, and it was willing to co-operate with the older societies provided it felt that there was a shared theological perspective. The CIM was the only inter-denominational society but its primary goal was, according to Searle Bates, "beneficial distance, not fellow-ship, and the key phrase was 'division of the field'."[6] In practice, it often functioned as a separate denomination with its own distinct congregations – a tendency that grew more marked as the conservative theological consensus amongst China missionaries began to break down. There can be no doubt, nevertheless, that the CIM made an enormous contri-bution to the establishment of the Protestant Church in China, and many of today's Chinese Christian congregations have their origins in its work.

Looked at, however, from the wider perspective of our con-cern with the question of the cultural encounter between Christian faith and Chinese culture, the CIM showed a total lack of interest in the question. Hudson Taylor may have followed his mentor, Gutzlaff, in adopting Chinese dress, but it was a superficial means of adaptation, masking a rigid and narrow theological understanding.

The nineteenth century was not an age for considering the relationship of Christian truth to non-European cultures and religions. The CIM was no different in this than the over-whelming majority of missionaries in China. One area, however, where it came increasingly to differ from the major denominational societies was in the matter of social concern. The development of bibilical criticism in Europe was chang-ing the attitudes of many Protestants away from biblical literalism. Gradually some missionaries moved towards a greater concern with social conditions in China, and while in the nineteenth century the overwhelming majority remained evangelical in their convictions, there was a real difference between those who adopted a pietist stance and those who espoused the social concern associated with some parts of the Evangelical Movement. The CIM from the beginning had little or no concern with wider social issues, and as new ideas gained currency amongst other missionaries so the CIM

closed its doors to those who did not accept its narrow theological position. In the twentieth century it was to remain in
its nineteenth-century mould, unable to come to terms with
developments in theology or in Chinese social and political
life. What was understandable in Hudson Taylor in 1860 was
less excusable in 1930.

In so far as the direction of the mission was located in China
and not in some Board in Britain, the CIM could claim to be
different, but in fact it was no less controlled by the foreign
missionary than many other parts of the Chinese Church.
While it is true that it recruited many Chinese assistants, they
were always subordinated to the foreign missionary, and the
mission itself remained firmly under the control of its director,
who for the first forty years was Hudson Taylor himself. It is
often claimed that the CIM in particular laid the foundations
for today's self-supporting, self-governing and self-
propagating Church in China (the famous "Three Selfs"). This
is to confuse evangelism with the nurture of the local church.
Few missionaries understood this, even in the twentieth
century. The critique of Roland Allen, himself a missionary in
China around the turn of the century, is vital for our understanding of the missionary movement. Allen maintained that
from the beginning:

> the very first groups of converts must be so fully equip-
> ped with all spiritual authority that they could multiply
> themselves without any *necessary* reference to us: that,
> though, while we were there, they might regard us as
> helpful advisers, yet our removal should not at all mutilate
> the completeness of the Church, or deprive it of anything
> necessary for its unlimited expansion.[7]

Allen, rightly, understood that the organization of Christians
under missionary societies was not the same as establishing an
indigenous Church: "Only a Church could propagate itself,
and beget Churches."[8] In this sense the CIM was more of an
obstacle to the development of a Chinese Church than many
of the denominational societies. Our criticism of the CIM may
seem to be very hard, but it has been made necessary by the

greatly exaggerated claims as to its achievements that are still being made in some quarters. Even if our theological critique is rejected, there remains the critique of missionary method. But let us also give credit where credit is due: recognition of the limitations of the CIM does not mean that its peculiar and important contribution in preaching the Gospel need go unacknowledged. It strength was in evangelism. It is in this light that the stories of CIM pioneers like J.O. Fraser of Yunnan, and George Hunter of Xinjiang, can be heard and acknowledged.

The English Presbyterians in Guangdong

A very different model from that of the CIM may be found in the work of British Presbyterian missionaries in South Fujian and North-east Guangdong. The work in the Xiamen (Amoy) area of Fujian was more advanced than that in Guangdong, but the Guangdong experience is of particular interest for a number of reasons. The Shantou (Swatow) area of Guangdong was the place where the Chinese Union of Gutzlaff was active, and it was the scene of early pioneering work by Rudolf Lechler and William Chalmers Burns, for whom the itinerant method of evangelism later espoused by Hudson Taylor was the preferred missionary strategy. It was also, incidentally, to experience the first Chinese Soviet of Haifeng County in 1927. Its history has recently been studied in detail by George Hood.[9]

The area covered by the English Presbyterian mission is known as Lingdong, the eastern part of Guangdong province, of which the city of Shantou is now the administrative centre. Lechler can be said to have laid the foundations of the Lingdong church in 1849, and within three years he had baptized thirteen converts. However, he was not able to continue his work owing to growing local hostility. Burns later continued the pioneering task, mostly in Shantou City itself, but it was only after 1858, that the mission could really begin work, under the leadership of George Smith.

Under the Treaty of Tianjin (1858) Chaozhou City and Shantou were opened up as a treaty port (Chaozhou is twenty miles upstream from Shantou). The British Consul in Shantou arrived in 1860 but it took him five years before he was allowed to visit the administrative centre in Chaozhou. Local opposition was led by the gentry, with the tacit sympathy of government officials who were, nevertheless, obliged to implement the provisions of the unequal treaties. It was possible, therefore, for a "Clean out the Barbarians" office to exist in Chaozhou and for it to issue public proclamations. One such threatened any person who dared:

> . . . league himself with these sons of devils, let him be killed immediately when discovered in the cities by the gentry, in the villages by the elders . . .[10]

The protection offered to Christian converts by the Sino-British treaties was invoked in these circumstances by the missionaries in Shantou to protect converts and Chinese assistants from persecution or unjust punishment, albeit with considerable reluctance. The treaties were also used on occasion to ensure official support for establishing a new mission station. Unfortunately, the degree of protection afforded to Chinese converts was thought by many Chinese to be much greater than was in fact the case. Moreover, an insensitive appeal for protection could lead to increased hostility. The fact was that the very existence of the "rights" was an affront to Chinese national pride; the missionaries by invoking their use, for whatever reason, showed that they were a part of the foreign invasion of China. As George Hood comments:

> The Treaty rights both enabled them to exist and sowed the seeds of future alienation, the distortion of the life of the Church and its relations to the community . . .[11]

By 1874 the Shantou mission had twenty stations with around four hundred converts. There were two foreign missionaries and seven Chinese preachers. Then in 1874 the most important figure in the history of the Shantou Church arrived. John Campbell Gibson came from an Evangelical Calvinist background, and he was a strong believer in the need to make "the Church in China strong and intelligent by giving it free access to the Word of God and a Christian literature".[12] He also advocated the development of a native Church, and in order to train adequate Chinese leaders in 1877 he established a Boys' School. Its purpose was to produce ". . . men of some independence and power of origination to make the Church a really independent, strong, *native* Church".[13]

The year 1881 was to witness a decisive step forward, the formation of a Presbytery. It had seven Chinese and six foreign members with six more Chinese associates, and meetings were in Chinese. The Founding Statement is an historic declaration, although it of course reflects the inherent disunity of Protestantism in advocating the Presbyterian form of church government as most appropriate. It is the third part of the Statement that is of most significance for the future. It read:

> For the present, those who have come from the West to preach the truth and guide the Church, whether ordained ministers or elders, inasmuch as they all hold the office of eldership, therefore ought to be united in the discussion of the business of the presbytery; but the native Church ought to be self-governing, self-supporting and self-propagating; therefore in the future, when the Church becomes stronger, and its members more numerous, all matters must revert to the native office bearers, as their own charge, that they may lead the people of our native country to turn to the way of salvation.[14]

1881

Gibson believed that the "Three Selfs" had been more or less implemented in Shantou, and at the nationwide Shanghai Centenary Conference of 1907 he spoke with enthusiasm and passion of the need for a Three Self Church and for the ending of foreign control – "Independence of foreign control is the inherent right of the Chinese Church", he stated. For Gibson this also meant liberty of confessional expression, and the doctrinal basis of the Shantou Presbytery was neither creed nor confession but "the fellowship of its members in spiritual life in Christ".[15] It was not a point of view that commended itself to many of his fellow missionaries, especially as it seemed to acknowledge that the organization of the Shantou Church along Presbyterian lines was derived more from historical necessity than doctrinal principle.

Origin of the Three Selfs

Gibson was by no means the only advocate of the principles of self-government, self-support and self-propagation. The origins of the Three Self idea can be traced back to Henry Venn (1796-1873) of the Church Missionary Society (CMS). Venn wrote:

> If the elementary principles of self-support and self-government and self-extension be thus sown with the seed of the Gospel, we may hope to see the healthy growth and expansion of the Native Church, when the Spirit is poured down from on high, as the flowers of a fertile field multiply under the showers and warmth of summer.[16]

Venn's views were shared by another missionary administrator, Rufus Anderson of the American Board of Commissioners for Foreign Missions. He wrote:

> When [Paul] had formed local churches, he did not hesitate to ordain presbyters over them, the best he could find; and then to throw upon the churches thus officered, the responsibilities of self-government, self support and self-propagation.[17]

Neither Venn nor Anderson had experience in the field, and they were not fully aware of the problems caused by the manner in which most missionaries set about their task. Roland Allen's criticism could be applied to all the attempts by missionaries in China to establish a native church. In the Shantou Church it became clear that the missionaries retained a commanding role in the affairs of the Presbytery, and that self-support never became a reality for the majority of local congregations. Hood shows, moreover, that after 1919 there were virtually no new churches opened. Self-propagation did not take place. Of course this lack of growth must be related to a whole range of factors, some of which we will need to look at in the next chapter.

Up to 1912, then, the Protestant community was still dominated by the foreign missionary. Nevertheless the developments in Shantou were important for the future, whatever their limitations, and were paralleled elsewhere. In Xiamen in Fujian the Presbyterians formed a presbytery in 1863, and similarly in Shandong in 1865. The Anglican Church was the next to follow this pattern, and in 1876 CMS created its first Chinese-run Church Committee for a local congregation in Zhejiang/Jiangsu. With even more success, the American Episcopalians developed local committees in Hubei.

There were also a few Chinese Christians who founded indigenous churches. In 1873 Chen Mengnan organized in Guangzhou the East Guangdong Zhaoqing China Evangelization Society. It began with two churches but later on it had as many as forty or fifty.[18] This was the first independent Chinese Church, and it was followed by other independent congregations established in Manchuria. In 1906 Yu Guozhen set up the "Chinese Jesus Independent Church" in Shanghai declaring:

> Give up the unequal treaties which protect the church . . . awaken churches in all areas and Christians with lofty ideals to plan for independence, self-support and self-propagation . . . absolutely refuse the jurisdiction of Western churches.[19]

As Philip Wickeri points out, "Yu became the first Chinese to speak of Three Self by combining a love of his country (*aiguo*) with a love of his Church (*aijiao*)".[20] The Chinese Jesus Independent Church was to continue into the 1950s led by Xie Yongqin, who became active in the Three Self Movement.

In Shandong in 1915 two Presbyterian converts established the "Independent Chinese Church" in Jinan, and further congregations started in Qingdao, Yantai, Enxian and Weixian, so that in 1926 a local Shandong Assembly was set up. The Church ran schools, housing projects, women's literacy classes and a hospital.[21]

All of these were small and limited undertakings, of some historical significance in that they reveal that Chinese Christians themselves were conscious of the need for independence from the missionaries. On the other hand there was a sense in which they simply helped to proliferate the number of Protestant groups in China. This was to be one of the major problems associated with the rise of large independent churches in the 1920s – the Little Flock and the True Jesus Church. But that is to anticipate!

What then was the over-all state of the Protestant Christian community in China by the turn of the century? In 1853 there were around 350 communicants, a tiny proportion of the people of China. By 1900 there were 100,000. It was a significant growth, especially if it is remembered that communicant members did not include either children or enquirers. Around 300 Chinese ministers served this community, whereas in 1905 there were 3,455 foreign missionaries. Until around 1900 almost two-thirds of the Protestant believers lived in the three coastal provinces of Zhejiang, Fujian and Guangdong. The Protestants had one-seventh of the Roman Catholic baptized membership, and the Catholic communities were scattered throughout the country, although with the main concentrations in the North and in the Jiangnan area near Shanghai. The difference in numbers was in part accounted for by a differing understanding of church membership reflected in baptismal practice.

There could be no doubt that by 1890 Christian activity was increasing rapidly. Work began in Guangxi and amongst the minority peoples in the South-west. The first attempt to enter Hunan with its strong anti-Christian tradition, was made in 1896, and work began in earnest after 1900. The 1890s were turbulent years in China, and Christian missionaries became caught up in the reform movement that was rapidly growing in strength. It was no wonder that 1900 also saw the climax of anti-Christian activity. The challenge of Western learning and the Western religion had to be faced.

The Anti-Christian Movement

The tradition of anti-Christian polemic by China's scholars that had started with Shen Que in 1616 and had found its most influential expression prior to the nineteenth century in Yang Guangxian's *Budeyi* (I Could Not Do Otherwise), was to continue in more vitriolic form in the late Qing. The most influential of the many tracts and books that appeared after 1860 was the notorious *Bixiejishi* (A Record of Facts to Ward off Heterodoxy). Its origins seem to be related to Zeng Guofan and the anti-Taiping campaigns, and it may well have been written in Hunan – a province that suffered greatly from the depredations of the rebels and, as noted above, had become the centre of anti-foreign sentiment. The *Bixiejishi* combined shrewd argument with crude polemic. Four Christian works are used in order to show the folly and heterodoxy of Christianity and its threat to traditional Confucian values. In the more polemical sections Christians are accused of sorcery, sexual perversion and of indulging in a whole series of revolting practices. There is no doubt that the influence of this work on the opponents of Christianity was profound, and many of the anti-Christian riots were fuelled by its invective.[22]

The most serious such incident took place in the city of Tianjin. In 1869 the Catholics constructed the church of Notre Dame des Victoires, together with an orphanage, on the site of a razed Buddhist temple. To obtain the children the nuns offered money, thereby unwittingly encouraging "child brokers" to kidnap them. This, and the high death rate due to the policy of baptizing the sick and dying children, led to rumours that the nuns used their eyes and hearts to make medicine. It was a not untypical example of anti-foreign propaganda, and it would probably not have provoked trouble if it had not been for the folly of the French consul who, without provocation, shot the servant of an investigating Chinese official who had, in fact, found no truth in the charges. As a result a riot started, and the consul and his assistant were killed; the church and orphanage were burnt down; fifteen other foreigners were killed, including ten nuns and two priests. Four other churches were also destroyed.

Not all Chinese reacted against the foreign teaching. We have considered in the previous chapter the reasons why Christianity appealed to a minority of Chinese from an educated but non-gentry background – men such as Liang A-fa. We have also seen how it appealed to Hong Xiuquan and the Taipings. It was this link to the older Chinese tradition of sectarian revolt that, as in Hunan, stimulated gentry opposition. The reactions of the common people were less predictable. After 1860 the expansion of missionary activity brought the missionaries into further contact with Chinese sectarians. Recent studies suggest that many Chinese sectarians, especially from White Lotus groups, became Christian converts during the period 1860-1900. This was particularly the case in areas of intense sectarian activity such as the North China plain, central Yangzi valley and Fujian. Much of the evidence comes from Shandong, and the conversion of sect members especially from the "Eight Diagrams", the main branch of White Lotus, is testified to by the missionaries who worked in the area. Thus F.H. James, an English Baptist based in Jinan in central Shandong, said in 1890 at the second all-China National Missionary Conference that "large numbers of Christians in this province have been gathered from these sects".[23] In southern Shandong the German Catholic Society of the Divine Word (SVD) took over whole groups of sectarians, with the sect leaders becoming Catholic lay leaders. Such a pattern was evident outside Shandong, with similar reports by Protestant missionaries in Fujian.

This interaction between the foreign heterodoxy and Chinese sectarians was of course further evidence against Christianity in the eyes of officials and gentry. However, the readiness of some sect members to convert to Christianity was also perceived as a threat by those who remained loyal to the original sect. Anti-Christian activity could therefore result from sectarian hostility. Conversions in the Gutian district of Fujian actually went in both directions, and in 1895 the Caihui (or vegetarian sect) rose against the Christians.

It is clear that both support for and opposition to Christianity was multi-faceted. The complex and changing relationship between Christianity and the sects helps to clarify the background to missionary success and failure. One of the reasons for sect members converting to Christianity was certainly the protection afforded by the missionaries under the Unequal Treaties, for in this way they could escape official persecution. On the other hand the protection given to converts was itself a source of resentment, especially where this involved access to privileges. There is no doubt that the Catholic missions made more use of the Treaties, and also sought to build up Catholic communities at the expense of their neighbours. In the winter of 1891 two White Lotus sects in the Rehe (Jehol) area of Mongolia rebelled. The causes of the rebellion were complex, but one factor was a feud between Chinese villagers and Catholic converts which, some months before the uprising, had erupted into violence at the village of Sanshijiazi in Jianchang County. A village official, who had gone to remonstrate with the Catholics for demanding a contribution of grain from every family, was shot in a fight. The official was a member of the Zaili sect, and the Catholics then, afraid of revenge, made cannons in the church compound. The upshot was that during the rebellion Members of the Zaili burnt the Catholic Church and killed all three hundred Christians. Two days later a similar fate overcame the Catholics in the nearby city of Pingquan. Up to twelve hundred Christians were said to have died before the rebellion was suppressed.[24]

Christian Social Concern

Evangelism certainly remained the overriding concern of the missionaries of the nineteenth century. At first involvement in the problems facing Chinese society was limited to areas which aroused the immediate sympathy or the dislike of the missionary. Opposition to opium smoking, foot-binding, concubinage and female infanticide expressed the concern of most missionaries. In the areas of medicine and education, however, a wider involvement in social reform was implicit, and as time went on so the implications for Chinese traditional social conceptions became apparent.

Christian Education Work

Morrison's early concern with education and the foundation of the Morrison Education Society in 1839 remained comparatively isolated attempts to include education in the work of Protestant missions. Between 1840 and 1877 there was less interest in education than before. However, at the first all-China General Missionary Conference of 1877 new ideas were put forward by the American Presbyterian Calvin W. Mateer, based on the school he and his wife had founded in 1864 at Tengzhou in Shandong. He stressed that education was not an evangelistic "cat's paw" but a means to bring up a generation of educated Christians of spiritual and moral maturity. Gradually these ideas spread, although many still opposed missionary involvement in "secular" education. Between the 1877 Conference and that of 1890 enrolment rose from 6,000 to 16,836, with half the schools run by the Methodists, Presbyterians and Congregationalists. In contrast, in 1890 the CIM had only 182 pupils in elementary schools, and in general it was opposed to providing anything more than basic education.

The 1877 Conference also formed a special committee to write textbooks for mission schools, and it was from this committee that two important institutions emerged: the Society for the Diffusion of Christian and General Knowledge (SDK) and the Educational Association of China.

It needs to be borne in mind that schools teaching Western learning were regarded with suspicion by most Chinese, although from 1861 a limited number of specialist training schools were established by the government. These were not, however, intended to replace the traditional educational system centred on the civil service examinations. A number of prominent missionaries served in these schools, notably the

American Presbyterian W.A.P. Martin, who was President of the Beijing Tongwenguan from 1869 to 1895. Protestant educators were convinced that Western-style education would eventually replace traditional education – and after 1895 Chinese officials began to accept the need for fundamental reforms in the educational system. A key development for the future role and influence of missionary education was the establishment of institutions of higher education – even though in the beginning the standard of education was only the equivalent of an American secondary school. In 1879 the Anglicans in Shanghai founded St John's College, and in 1888 the American Methodists established Nanjing University and Beijing University. Other foundations were to follow in Fuzhou, Guangzhou and Tongzhou near Beijing. By the 1940s there were thirteen Christian universities in China, with nine thousand students in Protestant colleges and three thousand six hundred in the Catholic colleges. The influence of these colleges on national life was considerable – the 1931 *Who's Who of China* shows that thirty-five per cent had been educated in Protestant schools and colleges.

The missionaries also pioneered women's education, giving a small minority the chance to break free of the subordinate position assigned to women in Chinese society. In 1907 the Ministry of Education added primary and normal (teacher training) schools for girls to the national educational programme, but before the May Fourth Movement of 1919 few girls received education in government schools. No government colleges for women were established until after this date. Christian colleges for women were established in Beijing (its first graduates qualified in 1909), Fuzhou (Huanan College 1908) and Jinling College, set up in Nanjing in 1915.

The Catholic Church had also established elementary schools for both girls and boys, but these offered only a very basic level of education and were mainly concerned with catechetical training. In the twentieth century the standards were raised, and by the time of Liberation in 1949 there were half a million pupils in Catholic elementary schools. However, at the secondary level the Catholics were unable to compete with the Protestants, who were educating seventy-five thousand pupils in their schools. Catholic leaders frequently expressed concern over the growing Protestant influence through education. The French Jesuits had established Aurora University in Shanghai in 1903, and a Catholic layman, Ying Lianzhi, was responsible for the setting up of Fu Ren University in Beijing. Overall, however, the Catholic Church failed to train a generation of Christian intellectual leaders – with incalculable consequences for the future. The story of Ma Xiangbo (1840-1939) is an illustration of the problem. He came from an old Catholic family and was ordained as a Jesuit in 1870, but he felt compelled to resign his orders as he could not adjust to the demands of a clerical life moulded by European assumptions. It was Ma who was instrumental in founding the Aurora Academy that was later to become Aurora University. He was also to serve as a member of Sun Yat-sen's Republican Government. His involvement in educational, political and religious affairs marks him out as the most outstanding of the few Chinese Catholic intellectuals of the period.

Christian Medical and Relief Work

Medical work had become generally accepted as an important adjunct of evangelizing far earlier than was the case with education. However, there were differing views as to how to go about the work of healing. Some mission societies, after initial pioneering work, concentrated on refining the medical work, offering an increasingly high standard of care. Others combined expansion of inland dispensaries with consolidation in the coastal provinces. The CIM once again adopted a different policy from other agencies, seeing medical work as the spearhead for evangelism. At first their doctors were itinerant, but by 1890 the CIM were assigning them to strategically placed hospitals. After 1890 all medical work was being professionalized, although the CIM sought to retain some limited role for the doctor as evangelist.

In 1881 there were thirty-four missionary doctors in China;

by 1890 there were a hundred. Between 1877 and 1890 the number of hospitals grew from sixteen to sixty-one, and dispensaries from twenty-four to forty-four. Medical schools began to train Chinese doctors, and in 1887 the Medical Missionary Association of China was set up – in 1925 it became the China Medical Association open "to all fully qualified physicians . . . without regard to race or creed". In the 1940s there were three hundred mission hospitals, providing the majority of available beds for patients. Catholic medical work was much more limited in scope, and while Catholic hospitals existed in places such as Shanghai and Wuhan, most Catholic medical care was conducted at an elementary level in the villages.

Christian social concern was greatly stimulated by the growing awareness of the extreme poverty of the Chinese people, especially in the North. Timothy Richard of the English Baptist Missionary Society was shocked by the famine conditions he found in Shandong. By 1876 the famine was assuming major proportions and Richard was able to persuade friends in Shanghai to set up a Committee for Famine Relief. In 1877 Richard moved to the even more afflicted province of Shanxi, and his vivid reports of starvation, slavery and cannibalism led to a massive relief effort. It was to be a turning point in the style of Christian missionary work. The death toll in the famine has been calculated as thirteen million. The missionaries who had worked in the field realized that more than emergency aid was required, and the Shanghai Committee in its final report stressed the need for improvements in agriculture, public health and transport. These were, however, seen as concerns for the Chinese Government, and there were to be no attempts at Christian rural reconstruction for the present. In 1888-9 another serious famine gripped North China and the missionaries mobilized for relief work. This time, however, other more radical remedies were suggested by the newly arrived American, Gilbert Reid. Reid felt that charity did little good without the concurrent "application of science". His ideas were not accepted by his colleagues, but they point to a new spirit in mission that in the twentieth century was to lead to the emergence of Christian reform programmes.

Modernism and Social Gospel

Around 1890 a revolution occurred in theological thinking in the West. The rise of Christian modernism associated with Albrecht Ritschl's teaching in Europe, and of the related Social Gospel movement in the U.S.A., was to make a major impact on the thinking of missionaries in China and on a small but key group of Chinese who received a foreign education. A similar ferment went on in Catholic circles, although in 1907 the papal encyclical *Pascendi Gregis* was to halt the progress of Catholic modernism. The rejection of pietist fundamentalism in Europe was associated with the new confidence in the power of science to transform the world. It was in many respects a very optimistic age, and the expansion of Christian educational and welfare work in China was clearly linked to the changing mood in Europe and America. It would seem, however, that some of the evangelically minded missionaries were themselves coming to realize the need for reform and modernization as a result of their experiences in China itself. The most ardent and articulate advocate of reform was Timothy Richard. Richard was an evangelical Christian but his experience in the great famines led him to formulate a theology that may be compared with that of the Social gospel. For Richard the Kingdom of God was "understood . . . to take cognizance of all in this world as well as the next, in a word, of man – *body* and *soul*".[25] Richard Bohr comments:

> In short, Richard's vision of the *"kingdom* of God in China"* amounted to a theologically-informed programme of modernization which called for the reform of Chinese thought and institutions through the adoption of the salient elements of Western civilization: science, technology and Christianity.[26]

The Rise of Nationalism

The 1898 Reform Movement

Without doubt Richard's views went beyond any ideas of "self-strengthening" advocated by Chinese officials associated with the Tongzhi Restoration. He was to assume a key role in the growth of the Reform Movement in the 1890s as General Secretary of the SDK. The goal of the SDK became that of influencing Chinese officials, and in this it had remarkable success. Its programme of translation introduced many aspects of Western learning to Chinese literati, who were rapidly changing their contempt for foreign learning and foreign religion to an attitude of respect. A few advocates of reform even attacked the Confucian consensus, although most endeavoured to suggest that reform need not imply the overturning of the Confucian polity. The crisis following the Sino-Japanese War of 1895 led the young Emperor to support the reform programme advocated by the leading proponent of reform, Kang Youwei. For one hundred days, from June to September 1898, reform edicts were issued by the Emperor. It was too much for the conservatives led by the Empress Dowager Cixi, and on 21 September she staged a coup in which six reformers were executed, the Emperor made a prisoner in his own palace and the edicts revoked. The failure of the "Hundred Day Reform" had demonstrated the inability of the political system to innovate, and it was to convince more radical intellectuals that China was in need of a fundamental revolution. From this time on the influence of the Protestant missionary educators and reformers was to prove a decisive factor in the birth of the Chinese Revolution.

The Boxers

Cixi's ultra-conservative attitude may have hastened the end of China's imperial system, but it must be doubted whether the Reform could have been successful even without such formidable opposition. Suspicion of foreign ideas amongst the conservatives had been reinforced by the reassertion of foreign military power against China. Japan's victory in 1895 not only humiliated China, it also created consternation amongst the Western powers and led to a scramble for concessions in China (it was at this time that Britain obtained the ninety-nine year lease on the New Territories in Hong Kong). The Boxer Uprising was the final outburst of popular indignation against the foreigners. What made it far more serious than previous incidents was the unofficial support it received from Qing officials, almost from the beginning. It is ironic that as, for the first time, China's educated class was turning towards the West, the most wide-ranging and savage attack on foreign things should break-out. It was to prove to be the beginning of the end for traditional China.

A knowledge of the history of Chinese sects is necessary to understand the origins of the "Righteous Harmony Fists" (*Yihetuan* or Boxers as they were known to foreigners). Without doubt White Lotus traditions lay behind the movement and it was not in the first instance pro-Qing, for the White Lotus were loyal to the previous Ming Dynasty. It was in fact made up of several unco-ordinated groupings united by a common hatred of foreigners and foreign teachings. The primary targets were Christian missionaries ("Primary Hairy Men"), Chinese Christians ("Secondary Hairy Men") and those who used foreign goods ("Tertiary Hairy Men"). "Hairy Men" were all to be killed. Significantly, in view of the previous relationship of White Lotus to Christianity, the revolt began in Shandong. At first there was no reason to think that it was any different from other sectarian revolts against oppression and extortion by local officials. It was skilful manipulation by officials that turned it against the foreign community, and it was with the support of the Governor of Shandong, Yü Xian, that the banner "support the Qing and exterminate the foreigners" was raised. In the political climate after the failure of the Hundred Day Reform, and of increased apprehension about the intentions of the foreign powers, the Boxers served the purposes of the Empress Dowager Cixi and she proclaimed her support for the uprising.

Attacks on foreigners culminated on 13 June 1900 with the Boxers rampaging through Beijing, burning churches and foreign homes and killing Chinese converts. The bodies of Ricci, Schall and Verbiest were exhumed, along with those of other missionaries. In the meantime a combined force of foreign troops was fighting its way towards Tianjin, and in response the Qing court took command of the Boxer armies. The foreign relief army took Tianjin on 14 July and on 14 August it defeated the Boxer and government troops in Beijing. Two hundred and thirty-one foreigners had been killed and many thousands of Chinese Christians throughout North China, Inner Mongolia and Manchuria. The allied forces now took their revenge, looting the countryside surrounding Beijing. The Peace Protocol of 7 September 1901 extorted a crippling indemnity from China. The survival of the dynasty was now at stake.

The Rise of the Guomindang

It is not possible to trace the history of the rise of the Chinese Nationalist Party (Guomindang) in any detail. There is no doubt that it owed a great debt to the influence of Christian modernism, not least through the ideals of its founder Dr Sun Yat-sen (Sun Zhongshan). Sun was born in Zhongshan near Guangzhou in 1866 but, leaving at the age of twelve, was to spend many years abroad. He was educated in Honolulu, where he became a Christian, receiving baptism in 1883, and trained as a medical doctor, graduating in 1892 from Hong Kong. In 1894, back in Honolulu, he founded the Society for the Revival of China, which soon had a Hong Kong branch. Many of the members were either Christians or had been educated in missionary schools. Sun's first attempted uprising in Guangzhou was led by Protestants, and a chapel was one of the main hideouts. Sun founded the Tongmenghui in Japan in 1905 and within a year had a thousand supporters amongst the Chinese students then studying in Japan.[27]

The mood in China itself had shifted even further away from traditional values. The Russo-Japanese War of 1904-5 was fought on Chinese territory, and Chinese nationalist feelings were aroused as never before. The death of Cixi in 1908 removed the strong hand that had held Manchu power together for so long. Unrest and rebellion broke out in Sichuan over government plans to nationalize the railway network, and the unrest soon spread. On the Double Tenth (10 October) 1911 the Wuchang Uprising took place. Two months later Sun Yat-sen was nominated President of the Provisional Republic Government. In reality power remained in the hands of conservatives and Sun was obliged to give way to Yuan Shikai, commander of the modernized Beifang Army, in return for the abdication of the last Emperor of the Qing, the boy Pu Yi (1906-67), on 12 February 1912. So began the struggle for the soul of China that was to plunge her into civil war, invasion and economic and political chaos until the victory of the Communist Party in 1949.

REFERENCES

1. Hall, Ronald *The Art of the Missionary* pp. 24-5, 29, International Missionary Council New York and London 1942.
2. Breslin, Thomas A., *China, American Catholicism and the Missionary*, op. cit., p 16.
3. For further details of the history of the Catholic Church in Inner Mongolia see the series of articles by Berg, Leo Van Den in *Tripod* Nos. 4 and 5, 1981 & No. 10, 1982.
4. *Yuyingtangde Douzheng*, Shanghai 1973.
5. Broomhall, A.J., *Hudson Taylor – China's Open Century*, Parts 1-5 so far published, Hodder & Stoughton and the Overseas Missionary Fellowship, 1981-85.
6. Bates, M. Searle, *Gleanings from the Manuscripts: The Protestant Endeavour in Chinese Society 1890-1950*, National Council of Churches of Christ U.S.A., 1984.
7. Allen, Roland, *The Spontaneous Expansion of the Church*, World Dominion Press, 1927, p.1.
8. ibid., p. 57.
9. Hood, *Mission Accomplished?*
10. Hood, George A., "The Planting of a Mission", *CSP Journal* No. 1, April 1986, p. 11.
11. ibid., p. 23.
12. Hood, George A., "Establishing the Church", *CSP Journal* No. 2, August 1986, p. 6.
13. ibid., p. 7.
14. ibid., p. 9.

15. ibid., p. 10.
16. Warren, Max, ed., *To Apply the Gospel: Selections from the Writings of Henry Venn*, Eerdmans, Grand Rapids 1971, p. 26, quoted in Wickeri *Seeking the Common Ground*, p. 85.
17. Beaver, R. Pierce, ed., *To Advance the Gospel: Selections from the Writings of Rufus Anderson*, Eerdmans, Grand Rapids, 1967, p. 37, quoted Wickeri, op. cit., p. 86.
18. "Chen Mengnan and the China Evangelization Society", *Tian Feng*, February 1985, translated in part in *CSP Documentation*, No. 18, December 1985.
19. Shen Yifan and Cao Shengjie, "*Cong Zhongguo jidujiao zili yundong kan aiguozhuyi chuantong zai zhongguo jidujiao nei de fanying*", ("The Patriotic Tradition within Chinese Christianity in Light of the Independence Movement in the Chinese Church"), a paper presented at the Institute for Religious Studies, Academy of Social Sciences, Shanghai 1982, p. 2, quoted Wickeri op. cit., p. 93.
20. Wickeri op. cit., p. 93.
21. "The Shandong Independent Church", *Tian Feng*, June 1985, translated *CSP Documentation*, No. 18, December 1985.
22. For details of the *Bixiejishi* and its background see Cohen, Paul A., *China and Christianity, the Missionary Movement and the Growth of Anti-foreignism 1860-1870*, Harvard University Press, 1963, p. 45f.
23. James, F.H., "The Secret Sects of Shandong", with Appendix, pp. 196-202 in *Records of the General Conference of Protestant Missions in China, Shanghai 1890*, quoted in Bays, Daniel H., *Christianity and Chinese Sects: Religious Tracts in the Late Nineteenth Century*, Barnett and Fairbank ed., *Christianity in China: Early Protestant Missionary Writings*, Harvard, 1985.
24. Shek, Richard, "The Revolt of the Zaili, Jindan Sects in Rehe (Jehol) 1891", *Modern China*, Vol. 6, No. 2, April 1980.
25. Bohr, Paul Richard, *Famine in China and the Missionary: Timothy Richard as Relief Administrator and Advocate of National Reform, 1876-84*, Harvard East Asian Monographs No. 48, 1972, p. 172.
26. ibid., p. 172.
27. Further details in Treadgold, Donald W., *The West in Russia and China*, Vol. 2: *China 1582-1949*, Cambridge University Press, 1973, pp. 70f.

V

Facing the Revolution
1912-1949

A host of dark, gaunt faces in the brambles,
Yet who dare shake the earth with lamentation?
I brood over our whole far-stretching land
And in this silence hear the peal of thunder.

Lu Xun, 1934[1]

The Years of Turmoil 1912-27

The new intellectual climate amongst Chinese scholars
after 1895 was reinforced by the students now beginning to
graduate from Western-run schools and colleges, and from
the increasing number of government-sponsored colleges
offering a Western-style education. The traditional academies
had been reorganized into new schools as part of the build-
up to the 1898 Reform Movement, and changes were never
rescinded. In this way the ground was prepared for the
abolition of the civil service examinations in 1905. The
revolution in official thinking can be gauged by the fact that
now the basic requirement for government service was an
overseas education. Small numbers of students went to
France, Germany and the United States, where they received
an academic training in an atmosphere of ideological ferment
in which Western ideas of social democracy, anarchism and
socialism contended for their attention. It was, however, the
Japanese experience that exerted the greatest influence at this
stage. Huge numbers of students went to Japan to study,
rising from two hundred and eighty in 1901 to eight thousand

in 1905 and 1906. The education received may have been of poor quality for most (in 1911, the peak year for graduation of Chinese students, only 691 did graduate), but the students were fired with nationalist sentiments as they witnessed the growing strength of the first modern Asian power.[2]

The Student Volunteer Movement

This receptiveness to foreign ideas in China coincided with the rise of a new enthusiasm for evangelism amongst the youth of Europe and America. The Student Volunteer Movement (SVM) was founded in December 1888, and by 1900 it had recruited thousands of young Americans under the slogan "The Evangelization of the World in This Generation". The SVM was closely linked with the YMCA and YWCA and through them to the World Student Christian Federation, founded in 1895. The Chairman of SVM was John R. Mott, who was one of the architects of the WSCF, and whose appointment as its first General Secretary was followed by a two-year world tour leading to the emergence of Student Christian Movements in Europe, Asia and Australasia. In 1902 Mott spoke at an international SVM conference in Toronto of:

the wonderful destiny before the great British Empire and the Republic of America . . . introducing into the unevangelized nations and setting at work among the depressed and neglected races those influences which alone can ameliorate the conditions of mankind, build up a lasting civilization and make possible the evangelization of the world.[3]

This great movement emerged out of the revivalist spirit promoted by Dwight L. Moody which swept America and Britain in the latter years of the last century. However, by the early 1900s there was a clear emphasis on the "Social Gospel" rather than the saving of individual souls, and this was reflected in the concern to recruit volunteers from institutions of higher education. The President of the Union Theological Seminary, Charles Cuthbert Hall, called for "men and women who have prepared themselves by years of academic discipline to grasp and apply the sociological functions of Christianity".[4]

The Chinese YMCA had been set up in Shanghai in 1889, and in 1901 Associations were formed in Tianjin and Hong Kong. The YWCA was set up ten years later, in 1899, although there had been work in individual schools since 1888. The "Y" concentrated on the great treaty ports, and the main emphasis of the work soon shifted from the expatriate community to the new student generation. Mott visited China in 1907 with the express purpose of extending the work into government schools. For the first time since the early Jesuits it seemed as if Christianity was appealing to the intellectuals. When in 1912-13, together with Sherwood Eddy, Mott made an evangelistic tour of China they faced huge audiences, with attendance averaging two thousand a night. Eddy went on further evangelistic tours in 1914 and 1915. His message was full of the "Social Gospel". He spoke of the evils of the capitalist system and preached the need for an intellectual, social and spiritual revolution. Most members of his audience were interested in his critique of the West rather than in his religious message, but to many Christians it seemed that at last the conversion of China was a real possibility.

The flow of volunteers, especially from North America, was impressive evidence of the strength of revival in the Anglo-Saxon countries. Between 1886 and 1919, 2,524 student volunteers sailed for China. The First World War hardly halted the flow from America, although the proportion of women was much increased. At the Eighth International SVM Convention in December 1919 Mott could declare: "We stand on the threshold of the greatest opportunity which North American students have ever confronted."[5] In 1920 and 1921 the largest ever number of volunteers sailed to the mission fields of the world. Unbeknown to them, the mood in China had turned decisively against Christianity, and the euphoria over things Western had evaporated. The World War was the watershed in both China and the West. Europe tore itself apart in a frenzy of blood-letting that put paid to facile assumptions about the onward march of progress. It is true that the self-confidence of the pre-war world was less pervasive than might appear on the surface, and that even in the nineteenth century warnings were being sounded by men such as Nietzsche and Kierkegaard, but we must agree with John Macquarrie who concludes that in this period there was to be found, generally speaking, "optimism, whether it rested on the perfection of the Absolute and the kinship of the world with the human spirit, or on the confidence inspired by the power of science and the belief in the perfectibility of mankind through scientific enlightenment".[6]

In Europe and America liberal theology never recovered from the collapse of man's self-confidence after 1914. In retreat before the onslaught of secular thought, it revealed its spiritual shallowness. No wonder that in the 1920s Western intellectuals found religion irrelevant in the context of the post-war world. Modernism simply faded from the scene, while Catholic theology remained fiercely conservative, and evangelical Christianity had entered into a period of steady decline. The most serious theological assault on liberal theology was contained in the passionate *Nein* of Karl Barth's *Commentary on Romans*, published in 1919. In continental Europe the Protestant churches were deeply influenced by Barth's dialectical theology, resulting in a turning inwards to a concern with the Church and its life, but Barth's influence on Britain and America only began to be felt in the 1930s, and it was never fully accepted, save by a minority. The rise of Anglo-Catholicism within Anglicanism was to introduce a new dimension into the life of the Church in Britain. In fact, it was not as new as all that, for it traced its origins through the Christian socialism of Gore, Scott Holland and others as far back as Frederick Denison Maurice, linking a sacramental theology to involvement in social issues. As time passed this open sort of catholicism came to influence almost all the non-Roman Catholic churches, and it also affected the thinking of a new generation of missionaries – men such as Bishop R.O. Hall of Hong Kong, Geoffrey Allen (Later Bishop of Derby), Gilbert Baker and David Paton.

In America, the major figure of post-liberal theology was

Reinhold Niebuhr who, while accepting Barth's rejection of the theology of "feeling", with its downplaying of God's transcendence, was also deeply suspicious of him, since he regarded Barth's thought as a "new kind of fundamentalism". Niebuhr maintained the political concerns of the "Social Gospel", and in the 1930s and 1940s helped to keep alive the enthusiasm of a number of North American Protestant missionaries for programmes of social reform in China, most notably that of M. Searle Bates and Randolph Sailer. In 1918 these new emphases were, in any case, waiting to be developed, and the post-war years were a time of questioning and transition. In China, the most immediate concern was with the after-effects of the First World War and the need for a believable ideology offering hope within a demoralized and divided society. The Christian churches were in no state to offer such an ideology.

The Father of the Nation

Sun Yat-sen's decision to step down from the Presidency of the new Republic in March 1912, in favour of Yuan Shikai, had been a clear indication that the forces of a new Chinese nationalism were still no match for the conservatives who now rallied behind Yuan. The next few years were to see a struggle between Yuan and the newly formed Guomindang (Nationalist Party) of Sun. In 1913 an attempt to overthrow Yuan failed, and Sun fled to Japan. Yuan then stage-managed affairs so that in 1916 he was able to declare himself Emperor. He had seriously miscalculated, and a series of provincial revolts led his closest followers to abandon him. He died suddenly on 6 June 1916, overcome with anxiety and shame. The legacy of his folly was to be the decade of chaos in which huge areas of China were controlled by warlords and the cliques around them. By 1921 the most important of these, the Zhili Clique, controlled North China, including Beijing. Meanwhile Sun had succeeded in establishing a revolutionary government in Guangzhou on 2 April 1921. After further warlord fighting, and the victory in Beijing of the "National

People's Army" led by the Christian warlord Feng Yuxiang, Sun was finally invited to Beijing, arriving on 31 December 1924. He died on 12 March 1925 without achieving an agreement between the various factions. Yet he is today revered as the Father of Modern China, by both the Chinese Communists and the remnant forces of the Guomindang who still rule on the island of Taiwan.

The Growth of the Church

In China the Catholic and Protestant churches had witnessed considerable expansion. The Catholic Church had grown from 720,000 in 1901 to almost one and a half million in 1912. Amongst the Protestants the number of missionaries had reached almost 5,500 by 1914 and the number of Christians was around 500,000. According to one source 253,210 of this number were communicant members – Presbyterians 65,786, Methodists 52,200, CIM 35,150, Baptists 33,256, Lutherans 24,422, Congregationalists 21,828, Anglicans 14,541 and others 6,027.[7] The period 1900-14 therefore witnessed the most rapid growth of Christianity in China to date. This, combined with the apparent interest amongst China's intellectuals, seemed to confirm the optimism of the missionary community.

A more careful consideration of the period reveals, however, a rather different picture. The growth in numbers was undoubted, but it still meant that at the most only two million Chinese people considered themselves to be Christian believers. Of these some were undoubtedly "rice Christians", Christians out of economic or social necessity, and we have already noted the unorthodox methods of some Catholic missionaries in attempting to fill their quota for conversions! The success of the modernist evangelism of Sherwood Eddy was not in terms of new, educated converts, but rather in encouraging the new generation of intellectuals to reject the capitalist model of the West in favour of some form of socialism. It is, moreover, essential to place the work of the "Y" and the teaching of the new breed of evangelists within the context of the general intellectual ferment in

China at the time, in which any and all new ideas were welcome.

The May Fourth Movement and the Founding of the Communist Party

While Gilbert Reid and Timothy Richard preached the need for Reform, others were spreading the gospels of liberalism or anarchism in China. Confucianism was under attack from the influential group of "returned students" – those who had been studying abroad. The most popular book with Chinese students in Japan was the translation into Chinese of Thomas Huxley's *Evolution and Ethics*. Chinese students in general were reading translations of Darwin, Adam Smith, John Stuart Mill, Rousseau and Spencer's works on sociology. Social Darwinianism was the vogue, and as time passed, so more and more came to understand that the social teaching of the missionaries could be separated from their religious proclamation, and that in Europe religion was on the defensive. Chinese liberals were, however, not anti-Christian as such, and some followed Sun Yat-sen and espoused Christian modernism. On the other hand the anarchists were self-consciously anti-religious, and their influence was considerable in the first two decades of this century, before the Russian Revolution of 1917 had made its impact. As Lucien Bianco puts it:

> . . . Chinese anarchism on the eve of the First World War could be defined as a combination of the most radical theories of the contemporary West and a violent repudiation of Confucianism. Repudiation and modernism – a modernism that naturally meant Westernization – lay at the heart of the May Fourth Movement.[8]

The May Fourth Movement was triggered by a student demonstration in Beijing (on 4 May 1919), against the decision of the Paris Peace Conference to transfer Germany's "rights" in Shandong to Japan. Japan had first put forward her claim to Shandong and other parts of China in her "Twenty-one Demands" issued in January 1915. Chinese resentment at the

Powers' encouragement of Japanese ambitions was natural, and was reinforced by the contribution made by China to the Allied war effort, many Chinese having died serving the Allied armies in Europe. Reaction against the foreign powers was an important ingredient of the nationwide movement that followed – but it was far more than an outburst of a new-style nationalism. It was an intellectual and cultural revolution in the name of science and democracy, that repudiated old China for a new, modern China that would be able to stand on her own feet. The impact of the Movement was immediate for it drew on the intellectual ferment of the past twenty or so years, and it is rightly seen as marking the real beginning of modern China.

Two of the most influential figures of this period were Hu Shi (Hu Shih) and Chen Duxiu. It was Hu Shi who inaugurated a literary revolution by promoting writing using the language of the people in place of the classical language – "something like the switch from Latin to the national vernaculars in Europe".[9] The next twenty years were to see a veritable flowering of a modern and experimental literature that was in the forefront of the search for social and political reform. Chen Duxiu spearheaded the cultural revolution itself. In 1915 he founded the *Xin Qingnian* (New Youth) journal, whose Editorial Board contained all the most prominent reformers of the day, so that its influence on the thinking of the May Fourth generation was overwhelming. At this stage, Marxism had hardly been heard of in China. It was the Russian Revolution rather than theoretical Marxism that inspired young Chinese with its anti-imperialism and utopian socialist vision. The Soviet Union also publicly renounced the privileges held by Tsarist Russia in China, demonstrating willingness to enter into a new relationship of equality. So at least it was thought, although Stalin never fulfilled these pledges. In 1918 Li Dazhao, Librarian at Beijing University, announced his conversion to Marxism, hailing the Russian Revolution as a "great, universal and elemental force". With his support in late 1918 a Society for the Study of Marxism was established in Beijing. Chen Duxiu also became a Marxist soon afterwards. Small communist groups began to be formed, including one in Changsha, capital of Hunan, of which the young Mao Zedong was a founding member. Chen Duxiu's Shanghai group was the strongest and *New Youth* became its organ. Contacts were established with the Comintern in early 1920, and the founding Congress of the Chinese Communist Party (CCP) was held in Shanghai in July 1921.

At this stage the CCP was tiny, and it only survived by linking itself to the Guomindang (Nationalist Party) of Sun Yatsen, which had by now assumed a positive attitude towards the Soviet Union. Yet the tiny beginning was the result of a radicalizing of the young intelligentsia of China which was to continue steadily until the final victory of the CCP in 1949. In 1918 Chen Duxiu wrote that China had either to choose the "enlightened path to republicanism, science and atheism" or "the obscurantist path of despotism, superstition, and theocracy". Marxism was the logical next stage in the thinking of radical intellectuals such as Chen. Yet even after his conversion to Marxism Chen was not unsympathetic to the personality and teachings of Jesus, but as he put it in 1917, "The value of a religion is in direct proportion to the extent of its benefit to society".[10] It was already becoming clear that Christianity would have little place in the thinking of the youth of China. Catholic and Protestant fundamentalism was simply irrelevant within this context, and Protestant modernism could offer no convincing reason for religious belief. As Donald Treadgold has commented, "beneath a Christian exterior and profession of faith was developing a corpus of ideas at radical variance with Christianity, in the shape of unlimited faith in progress and man's ability to create new institutions with reference almost entirely to reason and almost not at all to tradition – Western, Chinese, or other."[11]

Liberalism in either politics or religion became less and less attractive as the political and economic state of the country deteriorated. The steady rise in population during the nineteenth century continued, and a peasant family had no more than two to five acres at its disposal. Most peasants did not own their land and were forced pay excessive rent to the landlord who, increasingly, lived in the city, farming out rent collection to unscrupulous agents. Landlords also were, in effect, the representatives of the State at local level, and taxation was high, frequently levied in advance (thirty years ahead in Sichuan), and bribery was usually necessary when dealing with state officials. Famine and disease were rampant, and as the twentieth century progressed the conditions of the peasantry deteriorated still further. Many were forced to migrate, often overseas; or were forced into beggary; or to eking out a living in the great cities as casual labourers; or into joining one of the marauding armies of the warlords. Chinese traditional agriculture and the rural society it sustained was rapidly ceasing to be viable. The system of usury operated by the landlords brought far higher returns than investment in the land. There was no chance of rural capitalism succeeding in this context except in favoured locations near the cities.

The peasants formed the overwhelming proportion of the population. The industrial workers numbered about one and a half million in 1921, of whom one-third were employed by foreign companies. Conditions were atrocious, and women and children formed a large part of the industrial workforce. The year 1919 saw the beginnings of industrial organization by the workers, and by 1922 there were links being forged with the Communist Party. The next few years witnessed the growth of militant action by workers and its savage repression – in 1923 there was a massacre of railway workers by the warlord Wu Peifu, followed by a wave of repression throughout the country. There were also numerous outbreaks of peasant unrest, frequently linked to White Lotus or Triad groups as in the past.

The Protestant Church in Crisis 1912-27

The publication in 1922 of the book *The Christian Occupation of China* marked the peak of missionary self-confidence. Few had the slightest awareness of the tremendous forces now being unleashed through the May Fourth Movement and the subsequent leftwards drift of the intellectuals. The missionaries were, of course, all too aware of the chaotic political and military situation, and of the growing agrarian crisis, but they believed that the answers were to be found in liberal democracy and economic reform. Nor were the Christians the only ones to fail to read the signs of the times. John Dewey visited China from May 1919 to July 1921, and was convinced that his pragmatic social and political philosophy appealed to many educated youth. Bertrand Russell spent almost a year in China (1920-21), during which time he extolled the value of traditional Chinese virtues as opposed to the harmful effects of Western patriotism. It was not a message likely to commend itself to a generation who wanted to be patriotic and modern. Russell's failure to understand the meaning of Chinese patriotism (*aiguo*) was typical of liberal and moderate social democrats from Europe and North America through to our own time.

Both Dewey and Russell did, however, reinforce the growing anti-religious element in Chinese thought. Chinese students in Paris had already tried to impose a ban on religious believers joining the Beijing-based Young China Society. Then in early 1922 it was announced in the Chinese YMCA magazine that the forthcoming WSCF conference was to be held in Beijing. In response a small group of Shanghai students formed the "Anti-Christian Student Federation" and issued a manifesto on 9 March. The theme was taken up in Beijing, and the aims broadened to oppose all religions through the formation of the "Great Federation of Antireligionists". The Conference was held from 4 to 9 April, and in a letter the Anti-Christian Federation attacked Christianity and the missionaries, saying that Christianity was dead in the West and the missionaries make up the loss by:

> implanting in foreign areas the remnants of their superstitions in order to prolong their parasitic existence. Their governments and big business favour these enterprises because they open the way to colonization . . .

Gold and iron make our bodies slaves of the foreigner; the Gospel enslaves our souls.[12]

Chinese Christian students at the Conference responded by defending their faith but accepting many of the criticisms of the missions and of missionary education. It must be understood that the "Y"s were already led by Chinese, and that as large and powerful service organizations they had more influence on public life than did the churches. Chinese Christian students were themselves being radicalized. As David Paton has put it:

> The struggle among the educated – which was not usually overt – was between those who primarily wanted a Chinese Church responsive to the national need and the national mood and those who wanted a Chinese Church primarily faithful to the ecclesiological understanding(s) and cultural assumptions of the missionary movement.[13]

The momentum of the anti-religious movement was not sustained although there was a general anti-religious atmosphere amongst intellectuals by 1927. It may be, as David Paton suggests, that the net effect of the agitation against the WSCF meeting was helpful to those educated Chinese Christians who were looking for a Chinese Christianity that was both intellectually defensible and free from the taint of imperialism. Dr Y.T. Wu (Wu Yaozong) of the YMCA, and later leader of the Three Self Patriotic Movement, commented in 1925 that Beijing 1922 was a stage in the development of a truly Chinese national Christian movement. The "Christian Movement" was to play a key role in the years up to 1949.

Missionaries, most of whom lived far from the great cities, were generally unaware of the ferment amongst Christian and non-Christian intellectuals, and they dismissed the anti-Christian movement of 1922 as the work of agitators. At a National Christian Conference in Shanghai in July 1922 it was stated by the commission on the current state of Christianity in China that "opportunities for religious teaching in our Christian schools are practically unlimited, for nowhere is there any serious prejudice against it".[14]

Just how ill-founded were the perceptions of the missionaries was demonstrated dramatically in the "Restore Educational Rights Movement" in 1924. The movement was directed against Christian schools and colleges, and was stimulated by the publication of the report *Christian Education in China* by a commission of Western educators and theologians, Chinese Christians and missionaries. In fact the report recommended a number of major reforms, including greater independence for colleges and schools. However, it was attacked not only by the anti-Christian movement but also by Chinese Christians who felt it did not go far enough, and by many missionaries who felt it went too far! Significantly, many of the students in the Christian colleges themselves joined the educational campaign. It was the beginning of their integration into the general student movement of China.

On 30 May 1925 British troops in Shanghai killed a number of unarmed students who were demonstrating over the killing of a striking Chinese worker in a Japanese factory. It led to widespread protests against foreigners in China, and many colleges were closed, including Christian colleges such as St John's Shanghai. The internal political situation in China was about to experience a momentous change with the launch of the Northern Expedition by Nationalist forces in the South. As the troops moved north so nationalist fervour increased, merging with the campaign of boycotts and strikes against foreigners that had followed the May 30 Incident. There were many attacks on missionaries, and by July 1926 only five hundred out of eight thousand Protestant missionaries were left in the interior of China. By 1928 the over-all number of missionaries had dropped to 4,375. The success of the Northern Expedition also saw the rise and triumph of the right wing Guomindang under Chiang Kai-shek. The massacre of Communists and their supporters in Shanghai in April 1927 marked the end of the period known as the First United Front between the Guomindang and the Communists. It also demonstrated the fundmental weakness of the CCP's urban-based policy.

It is essential to grasp the general developments in China

during the years after the First World War in order to understand the relationship of Christianity to Chinese society in
this period. The growth in numbers prior to 1914 seemed to
suggest that Christianity would play a major role in twentieth-
century China. The impression was not destroyed by the
events of the 1920s, largely because few missionaries understood what was happening. By 1920 there were a hundred and
thirty Protestant missionary societies working in China (of
whom sixty-five were American and thirty-five British), and
the decline in 1926-28, while never fully reversed, was soon
forgotten as numbers of missionaries gradually increased
again, so that by the time of the Japanese invasion of China in
1937 there were around six thousand. Despite the attempts to
push into the interior and into the countryside, in 1920 Protestantism was very much a coastal, urban phenomenon. Sixty-
six per cent of missionaries and thirty-four per cent of
Christians lived in a hundred and seventy-six cities of over
fifty thousand inhabitants compared to six per cent of the total
population of four hundred and forty million. Seventy-one per
cent of Christians lived on the east coast. There were said
to be 366,524 communicant members and a total of 806,926
Christians.[15]

Towards a Chinese Church

Turning to look at the internal history of the Church in this
period, we will discover some important changes. The
Centenary Missionary Conference held in Shanghai in 1907
was the last major event in which missionaries formed the
overwhelming majority (over a thousand missionaries and
fewer than ten Chinese were present). John R. Mott's visits to
China after the 1910 World Missionary Conference in
Edinburgh marked a departure from the old denominational
and mission-dominated patterns. The Edinburgh conference
had resulted in the establishment of the International
Missionary Council, and Mott's 1913 visit to China was to pre-
side over five regional meetings. At these meetings Chinese
formed the majority, and at the subsequent national con-

ference in the same year about one-third were Chinese. The conference established a China Continuation Committee with two outstanding secretaries, Cheng Jingyi and an American Presbyterian, E.C. Lobenstine. The aim was the fostering of an indigenous church and church unity. The survey of 1922, *The Christian Occupation of China*, was the work of the Continuation Committee and formed part of the preparatory work for the important National Christian Conference that met in 1922. Some have claimed that the 1922 Conference marked the point "when the Chinese took the leadership in the Christian movement in China".[16] This is a considerable overstatement but it was based on the fact that most of the delegates were Chinese, its chairman was Cheng Jingyi and proceedings were in Chinese and English. Moreover, the theme of the meeting was "The Chinese Church". A public statement by the Chinese representatives declared:

> We Chinese Christians who represent the various leading denominations express our regret that we are divided by denominationalism which came from the West.[17]

The immediate result of the conference was the formation of the National Christian Council (NCC), whose first annual meeting was held in Shanghai from 10 to 16 May 1923 with thirty-eight of the sixty-four delegates being Chinese. David Z.T. Yui (Ru Jikun), lay General Secretary of the YMCA, was elected Chairman, and Cheng Jingyi and Lobenstine General Secretaries.

The formation of the NCC and the role it was able to assume in subsequent years represented a considerable step forward within the Protestant Church. It was, of course, a response to the growing spirit of Chinese nationalism even though many ardent nationalists now scorned Christianity. It was important in the formation of a new generation of Chinese Christian leaders. It also, however, in its own way, remained heavily dependent on foreign sources for funds and staff. Inevitably, it did not represent the church "in the field", for it was the expression of a metropolitan intellectual élite. On the other hand, it was the élite who understood more of the over-all political process in China and who in the next twenty or so years sought to respond both politically and theologically.

A related but distinct development in these same years was the formation of the *Zhonghua Jidujiaohui* or Church of Christ in China, which grew out of the First Assembly of the Presbyterian Church, which met in 1922 after the National Conference. The Church of Christ in China held its first General Assembly in October 1927. It aspired to become the expression of Chinese Protestantism and the Chinese involved resisted the use of "united" in the title as savouring of foreign denominational origins. In the event it succeeded in bringing together sixteen denominational groups representing between one quarter and one third of Protestants in China. Almost all, however, were of Calvinist background and of Presbyterian or Congregationalist polity. In December 1927 the Shandong Baptist churches joined, and these were to be followed later by Baptists in Shanxi and Shaanxi. There was also some Methodist participation, notably the former Methodist Church in Sichuan which in 1931 became the Sichuan Synod. The Church of Christ in China represented the most impressive attempt to overcome denominational division prior to 1949, but it could not in itself overcome that division. In this sense it must be seen as an important milestone on the road to a post-denominational church, but the vision of its founders was not fully realized. It was also a big step forward in self-government. As George Hood comments:

> It was self-governing, under no external authority either in matters of faith or discipline. But in the relations between the Assembly and its Synods, and Assembly and the related Mission Boards, there continued for the next twenty years unresolved questions concerning the appointment of staff and the channelling of funds.[18]

The influence of modernism in theology and in social and political attitudes amongst the missionary community in China was strongly resisted by those who still considered the saving of individual souls to be the sole duty of the missionary. There were many individuals who retained a strongly evangelical faith but who also had a concern with wider social issues, but the general trend was towards a polarization between liberal and conservative Protestants.

It was a division already affecting the life of the churches in Britain and North America, and in China it was far more acute, due in part to the existence of a large body of missionaries associated with the CIM and with other small societies representing conservative churches, mainly of North American origin. To counter "modernism" a Bible Union was established in 1920 with the express purpose of preventing the acceptance of "liberal" missionaries and to proclaim belief in the Bible as the inspired Word of God. By 1923 it had two thousand members, most being missionaries, and in May 1922 its first national convention was held in Shanghai. A new seminary was established in Shandong and a university in Shanghai to teach conservative views.

The division in the Protestant ranks seriously weakened the Christian witness in China at a crucial time. The move beyond fundamentalism was entirely necessary for the future of both the Protestant and the Catholic Church in China, even if "modernism" brought its own problems. Throughout the previous century the missionary body as a whole had shown little awareness of Chinese culture, and the possibility that it might have its own contribution to make to Christian understanding did not occur to them. So much that was good was vitiated by a theology that claimed to take salvation as its centre, but which in fact had no word of grace to speak to the cultures and religions of mankind. It offered to its converts a means of escape from an evil world, and the inevitable result was that Christian congregations became foreign enclaves. Beyond the problems arising from association with foreign national power or Chinese xenophobia lies this theological failure stemming from the captivity of the Church to European culture rather than from the "scandal of the Cross". Bishop K.H. Ting has commented,

For the Church in China to be Chinese is a prerequisite for communication. The gospel convicts man of sin. This is its intrinsic foreignness or scandal, which makes its acceptance hard for men and women in our natural human inclination. Thus, the communicator should refrain from putting in any other foreignness to make its acceptance even harder.[19]

The shortcomings of the missionary movement must not be allowed to detract from our admiration of the personal qualities and dedication of the missionaries. One has to say that the Gospel was preached, that the Holy Spirit was working through fallible human beings in that age as in this, and that the missionaries did lay the foundation of the Chinese Church.

Chinese Catholics 1912-27

The Roman Catholic Church in China in the nineteenth century had come to be dominated by fundamentalist missionaries whose main preoccupation was with baptizing as many as possible. The concerns of Ricci and the early Jesuits were far from their minds, and their treatment of traditional Catholic communities was, as we have seen, insensitive. The French protectorate of Catholic missions was exercised with little of the tact shown by many Protestants. In the twentieth century Catholics, while numerically superior to Protestants, were to exert far less influence on national life either directly or indirectly. Catholic Christianity was mainly a rural phenomenon, and it had made little contribution to the intellectual ferment discussed above. Catholic modernism had no impact on the China missions, and Catholic theology in China remained in a conservative mould. Our discussion of the Catholic Church will, in consequence, be comparatively brief, with the focus on the gradual moves towards a native Chinese Church rather than on the detailed story of missionary activity.

At the turn of the century changes were in the offing, and

they were to a great extent the result of the work of Father Vincent Lebbe, a member of the Lazarist Order, who arrived in China in 1901. Lebbe and his friend and colleague, Father Antony Cotta (who arrived in 1906), refused the protection of the French, and in 1916 Lebbe denounced the French consul in Tianjin for interfering in a land case, with the result that his superiors banished him to Ningbo. Like most of the missionary Orders, the Lazarists regarded Chinese priests as inferior to foreigners, and when the 1914 Lazarist Assembly expressed its concern over the lack of foreign priests able and willing to serve in China, Lebbe and Cotta began a campaign to accept Chinese priests on an equal footing with those from overseas.

The French domination of the mission to China was not only political. The majority of foreign priests and bishops were French (even by 1922 of 1,438 priests from overseas 680 were French, and twenty-four out of fifty-six bishops). Lebbe's objection to French control was not welcomed by the old hands, even though in 1905 the French Separation Act led to the severing of relations with the Holy See and the declaration by France that in future her protectorate extended only to French missionaries. The Vatican had been seeking direct relations with the Chinese government since 1886 but France had intervened to thwart any moves in this direction. In fact the Vatican's attempts only came to fruition in 1943 despite serious but abortive moves in 1918 which were opposed by both France and Italy.

It is not surprising in these circumstances that Lebbe received a sympathetic hearing in Rome. Lebbe was, however, proposing an entirely different missionary strategy from that conducted since the 1840s, and it is the acceptance of his over-all approach which is perhaps more remarkable. It was made easier because Lebbe was no theological radical – what he was proposing was more of a return to Ricci's understanding of mission. He, therefore, began work amongst intellectuals in Tianjin, formed Catholic lay associations and set up the first Catholic newspapers in 1912 and 1916. He sought for common ground with Chinese tradition and to build indigenous churches served by native priests. As a direct result of Lebbe's *Memoir on the Catholic Mission to China*, in November 1919 Pope Benedict XV promulgated the encyclical *Maximum Illud*. Benedict also appointed the Vicar Apostolic of Guangzhou, Guébriant, as Apostolic Visitor to China. It was, however, the arrival of Archbishop Celso Constantini as Apostolic Delegate in late 1922 that inaugurated the first moves in the formation of an indigenous Chinese Church. The French protectorate was finally brought to an end. The Catholic Church in China remained, nevertheless, directly under the control of Rome, with the country still divided into vicariates apostolic.

Benedict's successor, Pius XI, had been responsible for Contantini's mission, and under the sensitive guidance of the Apostolic Delegate two Chinese priests were appointed as Vicars Apostolic. In May 1924 the first plenary Council of the Church of China was held after seven regional synods had been convened. It was an important step forward, even though its findings were not published until they had been approved by Rome. In 1926 Pope Pius issued the encyclical *Rerum Ecclesiae* which reinforced the principles of *Maximum Illud*. As the culmination of this process he consecrated six Chinese bishops at St Peter's, including Simon Xu, descendant of the famed Xu Guangqi. None of the bishops, however, were placed in a major vicariate, and control remained firmly in foreign hands.

The arrival of American and Irish missionaries in 1918 and 1920 respectively was related to the Vatican's concern to diminish French control, although it was also the result of an acute shortage of personnel stemming from the recall of many French and Belgian missionaries in the First World War. The Vatican was further concerned to counter Protestant influence, and American Franciscans were ordered to work in Wuchang (part of the city of Wuhan) to "offset the most nefarious propagandism practised by the Englisch [sic] sectarians in China".[20] Needless to say, the American Franciscans were not keen to engage in such work! The new Orders brought new ideas of mission, and it might have been expected that their presence would hasten the process of creating a Chinese Church. In the event they frequently resisted the indigenization of the Church. In Jiangmen in Guangdong the Maryknoll Fathers managed to exclude Chinese priests, and in Jiangxi American Vincentians (Lazarists) in Yujiang used canon law to prevent Chinese clergy taking control over part of the vicariate. Chinese religious sisters were kept in an inferior position, and even in the new Chinese sisterhoods established by Maryknoll and the Sisters of Providence, Americans dominated. There were also ongoing disputes between old and new Orders, especially with regard to jurisdiction. The contradiction between the professed desire for a Chinese Church and the continuing exclusion of Chinese from key posts in favour of the foreign missionary was not resolved before 1949. Many missionary priests remained profoundly suspicious of their Chinese brothers. The anti-Japanese War drew them together for a time but mutual hostility was not far below the surface.

One missionary, Monsignor Misner of the Yujiang mission, while very critical of many missionaries, simply dismissed the Chinese clergy: "The best that can be expected from the natives is that they do not cause trouble."[21]

Anti-foreign feeling in the mid-1920s also affected the Catholic work, and there were numerous incidents which forced many missionaries to flee to the safety of the Treaty Ports. The trouble was most acute in South and Central China where Nationalist militants had more opportunities to express their opposition to Christianity. Much of the hostility towards Catholics was based on Catholic land ownership. Missionary policy towards their rural converts was to provide a secure environment through the ownership of land: convert families would frequently be brought together from different villages and settled in a Catholic village. There were two methods adopted in organizing Catholic villages: the earlier policy adopted in the nineteenth century was for the mission itself to hold the land; the later policy adopted by, for example, the Maryknoll Fathers in Guangdong, was to give up ownership of the land to the Catholic farmers. In neither case was there any attempt to introduce systematic rural programmes: the

Catholic Church tended to reinforce traditional patterns of ownership, and cultivated good relations with local landlords and officials.

This approach, while affording protection to converts, also isolated them from their neighbours, thereby perpetuating the ghetto-like nature of the Catholic Church in China. There were other serious problems caused by the policy. One such problem was the motivation of many converts, numbers of whom, without doubt, were attracted by the material benefits to be gained. An American Passionist in Hunan found that many Catholics joined the Church "simply for the sake of bodily protection, temporal goods or financial assistance".[22] Once admitted they often became no more than nominal Christians, and returned to former habits and traditions including polygamy, concubinage and opium addiction. In the place where Francis Xavier had died, the island of Shangquan off the coast of Guangdong, there was a supposedly strong Catholic community where in the years before the First World War there had been mass conversions. Fifteen years later there were only about a hundred practising Catholics with thirteen hundred nominal members. In 1927 it was a hotbed of anti-Christian feeling and activity. The Church was unable to collect rent on its seventeen acres of land, even though it offered terms which were one-seventh of the going local rate. Resentment of Catholic wealth and privileges fuelled hostility such as that in Shangquan, and conflict with non-Christian neighbours was frequent in many Catholic communities.

The political consequences of Catholic land policies were serious. As the Communists engaged in land reform, first in the Red Bases and then, after 1950, nationally, so the already difficult position of the Catholic Church was made worse. In the long run the compact nature of Catholic communities has enabled them to survive the pressures of later political movements, including the Cultural Revolution, and in the 1980s they were to re-emerge as vital centres of faith.

In 1924 there seemed little need to take the newly formed Communist Party seriously. The Catholic community was still growing and there were said to be almost two and a half million Catholics with a further half million catechumens. Many missionaries must have regarded the future with optimism.

The Nanjing Years 1927-37

1927 marked a watershed in China's political history. For ten years under the Nanjing-based government of Chiang Kai-shek most of China was to experience a period of comparative stability. The Guomindang was transformed into a powerful political machine drawing support from conservative social groups, the emerging business community in the cities, and the foreign powers. The forces of the left had been driven underground, and in the cities a new era seemed to dawn. The Guomindang in the beginning of the period was accepted by many intellectuals as a force for nationalism and moderniza-tion, and intellectual life took on a Western liberal veneer. Chiang espoused an ideology that combined traditional Con-fucian virtues with those of Protestantism (he was converted to Methodism in 1930). Behind the façade, however, were other, more sinister ideas drawn increasingly from Nazi Germany and Fascist Italy. The dominant slogan was "Nation-army-production". However, there can be no doubt that in some ways the years 1927-34 represented an era of relative stability and economic progress. Yet, economic growth was mainly in banking and transportation, little in industry, and not at all in agriculture. In the countryside during 1925-27 there had also been a revolutionary upsurge, but in the realign-ment of forces after Chiang wrested control from the Left Guomindang the landlords had largely joined him. The exploitation of the peasantry grew worse. Moreover, the power of the provincial warlords remained intact and the Nanjing government was forced to compromise with them.

The anti-Christian movement seemed to fade in the new atmosphere of order and discipline. As order returned to the country the missionaries moved back to their locations. Many now felt that Chiang Kai-shek represented the best hope for

China and for the Gospel in China. Largely oblivious of the feelings that stirred the intellectual youth in the 1920s, they failed to understand the significance of the growing force of Chinese Communism in the depths of the Chinese countryside. The defeat of the left in 1927 had seemed to mark the end of Communist hopes. It was, however, this very defeat which, by driving the urban intellectual Communists into the arms of the peasant masses, was to create a formidable rival to the Guomindang.

The Church and the Rural Challenge

The National Christian Conference of 1922 had steered a careful line between the theological extremes, and while affirming that "no outward adjustments can, of themselves, bring us near to the Kingdom of God" it also affirmed that "men whose hearts and minds are truly converted will, of necessity, seek such outward adjustment".[23] It called for church programmes in rural areas and in agricultural education. The NCC founding meeting appointed a Committee on Rural Problems and the Country Church (re-named in 1927 the Committee on Christianizing Rural Life). A number of proposals were made but little work was done until after the appointment of Zhang Fuliang as full-time Rural Secretary in 1927. Two themes emerged as major concerns: mass literacy work, following the principles established by James Yan's model literacy project in Dingxian (Ding County) in Hebei, which began work in 1926; and the promotion of rural industries, credit, marketing, processing and consumer co-operatives. This latter programme was directly related to the theme of self-support, for rural churches were in dire economic straits and the Depression in the West meant that mission funds were decreasing.

The Nanjing Government was committed on paper to national reconstruction. Following this line, in 1929 the NCC adopted a five-year "Movement", but rural work found little place within it. Nevertheless, rural work continued to develop, and in 1930 a two-week Dingxian Literacy Institute was held. James Yan was a Christian, but he had despaired of the Church paying attention to rural problems, and religion had had no place in the original Dingxian experiment. Yan's work had already expanded beyond the literacy field, and from now on Christian rural work had close links with Dingxian. Further impetus was provided later in the year by the visit of Kenyon L. Butterfield, who had come fresh from a study of Indian village communities. His proposals included a "community-parish, with a self-supporting rural church, indigenous in its methods, led by a specially trained pastor".[24] As a result of his visit rural work was reorganized and branch committees were set up in Hebei and Shandong. Eventually the North China Rural Service Union was established in 1933, which engaged in mass education, co-operatives, rural training centres, industrial projects and the publication of *Tian Jia*, a magazine for farmers.

Meanwhile an entirely new factor had entered the situation. It will be remembered that in 1927 the small Communist movement had been driven out of the major cities. It had attempted a series of urban uprisings during 1927, as well as a peasant revolt led by Mao Zedong in Hunan. Routed by superior Nationalist troops the tattered remnants retreated to the isolated mountain fastness of Jinggangshan on the borders of Hunan and Jiangxi, where they established the second Chinese soviet (the first had been in Haifeng, Guangdong led by Peng Pai), from which they would conduct an armed struggle using the peasantry as the main force. In early 1929 the growing Communist forces moved to a new base on the Jiangxi-Fujian border, an area which included several market towns such as Ruijin and Ningdu where there were also Catholic mission stations. Communist policy at this time was strongly anti-Christian, and mission properties were sacked and converts murdered. The situation in the whole Jiangxi-Fujian border area was fraught with difficulties, and the Guomindang troops who were supposed to offer protection often showed scant respect for church property, especially when it was manned by Chinese clergy. The result was a dramatic decline in church activities – the Ganzhou vicariate in Jiangxi, for instance, suffered heavy losses, and adult conversions in 1928 were less than half those of two years before.

Chiang Kai-shek's reaction to the rise of the Red Army was an attempt to exterminate the Communist "bandits" in a series of encirclement campaigns. The first two campaigns saw the defeat of the government armies, and the third, in 1932-33, failed to dislodge the Communists from their main Jiangxi base. However, the fourth campaign was successful in driving the Communists out of the base, forcing them to move westwards on what was to become one of the great epics of modern history, the Long March. After the Communist retreat in August 1934, the government was faced with the task of reconstruction in the war zone. As part of its effort it turned to the NCC for help.

Christian concern over the "Red bandits" had been growing over the years. In the summer of 1932 a group of American Protestant missionaries had met at the mountain resort of Guling in Jiangxi, to discuss the problem posed by Communism and by the growth of Marxist-Leninist ideas amongst students and intellectuals. In the following year the group met again, but this time in very different circumstances, for Guling was now the informal summer capital of Chiang Kai-shek, who was masterminding the anti-Communist campaign. The missionary group developed warm relationships with Madame Chiang, and subsequently it was through William Johnson, a member of the group, that the government invited the Church to undertake the rehabilitation of the Communist areas. The result was the establishment of the NCC Jiangxi Christian Rural Service Union, with its centre in Lichuan. Despite some limited success the Lichuan project did not fulfil its original goals. This was in part due to the objective difficulties, but in the main it was the result of an inability of the Church to cope with the rural challenge.

The concern for agricultural education also did not find a satisfactory expression in the Christian schools and colleges – with the notable exception of the Nanjing University College of Agriculture and Forestry (founded in 1914). In 1923 a ten-year programme of famine relief was started with an American grant. The College co-operated with various mission agencies, and held numerous extension meetings throughout China. Its most impressive achievement was the survey work conducted by John Lossing Buck, published under the titles *Chinese Farm Economy* and *Land Utilization in China*. Both books had considerable influence, and it is probable that they were used by the Communists in their agricultural development programmes after 1949.

The Nanjing Theological Seminary's Rural Training Centre began work in 1930 under the direction of Frank Wilson Price in the market town of Shunhuazhen, Jiangning County, not far from the city of Nanjing. Considerable development took place over the years up to 1937 in association with the dynamic local pastor, Chu Chin-ih [*sic*]. However, from 1932 the involvement of the local and national governments who chose to develop the County as a model in self-government and rural reconstruction, actually prevented it becoming an example to other rural Christian communities.[25]

R.H. Tawney in his study, *Land and Labour in China*, written in 1931, said:

> Privation is one thing, poverty to the point of wretchedness – *la misère* – another. A sturdy and self-reliant stock may grow in a stony soil. But when due allowance has been made for the inevitable misconceptions, it is difficult to resist the conclusion that a large proportion of Chinese peasants are constantly on the brink of actual destitution.[26]

After 1931 it was to get worse. Reformism offered no hope to the peasants – it is no wonder they turned to the Communist Party. The ultimate relevance of the various church-sponsored rural work programmes to the problems of China's poverty-stricken countryside must be doubted. A small number of well-intentioned experiments could do little more than alleviate distress in a few places. The departure in 1934 of the NCC Rural Work Secretary, Zhang Fuliang, for government employment led, in any case, to the rapid decline of the rural programmes.

It must also be said that the supporters of rural reconstruction work received scant back-up from the majority of missionaries and mission boards. In surveys conducted by W.A. Anderson in 1930-31 and by F.W. Price in 1936 it was found that most rural church leaders considered evangelism to be their main priority, and in general they opposed any stress on secular education. Price found three main systems of church organization: the Circuit with several churches linked under one pastor or supervisor; the episcopal, with each local church related directly to a superior body; and the congregational, with or without some degree of linkage both horizontally and vertically. The quality of leadership was poor, with rural churches receiving few seminary-trained clergy. Most missionaries were themselves trained in seminaries offering a stereotyped and narrow theological approach. Rural worship was an imitation of that to be found in the West, with the main focus on the sermon and Sunday School lessons. Weekday activities were generally limited to prayer meetings.

The urban bias of Protestant missionary work was evident, both in the failure to respond to the social needs of the countryside and in the inadequate response to nurturing the rural church. This was the case even in the advanced areas such as Shantou where the "three selfs" had long been implemented – according to the claim of John Campbell Gibson at the 1907 Missionary Conference. In reality, as reported by Gibson's son, Tom, in 1931 out of eighty-eight congregations only twenty-eight were self-supporting, a situation which remained basically unchanged up to 1937.[27] Compared to other areas Shantou was, however, well ahead. In the three provinces of Jiangsu, Zhejiang and Anhui by 1937 there were three thousand rural Christian communities representing one-fifth of all Protestant work in China, but of these only one-third had a church, organized Christian group, or regular place of worship.[28]

The link between Christian rural reconstruction and government programmes that emerged in the early 1930s was more than fortuitous. It marked a wider co-operation, that was based on the support of the American missionaries in particular for gradualism over against revolution. Disillusion with the

Guomindang set in rapidly amongst the strongly nationalist intellectual community in China. Increasingly, as the situation polarized, there was no middle road to be followed. The New Life Movement launched by Chaing Kai-shek in 1934 was an attempt to provide his regime with an ideology that could counter the appeal of Marxism. As such it received the enthusiastic endorsement of many Christian missionaries. Yet it was an impossible mixture of traditional Confucian values, the values of the Boy Scouts (cleanliness, temperance and physical fitness), with the values of the fascist national state. Chiang's professed aim to eliminate "beggary and robbery" together with official corruption, and the creation of productive enterprises, was to be achieved through moral suasion, "A mass campaign for national regeneration was to be built on the toothbrush, the mouse trap, and the fly swatter".[29]

Catholics and Nationalists

The shift in consciousness within the Protestant missionary community from evangelizing to social engineering was not shared by most Catholic missionaries, who generally remained suspicious of the forces of modernization and continued to direct their mission at the poor and marginalized. Lebbe's awareness of the need to adopt Ricci's method of appealing to China's intellectuals was not shared by many other missionaries. Lebbe himself was unable to develop an effective programme amongst this group, despite his attempts to work out a strategy through his work amongst the laity, largely because his respect for traditional Chinese culture was no longer shared by Chinese intellectuals themselves. There was an attempt to establish a group of highly educated Jesuits in Nanjing to work with the government on educational, economic and agricultural problems, but this failed to get under way before the Japanese seizure of the city brought all such schemes to an abrupt end. The proposal demonstrates the concern of the Vatican and the missionary hierarchy in China over the inability of the Church to speak to the intellectuals and government leaders, but it also reveals their failure to see that intellectuals were less and less prepared to continue support for Chiang Kai-shek.

Chiang's conversion to Methodism in 1930 was an obvious factor in the support he received from Protestants and Catholics alike. The Catholic hierarchy was concerned to offer an effective alternative to the Protestant challenge, and it therefore responded with enthusiasm to the New Life Movement. Archbishop Constantini was able to engineer a rapprochement between the Vatican and the Guomindang. The Chinese Catholic Church translated and published the papal encyclical against atheistic Communism, and it agreed with the Guomindang on total opposition to Communism. On 8 December 1939 Rome issued revised instructions on the question of participation in the Confucian rites, thereby reversing the ruling of 1715. The Bishop of Nanjing, Yu Bin, hailed this as the beginning of a new era in Catholic mission, advocating a return to Ricci's method of approach to the literati: "Once they are converted to Catholicism, the conversion of the rest of the nation will follow as a matter of course."[30]

The New Life Movement and China's Scholars

Chiang Kai-shek's New Life Movement was indeed rejected by the overwhelming majority of intellectuals, and as the '30s progressed so more and more came to identify themselves with the Marxist cause. Not all missionaries approved of Chiang's government or the New Life Movement, but in general the missionary community failed to sense that Chiang's government had lost the support of the two key sources of power throughout the history of China, the peasants and the scholars. There were, however, a small number of Chinese Protestant intellectuals, who understood the way things were going. A good number of these had distanced themselves from the churches and formed the "Christian Movement" referred to earlier. The Student Division of the YMCA and YWCA was a main focus of this movement, linked as it was to the more general student movement. The City Division of the YMCA was far more conservative, and the YWCA was more radical than the YM.

Jiang Wenhan, Executive Secretary of the YMCA Student Division, in a paper presented to the Christian Council for Higher Education in February 1937, spoke frankly about the secularization of Christian colleges and the increasing concern of students with politics. Student concern had shifted and "We begin to see . . . an increasing feeling of disillusionment about such isolated rural experiments as fundamental solutions of China's problems. The interrelatedness of political and economic problems seems to be too obvious to ignore." Students "are not so easily satisfied with religious principles and generalities."[31] By 1937 it was obvious that Christianity could not compete with Marxism for the hearts and minds of China's intellectuals. When in October 1935 the decimated columns of the Red Army arrived in the remote and poor country around the city of Yanan in North Shanxi, after their epic march through three thousand miles of wild and hilly terrain, the history of China was about to take another decisive turn.

The Anti-Japanese War and the Second United Front

The rise of Japanese militarism and its expansionist plans in East Asia resulted in the occupation of the whole of Northeast China in 1931 and the establishment of the puppet regime of Manzhouguo, with the last emperor of the Qing, Pu Yi, as nominal emperor. In 1933 the Japanese began an offensive against North China and by 1935 had occupied Mongolia, Hebei and the former provinces of Jehol and Chahar. The Guomindang failure to resist the Japanese was a major reason for their loss of authority, and from now on Chinese patriotic feelings were to combine with desire for radical economic reforms to win increasing support for the Communist armies, who were using guerrilla tactics to fight the Japanese behind their own lines.

Chiang Kai-shek's desire to exterminate the Communists before dealing with the Japanese was to be thwarted by his own generals, as popular pressure for a "united front" against the invaders culminated in the famous "Xi'an Incident", in which Chiang was kidnapped by the very troops who were supposed to be fighting the Red Army. From 1937 the policy of the "United Front" was to maintain a precarious existence throughout the long years of war until 1945. The Japanese invasion turned into a general war against China in July 1937, after the minor incident at Lugouqiao (Marco Polo Bridge). Shandong, Shanxi, Shanghai and the capital Nanjing fell by the end of the year, while other armies moved on South China, taking Guangzhou in October. By October 1938 "Free China" consisted of the South-west, with the capital in Chongqing, Sichuan, the North-west (including Shaanxi) and parts of the countryside in northern, central and eastern China.

The war inevitably meant serious disruption to Christian life, especially in Japanese-occupied areas. The suffering of the Chinese people was horrifying, and both Catholics and Protestants organized to respond. The Christian Forward Movement was established in 1937 with three aims: relief work, spiritual uplift and closer co-operation. The NCC was deeply involved in relief programmes, and it also held a series of regional conferences during 1939-40. The Chairman of the NCC at this time was Dr Wu Yifang, Principal of Jinling Women's College and a Vice-Chairman of the International Missionary Council. She was active with Deng Yingchao – wife of Zhou Enlai (Chou En-lai), the future Premier of the People's Republic of China – in the care of children affected by the war, a link that was to enable her to play a prominent role in society after 1949.

Christian activities became more difficult after Pearl Harbour on 8 December 1941, when all mission property was taken over by the Japanese and many missionaries were interned. It thus came about that in many areas Christian congregations were compelled to run themselves without foreign support. It must have provided a good preparation for the situation after 1949 when the churches were thrown entirely on their own resources. In the areas outside Japanese control Christian relief work brought greater sympathy for Christians and an increased number of conversions.

Chinese Protestants: Evangelists and Theologians

The Protestant Church that emerged out of the years of war in 1945 was a church that was coming to rely more and more on its own resources. The missionary domination, still so obvious in the 1930s, was under challenge from two very different quarters. The radicalism of the May Fourth generation affected the thinking of Chinese Christian leaders in the urban centres and a number of these sought for an indigenous Chinese theology. At the same time, there was a growth in independent Chinese evangelism and the emergence of such groups as the "Little Flock" and the "True Jesus Church". Both movements sought to bypass missionary control and both can be seen as manifestations of Chinese nationalism within church life. However, in all other ways they represent opposite poles of Christian understanding. The one deeply influenced by "Social Gospel" and seeking an authentic Chinese theological expression; the other consciously rejecting social concern, stressing the doctrines of Heaven and Hell and the Second Coming, and expressing itself in a theological language drawn from revivalist groups in the West but mixed with elements drawn from indigenous tradition.

Chinese Revivalism

Watchman Nee (Ni Duosheng), founder of the "Little Flock", was born in Shantou, Guangdong in 1903 but was later taken to Fuzhou in Fujian by his parents where he studied at Trinity College (established by the Dublin University Far Eastern Mission), and attended a Methodist Church. At the age of nineteen he had rejected infant baptism and had helped establish an independent group of Christians. He was greatly influenced by a former Church Missionary Society (CMS) missionary, Margaret Barber, who had become associated with the Brethren Movement and been re-baptized in England before returning as an independent missionary in 1920. Nee believed in one church for each locality – a principle that was to become the hallmark of the Christian Assembly which he founded (the term "Little Flock" was never accepted by him). It was also this principle which distinguished him from the Open Brethren, with whom he maintained close relations in future years. In 1928 Nee settled in Shanghai and completed his book *The Spiritual Man*. Here he founded the Hardoon Road Assembly. In 1933 he visited England and established relations with the Exclusive Brethren, but his refusal to limit his fellowship to this group led them to exclude the Little Flock in 1935. Links with the Honor Oak Fellowship of Mr T. Austin-Sparks were, however, maintained and in 1938 Nee made this his base while on a further visit to England. He also continued to have friendly relations with the Open Brethren.[32]

Nee must, therefore, be related to the Brethren movement from whom much of his theology was drawn. He was a biblical literalist who also espoused a dispensational interpretation such as that adopted in the Schofield Bible, following along the lines of the founder of the Brethren Movement, John Nelson Darby, grandson of Lord Nelson and a clergyman of the Church of Ireland. This perspective sees history as divided into different dispensations and implies a complex eschatology in which the Kingdom of God is seen as wholly future. So Nee was able to relegate Christ's teaching on serving those in need (such as Matthew 25:35-40) to a future prophetic period. At no point did he show concern for the plight of the poor of China. His concern was with the saving of souls, for he believed that in this way the Second Coming would be hastened. Nee added to this fundamentalist heritage a number of his own peculiar doctrines, including his ecclesiology with its naïve belief in one church for one locality. His notion of authority was essentially élitist – based on a misreading of 1 Corinthians 7 – claiming that Paul had reached a spiritual perfection in which "he had the Word of the Lord, whether or not it was put in his mouth".[33] Such a doctrine led to the development of an élite of "apostles", unaccountable to any but themselves, whose task was itinerant evangelism. On founding an assembly the "apostle" appointed elders, and the assembly continued as self-supporting and self-governing. The élitist tendency was to lead in the long run to the emergence of the strongly authoritarian and heterodox "Local Church", led by Witness Lee (Li Changshou), in opposition to the more orthodox Little Flock assemblies that by the mid-1980s could be found in Chinese communities around the world.

The history of the Little Flock, first in Shanghai and then in Shandong, Jiangsu, Zhejiang and Fujian, cannot be told in detail. Its rapid growth was due in part to whole congregations defecting to them from the traditional denominations or the CIM. After 1950 some conservative missionaries handed over their local churches to the Little Flock. Witness Lee, who was Nee's right hand man in Shandong, was responsible for the policy of "evangelism by migration" that led one party of seventy families to leave Yantai for Taiyuan in Shanxi, and one of thirty families to emigrate to the North-east. Forty assemblies sprang up in Shanxi as a result. A similar policy of migration was adopted in Shanghai during the 1950s.

There can be no doubt of the appeal of this independent and enthusiastic movement within a situation of war, social deprivation and political upheaval. It offered adherents both spiritual security and hope within an insecure and seemingly hopeless human situation. It also had all the hallmarks of a sect, and its future history outside China was to underline this fact. Nee's theology was faulty at certain crucial points, and must be subjected to the same critique as we have applied more generally to the pietist and fundamentalist tradition. However, his adoption of J.N. Darby's ideas led to a more serious omission of the social aspects of biblical teaching, and this in a context of extreme deprivation. It must be judged as a momentous and crucial distortion of the Christian Gospel, which made a serious contribution to the conflicts of the 1950s and the ongoing problems in some parts of the Protestant Church in China today.

On a more positive note, Watchman Nee's own contribution to Christian spirituality can be acknowledged for it went beyond the sectarian aspects of his thought. Nee's writings on sanctification and holiness draw attention to areas all too frequently ignored by mainstream Protestantism. He was critical of the excesses of the "Holiness Movement" which had manifested itself in Shandong in 1931, with its emphasis on visions, dreams, exorcisms, faith healing and the gift of tongues. Many of these groups taught that sin could be eradicated after conversion through a "second blessing", or "baptism of the Spirit" – an idea which Nee strongly repudiated, although he did teach the possibility of "spiritual illumination" for the few, whom he opposed to the "carnal" Christians. On balance his legacy to the wider Protestant movement in China in this regard was a positive one, although the quietist tendency has inhibited the development of a more rounded understanding of spiritual experience amongst Christians deeply influenced by the Little Flock.

There were other important revivalist movements in these years. The True Jesus Church was started by Barnabas Tung after a vision in 1909 or 1910 and it stressed faith healing and speaking in tongues. Another founding leader was Paul Wei in Tianjin. Its main base, however, was in Fujian, and it drew support from pastors and members of other churches. Unlike the Little Flock it had no links with other Christian groups, and its teachings were much less orthodox. The Jesus Family was started in the village of Mazhuang in Shandong in 1921, by a converted Buddhist, Jing Dianying. By 1941 there were a hundred and forty communities in eight provinces with six thousand members. The life of the Mazhuang community was a model of orderly production centred on a communal life with a strict spiritual discipline. It was also exclusive, and according to Leslie Lyall its origins were in extreme Pentecostalism, with a stress on direct revelation through dreams and visions, mass prayer, emotionalism and "notorious lawsuits to obtain possession of church property not theirs, its spiritual 'love-ins' etc.".[34]

Wang Mingdao was an independent evangelist who was born in Beijing in July 1900 and educated in a school run by the London Missionary Society. He started preaching in 1925, and in 1936 built a large church in Shijia Hutong in Beijing. He was a fundamentalist who preached a similar message to that of Watchman Nee, but without any pretensions to establishing his own sect and without the more unorthodox aspects of

Nee's theology. The general tenor was, however, other-worldly, and his appeal was not dissimilar to that exercised by the Little Flock. Wang's *Spiritual Food Quarterly* was widely read for twenty or so years, and in the years 1948-50 his influence was probably at its greatest. Unlike many of the other evangelists, Wang addressed an urban audience, including many students, and this was to provoke a major confrontation with the Communist authorities after 1949.

Towards an Indigenous Theology

Revival and independent evangelism were certainly all part of the movement within the Protestant community in China towards self-support, self-government and self-propagation. The legacy of these movements is with us today, and its contribution to the survival of the Church is undoubted. Nevertheless, despite their seemingly indigenous character, these movements were heavily dependent upon particular types of Western theology which they took over and, to some extent, modified. It is noticeable, however, that these modifications were rarely in the field of theological adaptation. Where this was the case, as in parts of Watchman Nee's thought, the results were unimpressive. This is hardly surprising given the fact that their whole position was rooted in a rejection of the "world" in favour of the gathered community of the elect. Chinese tradition and culture was ignored as irrelevant, as were her social problems with the accompanying human suffering. By way of a provisional conclusion we may say that this type of Christian belief provided the faithful with a means of survival in a hostile environment, but could not provide an adequate framework for living a Christian life which combines spirituality and social action in a theology that affirms that which is best in culture and society. It is, therefore, with a realization of the outstanding theological task, that we turn to look briefly at those few Chinese theologians who sought to probe beyond the familiar categories of the various European theologies to discover an authentic expression of a Chinese theology.

The May Fourth Movement had made more thoughtful Chinese Christians acutely conscious of the unacceptable face of a Christianity buttressed by unequal treaties and force of arms. The "rights" in the treaties were no longer invoked by missionaries, and the treaties themselves had been inoperative for many years by the time of their formal abrogation in 1943, but the psychological burden carried by Christians sensitive to the cultural and national aspirations of their society was considerable. It was in response to the cultural revolution of 1919 that some sought for the indigenization of Christianity. Although for a period this was expressed in terms of a debate on the relationship of Confucianism and Christianity, by the 1930s interest in this approach was on the wane amongst Chinese theologians, and it was left to the superficialities of those missionaries who supported Chiang Kai-shek's New Life Movement. The fact was that Confucianism itself was the prime target of the May Fourth intellectuals. Theoretical discussions on Christianity and traditional Confucian culture were irrelevant to the rising generation, and only served to demonstrate that both Confucianism and Christianity were equally obsolete. By the mid-1930s Wu Leiquan, in the '20s a leading exponent of indigenization, was saying: "Chinese culture itself is now seeking a new direction of development. It is therefore only futile for Christianity to identify itself with traditional Chinese culture."[35]

Foremost amongst Chinese theologians was T.C. Chao (Zhao Zichen) who studied in America from 1914 to 1917, where he imbibed the spirit of the "Social Gospel". On his return to China, in 1918 he published his article "The Appeal of Christianity to the Chinese Mind". It was followed during the 1920s by articles on the indigenization of Christianity, in which Chao sought for linkages between traditional thought and Christian teaching. His search went far deeper than a merely superficial attempt at accommodation. Chao was not merely an academic, he was also a poet, and his knowledge of both Western and Chinese philosophy was supplemented by his intuitive appreciation of the expression of Chinese spirituality through the medium of art. Chao was one of the

very few Christian thinkers in China who refused to allow the
Chinese dimension in his background to be subsumed under
the thought patterns of a theology developed within an entirely different cultural milieu. Another figure of importance at
this time was T.T. Lew (Liu Tingfeng), author of many
hymns, and the centre of a circle of much younger YMCA/
YWCA Christians who looked upon him as a kind of sage.

In our earlier discussions of the distinctive elements of the
Chinese world-view we have noted its organic and dynamic
understanding of the universe, with its concern for harmony
between man and nature and man and his social world.
Chao's poetry seeks to express the dynamic of human self-
realization within the organic unity of the cosmos. Art and
friendship, food and wine, these are the mediums of the spirit.
In Chinese landscape painting the human figure does not
dominate; it is one with the rivers and hills, taking its fitting
place. Chao was heir to this tradition. In 1929 he published an
article entitled "Religion in the Poetry of Tao Yuanming (A.D.
365-427)", and obviously found a kindred spirit in him. Tao
was a Confucian but he also moved beyond the Confucian
concern with status towards the Taoist and Chan Buddhist
search for the simplicity of the *Dao*. Winfried Glüer, in his
important study of the theology of T.C. Chao, discusses the
influence of Tao Yuanming on Chao.[36] He quotes Tao's poem,
"Drinking Wine V:"

> I built my hut amid the throng of men,
> But there is no din of carriages or horses.
> You ask me how this can be.
> When the heart is remote, earth stands aloof.
> Culling chrysanthemums by the eastern hedge,
> I see afar the southern hills;
> The air of the hills at sunset is good;
> The flying birds in company come back to their nests.
> In this is the real savour,
> But, probing, I can find no words.[37]

Chao's comment on this poem is, "one may regard these
verses as the essence of our Chinese religion, providing Holy

Scripture for everyone".[38] As Glüer glosses, "Life transcends the daily worries; the objective disparity of human consciousness, the notion of 'I', and of the material world are absorbed in the apparent beauty which reveals true meaning and divine reality."[39]

Chao was wrestling with a key question in Chinese theology. This search within the tradition was no mere escapism, for Chao, like Tao Yuanming, never abandoned the search for a relevant social ethic. It was for this reason that the liberal theology of the "Social Gospel" was important to T.C. Chao, for it demonstrated a similar ethical concern, relating salvation to human self-realization through following the example of Christ. His concern with the realization of values within society was central to the Confucian tradition (the saying of Wang Yangming may be recalled, "Knowledge is the beginning of action and action is the completion of knowledge"), and it had become so much a part of the general consciousness of Chinese culture that the overt rejection of Confucianism by no means meant a rejection of this concern. It was, indeed, to remain central to the Chinese Communist understanding, albeit explicated within a dialectical materialist framework – Mao, for example, wrote in *On Practice*, "Discover the truth through practice, and again through practice verify the truth".[40] Chao in his theology makes explicit the reason why many Chinese converted to Christianity – they saw it as offering an effective means of moral transformtion (thus Liang A-fa in the early nineteenth century).

The "Christian Movement" had a mainly negative significance, rejecting the Church as foreign, and orthodox faith as incredible. In his early writings T.C. Chao fails to develop an adequate Christology, accepting an Adoptionist framework ("Jesus . . . achieved character and became God's only begotten Son"). This was replaced in the 1930s by an emphasis on the transcendence of God and on the activity of the Spirit of Christ, manifested in the self-giving love of God. Chao's pilgrimage was to lead him towards the Anglican Catholic tradition, and under the guidance of Bishop R.O. Hall he was ordained in July 1941. David Paton suggests that the question for Chao was similar to Bonhoeffer's, "Who is Jesus Christ for us today?" but transposed into a Chinese context: "Who is Christ for Tao Yuanming?" It was a question that could receive no satisfactory answer from within the Protestant theological tradition, and it is a mistake to interpret Chao's new concern with the Church as the result of the influence of Barth's dialectical theology. Within Anglicanism he sensed a different ethos, with its sacramental understanding of the relationship between matter and spirit. To quote C.S. Lewis on Richard Hooker:

> If "nature hath need of grace", yet also "grace hath need of nature" . . . We must not think that we glorify God only in our specifically religious actions. "We move, we sleep, we take the cup at the hand of our friend" and glorify him unconsciously, as inanimate objects do, for "every effect proceeding from the most concealed instincts of nature" manifests his power . . . We meet on all levels the divine wisdom shining through "the beautiful variety of all things" in their manifold and yet harmonious dissimilitude.[41]

In his search Chao was, of course, moving close to the patristic world and to Eastern Orthodoxy and the best of medieval spirituality, but these had little influence on Catholic or Protestant missions in China.

Anglicanism was in another sense, however, an inappropriate model for China. Christianity as a Chinese national religion was a non-starter. Yet T.C. Chao in his essay "Can Christianity Be the Basis of Social Reconstruction" had clearly indicated the link between the call for indigenization and the desire for national reconstruction. In the early 1930s Christianity was seen as providing the basis for a new spirit in society which would lead to national regeneration. It was not to be, and as Ng Lee-ming points out:

> As China's situation became worse, the "liberal" approach was found by most Chinese to be too slow for the occasion. With the burst of this liberal bubble, indigenization also lost its place in the all important task

of national reconstruction, and accordingly stopped being the entering point to the hearts and minds of the Chinese people.[42]

As China faced the problems of reconstruction and then of invasion and war Christians were faced with a fundamental challenge: why be a Christian at all? The importance of Christian faith was not to be demonstrated by assertions on spirituality in a social context of injustice, overwhelming human misery and the rape and pillage of the marauding Japanese armies. T.C. Chao and others understood this, and their writings reflect this concern. At the same time it was increasingly clear that Christianity was unable to offer solutions to the pressing social problems. The "Social Gospel" was ultimately revealed as a hollow gospel, and Communism a more satisfactory path to national reconstruction. Conservative Christian criticims of liberal modernism received their partial justification in the years up to 1949, but conservative Christianity in ignoring social questions offered no way forward either. What they failed to understand was that Christianity had in a sense lost its right to make claims for itself.

Ng Lee-ming comments:

We see here that theologians in China were forced by the peculiar circumstances there into a "no-win" situation. They were forced to state the case of Christianity in a particular context in which no specific Christian claim could properly be made. In not being able to convince the Chinese people of the social necessity of Christianity, they failed to convince the same people of its religious validity.[43]

T.C. Chao in his essay "The Future of the Church in Social and Economic Thought and Action", published in 1938, revealed his personal awareness of this problem, stating, "It may almost be said that in the necessity of making the social impact upon China, the Church has become a Christian movement, with far-reaching radii but with an often weakened centre, the Church itself." In a searching and prophetic analysis published in 1948 Chao wrote:

> The Church in general lacks passion for Christ in the present world. The most popular religious appeal in China today is contained in selfish preaching and selfish enthusiasm for individual salvation. Instructed by evangelists to seek the glory of heaven, not of earth, where wars rage and mankind suffers, where the atomic bomb may descend and whole civilizations may be wiped out, many followers of Christ seek to save their souls away from society. They give money freely, have fellowship wherever they form their groups, and possess a sort of radiant faith and unfailing hope. On the other hand, where the preaching is a call to bear the cross, to leave heaven in the hands of God, and to offer oneself in the spirit of sacrifice, there seems little incentive to gain and the following is therefore weak. There are numerous youths who do not value their heads and go over to the Communists. They see slight hope in the Church for the salvation of their nation. They desire to hear the Church lift its prophetic voice against corruption, oppression, cruelty, totalitarianism, and war. They want the whole Church, all denominations combined, to take a stand against the evils that devour China today. Since no such stand has been made, they are turning away from Christianity.[44]

Winfried Glüer points out that Chao's approach to ethics was personalistic; he failed to develop a satisfactory alternative to the "social gospel" after realizing the inadequacies of liberal theology. His struggle was for a comprehensible orthodoxy which avoided Barth's neo-orthodoxy. Faced with the failure of the Church to offer an answer to the Communist challenge, he was left with a breakdown between the unity of faith and action, which drove him to retreat into a self-cultivation that in the 1950s was to lead him back to a Chinese spirituality and away from Christianity. "I have not been a true theologian . . . I have not been able to bear the burden that should be mine", he said in a letter to Glüer just before his death in 1979.[45] As

China once again allowed freedom of religion after the end of the Cultural Revolution, Chao refused to describe himself as a Christian; but in a letter to his former pupil Luo Zhenfang he wrote on 26 July 1979:

> For three years now I have not left my house, as I can only walk five hundred paces a day. But since the death of my wife last September, I have been reading the Old and New Testaments. The New I have already finished and am as far as the Book of Joshua in the Old. I want to see the historical development of religion, to see if the boundless universe is under the governance of God or is simply a natural process.

Luo comments on the question of Chao's faith:

> On his new road of seeking, before he could reach his goal, Chao parted from this world. Because of this his search for the truth is an "unfinished symphony". But what does it matter? It is still a masterpiece passed on to those who would continue the work of composition.[46]

It was fitting indeed that he was given a Christian burial, the funeral address being given by Professor Zhao Fusan, another Anglican priest.[47]

T.C. Chao's spiritual struggle is an eloquent testimony to the outstanding theological questions facing Chinese theology. Looking back from the perspective of today, however, it is clear that what would now be termed the "contextualization" of theology within a Chinese cultural milieu was a task rightly begun, even if the terms of the discussion were inadequate. Chao has pointed to the truth that many non-Western theologians are now also stressing: It is the over-all context of a culture that must be taken into account, with all its implicit as well as explicit value, its popular as well as its intellectual culture, its stories and its art as well as its philosophy and theological systems. For Chao personally the settlement he reached "lies in the wider horizon of reality such as Tao Yuanming and others have attempted to attain. Chao at one time felt that his was not unrelated to Christianity. But after a long, wearisome journey he . . . returned to this wider spirituality of China from which he originated."[48] Who are we to pass judgement, who understand so little of the splendours of the Chinese Way and who, indeed, may be called, in the poverty of Spirit of the Western world, to pass this way ourselves?

The Struggle for China 1945-49

Many Christian leaders felt that the contributions of the churches to the war effort, the relief programmes run by Christians, and the fact that Christianity could offer "a moral and spiritual foundation and a dynamic for real democracy",[49] would enable Christianity to play a new role in postwar China. In reality, T.C. Chao's analysis of the weakness of Christian faith in China's struggle was more realistic than his and others' view of its strengths. After the war Christian work revived, and substantial resources were sent by mission boards for the work of restoration. A whole new generation of missionaries began work in 1946 and 1947, bringing updated ideas of mission. But already the co-operation between the Guomindang and the Communists was breaking down, and in June 1946 a government army of almost two million men attacked the Communist-held areas in North and Central China. Many believed that the Communists would soon be defeated, but by late 1947 Communist armies were striking back, inflicting heavy defeats on the numerically superior government troops.

The Civil War appalled many democrats and leftist intellectuals. In early 1947 a group of fifteen prominent Protestant church leaders presented a statement to the United States, asking the U.S.A. to reconcile the Nationalists and Communists. The Guomindang were rapidly losing whatever goodwill they had gained as the governing party of "Free China", and the Communists were the beneficiaries. Reformism in the mood of the early 1930s was doomed, and the calls of liberal

Christian leaders for reform and social democracy showed their failure to understand the forces now at work in China. Thus the launching of a three-year nation-wide Forward Movement by the NCC in December 1946, "which will aim at strengthening the inner life of the Church and at making the service of the Church to the nation more far-reaching and significant", was commendable if ultimately irrelevant. Indeed, the future of China, and the future of the Church in China, was being decided elsewhere by those who at best saw religion as irrelevant, at worst as a superstition to be eradicated. As the economy in non-Communist China collapsed so the initiative passed to the Communist Party led by Mao Zedong. In the spring of 1948 their armies occupied important cities along the Yellow River. In the next year huge areas of the country passed under Communist control. By January 1949 the Guomindang had effectively lost. On 1 October 1949 Mao Zedong declared the establishment of the People's Republic of China with the famous words, "The Chinese people have stood up".

There were a few, both missionaries and Chinese Christians, who had expected the Communist victory. An even smaller number had come to feel that the Communist Party represented the best hope for the future of China. Amongst missionaries there were those whose standpoint had been changed as a result of direct experience of the Communists in the period of the United Front, when the Communists adopted a more moderate policy towards religious believers than in earlier years. American Congregational missionaries in rural Shaanxi discovered this for themselves in 1937-39, and hostility turned into cautious approval of some aspects of the Communist programmes, especially economic reform, education and the exemplary behaviour of the soldiers towards the common people. At the same time they were at pains to stress the non-Communist aspects of the programme in the Red areas. Hugh Hubbard wrote in his diary that "The brand of communism taught in this army is quite different from the Russian brand".[50] Japanese harassment also tended to drive the missionaries in the Communist areas towards a sympathetic stance. Nor was this change in attitude limited to liberal Protestants. Agnes Smedley in her book *Battle Hymn of China* tells the story of a young Irish Catholic priest who smuggled medical supplies from behind Japanese lines to the Communist guerrilla armies.[51]

For the majority of those who came to some sort of tacit alliance with the Communists during the anti-Japanese war, their sympathy was founded on a degree of shared interest and was in no way a consciously thought out taking of sides. In 1945 most missionaries hoped for a continuation of the United Front, and when the Civil War broke out few indeed would have agreed with James G. Endicott, of the United Church of Canada, who urged Christian co-operation with the Communists. It is significant that Endicott was deeply influenced by Wu Yaozong (Y.T. Wu), the foremost Chinese Christian exponent of Christian-Marxist co-operation. Wu, of the YMCA Association Press, had started *Tian Feng* (Heavenly Wind) in February 1945 as a liberal Christian journal. On 10 April 1948 he published an article "The Present Day Tragedy of Christianity", which caused a furore and forced him to resign as editor. He attacked the association of Christianity with capitalism and in particular its subservience to American policy in China. "Christianity has no understanding of today's revolutionary movement." He added:

> If our thinking had remained the same as Western Christian thinking, we should indeed have become unconscious tools of imperialism and cultural aggression. If the religion we preach should avoid reality, and be concerned only with individualism and revivalism, then, in the eyes of the great masses who are demanding liberation, Christianity would be nothing but an opiate. The times demand a move forward; if our religion is superstitious, backward, and opposed to the interests of the people, then all we stand for will be swept away under the ruthless judgement of history. It will indeed be tragic if at that time we still think we are being persecuted for righteousness' sake and are bearing the cross of Jesus.[52]

Wu's outspokenness was the result of many years' thought, not the product of an expedient response to the immediate political and military situation. In his 1940 essay, "The Significance of Christian Faith in these Critical Times", he had already reflected on the relationship of Christianity and Communism.[53] Unlike many other members of the "Christian movement" Y.T. Wu was deeply concerned with theology. He insisted on the need to maintain a dialectical unity between God's transcendence and his immanence, and in response to what he saw as the unduly pessimistic vein of much contemporary Western theology he came to stress the importance of the immanence of God, indwelling in man:

> If we see God only in his transcendence, we are bound to arrive at a pessimistic view of man . . . According to this one-sided emphasis, man is sinful, miserable and utterly depraved. God and man are separated from each other by an absolute chasm . . .

He went on to argue that this view was responsible for the split between evangelism and social involvement in which being "above politics" is "but a service to reactionary politics". For Wu, "The religious person is . . . full of joy and confidence. In realizing that his vocation is to co-operate with God in the working out of his will in history, he finds his place in God's economy for the recreation of the world."[54] Unlike T.C. Chao he saw the Christian as sharing in the secular movement for social change without claiming a special role for the Church. It was a key insight. Wu brought to the "Christian Movement" a depth which had been absent in earlier years. Theology was central, not peripheral. Wu's leadership of the informal "Christian Movement" was based on his combined theological and political perception. Bishop K.H. Ting later wrote that Y.T. Wu allowed "many Chinese Christians to take their place in the movement for national salvation with their faith intact, as well as for intellectuals mindful of the national fate to take their place among Christians."[55]

The Catholic Church had no such group within their ranks. Bishop Yu Bin was an outspoken supporter of Chiang Kai-shek. In 1942 the Guomindang had named its first minister to the Vatican, and these close relations continued after the war. The Vatican moved rapidly to improve the status of the Chinese Church, and in 1946 it established a Chinese hierarchy with twenty archiepiscopal metropolitan sees, and seventy-nine suffragan episcopal sees. Thirty-eight vicariates remained in the less settled areas. Pope Pius XII also appointed the first-ever Chinese Cardinal, Thomas Tian of the Society of the Divine Word. It was to be too little and too late. It was, however, too much for many missionaries – one wrote in August 1947, "I have heard time and again here in Tianjin – the big danger to the Church in China is not the Communists, but the native clergy".[56]

It is unfortunate that we do not have any firm information on the attitudes of Chinese Catholic clergy and laity to the missionaries and the issues that faced the Church in the late 1940s. It certainly seems from missionary sources that there were many tensions, and that in some areas lay Catholics welcomed the incoming Communist troops. The Catholic Church as an organized body was ill-prepared to encounter the revolution. The sinification of the Church had hardly begun. In 1946 there were still 3,064 foreign missionaries compared to 2,073 Chinese priests, and while the increase in Chinese priests since 1900 (when there were less than five hundred) was notable, their status was still an inferior one. By the time of Liberation in 1949 there were only nineteen Chinese bishops and seven prefects apostolic out of a total of 139 diocesan units, and of these, eleven were appointed in 1949 on the eve of the Communist takeover. Theologically the Church was even more unprepared. The theology taught in the seminaries in China was thoroughly Western in its ethos and politically ultra-conservative. The catechists, who conducted much of the teaching work in the villages on behalf of the clergy, were poorly educated. Finally, the fact that most Catholic converts were from the rural poor and many of these were also illiterate, meant that there were few members of the laity who had any grasp of the over-all situation in China and who might have been in a position to make an appraisal of

Marxism that went beyond the stereotypes of conservative Catholic thought. The Catholic Church in China knew how to survive in a hostile environment, and there were parts of the country with a strong Catholic tradition linked back to the original Jesuit mission. What the Chinese clergy lacked in training they made up for in their dedication to the Church, and the village focus of much Catholic life was to prove a strength in the coming trials. It was, however, a return to the essentially negative relationship to the surrounding culture, that marked the Catholic Church as a heterodox sect from 1724 to 1927.

So it was that in very different ways, and from very different histories, the two Western branches of Christianity were about to meet with a historical reckoning. Y.T. Wu was right, the times were demanding a move forward, but the churches in the West would not be able to hear his message as they recoiled in horror before the revolutionary dawn.

REFERENCES

1. Lu Xun, A Poem, 1934, translated by Yang, Gladys, in *Silent China, Selected Writings of Lu Xun*, Oxford University Press, 1973, p. 133.
2. Saneto Keisho, *Chugokujin Nihon ryugaku chi* "History of Chinese Students in Japan", Kuroshio Shuppan, Tokyo, 1960; quoted in Fairbank, John K., and Liu, Kwang-Ching, *Cambridge History of China Vol. 2, Later Ch'ing 1800-1911*, Part 2, Cambridge University Press, 1980, p. 351.
3. *World-Wide Evangelization, the Urgent Business of the Church; Addresses Before the Fourth International Convention of the Student Volunteer Movement for Foreign Missions*, New York, 1902, p. 28., quoted in Fairbank, John K., ed., *The Missionary Enterprise in China and America*, Phillips, Clifton J., *The Student Volunteer Movement and Its Role in China Missions 1886-1920*, p. 102.
4. Hall, Charles, C., 'The Responsibility resting on Christian Colleges and Theological Seminaries in View of the Student Missionary Uprising", Report of the Third International Convention of the SVM (1898), p. 185, quoted ibid., p. 103.
5. Mott, John R., 'The World Opportunity", Report of the Eighth International Convention of the SVM (1914), p. 17, quoted ibid., p. 109.
6. Macquarrie, John, *Twentieth Century Religious Thought*, SCM Press, London 1963, p. 116.
7. *China Mission Yearbook, 1914*, p. 17.
8. Bianco, Lucien, *Origins of the Chinese Revolution 1915-1949*, Stanford University Press, California and Oxford University Press, London 1971, p. 31.

9. ibid., p. 33.
10. Chen Duxiu, *Xin Qingnian*, Vol. 3., No. 3, 1 May 1917.
11. Treadgold, Donald, W., *The West in Russia and China, Vol. 2, China 1582-1949*, Cambridge University Press, 1973, p. 79.
12. For details see Lutz, Jessie Gregory, *China and the Christian Colleges 1850-1950*, Cornell University Press, 1971.
13. Paton, David M., *"R.O.": The Life and Times of Bishop Ronald Hall of Hong Kong*, Diocese of Hong Kong and Macao and the Hong Kong Diocesan Association, Alan Sutton Publishing, Gloucester 1985, p. 46.
14. Rawlinson, Frank, ed., *The Chinese Church as Revealed in the National Christian Conference, 1922*, p. 117, quoted Lutz, op. cit., p. 230.
15. Stauffer, M. T., ed., *The Christian Occupation of China*, China Continuation Committee, Shanghai, 1922.
16. Fisher, Dr A.J., quoted in Merwin, Wallace C., *Adventure in Unity: The Church of Christ in China*, William B. Eerdmans, Grand Rapids, Michigan 1974, p. 27.
17. ibid., p. 28.
18. Hood, George A., *Mission Accomplished?* p. 214.
19. Ting, K.H. "The Church in China", Lecture at School of Oriental and African Studies, 14 October 1982, British Council of Churches, London 1982.
20. The Very Rev. Seraphim, Minister General, to the Very Rev. Fathers Provincial U.S.A., Rome, 14 July 1920, quoted Breslin, Thomas A., *China, American Catholicism and the Missionary*, Pennsylvania State University Press, 1980, p. 28.
21. Misner to Father Winne, Yujiang, 10 August 1938, Archives, Congregation of the Mission, St Louis, Ma., quoted in Breslin, op. cit., p. 44.
22. Ubinger, Paul, to Grennan, Chenxi, 10 July 1923, quoted in Breslin, op. cit., p. 44.
23. Rawlinson, Frank, ed., ibid., pp. 323-4.
24. Butterfield, Kenyon L., "The Christian Church in Rural China", *The Chinese Recorder* 62:744, June 1931, quoted in Thomson, James C., Jr., *While China Faced West: American Reformers in Nationalist China 1928-1937*, Harvard University Press, 1969, p. 53.
25. For further details see Brown, William A., "The Protestant Rural Movement in China 1928-1937", in *American Missionaries in China, Papers from the Harvard Seminars*, ed., Liu, Kwang-Ching, Harvard East Asian Monographs, 1966, pp. 238f.
26. Tawney, R.H., *Land and Labour in China*, Allen & Unwin, London and Harcourt, Brace and Co., New York 1932.
27. Hood, op. cit., p. 296.
28. Price, Frank Wilson, *The Rural Church in China*, New York: Agricultural Missions, 1948, pp. 18-19, quoted Brown, op. cit., p. 220.
29. Thomson, op. cit., p. 158.
30. Hanson, Eric O., *Catholic Politics in China and Korea*, Orbis Books, New York 1980, p. 23.
31. Jiang Wenhan, "Secularization of Christian Colleges in China", *Chinese Recorder*, 68: 302-5, May 1937, quoted Thomson, op. cit., p. 233.
32. I am indebted to Norman Cliff for the information in this section which is

drawn from his Doctoral Dissertation, "The Life and Theology of Watchman Nee, Including a Study of the Little Flock Movement which he Founded", Open University, 1983, mimeographed.

33. Cliff, op. cit., p. 180.
34. Lyall, Leslie, *Three of China's Mighty Men*, OMF Books, London 1973, p. 79.
35. Ng Lee Ming, "The Promise and Limitations of Chinese Protestant Theologians, 1920-50", *Ching Feng* Vol. 21 No. 4, 1978, p. 178.
36. Glüer, Dr Winfried, *Christliche Theologie in China: T.C. Chao 1918-56, Missionswissenschaftliche Forschungen*, Vol. 13, Gutersloher Verlagshaus Gerd Mohn, Gutersloh 1979.
37. *The Penguin Book of Chinese Verse*: verse translations by Kotewall, Robert and Smith, Norman L., Penguin Books, 1962, p. 9.
38. Chao, T.C., *Religion in the Poetry of Tao Yuanming, 1929*, quoted in Glüer, Dr Winfried, *T.C. Chao and the Quest for Life and Meaning*, *China Notes*, Vol. 18, No. 4, Fall 1980.
39. Glüer, ibid.
40. Mao Zedong, *On Practice*, July 1937.
41. Lewis, C.S., *English Literature in the Sixteenth Century*, Oxford University Press, 1954, pp. 459-61, quoted Allchin, A.M., *The Dynamic of Tradition*, Darton, Longman and Todd, London 1981, p. 136.
42. Ng Lee Ming Op. cit., p. 177.
43. ibid., p. 181.
44. Chao, T.C., "The Christian Spirit Tried by War", in Miao, Chester S., ed., *Christian Voices in China*, Friendship Press, New York 1948, p. 17.
45. Glüer, *T.C. Chao and the Quest for Life and Meaning*, op. cit.
46. Luo Zhenfang, "Dr T.C. Chao's Last Letter to Me", *Nanjing Theological Review*, December 1985, translated *Chinese Theological Review* 1986, pp. 75-8.
47. Paton, op. cit., p. 104.
48. Glüer, *T.C. Chao and the Quest for Life and Meaning*, op. cit.
49. T.C. Chao, *The Christian Spirit Tried by War*, op. cit., p. 20.
50. Butterfield, Fox, "A Missionary View of the Chinese Communists (1936-1939)" in *American Missionaries in China*, op. cit., p. 277.
51. Smedley, Agnes, *Battle Hymn of China*, Victor Gollancz, London 1944, pp. 319-20.
52. Wu Yaozong, "The Present Day Tragedy of Christianity", *Tian Feng*, 10 April 1948, translated in *Documents TSPM*.
53. Wu Yaozong, "The Significance of Christian Faith in these Critical Times", translated by Wickeri, Janice, in *Ching Feng* Vol. 28, No. 1, March 1985.
54. Wu Yaozong, quoted in Endicott, Stephen, *James G. Endicott: Rebel Out of China*, University of Toronto Press, 1980, p. 225.
55. Ting, K.H. "Forerunner Y.T. Wu", in *Huiyi Wu Yaozong*, Three Self Patriotic Movement, Shanghai 1982, p. 90.
56. Haggerty, George M.M., to Father General, Tianjin, 16 August 1947, quoted Breslin, op. cit., p. 100.

VI

The Tide of History

1949-1957

> Under a strong challenge from the outside, the power and the glory of self-concerned church institutions was utterly shaken. Thus the traditional temptations of such institutions diminished. At the same time, their genuine possibility emerged: to once more become modest, functional centres of common Christian life and activity.[1]

The experience of the Church within socialist societies has been an experience of negation in which at times it has seemed that the Church is being overwhelmed by the tide of history. For the Church of the West, this is a scarcely credible possibility, accustomed as it has been, since the triumph of Constantine, to being the bearer and transmitter of the values of a whole civilization. It was, as argued in earlier chapters, these values that the missionaries presumed to export to another distinct and equally proud culture. Few of the thousands of men and women who gave the best of their lives to China and her people ever came to terms with that culture or understood that, unlike Europe or India, Chinese spiritual values were expressed within the subtleties of human intercourse; in art and friendship; in the essential humanism of her religions; rather than through a dominant and transcendental religious system.

The rise and consolidation of Marxist societies in the twentieth century has presented Western Christianity with its biggest overt challenge. Whether it is in Cuba or in the Soviet Union and Eastern Europe, the power and the glory has departed and the foundations have been shaken. In the remainder of the West, while the challenge of secularism has been felt, the retreat of the Church has been less fundamental and certainly less threatening. In Western Europe the Church is in most countries marginalized, but in such a way as to leave many Christians with the illusion that Christianity matters to society at large. In America, Christianity has not been marginalized to the same extent, and the secularization of society has been masked by a veneer of religiosity. For many Americans Marxism is seen as a political threat but otherwise as remote and alien, and the dominance of American missions in China in the twentieth century may help to explain the failure of the Church in China to understand the challenge of Marxism until after the Liberation of 1949. However, the understanding of most Europeans was also limited. Even in the socialist countries of Europe there has been a history of strong Christian influence, and the Church, while on the defensive, has also been able to benefit from its former role as the custodian of traditional values. In East Germany, Protestants have been helped to sustain themselves by their links to Martin Luther and the Reformation; in Poland, the Catholic Church retains the loyalty of the vast majority; in Russia, the Orthodox Church remains for many the authentic expression of the Russian spirit.

In contrast the Christian presence in China has always been marginal. That, at least, should be clear from the earlier pages of this book. For the hundred or so years from 1842 to 1949 foreign missionaries were able to operate within a weakened and demoralized China, and they played a considerable role in the introduction of modernizing Western values into the society. The manner and the style of Christian mission in China was, however, disliked by most Chinese, including, it is important to note, many Christians. How else can we account for the resentment amongst old Catholic families at the imposition of European norms and the patterns of order in the nineteenth century; at the mutual suspicion of foreign Catholic and Chinese priests; at the rise, from the turn of the century, of indigenous Protestant congregations such as the

Chinese Independence Church, and the later phenomenal growth of the True Jesus Church and the Little Flock? Amongst Protestant intellectuals we have spoken in some details of the origins and rise of the "Christian Movement" during the 1920s as a component part of the "May Fourth" cultural revolution. Chinese Christians expressed themselves on numerous occasions on the need to overcome denominational divisions, and the history of the Church of Christ in China represents a sustained, if flawed, attempt to foster unity. The growing influence of Chinese Protestants by the middle of the century is reflected in their increasing participation in international ecumenical affairs. According to David Paton, the Chinese delegation at the World Missionary Conference at Tambaram in 1938 was "generally reckoned to be the strongest national delegation".[2] In 1948 T.C. Chao was elected one of the Presidents of the newly-formed World Council of Churches. At home, Chinese Christians were increasingly restive over foreign control, and the realization of the Three Selfs (self-government, self-support and self-propagation) was an urgent task if the Church in China was to adapt itself to the growing nationalist tide. In the late 1940s patriotic Chinese from all walks of life came to see the Communist Party as the focus of nationalist sentiment. The prestige of the liberated zones was considerable, and more and more intellectuals, students and young people left the cities to join the Communists.

In 1945 the Communists controlled nineteen liberated zones, extending from the northern border with the Soviet Union to the tropical island of Hainan off the coast of Guangdong. It was from these bases that they gradually expanded their power and in 1948 began to occupy the first major cities, intially in Manchuria. With the end of the United Front with Chiang Kai-shek the Communist Party launched a mass movement against Japanese collaborators, followed in 1946 by a renewal of the agrarian revolution under the slogan "The land belongs to the tillers". The October 1947 Agrarian Reform Law called for the confiscation of the lands and goods of the landowners without compensation, launching the pent-up anger of the peasant masses in an explosive and violent movement that the CCP could only partly control. The senior party leadership was dependent on a membership that had expanded from around 30,000 to 2,700,000 in ten years. "Liberation" was not a tidy, carefully controlled process, but an unexpectedly speedy and barely controllable one. The just grievances of poor peasants and other socially deprived groups found redress in the exercise of rough justice against their former oppressors, while the collapse of traditional social order in the countryside allowed old scores to be settled. Moreover, not uncommonly, inexperienced leaders either failed to lead, carried things to excess, or became corrupted by their new-found power. Despite these problems there can be little doubt that the 1949 Revolution was a popular revolution, and as Mao himself had said, "A revolution is not a dinner party!" This was the new reality facing the Christian churches. How were they to respond?

The Churches in 1949

It must be remembered that the majority of Chinese Christians and foreign missionaries had had no direct contact with the Chinese Communists. Few knew what to expect when the Communist armies arrived to "liberate" them, but most were apprehensive and many expected the worst. Economic and political collapse meant that everyone was anxious for some sort of resolution of the situation. Those Christians who had been living in Communist areas for some time did already realize that the Communists were different from the corrupt and inefficient officials of the Guomindang and offered a real chance of order within a ravaged society. The Rev. Dr A.J. Weir, one of the last missionaries to leave Manchuria, writing from within a situation where the Communists had already been in control since early 1948, detailed the attitudes of Christians in the North-east, in a memo of August 1950:

There is a group – perhaps the most obvious amongst

intellectuals and "liberals" in theology – who really seem to feel that there are good grounds for much positive co-operation with the new Democracy . . . The solution to a positive Christianity in a Communist-dominated society may perhaps come from their initiative, though there is always the danger of them trying to be "too clever by half". Probably the large majority of Church members feel that the present order in China is the only live option in the foreseeable future – apart from the outbreak of a third world war: or even as offering the best and most effective government they have had this century. They would seek to carry on their accustomed faith as best they may within the permitted "Freedom of Religion" policy. These would form the bulk and ballast of the Church, not very vocal and a bit bewildered which way to turn, and carrying on under the existing momentum of their habits and traditions rather than with the power for new evangelism. A third considerable group is much affected by hopes of an approaching end of all things, by a concern with times and seasons, with visions and revelations and holding fast the faith, and by much indulgence in tongues and trances and "separation from the world" . . . There seem to be a few deliberate charlatans exploiting the situation, and the obvious functioning of a rather negative escapist mechanism for many in their difficulties; but it must be said that it is amongst this group that the boldest professions of belief are to be found, and the greatest "evangelistic" zeal, impressing many both inside and outside the church.[3]

In provinces such as Fujian, the arrival of the People's Liberation Army (PLA), was awaited with a mixture of anxious trepidation and a longing for the end of social chaos. In Fuzhou the arrival of the Communist troops was assisted by the locals, including local Catholics, according to the Archbishop of Fuzhou, T. Labrador, who tried to explain this by saying that they did so out of hunger and ignorance.[4]

Numbers of Christians

Some attempt to enumerate the number of Christians must be made before we move into detailed discussion of the post-1949 era, as the statistics to be found in Christian sources in the late 1940s are the last reasonably reliable figures available. They represent, therefore, an important benchmark, although it must be stressed that the degree of accuracy varies considerably. In the case of the major Protestant denominations the figures only include adult members and exclude enquirers and children. In the case of groups such as the Little Flock, the figures are little more than informed guesses.

The Catholic Church

The Catholic Church is said to have had 3,274,740 members and 194,712 catechumens in 1949. In view of the fact that by 1924 there had already been 2,250,000 members with over 500,000 catechumens, the rate of growth had slowed considerably. On the other hand, it may well be that, especially in the ten years from 1927, there had been a considerable improvement in the training of the Catholic membership so that by 1949 the number of nominal Catholics had decreased. It is worth reminding ourselves of the fact that out of a total of a hundred and thirty-nine diocesan jurisdictions, only twenty-six were occupied by Chinese by the time of Liberation, although it is true that this included some of the important dioceses, including Shanghai. There had been a steady increase in the number of Chinese priests, rising from the figure of 2,073 in 1946 to the last available figure of 2,698, with the number of foreign priests reducing from 3,064 to 2,090. There were 924 major seminarians in training. Total missionary personnel amounted to 4,441.[5]

The Protestant Church

The Protestant churches present a more complex picture. The total number appears to have been around one million with perhaps as many as 600,000 enquirers. There were 2,024 Chinese and 939 foreign clergy, with a total of forty-four theological seminaries and twenty-one Bible schools. There was a total of 4,091 missionary personnel. The breakdown of the one million as given in the 1950 *Revised Directory of the Protestant Christian Movement* is as follows:

	Thousands
Church of Christ in China	177
Presbyterian (joined above in 1949)	30
Methodists	147
Baptists	81
Anglicans	77
Lutherans	65
China Inland Mission	86
True Jesus Church	125
Chinese Independent Church	30
Seventh Day Adventists	21

Adding to this the combined total for smaller churches such as the Salvation Army (4,000 in 1935); Assemblies of God (12,000); Christian and Missionary Alliance (20,000); churches such as the Zong Zhenhui (21,000), Gonglihui, etc., and the Little Flock (70,000 at least) and Jesus Family (6,000), we arrive at the one million total.

Other Christian work, notably in medicine and education, was still considerable, despite major disruption and some decline during the war years. There was a total of thirteen Protestant-run universities compared to three Catholic. There were 240 Protestant Middle Schools and 189 Catholic; 322 Protestant-run hospitals and 216 Catholic.

The Russian Orthodox Church

One church not so far mentioned at all is the Russian Orthodox Church, which is said to have had 200,000-300,000 members in 1949. Almost all these were Russians, concentrated in North-east China, Shanghai, and also to a lesser extent in Xinjiang. The Russian Orthodox mission had begun in Beijing in 1858 but its intentions were very different from those of the Catholics and Protestants. Active proselytizing was not its style, and the community remained as a small Russian enclave within areas where Russians settled. The church grew as a result of the influx of thousands of White Russians who fled the 1917 Russian Revolution. Many left China in 1949, leaving a small Orthodox community in a few cities. In 1952 in the North-east there were said to be sixty parishes, two hundred priests and a hundred thousand members, with another one hundred and fifty parishes in the rest of China with up to two hundred thousand members. The first Chinese Bishop, Simeon Dou (Du) was consecrated on 27 July 1950 as Bishop of Tianjin, later moving to Shanghai. The church, however, steadily declined. By 1955 there were few Russians left and the community consisted mostly of about twenty thousand Chinese converts. In 1957 it became an autonomous church under the Moscow Patriarchate. Bishop Basil Shouan was consecrated in Moscow in that year and resided in Beijing, where there were about eighty orthodox families and eleven clergy at St Innocent's Church.[6]

The Challenge of Marxism

During 1948 and 1949 this mixed and diverse Christian community faced the most serious challenge to its presence in China since the 1721 edict of Kang Xi banning Christianity. Over one hundred years of renewed missionary activity now left the Church in an ambiguous position. Undoubtedly there had been significant moves towards indigenization in the sense of handing over to a Chinese leadership, even though the process was far from complete in 1949. Yet genuine self-support had proved an elusive goal for all but the indigenous churches. Self-propagation had indeed taken off amongst the indigenous groups, but a good part of the growth of the Little

Flock, for example, was due to their adoption of congregations from other traditions. Overall, church growth had slowed considerably since the optimistic years after the Boxer rising of 1900, and, most crucially, Christianity had lost the battle for the minds of the intellectuals.

Fundamentalist Christianity (Catholic or Protestant) is, not unfairly, to be understood as akin to many other branches of Chinese heterodoxy. Its appeal, if successful, was to the poor and marginalized. Although very different from Chinese popular religion its stress on rewards and punishments coincided with popular religion's concern with prosperity in the here and hereafter, a similarity which the missionaries, for the most part, failed to see. This was its strength and its weakness. It competed with other groups such as the White Lotus, and the nearest it came to making a more universal appeal was in the Taiping Heavenly Kingdom, a movement that the missionaries soon found was not to their liking! In the twentieth century it continued to attract converts but it faced a new challenge for the hearts and minds of the rural and urban poor in the rise of Chinese Communism, which, in the perspective of our present discussion, may be seen as the latest and most successful Chinese heterodox movement. Conservative forms of Christianity were bound to limit Christianity to the margin of society. They offered their adherents an ideology that would enable them to face persecution in the coming years but would also help to ensure that the encounter with Communism was one of confrontation rather than accommodation.

Liberal Christianity (almost entirely a Protestant phenomenon in China), sensed the danger of a Christian ghetto and in the twentieth century sought for a way forward in which Christianity could enter the mainstream of Chinese life. In the context of the social realities of the day this meant facing the task of social reconstruction. The failure of social democracy in China inevitably meant the failure of the social gospel. Thus by the later 1940s Christianity in China may be said to have reached an impasse. There seemed to be no way forward other than into the ghetto. In drawing this conclusion we have not forgotten that the faith was of immense personal importance to many thousands of devout individuals. Our concern, however, is with the larger question of the long-term relationship between Christianity and Chinese culture – which is ultimately a theological question with profound implications for the future of Christianity worldwide. It is from this perspective that the "Christian Movement" discussed in the last chapter becomes of such importance. This small minority of Protestant intellectuals assumed a leading role in the events surrounding the Liberation of 1949 as far as the Church was concerned. The NCC was quickly rendered powerless, as were the major Protestant denominations. The Catholic Church moved inexorably towards confrontation. The only possible ground for co-operation was being laid by these Protestant radicals.

Many commentators have interpreted the actions of this group as a betrayal of the Church. Y.T. Wu has been criticized as a time-server and Party stooge. The undoubted fact that all Christian leaders were compelled to operate within a framework that was not of their choosing, does not imply that the decision of the majority, led by Y.T. Wu and his close associates, to accept the constraints and conditions laid down by the CCP, was wrong in principle. Inevitably, in an unprecedented and rapidly changing situation, wrong judgements were made, extreme things were said, but in principle the series of decisions and actions that culminated in the setting up of the Three Self Patriotic Movement in 1951 must be judged as the appropriate response to the situation. The context was one in which Christians were challenged to reveal their love of the motherland (*aiguo*) – a challenge which in the context of Christian history in China was not inappropriate. Throughout the 1950s Chinese Christians found themselves wrestling with the relationship between *aiguo* and *aijiao* (love of the church). Most had been taught to believe that Church and State must be separate: it was a theological option which was inappropriate in the New China, and the Three Self Movement was an important stage in the re-orientation of Christian thinking on this question. The problems encountered along this road were many, and indeed the process is by no means over yet. The excesses and failures of the Three Self can be validly criticized but the over-all direction was, and remains, a necessary stage along the hard road to a truly Chinese Church.

What the "Christian Movement" had grasped, and which few others, Chinese or missionary, had even begun to understand, was the fundamental challenge of Marxism. Many perceived Marxism as a threat, others were perhaps prepared to work out a *modus vivendi* if necessary, very few were prepared to risk an encounter with Marxism. Such an encounter would be a risky affair, especially given the often shaky theology of many of those who were involved in the "Movement". Here, however, was the cutting edge of the Christian encounter with China at this particular historical moment. Ultimately, the important question is not how far Y.T. Wu was representative of Christian opinion, but how far he had discerned the signs of the times.

David Paton wrote in 1953:

Since we never thought through our own problems theologically – always asking the question, "What are we really trying to do?" – and never fostering that habit among the Chinese, the Faith never acquired a truly Chinese expression. There are Chinese intellectuals: most of them have no theology worth speaking of, and what they have is seriously, not to say appallingly, heretical. There are orthodox Christians: there are simple minded fundamentalists, or educated clergy whose thought is not at bottom their own or Chinese but remains woodenly in Western categories. There is a vacuum. It has been filled mainly by dialectical materialism. If today there are signs of a Chinese theological movement, it is due principally to the realization, tragically belated, that Marxism must be encountered and mastered.[7]

Imagine a picture of Chinese Christianity some time in the mid-1950s. Four figures stand out as symbolic of the era. On the right is Wang Mingdao, the "man of iron", who, in utter integrity and out of deep Christian conviction, refused all compromise. He was the best of the Church on the margin. He is joined by an unlikely companion: the Catholic Bishop of Shanghai, Gong Pinmei, descendant of an old Catholic family, commanding the loyalty of many Chinese Catholics; a symbol of a frustrated hope and future possibilities. Then in the middle of our imaginary picture there is T.C. Chao, symbolic of those torn between two worlds: China's greatest modern theologian who in his own person was to suffer the agony of a spiritual darkness induced by his refusal to separate theology from life and who, at the beginning of the rebirth of organized Christianity in China, stands as a figure of ambiguity, pointing to the task ahead. Finally, and fittingly, on the left is the figure of Y.T. Wu. Of him it has been said:

> Y.T. Wu is like an Old Testament prophet: his soul is seared by the social sins and injustices that he sees around him, and his words, though quietly spoken and written, lash and cut. He has made a thorough study of socialist and Communist theories and seeks a truly Christian answer to their challenge: some, therefore, think of him as a radical. But he is also mystical and a man of prayer.[8]

Communism, Nationalism and the United Front

Chinese nationalism expressed itself in terms of hostility to the West and, very understandably, to the religion of the West. There was a whole tradition of anti-foreignism and of anti-Christian polemic to draw on, beginning with Shen Que in the sixteenth century and reaching its peak in the *Bixiejishi* (Record of Facts to Combat Heterodoxy) of 1860. Marxist hostility to religion merely reinforced a hostility that was already present – and as we shall see, the Chinese Marxist theory of religion has been little more than a rather unsophisticated version of the standpoint adopted by Marx, Engels and, above all, Lenin. No more was necessary, for policy was dictated by nationalist feeling and practical expediency.

Early Attitudes to Religion

The CCP had never elaborated a coherent policy on religion. As early as 1926, in his report on the peasant movement in Hunan, Mao had written:

> It is the peasants who made the idols, and when the time comes they will cast the idols aside with their own hands; there is no need for anyone else to do it for them prematurely. The Communist Party's progaganda policy in such matters should be, "Draw the bow without shooting, just indicate the motions".[9]

As we have seen, in practice Communist policy towards Christianity varied from active suppression in the late 1920s and early 1930s to toleration in the period of the Second United Front from 1937 to 1945. Moreover, it is doubtful if the vast majority of Communist cadres had any thought-out policy concerning religion, beyond an instinctive dislike of "superstition" and of foreign missionaries. It is not surprising, therefore, that the experiences of Chinese Christians and missionaries during the process of Liberation varied from almost friendly toleration to ruthless persecution. As a generalization it is true to say that Protestants were treated with more respect than Catholics and there can be little doubt that the major reasons for this were the Catholic ties with Rome and the status of the Catholic Church within rural society.

The United Front Policy

Communist theory was of far less importance than the political context in which the CCP found itself operating. The context of the late 1940s was one in which the CCP moved out of its rural bases into the unfamiliar terrain of the cities. The most urgent political issue became the winning over of key non-Communist groupings, and the political instrument to hand was the already tested policy of the United Front. It was, therefore, within the parameters of this policy that the Church found itself expected to operate.

It is not possible to enter into a lengthy consideration of the policy of the United Front, but some discussion is essential to our understanding of the place of religion in post-Liberation China up to today.[10] The United Front was the context for religious policy in the early years of the post-1949 revolution. Philip Wickeri has pointed out, in his detailed and important discussion of Protestant Christianity and the United Front,[11] that most discussions of religion in contemporary China have virtually ignored the question of the United Front, and in so doing they have seriously distorted our understanding of the situation.

New Democracy

At the end of the war the CCP attempted to form a coalition government with the Guomindang. It was agreed that a Political Consultative Conference should be convened, and this actually met in January 1946 – only to be dissolved by Chiang Kai-shek in March. In May 1948 the CCP Central Committee called for a new Political Consultative Conference, but this time excluding the Guomindang. The preparatory committee met in Beijing in June 1949. It was followed in July by the issuing of Mao's key work *On the People's Democratic Dictatorship* in which he adumbrated the theory that was to lie behind the formation of the People's Republic of China later in the year. The leading role of the Party is clearly stated, but within the context of a "New Democracy" receiving general support from democratic and patriotic groupings of all kinds. In other words, the idea of a "united front" is seen as fundamental to the existence of the New China.

The United Front idea represents a distinctive Chinese addition to Marxist theory and for this reason has always been vulnerable to "leftist" attack. At the same time it draws on the Chinese traditional ideal of Universal Harmony *datong* which in modern times inspired the Taiping, the reformer Kang

Youwei and San Yat-sen. It also inspired the young Mao, and it was to re-emerge in his 1949 speech "On the People's Democratic Dictatorship" in which he looks forward to the time when "mankind will enter the realm of Great Harmony *datong*.[12] As Wickeri suggests, Mao is in effect suggesting a United Front State. The meeting of the Chinese People's Political Consultative Conference (CPPCC) in September 1949 proclaimed the establishment of the People's Republic, and ratified the "Organic Law" and the "Common Programme". The Organic Law created the Central People's Government, and the Common Programme gave legal expression to the United Front. The CPPCC was to remain as a national assembly until 1954, when it was replaced by the National People's Congress, and the Common Programme by the first Constitution. The CPPCC remained in existence as a sort of "Upper Chamber", albeit with no effective power. It still exists today as a consultative body with a degree of investigative powers. However, its primary function is a bridge-building one between the Party and the eight non-Communist parties that still exist, together with other special interest groups, including religious believers.

The Common Programme did not mention class struggle, although it did stress the severe punishment of counter revolutionaries, traitors and accomplices of imperialism. In general it adopted a reassuring tone, with aims that must have been generally acceptable to the majority of the people. Under Article 5 of the Common Programme various individual rights were guaranteed, including the right to freedom of religious belief. This was the first formal statement of religious policy, and it makes clear the fact that religion was to be treated within the United Front. This is important as it indicates that in principle religious believers were accepted as having a legitimate place within New China. The principle was to be re-confirmed in the 1954 Constitution under Article 88 which simply stated, "Citizens of the People's Republic of China have freedom of religious belief".

Work Style

There is an obvious sense in which the United Front after 1949 was different from before. The CCP in power had no need to justify itself to the people: the political mandate had fallen on its shoulders and this gave it legitimacy in its own eyes, and indeed in the eyes of the masses. C.P. Fitzgerald has remarked:

> The Chinese people looked now for a government which could govern, which knew its mind, its power and purpose, a theory and a practice which fitted together – in fact for a modern version of the government under which they had lived for so many centuries.[13]

It is this deeply traditional aspect of the rule of the CCP which is all too frequently forgotten by those who would see all Communist states as of one type. The United Front in this context was a political instrument, and the United Front Work Department of the CCP was the agent through which the Party exercised ultimate control. Acknowledgement of this indubitable fact does not, however, lead to the conclusion that the United Front was a sham, or a cynical exercise in political manipulation. The traditional totalitarianism of the Chinese political system did not exclude a degree of consultation and even criticism. Thus in the modern context the United Front policy had certain implications for the CCP itself, especially in the style of work of cadres at all levels. It implied a willingness to listen and to take account of non-Communist points of view. In the adoption and application of policies it implied "democratic consultation" and the acceptance of criticism within the limits of the over-all political consensus. In this sense it can be related to the "mass line" theory of leadership developed by Mao, and given its earliest and classical expression in the Poilitburo resolution of 1 June 1943 on "the Methods of Leadership":

> The two methods which we Communists should employ in carrying out any tasks are, first, the linking of the general with the specific, and second, the linking of the

> leadership with the masses . . . In all practical work of
> our Party, correct leadership can only be developed on
> the principle of "from the masses to the masses". The
> basic method of leadership is to sum up the views of the
> masses, take the results back to the masses so that the
> masses can give them their firm support and so work out
> sound ideas for leading the work on hand.[14]

In so far as the CCP has followed the "mass-line" principle, its
work-style has been democratic in the sense that there has
been a real interaction between the leaders and the led. On the
other hand the whole conception assumes the right of the
CCP to lead the masses, and its understanding of consultation
is fundamentally élitist. It is also true that the policy was
frequently ignored and that in practice "commandism" and
coercion were all too common. These are serious provisos but
they should not blind us to the fact that the United Front
policy did enable a whole range of non-Communist groupings
to contribute to the discussion and the decisions taken in the
early 1950s.

"The goal of the United Front is not uniformity of opinion
but the establishment of a community of interest around a
common political stance."[15] The United Front implies not
only community of interest but differences. On the positive
side this implies that differences can be reserved within the
general community of interest – as it is put in China, "seeking
the common ground while reserving differences". On the
negative side this implies that certain differences may preclude the search for unity. In the terms of Mao's important
essay of 1957 "On the Correct Handling of Contradictions
Among the People" there are antagonistic contradictions with
the enemy and non-antagonistic contradictions among the
people. Crucial then within the whole policy of the United
Front is the prior definition of who are enemies and who are
friends, and here the initiative lies entirely with the Communist Party. It follows that the United Front must always be
an unequal partnership, and that the bounds of the United
Front can be drawn more or less widely, according to the

wishes of the CCP at any one time. This limitation does not invalidate the positive role of the United Front within the context of China's political system. Yet, for this reason, it has frequently been dismissed by observers. One has only to look at the long period in China's recent history when the United Front was inoperative to see its positive role in the periods when it has been an instrument of policy. This is not to imply that the policy always succeeded, and in certain areas it had very limited success; but it is to suggest that in attempting to assess the application of a policy such as the right to believe, the role of the United Front cannot be ignored.

Opposition to the United Front policy has been consistent within the CCP itself from the very beginning. It was found immediately after Liberation: some "comrades" felt after 1949 "that we have conquered rivers and mountains, what further need do we have for the United Front?"[16] Moderate elements around Zhou Enlai and Liu Shaoqi argued strongly that the United Front was essential within the foreseeable future. While it is true that the United Front is seen as a means to an end, the end is recognized as a very long-term goal. Those who have supported the United Front have accepted the need to consult and to minimize overt methods of coercion, "leftists" have argued for overt class struggle. The history of China since 1949 has seen a constant struggle between these two positions or "lines", although in practice many individuals have taken different positions at different times or have attempted to combine the two. The attempt to bypass the United Front reached its logical conclusion in the Cultural Revolution, with disastrous results for the whole society. The restoration of the United Front from 1978 as a central part of the new strategy for modernizing China is an indication that the current leadership has recognized its continuing importance.

Thought-Reform

Mao's theory of contradictions also implied that people could change and be changed. Thus the United Front was seen also as a part of an educational process. Thought-reform was an important aspect of the Party's work in the years after Liberation, and it involved precisely those groups who formed the core of the United Front – intellectuals and cultural workers, the business community, members of the democratic parties, religious believers. We shall deal with this further in discussion of the process of thought reform amongst Christian leaders, but for the moment need only to understand its place within the over-all United Front policy.

Fosterage, in the sense of changing the thinking of individuals in a socially acceptable direction, is rooted in the traditional Chinese concept of man and his place in society. In Confucian society the individual was constrained by the nexus of family relationships and could not be said to have individual "rights" – as Hugh Baker puts it, "His existence as an individual is necessary but insignificant beside his existence as the representative of the whole".[17] The state as the moral arbitrator of ultimate values is also very much a part of Chinese tradition, but in traditional China the state remained at a distance from the individual whose life was defined by the complex of kinship relations supplemented by other networks of personal relations of a quasi-kinship type, of which the most important was that of friendship. The CCP has endeavoured through the process of thought-reform to draw the individual and the state into an immediate relationship. As one Chinese theorist expressed it:

> Purity of thought consciousness is a matter of inserting proletarian thought-consciousness with self-awareness into the brain, and continually overcoming and cleaning up all non-proletarian thought consciousness in the brain. This kind of purity amounts to being in an awakened state.[18]

The elaborate system of control and surveillance established by the Party and its organs has been the institutional expression of this, but the key element has been the study class in which the process of criticism, self-criticism and re-education could take place with the assistance of one's fellows. The goal is the inner transformation of the individual and, according to the theory, this can only be a voluntary process. In practice, it frequently turned into coercion, especially in the midst of the major political campaigns that were a constant feature of political life until the end of the Cultural Revolution in 1976. Nevertheless, the process of thought-reform was not altogether a negative one, and we should be careful not to dismiss too readily all the reports of the benefits obtained by some people from the experience.

Overall, however, thought-reform when carried out under the auspices of a powerful state, is a dangerous process. Ultimately it must destroy the foundations of the United Front. It is this process that went on in the 1950s and early 1960s, and it is significant that today there is little emphasis on thought-reform but a great deal of emphasis on seeking the common ground and reserving differences.

The Religious Affairs Bureau

The specific political instrument used by the CCP for the supervision of religious affairs was the Religious Affairs Office under the Committee on Cultural and Educational Affairs of the Government Administrative Council. It was established in January 1951. In 1954 the office became the Religious Affairs Bureau under the State Council of the National People's Congress. In late 1951 offices were being established in all provinces and municipalities, and in 1954-55 in counties with a high level of religious activities. There were four sections in each bureau, Catholic, Protestant, Local religions (including Buddhism and Taoism), and Secretarial. Muslim affairs were handled under national minority affairs. It seems likely that in general the Bureau adopted a moderate line, although this depended on national policies. However, until 1956 it was the police who controlled religious affairs, thereby ensuring that the Religious Affairs Bureaus possessed only limited authority. This points to a fundamental problem in the political organization of the People's Republic under the CCP. Mass mobilization, the political campaign, were likely to over-

whelm the political instititions which had no legally established autonomy from the party. In the end, the United Front
was only effective in so far as the CCP allowed it to be so.

Let us conclude this discussion with two thoughts. First,
the United Front policy represented a genuine option within
the over-all context of Party control, an option that favoured
discussion and moderation even when in practice the organs
of control over-stressed supervision. Second, the United
Front policy was carried out within the parameters of a view
of politics in which the CCP was assumed to play the leading
role. The tensions and contradictions between these two
aspects of policy would lead to many of the problems
associated with the implementation of the United Front
policy in succeeding years.

Christians and the United Front 1949-51

For many Chinese Christians the doubt was not so much to do
with the politics of the Communists as with their attitude to
religion. Amongst Protestants it was, indeed, the liberals who
would provide a natural bridge with the United Front, but they
were joined in many places by more conservative Christians.
Amongst Catholics there was no group with a prior commitment to the socialist road, or even to social reform. Many of
the most outspoken members of the "Christian Movement"
were already known to the Party, and it was they who were
invited to attend the national CPPCC meeting in June 1949.
Four official delegates attended, Y.T. Wu, Cora Deng, T.C.
Chao and Zhang Xueyan, editor of the *Christian Forum*. Wu
Yifang, Shen Tilan and Chen Sisheng attended in other
capacities. In late November 1949 the delegates set out on a
visitation team, together with representatives of the NCC and
the "Y"s. Their task was to explain the United Front policy and
to investigate the application of religious policy. They discovered serious problems in some rural areas, notably in
Shandong, and these were later raised with Premier Zhou
Enlai.[19]

The NCC was involved in this process but it had not been

asked to nominate the representatives to the CPPCC. The NCC was regarded with some suspicion by the Communists because of its past associations with the Guomindang and its continuing overseas links. In 1949 it issued two messages to Christians in China, reflecting the anxiety felt by the leadership over the position of the Church as Liberation approached. It was followed in December 1949 by a third message stressing the contribution that the church could make to society, and calling for a willingness to "accept criticism, and engage in . . . self-examination".[20] In the new situation the initiative had passed to the group around Y.T. Wu, but the differences between this group and the leaders of the major denominations within the NCC should not be exaggerated. Both groups recognized that the time had come for a radical re-orientation of church life, and many welcomed the chance to implement the long-standing principles of self-government, self-support and self-propagation.

The Christian Manifesto

The next stage in the story is surrounded by disagreement amongst observers. Nineteen Protestant leaders went to Beijing in late April 1950 to meet with Zhou Enlai and other officials. It was in the course of four meetings on 2, 6, 13 and 20 May that the "Christian Manifesto" was discussed and agreed. According to many earlier commentators, these meetings were called by the government to discuss how the Church might best express its loyalty to New China. Some have argued that the Manifesto was actually written by Zhou Enlai himself. According to Wickeri, who, during 1980-83 was able to conduct extensive interviews with some of the individuals involved, the meeting was requested by the Christians themselves to discuss the problems they had encountered in the implementation of religious policy during their visitation in late 1949. The recent publication in China of the official summary of the four conversations has helped to clarify what was actually said.[21]

Present at the meeting from the Christian side were the

delegates to the CPPCC with the addition of Liu Liangmo (an alternate member), Bishop Z.T. Kuang (Jiang Changquan) (Methodist), H.H. Ts'ui (Cui Xianxiang) (Church of Christ in China), Y.C. Tu (Tu Yujing) (YMCA), Ai Niansan (Lutheran) and seven other leaders from North China. The record of the meetings shows that Zhou's concern was with the relationship of religion to society. He explicitly states, "we are not launching an anti-religious movement". The summary for 13 May reads in part:

> You are theists and we are atheists, but we are not trying to open up a debate on atheism and theism with you. We believe that materialists and idealists can coexist and co-operate with one another on a political level, and that we should practise mutual respect. It is our sincere hope that between us, we can follow a path of co-operation.
>
> . . . Our principle is: "No commonality of views shall be enforced, but we shall respect one another and be flexible."
>
> China has consistently upheld the separation between church and state. Today, the government and people from religious circles are co-operating on the basis of the guiding political principles which have been set by the "Common Programme".

The Premier constantly stressed during the conversations the need for the churches to sever their links with imperialism, and he indicated that "religious organizations themselves must be independent and self-reliant, and they should establish churches which are self-governing, self-supporting and self-propagating. In this way, the Christian Church can become China's Christian Church."

It is in the summary for 20 May that Zhou refers to the Manifesto. It had been discussed in great detail on previous days, and the fifth revision was now brought to the Premier. The original intention had been to issue a statement concerning the difficulties facing the Church, but in the light of the issues raised by Zhou this was withdrawn in favour of a document dealing directly with the question of the Church's political standpoint. As Wickeri has written:

> . . . the conversations with Zhou Enlai forced the issue and brought together the various impasses which the churches had to overcome. Some of those who attended the meetings probably believed that they had to do something in order to placate the Communist authorities and save the Church. Others saw more clearly how the churches had become isolated from the society around them, and they now wanted to identify with the New Democracy. Still others had an analysis of the situation which, from a political standpoint, was substantially the same as Zhou Enlai's.[22]

Zhou states that "The language of the Manifesto is not the same as our language, and we see no need why it should be". In an address in January 1951 Zhou commented on the process:

> . . . Of course, if I had drafted the Manifesto and brought it out for them to sign, they would have agreed to it. But what use would there have been in that, for everyone would have said that so-and-so had drafted the statement for them? It is better for them to speak about reform on their own. As long as they are close to our national policy and correct in their general orientation, there is no need to interfere.[23]

The Manifesto must be seen then as a response to the clear demand by the CCP for the Church to break with its past and identify with the new. While Zhou speaks as one who expects to be obeyed, his tone, while somewhat patronizing, is friendly and conciliatory. Those present must have felt that the Manifesto represented a genuine way forward for the Church.

In its first draft the Manifesto had been strongly criticized by church leaders in Shanghai, and the fifth draft took their criticisms into account. It was published in July 1950 with a covering letter signed by forty leading Christians, and its publication can be reckoned as the unofficial beginning of the

Three Self Patriotic Movement (TSPM). The text of the preface stated that:

> It is our purpose in publishing the following statement to heighten our vigilance against imperialism, to make known the clear political stand of Christians in New China, to hasten the building of a Chinese Church whose affairs are managed by the Chinese themselves, and to indicate the responsibilities that should be taken up by Christians throughout the whole country in national reconstruction in New China.[24]

The main text indicates that the general task is to support the Common Programme, and the fundamental aims include purging imperialist influence, supporting agrarian reform, cultivating a patriotic spirit and promoting the Three Selfs. The methods to be adopted include pursuing the search for church unity and reforming church organization.

The Manifesto had attracted 1,500 signatures by the end of August. In October the Fourteenth Biennial Meeting of the NCC endorsed it, marking a decisive turning point in so far as such an endorsement encouraged local Christians to sign. Within two months 180,000 people did so, and within two years almost half the Protestants in China had signed, a total of 417,389 people. At first the bishops of the Anglican Church (by now all Chinese) refused to sign, and issued their own pastoral letter in which they avoided any suggestion that the Church was identified with imperialism, but later they deemed it expedient to support the Manifesto. There can be no doubt that the Manifesto faced many Christians with a crisis of conscience, but it also confronted many with questions about the Church and politics which they had sought to avoid in the past. The widespread assumption by many Christians that they need have no direct involvement with politics was being challenged, and they were being asked to investigate themselves to see how they might indeed have taken a political stance without realizing it. The identification of Christians with political liberalism in the past was clear. The failure of Christian social reform programmes to offer viable methods for tackling China's immense social and economic problems had to be recognized. Indeed, it was precisely because many did acknowledge this failure that they found themselves unable to answer the Communist challenge. As David and Alison Paton wrote perceptively from Fuzhou in May 1949:

> There is already some apostasy, and there will be more: Christianity has so often been recommended to the educated as the best way to save and reconstruct China that many younger Christians are unprepared with answers to the argument: "You Christians have had two thousand years to improve the world, and have not done much. Now it's time to try our method."[25]

The End of the Missionary Era

Initial Optimism

As Chinese Christians sought to discover ways of responding to the new situation the missionary community was anxiously awaiting a clear declaration of intent towards the missionary presence by the CCP. Most missionaries doubted all aspects of Communist policy in any case but, whilst most Protestant missionaries were in principle prepared to co-operate if allowed to do so, Catholic missionaries were hostile from the start.

Just before and in the course of Liberation there was uncertainty as to the future role of foreign missionaries in China. The Patons wrote in their May letter:

> So it seems to most of us that that period of the change-over will not be very dangerous, that for some time at least thereafter we can go on with our work, and that most of our colleagues hope we shall stay . . . The further outlook is quite uncertain. We may be able to stay indefinitely. Perhaps in the end only doctors, nurses, agricultural

experts and others whose skills are considered "productive" or "useful" will be able to stay. Perhaps we will all be kicked out. Our own guess, for what it is worth, is that we shall be able to stay for a while, and may then be forced out; and that it will have been well worthwhile staying.

Most missionaries and mission boards believed that their work would be able to continue, although some withdrew. In late 1948, for example, the American Lutheran Church withdrew all its missionaries. Most, however, made preparations for handing over work to Chinese, for they perceived that whatever links might be maintained they would have to be within an entirely new famework. This cautious optimism seemed to receive confirmation from a "Message from Chinese Christians to Mission Boards Abroad" issued by an informal group of prominent Chinese Christians, most of whom were later active in the Three Self Movement. The "Message" points out the links of Christianity to imperialism but exonerates the missionaries from direct involvement. It suggests that "the authority of policy determination and financial administration must pass over to Chinese leadership" and the objective of self-support be achieved. However, within this context missionaries can still serve provided they can adjust to the changed circumstances.[26]

Severing the Links

CCP policy with regard to the missionaries was, as it turned out, rather different. It was first put forward by Premier Zhou Enlai at the conversations in May 1950, and several of those present on that occasion had signed the "Message". According to the published Summary Zhou, in the context of more general remarks about the need to sever links with imperialism, had stated on 6 May 1950:

We will no longer invite foreign missionaries to China, because, consciously or not, they may easily become tools of imperialism, and it is difficult for we Chinese to determine if this is the case. It will not hurt Christianity if there are no foreign missionaries. Those who are already in China do not have to leave immediately, unless they voluntarily request to do so, or if there is proof that they have been involved in reactionary activity. In other cases, foreign missionaries can wait until their term of service expires.[27]

He also indicated that "In so far as Christianity wants to sever its links with imperialism and become a self-reliant Church, there should no longer be fund raising overseas. Chinese should prepare to run their own Church." With regard to Christian educational organizations, contributions from overseas could be accepted provided there were no strings or conditions attached.

The missionary era was clearly over, but there seemed no reason to think that the transition could not be carried through with comparative smoothness. There had been instances of brutality against missionaries by local Communists and some deaths, especially amongst Catholics, but these might be deemed as exceptional. Yet within two months of the meetings with Zhou the missionary community was on the defensive, with increasing numbers of arrests and denunciations. On 29 December the state Council under the Chairmanship of Zhou Enlai issued a promulgation, "Regulations Governing All Organizations Subsidized With Foreign Funds". Its tone was notably different from Zhou's earlier comments. What if anything had happened to change the mood of the government?

The Korean War

On 25 June 1950 North Korean troops moved across the 38th parallel. By September the North Koreans were being driven back by a United Nations force (mostly American) under General MacArthur, who were advancing rapidly towards the Chinese frontier. The Chinese were caught unprepared and had even started to demobilize part of their army, but fearful that America might use the chance to attack China, on 16 October 1950 the first Chinese units crossed the Yalu River. The war was to influence every facet of Chinese life and above all it created a patriotic fervour within the country that gave the CCP a chance to push ahead with socialist transformation at a far greater speed than had been originally envisaged.

The December Regulations were, in fact, an instant response to President Truman's freezing of all Chinese assets on 16 December. The immediate result of this action was to plunge many foreign-run or aided institutions into crisis, and the Chinese response is understandable. The 29 December regulations were followed in April 1951 by an even more stringent set of regulations, published in July of that year. Vice-Premier Guo Moruo had spoken in December of the need for religious institutions to be self-supporting, and the April regulations dealing with American-funded organizations were designed to speed up this process. The regulations stated:

> Chinese Christian churches and other organizations should immediately sever all relations with American Mission Boards . . . Such Mission Boards shall immediately cease all activities in China.
>
> Americans who are now working in Chinese Christian churches and other organizations shall be treated according to the following rules:
>
> (1) Those who by word or deed work against the People's Government shall be dismissed from their work, and given appropriate punishment . . .
>
> (2) Those desiring to leave the country may do so.
>
> (3) Those who are not reactionary and whom the church or other organization wishes to employ and support may continue their work, but not hold any administrative position.[28]

The draft regulations were presented to a meeting of 151 Protestant leaders at a conference in Beijing, called by Zhou Enlai, which met from 16-21 April. This conference was the next stage in the foundation of the Three Self Patriotic Movement. Its whole tone was dominated by the atmosphere of strident nationalism fostered by the Korean conflict. At the conference the Chairman of the State Council's Committee on Culture and Education, Lu Dingyi, denounced the utilization of Christianity by American imperialism and singled out the American Presbyterian missionary and rural reformer Dr Frank Price, for attack:

> The American imperialist, Frank Price, wearing the cloak of a missionary, was most intimately related to Nationalist counter-revolutionary rebels; he at one time acted as adviser to rebel Chiang, writing for Chiang the anti-communist, anti-people's "Education Plan".

It is worth remembering that as a young man Price had taken a "progressive" stance in comparison with the majority of missionaries and he had translated Sun Yat-sen's "Three Principles of the People". His close links with Chiang Kai-shek are an illustration of how he and others like him failed to adapt to the changing political realities in later years.

Criticizing the Past

The signal had been given for the Denunciation Movement which was formally launched at the meeting in Beijing on 19 April. Although specifically directed at the churches, and concentrating initially on links with imperialism, the movement was a part of a general campaign of criticism aimed at ideological remoulding. It was conducted in an atmosphere of mistrust and fear as the Party implemented the land reform law of June 1950 and the law of 21 February 1951 on the suppression of counter-revolutionaries. Arrests and executions were widespread, and much of the initial support for the CCP's policies amongst non-Party intellectuals and the bourgeoisie was replaced by fear. The tense atmosphere was to continue until the end of the Korean War in July 1953, with the Three-Anti Campaign of August 1951, directed against officials (cadres) and corruption, waste and bureaucracy; the Five-Anti Campaign of January 1952, directed against the private business sector; and the purge of the head of the State

Planning Commission Gao Gang in 1953. The change in emphasis, from consultation and toleration, to suppression and denunciation, can in part be explained as the reaction to the perceived American threat to China. It looked to the Party as if the "war of intervention" had been launched, and it must be remembered that Chiang Kai-shek posed a continuing threat both from the island of Taiwan and from the presence of nationalist armies in parts of China. The CCP was, moreover, inexperienced in urban affairs, and faced formidable tasks of government and rehabilitation.

The April Conference witnessed a series of denunciations by leading Chinese Protestants of former missionary friends and colleagues, but also of fellow Chinese Christians. The principal objective was to speed up the break with foreign churches, and this meant that certain symbolic targets were singled out for attack and, as far as the Protestant missionaries were concerned, very few who were named actually suffered punishment or imprisonment. Frank Price, the main target of attack at the meeting in April 1951, was never arrested, and after a two-year wait for an exit permit was able to leave China in the autumn of 1952.

Life in general became very difficult for the remaining missionaries and many were subjected to criticism. Ethel Izzard, an Anglican medical missionary in Fuzhou, has written of her denunciation as an imperialist at the hospital were she was matron. What hurt her most was the fact that the accusations were made by the nurses whom she had selected and taught. After this she faced the task of obtaining an exit visa, which meant having to write her life history in triplicate, advertising her departure in the local press for three weeks and then facing an arduous journey overland to Hong Kong.[29] Her story could be repeated many times: clearly it was a time of hurt for all who were involved, but, provided they did not infringe regulations and followed procedures, most were able to leave without serious mistreatment.

There were those who for various reasons suffered more severely, often as a result of the general ambiguities in the situation or through misunderstanding or mis-information.

Again in Fuzhou, the American Methodist Bishop, Gene Carleton Lacy, was placed under house arrest for a year from December 1950, for breaking the regulations that one must seek permission to travel outside the city, when he visited churches in the province. He died while under arrest and was buried by his cook, who alone attended his funeral. The treatment of Catholic missionaries was in general harsher. The Vatican was strongly anti-Communist and all priests in China, foreign or Chinese, were linked directly to Rome. Many foreign priests were expelled, in contrast to the Protestants who were "frozen" out. Deportation usually followed on arrest and periods of imprisonment, and there were a number of deaths soon after expulsion as a result of ill-treatment and lack of proper food. One of the most notorious cases was that of Bishop Ford of Maryknoll, who was placed under house arrest in December 1950 and then ordered to be deported. He was maltreated at each stop along the way, and eventually died in prison in Guangzhou on 21 February 1952.

In retrospect there does not seem much doubt that, whether consciously or not, many Catholic missionaries became the focus of opposition to the government. The process of land reform in the countryside inevitably involved many of them, for the church was stripped of its rural holdings, including mission chapels and stations. The movement to create a national Catholic Church was, understandably, totally unacceptable to missionaries, and many advised Chinese Catholics to resist. Monsignor Gaetan Pollio, Italian Archbishop of the archdiocese of Kaifeng, Henan, who was placed under house arrest, imprisoned and then deported in October 1951, was charged with resisting the movement for church reform, including threatening the excommunication of those who joined the national Church. He was also accused of being an American spy and of collaborating with Chiang Kai-shek. While denying the last charges he subsequently admitted to the former.[30]

It is clear that the main purpose of the campaign was to ensure the ending of all foreign connections. It was a task that was far easier for Protestants than for Catholics and it could, therefore, be a more perfunctory process. The aim was to change the thinking of Chinese Christians themselves, a process that Protestants did little to obstruct deliberately, in contrast to the Catholics. The confession of the Anglican Bishop of Fuzhou, Michael Zhang, published in *Tian Feng* in 1951, demonstrates this clearly. 1950 was the hundredth anniversary of the diocese and Bishop Zhang had publicly praised the missionaries in a pastoral letter. He now felt compelled to acknowledge his mistake and he singled out three representative missionaries for criticism, John R. Wolfe for the period 1850-1900; W.P.W. Williams for 1901-44, and David Paton for 1945-50. Michael Zhang was, and remained, a close personal friend of David Paton. It was, perhaps, for this very reason that it was Paton who was singled out – for Bishop Zhang knew who would best understand. It is fitting that we close our account of the missionary era with David Paton's own words:

> The right word to describe what has happened to Christian missions in China is 'débâcle". The practical reasons for the ending of the missionary era in China are of course external to the Church and the Mission; they are political. But in the months between the realization that we should be leaving much earlier than we thought and our actual departure, months in which we had un-accustomed leisure and every opportunity for thoughtful self-examination, it became evident to some of us, and to many more of our Chinese friends, that our mandate had been withdrawn; that the time for missions as we had known them had passed; that the end of the missionary era was the will of God.[31]

By early 1953 almost all foreign missionaries had left China. Amongst Protestants, a handful remained, mainly those who had opted for Chinese citizenship. More Catholics stayed longer, with 750 still there in 1953, under 250 a year later, and under 90 by early 1955. In 1956 there were sixteen priests and eleven sisters (thirteen of the priests were in prison). Needless to say, all medical and educational work was taken over by the new government. Chinese Christians were on their own.

International Contacts

International ecumenical relations became almost impossible in the climate of mutual suspicion that now developed. The Korean War exacerbated this hostility, and the "Statement on the Korean Situation and World Order" of the World Council of Churches Central Committee in July 1950 finally estranged the Chinese churches from the WCC. The Statement unequivocally condemned the North Koreans as aggressors, and went on to call for the overcoming of the evils of "totalitarian infiltration". The resignation of T.C. Chao as one of the Presidents of the WCC, and the withdrawal from active membership of three Chinese member churches was the inevitable result. The Statement has never been withdrawn, despite the immense changes that have taken place in the thinking of the WCC since the Uppsala Assembly of 1968. In 1951 it was left to one of the few non-Western Central Committee members, Bishop Bereczky of Hungary, to sound a lone voice of dissent:

> There is little hope that the voice from the other side can be heard and understood . . . We take it for granted that there was pressure on T.C. Chao. He *is* under pressure, but not the pressure you think. Why did Dr Chao make this decision? The source of the decision does not come from Dr Chao or from Chinese Christians. It comes from the fact that the churches of the West and the WCC in the West have not understood the world situation accurately. We have to decide whether it was a mistake to elect Dr Chao as President, or whether we do not understand what is happening in China.

On the Chinese side, ecumenical relations came to be expressed mainly in terms of the World Peace Council and this too may be seen as a result of the Cold War. The first foreign church group to visit was a delegation of six Quakers from Britain, invited by the China Peace Committee. In fact they were able to meet with many Christian leaders, several of whom were active in the Peace Committee. During 1956 there were a number of ecumenical visitors to China, including Bishop and Mrs Hall from Hong Kong and a delegation of Australian Anglicans led by Archbishop Howard Mowll. The "Red Dean", Hewlett Johnson, was a frequent visitor, although his position was exceptional. The formation of an International Affairs Committee by the TSPM was an important development, and the newly-consecrated Bishop of Zhejiang, K.H. Ting and his wife, Kuo Siu-may (Guo Xiumei), attended the Lambeth Preparatory Conference in 1956 as well as the WCC Central Committee. Under the circumstances it was most unfortunate that the Archbishop of Canterbury, Geoffrey Fisher, showed no interest in their visit, although Bishop George Bell and Bishop Leslie Hunter endeavoured to make them welcome. It was Ting who, in 1957, told an Indian visitor,

> We do not automatically support everything the Communists do. They have done certain things that I regard as extreme and haphazard. Some of these things I later understood to have been quite reasonable, but there are others of whose necessity I remain unconvinced even today.[32]

The next year was to see the virtual demise of all such exchanges until the 1980s, and Bishop Ting was unable to attend the 1958 Lambeth Conference itself. The reason for this sudden change will become apparent in the next chapter.

The Three Self Patriotic Movement

The Fourteenth Biennial Meeting of the NCC, which met 18-25 October 1950, was an entirely Chinese affair. It was a difficult meeting, and the eventual acceptance of the Manifesto masked the conflict that helped to ensure that the NCC would be bypassed in future. Chester Miao (Miao Qiusheng) later confessed that he had worked with a committee of delegates to prevent the Manifesto being presented to the Conference, on the grounds that religion and politics did not mix. After the meeting the initiative passed to the Manifesto group. The need to demonstrate political loyalty was apparent to increasing numbers of Christians as time passed, and the April 1951 Beijing meeting was a decisive turning point. The Denunciation Movement that started at the meeting was, as we have already seen, designed to break the connections of the Church with the missionary past. As well as denunciations of symbolic missionaries, the movement also involved the denunciation of a number of Chinese Church leaders. Thus at the April meeting, Bishop Z.T. Kuang (Jiang Changchuan) denounced his fellow Methodist Bishop Chen Wenyuan, and Bishop Robin Chen Jianzhen denounced his fellow Anglican Bishop Y.Y. Tsu (Zhou Youyu), who had in fact already left the country.

The denunciations continued for about fifteen months. There were meetings to criticize the NCC, the YMCA and the YWCA, the Christian Literature Society and also individual denominations. Y.T. Wu stated that there had been 169 "rather large scale" denunciation meetings by mid-1952, and by September 1953 the total was 227 in 113 cities.[33] The style of the meetings was very similar, based on recommendations in Liu Liangmo's article in *Tian Feng* "How to Hold a Denunciation Meeting" published 19 May 1951. The pattern was a general denunciation, a list of particular "crimes" and a call for due punishment. The "crimes" were usually minor, and were generally either absurd or wildly exaggerated. There is some evidence to suggest that the published record did not always reflect what was actually said.[34] The aim of the Movement was not in fact to punish people but to get them to reform their thinking – it was an intensification of the thought-reform process. However, as has happened so often in China since 1949, what is supposed to be a voluntary process has turned into a coercive one. The Movement was conducted in the midst of a whole series of political campaigns in which the "ultra-leftist" tendency within Chinese Communism came to the surface.

The treatment of some individuals was inexcusable. The

imprisonment of men such as the Methodist Bishop Chen Wenyan and the Anglican Bishop of Zhejiang, Kimber Den, the dismissal of T.C. Chao as Dean of the Yanjing School of Religion and from Anglican orders, the disappearance of the evangelist Gu Ren'en; all were examples of serious abuses. An Anglican priest from England, the Rev. Francis James, had an interview with He Zhenxiang, Director of the State Council's Religious Affairs Bureau, during which the Director admitted that Bishop Kimber Den's imprisonment had been an injustice. At the same time the process enabled others to "speak bitterness", to express their resentment of missionary power and control. The extent of this resentment was not fully understood by many missionaries, most of whom maintained good working relations with their Chinese colleagues but rarely had a real friendship with any of them. Wickeri points out that:

> Even the excesses of the times are understandable, for they have been present in the formative stages of most religious and political movements. Severing the linkages with the past is aptly summarized by the Chinese expression, "breaking the cauldron and sinking the boat", that is, cutting off all possible means of retreat . . . in the light of their history, it was the Christians who had a special responsibility to "draw a line" between themselves and imperialism.[35]

The Establishment of the Three Self Patriotic Movement

At the end of the April Conference in 1951 a twenty-five person Preparatory Committee of the Chinese Christian Resist-America-Aid-Korea Three Self Reform Movement was set up. Y.T. Wu was Chairman and there were a number of Divisions. The Propaganda Division was headed by Liu Liangmo, the Liaison Division by Zheng Jianye, and the General Affairs Division by Y.C. Tu. The Committee was gradually to draw in more and more prominent Church leaders as it spread through the country by means of local visitations and the establishment of local Three Self Committees. The Manifesto campaign, the denunciation meetings, both involved local Christians, and despite the excesses it would seem that in many places it was possible to recruit the support of many ordinary Christians. Church life, especially in rural areas, was by no means normal, and the presence of a Three Self committee must have served to protect the local church from persecution. The visitation team that went to Fujian and Zhejiang in the Spring of 1953 involved several outstanding Christian leaders, including Y.T. Wu and H.H. Ts'ui. Their task was to further church reform, but also to report on any problems facing Christians.

An important instrument used by the Preparatory Committee was the extended study class. One such class began in Shanghai on 20 August 1953 and finished on 16 November. Ninety-nine men and women church workers took part, and the class concentrated on the criticism of imperialism and the meaning of Three Self. Each person had to write a personal and autobiographical review essay which was then discussed in small groups. Shen Yifan, son of Anglican Bishop T.K. Shen (Shen Zigao), and later senior pastor of the Community Church in Shanghai, had his concluding essay published in *Tian Feng*. His description of the change in his thinking is fairly typical of the process that went on in many people's minds:

> Until this study I thought that participation in the Three Self Movement was just the price we Christians had to pay for tolerance by the Communist government, so I was only a passive participant. Now I realize that it is necessary to purify the Church in this way, in order to oppose imperialism and implement our patriotism. Only the Three Self Movement will close the gap between the people and the Church, only the Three Self Movement can break the shackles that have bound the Christian Church in China and thus allow the Church to make known its pure truth and inner vitality. From now on I will actively and positively participate in this movement, and work for a real Chinese Church.[36]

The fostering of the Three Self Patriotic Movement in the political atmosphere of the time was not always conducted with tact and sensitivity. At the first National Christian Conference, held in Beijing from 22 July to 6 August 1954, Y.T. Wu admitted:

> There have been varying degrees of "sectarianism" within the Three Self Movement and we have often looked on fellow Christians who do not take part in the movement as backward. We have not entered deeply enough into others' situations or understood their problems in order to seek those common points on which we could co-operate.[37]

Church Reform and Mutual Respect

It is often assumed that the original founders of the Three Self Patriotic Movement were in fact all theological liberals. While this may be the case with the core group who took the first initiative, many of the leaders of evangelical churches became involved at an early stage. The most notable evangelical participant was Marcus Cheng (Chen Chonggui), who had been an itinerant evangelist and had worked closely with the China Inland Mission and had founded his own conservative seminary in Chongqing. The 1954 Conference seemed to mark a new stage in the drawing together of Christians within the TSPM. It was widely representative of mainline Christian opinion and it led to the appointment of a 139-strong committee of the TSPM. The possibility that "unity" might involve church merger was rejected in the Constitution: "Its purpose shall be to unite the Christians of China and stimulate churches to achieve the Three Self goals and to work for world peace. It will respect the creeds, organizations and rituals of the various churches, and encourage each church in the same spirit of mutual self-respect."[38] There was, therefore, no question of interference in the internal affairs of the separate denominations. The Three Self was to be a political mass movement of

Christians within the United Front, not a new church.

The original title of the Three Self Patriotic Movement contained the word "Reform". It was dropped at the National Christian Conference, out of respect for those Christians who had always suspected that one objective of the Movement was the reform of church doctrine. The Conference issued a "Letter to Christians Throughout China" in which the principle of "mutual respect" was spelt out:

> The goal of self-propagation is not the unification or modification of belief, but the thoroughgoing eradication of vestiges of imperialist thought, and the bringing into harmony with the true Gospel of Jesus Christ. We should have mutual respect for the differences that exist among the churches in creed, organization and ritual.[39]

The inclusion of "patriotic" in the title was unique to the Christians. Neither the Muslims nor the Buddhists included the word in the names of their Associations, which were established at around the same time. Nothing demonstrates more eloquently the marginal nature of Christianity within Chinese society up to then.

The role of the TSPM was to act as an intermediary between the Party and the churches: reacting to the demands of government while seeking to defend the Church from attack. That it sometimes found itself pushed into extremist positions or unable to correct abuses by local officials in some parts of the country, should not blind us to its positive function in moving the mass of church people away from attitudes that could only have condemned them to a negative existence and continual confrontation. For all its exaggeration and unfairness, the Communist charge that Chinese Christianity was linked to imperialism was historically justified. The painful and hazardous road towards discovering a self-hood for the Chinese Church could only begin by the acceptance of a role within the United Front.

Protestant Church Life

The Church as it emerged from the turmoils of the Korean War period was certainly changed. It had been a difficult period in which Christians were seeking to adjust to the new social and political realities. The majority had adjusted and had come to accept the new situation.

The next two years were to see an increasing amount of freedom for the church. The CCP must have felt that the break with the past had been sufficient. The task now was to balance *aiguo* with *aijiao* (love of country with love of church). The Second Enlarged Plenum of the Three Self Patriotic Movement was held in March 1956, with 49 delegates representing all churches and denominational groupings in China. Y.T. Wu's report claimed considerable progress in church life. In Zhejiang alone in three years membership of the Church of Christ in China grew by 2,587; Anglicans by 1,473; Baptists by 1,312, and the China Jesus Independent Church by 2,968. Nationally the Anglicans consecrated three new bishops in June 1955, and in August that year the Seventh Day Adventist Church held a nationwide conference. In 1955 a total of 275,000 Christian publications had been printed. Wu then listed ten tasks facing the churches: enlarging unity; reorganization of the structures of each denomination; solving the continuing problem of self-support in some places (this including the establishment of a Committee for Promoting Self-Support); preaching the Gospel; publishing work; original research; training of church workers; participation in socialist construction; promotion of international peace; conduct of patriotic study. It is clear from the whole tenor of the meeting that the Christian leadership anticipated a period of consolidation and gradual growth.[40]

Local Church Life

Information about the life of the local church during this period is rather limited. Most of the reports in *Tian Feng* concern the organization of Three Self committees, the reform of

234

structures and the holding of meetings. It is obvious from these reports that the transformation of church life was carried through in all parts of the country, but the actual day-to-day life of Christians is not so apparent. Life in the cities continued without too much disruption to the normal pattern of church activity, but in the countryside land reform led to the closure of many churches for some considerable period, sometimes permanently. Inevitably, there were many villages where the Church was a source of tension, or where it had close links with the landlord. On the other hand, according to one observer, in some areas Christians became leaders in villages because of their experience in leadership, their literacy and the trust put in them by the villagers.[41]

George Hood has a brief but useful discussion of the situation of the church in the Lingdong Synod in Guangdong.[42] A particular problem here, due to its many overseas links, was the departure of a large number of wealthy laymen and office-bearers, as well as a smaller number of pastors and church workers, for Hong Kong and elsewhere. During land reform churches closed for at least three months. Hood continues:

> When it was over, the main financial supporters of many congregations, often the comparatively rich doctors who had become landowners, had neither the will nor the means to carry their former responsibilities. In some places the church buildings were taken over permanently for public purposes . . .

Yet further difficulties in Lingdong resulted from time spent in study classes, for there was already a permanent shortage of manpower. The Presbytery ceased to function in 1951, and with it the means of support for rural churches through the central Preaching Fund. The new taxation policy meant that while churches and accommodation for church workers were exempt, other church-owned buildings were not, with the result that most were rented out and the rent used to help pay pastors and preachers.

It can be assumed that similar problems confronted many other local churches, although it may be that in areas where the Church had not relied on wealthy patrons the new situation actually brought an increase in income. One report from Shaanxi in February 1954 spoke of a new church building in a village that had never had a church, due to the increase in peasant income as a result of land reform.[43] Similar reports during the same year were received from Shunan, Anhui, Baoma in Shaanxi and Guotan in Henan.[44] Another report concerned the village of Shunhuazhen near Nanjing, the site of F.W. Price's rural reform work in the 1930s. Church activity was suspended in the summer of 1951 owing to land reform, and it was only able to get going again on 27 August 1953.[45]

An investigation in Anhui province in late 1956, by Y.T. Wu and Cora Deng in their capacity as TSPM leaders and members of the National People's Congress, published in *Tian Feng* in January 1957, revealed more than 500 churches covering sixty of the seventy-two counties, with over 400 church workers and a total membership of 40,000. In Huoqiu County all twenty-eight CIM Churches had re-opened after Land Reform, and membership had grown from 2,000 in 1949 to almost 4,000. On the other hand, in Puyang County of fifty-two country churches only seventeen had re-opened. These differences reflected the varying attitudes of local cadres, and in general the problems were always worse in the countryside, where there were no cadres specializing in religious work.[46]

Another report by central leaders came from the region of the city of Wenzhou on the coast of Zhejiang, where there were 1,050 churches with 70,000 members and 200 church workers. Christian life was thriving, except in the military zone of Wenling County, although there were problems with untrained voluntary workers, some of whom were said to be susceptible to superstitious extravagances such as "spiritual dances", clairvoyance and "spiritual firecrackers". The main problem in the area, however, concerned property, with difficulties in demarcating between school property to be taken over by the government and church property, and with local officials "borrowing" church buildings.[47]

One brief but interesting report in *Tian Feng* came from a Miao tribe Christian studying at the seminary in Chongqing.

He reported thirty organized churches amongst the Miao people, with the central church in Qiupushan, Wuding County. The churches closed during land reform but most had now re-opened, and since 1954 had received over 300 new members.[48]

It is apparent from these various reports that church life was able to be restored to a degree of normalcy in the mid-1950s. Christians were also adapting to the changed circumstances, and the growth in home meetings was a harbinger of things to come. Meetings in homes had long been an important aspect of church life. In many rural communities it was the norm, as they were too poor to build churches. The closure of churches during land reform meant that many rural Christians gathered in their homes for weekly worship. There were also home meetings held by religious leaders who did not want to co-operate with the TSPM. A report in *Tian Feng* in August 1953 quoted the Chairman of the Shanghai Religious Affairs Bureau as expressing disquiet at the rapid increase in home meetings: "We don't object to meetings in the home in general, but such meetings should be supplementary to the church programme. Are these meetings held in secret so that people can say what they please? It is a significant fact, that these home meetings are held precisely by the religious leaders who refuse to enrol in study groups."[49] It appears therefore that there were three sorts of home meetings: traditional meetings held either because no church building existed or as a supplement to the Sunday worship; new meetings held after the closure of church buildings, some of which would cease after re-opening; meetings established as a result of refusal to join the TSPM.

Evangelism, in the sense of meetings in the streets and other public places, was not tolerated by the authorities, as was made clear by He Zhenxiang in his talk with Francis James. He also stressed, however, that Christians had many other ways to meet, including meetings in private homes. It would seem then that home meetings were considered legitimate at this stage, despite the obvious disquiet of some officials. The prohibition on open-air evangelism was justified on the grounds that it might cause offence, especially since Christianity was still regarded by many as a foreign religion.[50]

Theological Education

Forty-four different theological seminaries had existed up to 1949, but their continuation became questionable as the flow of foreign funds stopped. Moreover, the denominational basis of ministerial training seemed inappropriate to many church leaders. The result was a complete reorganization along regional lines. A major conference on seminary reoganization was held in Shanghai 25-29 August 1952, with representatives of about fifteen seminaries. All reported problems of funding, lack of students, inadequate teaching materials, lack of professors and no future for graduates. It was agreed to establish a united seminary in Nanjing, covering East China. The general principles stressed its biblical basis, mutual respect for different theological points of view as well as each church's tradition, order, organization and ritual. They also emphasized support for the Common Programme and the Three Self Movement. The new seminary opened on 1 November 1952 with 105 students, and represented a union of eleven seminaries. Teaching was in two parallel streams, with one offering a conservative and the other a more liberal approach, although worship was united.[51] The seminary also produced a statement of faith, of considerable interest as it is the only such statement known from this period. It reads:

1.   All scripture is inspired by God (*shen*). It includes everything necessary for salvation and [is] the basis of the Christian's faith and the standard of conduct.

2.   The one God (*shangdi*) is the creator of all things and the Father of humankind, full of justice and love.

3.   Jesus Christ is the Son of God who became flesh and was crucified in order to save humanity, who rose from the dead to become head of the Church and saviour of the whole world.

4.   The Holy Spirit is the third person of the Trinity, the

source of regeneration and sanctification, and in the Church, gives believers every kind of grace.[52]

The statement is not a creed as such, rather a minimal basis for faith around which differences can be respected. All students were expected to subscribe to it upon entry. The statement hardly lends credence to those who argued that the Three Self Movement rejected the historic doctrines of the faith. The deliberate use of the two terms for God was designed to avoid offence to any group.

The Yanjing Union Theological Seminary was established in Beijing in 1953 as a union of a further eleven seminaries, offering three parallel courses to a student body of twenty-one, which grew to seventy-six in 1956. A similar union seminary was established in Guangzhou on the site of the Dongshan Baptist College. In October 1956 three Bible schools in Shanghai merged to form the Spiritual and Theological Institute with sixty-five students.[53] It would seem that the policy of rationalization was to continue, but with considerable care being taken to respect the various traditions within the churches. Unfortunately, the next year was to see an abrupt end to the process.

Publication and distribution of the Bible had continued throughout this period. From June 1949 to the end of 1955 the China Bible House had sold 171,278 Bibles, 170,493 New Testaments and 3,199,282 Bible portions. Subsidiary Bible Houses existed in Shenyang, Kunming, Wuhan, Beijing, Chongqing and Guangzhou, with agencies in six other provincial capitals. There were plans afoot for a revised edition using the recently introduced simplifications of some of the commonest Chinese characters, but there was still deep disagreement over the term for "God", (*shen* or *shangdi*).[54]

Protestant Resistance

Some of the conflicts of the period of the political campaigns of 1951-53 had not been resolved in time for the 1954 National Conference. There were a number of fundamentalist groups and individuals who resisted the search for a *modus vivendi* with the CCP. The story of this conflict is only partially known, but an adequate appraisal depends upon keeping the underlying theological issues distinct from the story of personal suffering. The problem related specifically to some of the indigenous sects whose origins we have already discussed. The history of these groups after 1949 is important, especially as they constituted a significant portion of the Protestant Church.

Not all indigenous groups found themselves in opposition to the new political reality. The Chinese Jesus Independent Church led by Xie Yongqin was able to co-operate with the Three Self Movement, and Xie became one of the TSPM's leaders. Others, however, found it more difficult. Wang Mingdao refused to co-operate altogether. The Little Flock and the True Jesus Church were both sectarian and other-worldly, and their whole ethos militated against co-operation with other Christians and against any compromise with worldy authority. The Jesus Family appears at first sight to be different, for their whole form of organization seemed akin to the Communist rural programmes. Let us look briefly at the fate of these various fundamentalist groups.

The Jesus Family

The Jesus Family of Jing Dianying, centred on Mazhuang in Shandong, was thought by many to be ideally placed to co-exist with the CCP. Indeed, the members of the family were amongst the earliest signatories of the Christian Manifesto. Then in 1952 Jing was arrested after being accused by his nephew. Subsequently Jing was accused of a whole range of offences, detailed in a book published in 1953 by the *Tian Feng* press. In the circumstances of the day it is hard to be sure how much truth there was in the accusations, but Leslie Lyall's reservations noted in the last chapter do suggest that the Jesus Family was not the idyllic community living along the lines of a primitive Christian communism as portrayed, for example, in Dr Vaughan Rees' book, *The Jesus Family in*

Communist China.[55] The "spiritual love-ins" mentioned by Lyall point to some truth behind the accusation of Jing's personal sexual immorality. Jing was sentenced to twenty years in prison for his alleged links with the Guomindang. The family was reorganized at Mazhuang and some other centres into a normal church, and in others it was simply dissolved.

The True Jesus Church

The True Jesus Church was dubiously orthodox, and it was its emphasis on faith healing and the ecstatic nature of its worship which led to the arrest in 1952 of Isaac Wei, the son of Paul Wei, one of the founders of the Church. Wei's "Self-Examination" was published in *Tian Feng* in February 1952.[56] The leadership of the church was brought within the Three Self organization, but the church continued its own life, although from 1954 it was subjected to increasing criticism. It was not until 1958, however, that the church was singled out for attack. Thus in a Hunan report preachers of the church were accused of unlawful activities, including causing the death of sick people through the refusal to allow medical treatment, and causing illness and death through baptism in freezing rivers.[57] While such accusations must be set in the context of the decisive swing to the left in Chinese politics at the time, there could well have been substance behind some of the reports. The extreme manifestations seen in certain indigenous movements in the pre-1949 period were to re-emerge in the 1980s, and there is no reason to think that they did not exist in the intervening years.

The Little Flock

The story of Watchman Nee's arrest in 1952 and the gradual separation of the Little Flock from Nee has been often told.[58] His initial problem was of course his refusal to go along with the United Front policy in the light of his conservative theological understanding. His arrest was, however, part of the Five-Anti Movement against corrupt capitalists, and the charge related to his involvement in 1940 in the establishment of the Sheng Hua Drug Manufacturing Factory. This unfortunate enterprise was a financial disaster. It also resulted in his exclusion from the Assembly in Shanghai until he publicly repented in 1947 and handed the factory over to the Assembly. Following his example other wealthy members "handed over" their factories and private property, leaving the Church with the task of running the various concerns. Nee's difficulties were compounded by his attempt in late 1951 to obstruct land reform in Fuzhou. According to a former close associate in Shanghai, Tang Shoulin, interviewed by Philip Wickeri after 1980, Nee had much property in Fuzhou, and he collected 30,000 signatures on a petition against the confiscation of the lands on the ground that they were used for church purposes. In fact, the people signed twice on two different petitions, and when the government rejected the petition Nee asked Tang Shoulin to give the other list to Y.T. Wu as signatures for the Christian Manifesto.[59]

Nee was sentenced to fifteen years in prison for selling to the state at inflated prices. He was attacked again in 1956, at a time when the general church situation was relatively relaxed, and in a new trial the previous sentence was simply reconfirmed. The reason for the 1956 publicity campaign against him may well have been the need to destroy his authority within the Little Flock. Tang Shoulin maintains that Nee, together with Witness Lee, had organized the Little Flock to oppose the CCP under the slogan "use the gospel to eliminate the revolution". The Little Flock was, certainly, strongly anti-Communist, and the authorities wished to bring it under control. After 1956 it was completely reorganized. Four of Nee's associates in Shanghai were arrested in January 1956 and other arrests followed elsewhere. It was, however, made clear that the Little Flock itself was not a counter revolutionary organization. Nee remained in prison throughout the Cultural Revolution, but in April 1972 was transferred to a labour camp in Anhui. He died there on 1 June 1972.

The charges against Nee were never detailed. Like many others he was sentenced as a "counter-revolutionary" because he was opposed to the government. Yet, there was sufficient in his background to suggest that his opposition was more than passive and that his original arrest in 1952 was "political" rather than "religious". That does not excuse it, but does suggest that we should be cautious of the interpretation that it was a purely religious persecution.

Wang Mingdao

The case of the independent preacher Wang Mingdao bears some superficial resemblance to that of Watchman Nee, but in fact they were very different. Wang is an outstanding example of a devout and orthodox Christian who found himself in conscience unable to accept the demands of the secular authority. As an independent evangelist he could not be accused of direct links with imperialism. Wang was never accused in the Denunciation Movement, and his refusal to join the Three Self Patriotic Movement was not used as an excuse to attack him. This suggests a degree of respect for him amongst the Christian leadership and even amongst government officials. He refused to join in the broadly-based first National Christian Conference in 1954. In September of that year he was criticized for the first time at a TSPM special meeting in Beijing, albeit with little effect, for soon after he preached a sermon, "Betraying the Son of Man with a Kiss". In June 1955 he published a pamphlet, *We, Because of Faith*, in which he discussed in detail his objections to the Three Self. There was never any doubt that his opposition was based on theological criteria and not on political grounds. Wang Mingdao was not open to the "counter-revolutionary" accusation, but his own theology led him to a position that was, objectively speaking, anti-Communist: Christians could have no truck with the world, and social reform was irrelevant in the light of the expected and immediate return of the Lord. However, his attack on the leadership of the Three Self was based on his rejection of Christian "modernism", on the incorrect assumption that all the Three Self leaders were theological liberals. Actually, he considered that evangelicals

243

who were prepared to associate with "modernists" were themselves tainted. As Wang wrote in his pamphlet:

> Some large denominations have both fundamentalists and modernists in their leadership, in which case the leaders have but two choices; either they must "share the same bed but dream different dreams" and put up a mutual bluff, or they must break off all relations and "turn their horses in different directions" . . . I have cried: "Beware of them, oppose yourselves to them, separate yourselves from them, have no fellowship with them."[60]

Wang was arrested on 8 August 1955 and released a year later after making a "confession". On his release he repudiated his confession, was re-arrested and remained in prison until 1979 when he was finally released. He now lives quietly in Shanghai. As far as is known his attitude has not changed, and in a message at the time of his release he is reported to have said, "During my years of imprisonment I may sometimes have been like Peter, but never like Judas".[61] The treatment of Wang Mingdao was unjustified, and there is every reason for thinking of him as having been a prisoner of conscience.

There has been a continual tendency in the West to confuse the issue of "human rights" with the consideration of whether the ideas for which a person was imprisoned represented a satisfactory or adequate viewpoint. A careful consideration of the criticisms of Wang's theology in *Tian Feng* in 1955-56, suggest that the critique was justified. The intemperate language that was used by some contributors has obscured the genuine grounds for criticism.[62] K.H. Ting relates the whole matter to the question of "mutual respect" and finds Wang woefully lacking in Christian charity.[63] It was, indeed, the case that Wang rejected the TSPM, and in this way opened himself to a legitimate theological attack. The intervention of the state was, therefore, quite inappropriate, but, in the context of New China, completely predictable. Wang's personal suffering was, in the end, the price paid by a Christianity that had never attempted to take seriously the context in which it was set.

The Catholic Church and the United Front

The reaction of the Catholic Church to the Communist takeover was to attempt to organize for survival. A primary instrument in this task was the Legion of Mary, established in 1948 by Antonio Riberi, the apostolic nuncio, who arrived in December 1946. With the demise of the Chiang Kai-shek government and the failure of the Vatican to recognize the new government, Riberi's position was irregular after 1 October 1949. The Legion of Mary was organized into about a thousand chapters throughout the country, and during 1950 the Catholic Church continued to flourish despite the persecutions in some places. There was, however, no question of a real accommodation with the new government, and the Catholic Church remained strongly anti-Communist. The origins of the Three Self within the Catholic Church were therefore utterly different from those within Protestantism.

The first move came from Sichuan province in the South-west, in the town of Guangyuan. Five hundred Catholics, reported to have been led by a priest, Father Wang Liangzuo, issued a manifesto on 30 November 1950, calling for a break with imperialism and the establishment of a self-governing, self-supporting and self-propagating Church. Soon afterwards a similar manifesto was published in Chongqing in the same province, signed by fourteen priests, eight religious and 695 laity. It is notable that these moves were made only after the outbreak of the Korean War.

Catholic leaders requested a meeting with Zhou Enlai and this took place on 17 January 1951. Zhou is reported to have acknowledged that "the Vatican is the heart of Catholics",[64] but to have insisted on the creation of a national Church. He distinguished between "ideological" matters and "practical" matters.

The reaction of the Catholic hierarchy came swiftly; in February 1951 the bishops published "The Church in China: Declaration of Principles". The statement was drafted by five bishops and three priests, of whom respectively four and two were foreigners. It was an uncompromising document rejecting the allegation that the Church was allied with imperialism, and arguing that self-government meant the establishment of a native hierarchy; self-support, the refusal of those subsidies with political implications; self-propagation, that the missionaries work in the interests of the local church. As one Catholic writer has remarked:

> The assertions of the document may be true according to Catholic theology *sub specie aeternitatis*. However, the *Principles* seemed oblivious to the political, historical and social currents of the time. It offered no possibilities for dialogue or rapprochement.[65]

The government, not surprisingly, rejected the document. *Guangming Ribao* (the intellectuals' daily newspaper) commented:

> As we all know, the Catholic Church has been established in China for more than three hundred years. During this time, the administrative and financial powers of the Church in China, together with all the policies having to do with the propagation of the faith, always having been held in the hands of foriegn priests who never had the desire to help us establish our own Church.[66]

On 31 March Riberi wrote to all the bishops, attacking a Nanjing declaration in favour of the Three Selfs by the vicar-general of Nanjing, Li Weiguang. He followed this in April with an even stronger letter, drawing attention to the ecclesiastical penalties of seeking to overthrow the authority of the Church. The government reaction came quickly. On 26 June he was placed under house arrest, on 7 September the Shanghai police arrested the Catholic Central Bureau's four departmental heads, and Riberi was expelled on the following day.

The Catholic Resistance

There seems little doubt that the government found itself
unable to persuade the overwhelming majority of Catholics to
co-operate with their demands for the creation of a national
Church. It was also angered by the uncompromising position
taken by Riberi and the hierarchy. The political atmosphere in
China during 1951-53 was, as already described, extremely
tense. A confrontation was almost inevitable. The authorities
seriously misjudged the mood amongst Catholics, and in seeking to compel them to adopt the Three Selfs it lost all chance
of commanding the political loyalty of the Catholic population. The story of Catholic resistance in Shanghai is the best
illustration of this.

The government looked to a Catholic layman, Hu Wenyao,
to lead the patriotic Catholic movement in Shanghai. It was a
quite inappropriate choice and revealed a lack of understanding as to the nature of the Catholic community in the
city. As mentioned in previous chapters, the centre of the
Shanghai community was in the part of the city known as
Xujiahui (Ziccawei). This was the home of Xu Guangqi, the
most famous Ming Catholic convert, and it was the centre of
the Catholicism of the Jiangnan Region. The Catholic community there had been much strengthened during the Taiping
Rebellion by Catholic refugees from the great cities of
Jiangnan along the Yangzi River. Many traced their origins to
the Catholics of the Ming time. Nor was this community
necessarily very fond of foreign priests – the memory of
French Jesuit interference in the last century helped to ensure
that. The Bishop of Shanghai, Gong Pinmei, was himself an
"old" Catholic, and commanded tremendous loyalty. The
authorities, therefore, found themselves confronting a well
organized and united community which could legitimately
claim to be indigenous. Careful and sensitive handling might
have won the loyalty of this community. Hu Wenyao,
however, was a layman and a "new" Catholic, and consequently his authority was derived solely from his political
position. His efforts were counter-productive and his advice

to the Religious Affairs Bureau to deal with Father Beda Zhang, rector of St Ignatius College, was a catalyst to Catholic resistance. Father Zhang was arrested in August 1951 and died in prison on 11 November. The authorities forbade a funeral procession, and he was buried quietly on 13 November. This did not prevent churches throughout the city holding Requiem Masses, and his tomb became a place of pilgrimage.

Bishop Gong maintained that he was anti-imperialistic but that in spiritual matters he must follow the directives of the Church. Catholic students organized themselves within a catechism group movement, and militants within this informal organization dedicated themselves to defend the Church. Bishop Gong responded to government political campaigns by issuing directives on the basis of opinions gleaned from parish discussions. He did not refuse all political co-operation, especially in regard to patriotic activities linked to the Korean War. Gong's activities were basically open and public, and it is significant that during these early years he was not arrested for political offences. His refusal to tolerate the patriotic position, however, provoked confrontations in churches, as police sought to ensure that patriotic Catholics were able to receive the sacrament, forbidden to them by the Bishop. The confrontation continued from 1951 to 1955 when it reached its culmination in the arrest of Bishop Gong on 7 September, together with twenty-one priests, two nuns and three hundred lay Catholics. A further 600-700 laity and fifteen to twenty priests were arrested on 26 September. This was the beginning of the end of organized resistance in Shanghai. In fact, it took the authorities several more years to sort out the situation to their relative satisfaction, and Bishop Gong was not sentenced until 1960. In 1955 the priests of the diocese were ordered to elect a sucessor to Gong, and they chose as a compromise candidate an elderly priest, Zhang Shilang. In March 1956 he was replaced by Zhang Jiashu as vicar capitular.[67]

Organized resistance in the rest of the country was already virtually over. A Beijing Catholic Reform Committee had been established in late 1951 and here resistance was much weaker.

Some priests joined the reform movement and a number of churches were soon under "patriotic" auspices. In the adjacent province of Hebei there was considerable resistance, and the minister of public Security, Luo Ruiqing, spoke in July 1955 of the discovery of almost two hundred Catholic dugouts in the Yongxian and Xianxian districts.[68]

The Origins of the Catholic Patriotic Association

During late 1952 to mid-1953 the government evidently re-thought its policy on the Catholic Church. The movement within the Catholic Church was re-styled the "Anti-imperialist Movement for the love of Country and Church" (*aiguo/aijiao*). Bishop Gong was approached to head the movement. His refusal led to the placing under house arrest of fifty or so priests in Shanghai. Then in August Li Weiguang of Nanjing called a congress and "Ten Articles" were drawn up for priests to sign. The exact content is not known but loyalty to the pope was allowed. Li had, in fact, been excommunicated by Rome in February 1952 but the decree was not published in the hope that he might change his stand. It was made public in March 1955. In October 1954 Pope Pius XII issued his encyclical *Ad Sinarum Gentes* in which he defended the missionary enterprise and rejected the Three Self principles and the Patriotic Catholic position.

The encyclical came at a time when Catholic resistance was weakening. 1955 was the turning point. In Beijing the vicar general took the patriotic line, and according to one source the number of lay people refusing to have contact with the patriotic churches in the city had fallen to thirty per cent. Ten per cent accepted the patriotic line, and the remainder were content to keep quiet and to receive the sacraments. Four churches and three chapels served the city (compared to thirty and thirty-three in 1949).[69] The government now felt itself strong enough to move decisively against those refusing to co-operate with the United Front position, which had been adopted without much difficulty by all other religious groups apart from the Catholics. Bishop Gong's arrest was the signal for a general clamp down. In Zhejiang Bishop Joseph Hu of Taizhou (one of the six bishops consecrated in 1926) was arrested, and in Haimen, Wenzhou, Ningbo and Pingyang in the same province so were several Catholic leaders. Arrests also occurred in Anhui, Sichuan, and in Wuhan, Guangzhou and Fuzhou cities.[70]

Thus by 1955 effective resistance was finished. The witness of Bishop Gong and others who chose imprisonment and even death for the sake of their faith would help to sustain the Catholics of China in the years ahead. At the same time, while perhaps they had no other way forward in the circumstances in which they found themselves, the failure to find a common ground with the CCP in these years, was to find the Catholic Church in the 1980s in a passive and negative position *vis-à-vis* Chinese society. One cannot help wondering what might have happened if both the government and Bishop Gong had adopted a more moderate line.

The next stage was the widening of the patriotic movement which began in earnest in 1956 and reached its culmination in the 1957 First National Congress of the Chinese Catholic Patriotic Association (CCPA). The details of this process are best left for the next chapter. It will be as well, however, to attempt an over-all evaluation of the events leading up to the 1955 clamp down before closing this chapter.

Eric Hanson has suggested that we need to understand these events in the light of the traditional concerns of the Chinese State with regard to religion. The aim of the State has always been to penetrate, regulate and control institutional religions and obliterate heretical sects.[71] From this perspective the religious policy of the early 1950s must be understood as aimed at control rather than suppression. The policy worked reasonably well with Protestants, Buddhists and Muslims, but with the Roman Catholics it met with a group more resistant to penetration and control. The ecclesiology of pre-Vatican II Catholicism did not allow for a real autonomy for the "local" church, and this ensured that traditional Chinese and foreign priests and most Chinese lay Catholics would find the demands of the State unacceptable.

The history of the Catholic mission to China makes it clear that Catholics were socially isolated and, after 1721, had come to define themselves over against the Chinese State. Hanson suggests that State toleration of religion has been based on four factors: the religion offers domestic and international services to the State; it offers some ideology of State support; its linkages within society are not useful for rebellion; it is internally united, making suppression difficult. He points out that in 1949-55 Catholicism fulfilled the last two conditions, but not the first two.

The isolation of the Catholic Church was, therefore, its short-term strength and its long-term weakness. The choice facing the Catholic leadership in 1949 was far more restricted than that facing the other religious groups in society. A more friendly attitude by the Vatican; the absence of the Korean War; these might have made matters different to a limited extent, but essentially the foundations of the conflict were laid over a long historical period. It is for this reason that the confrontation took place in the stronghold of "old" Catholic faith. Imperialism was not the central issue. At issue was the nature of the relationship of Christian Faith to Chinese culture and tradition – the unfinished encounter to which in this book we have constantly returned. The question that faced all Chinese Christians in 1949 was the question of how to combine faithfulness to their Lord with loyalty to their country. It is wrong to narrow this question down to the issue of Christianity versus Communism. What Christians confronted in 1949 was a newly revived Chinese State which could at last free itself of foreign interference and which could therefore pursue certain traditional concerns of Chinese government through to the end. The methods used to exercise control were, at least in some degree, new and refined through the experience of Marxist organizational techniques, but the objective was not so different from that of successive dynasties throughout Chinese history.

REFERENCES

1. Lochman, Jan Milic, *Church in a Marxist Society: A Czechoslovak View*, SMC Press, London 1970, p. 87.
2. Paton, David M., *"R.O.": The Life and Times of Bishop Ronald Hall of Hong Kong*, Diocese of Hong Kong, 1985, p. 47
3. Weir, A.J., Memo. The Church Situation in Manchuria, August 1950; quoted in Fulton, Austin, *Through Earthquake, Wind and Fire: Church and Mission in Manchuria 1867-1950*, The Saint Andrew Press, Edinburgh 1967, pp. 301-2.
4. Breslin, Thomas A., *China, American Catholicism and the Missionary*, The Pennsylvania State University Press, 1980, p. 103.
5. Figures based on Digan, Parig, *China and the Churches in the Making of One World*, Pro Mundi Vita, Brussels 1975, Appendix 4.
6. Bush, Richard C. Jr., *Religion in Communist China*, Abingdon Press, Nashville, Tennessee 1970, pp. 239-40.
7. Paton, David M., *Christian Missions and the Judgement of God*, SCM Press, London 1953, p. 50
8. Price, F.W., "Y.T. Wu (1893-1979): A Christian of Revolutionary China", *China Notes*, Vol. 17, No. 4 and Vol. 18, No. 1 Autumn-Winter 1979-80, p. 85.
9. Mao Zedong, "Report on an Investigation of the Peasant Movement in Hunan", *Selected Works* Volume 1, Foreign Languages Press, Beijing 1965, p. 46.
10. For further details on the United Front see van Slyke, Lyman P., *Enemies and Friends: The United Front in Chinese Communist History*, Stanford University Press, 1967.
11. Wickeri, Philip L., *Seeking the Common Ground*.
12. Mao Zedong, "On the People's Democratic Dictatorship", *Selected Works*, Volume 4, Foreign Languages Press, Beijing 1969, p. 412.
13. Fitzgerald, C.P., *The Birth of Communist China*, Penguin, London 1964.
14. Mao Zedong, "On The Methods of Leadership", ibid., pp. 111-14.
15. Wickeri, op. cit., p. 118.
16. ibid., p. 134.
17. Baker, Hugh D.R., *Chinese Family and Kinship*, Macmillan, London 1979, p. 27.
18. Yu Tingying, "Strengthen Political Thought Education Towards Adolescents", *Red Flag*, No. 9, 1963, quoted in Munro, Donald J., *The Concept of Man in Contemporary China*, University of Michigan Press, Ann Arbor 1977, p. 179.
19. Wickeri, op. cit., p. 247, quoting interview with George Wu Gaozi.
20. Documents TSPM, pp. 6-11.
21. Zhou Enlai, *Selected Writings on the United Front*, People's Publishing House, Beijing 1984, pp. 180-7, translated with commentary by Philip Wickeri in *CSP Journal*, Vol. 2, No.1, April 1987, pp. 4-11.
22. Wickeri, *Seeking the Common Ground*, op. cit., p. 251.
23. Zhou Enlai, Address at a Tea Party hosted by the Central United Front Work Department, 20 January 1951, translated Wickeri, CSP Journal op. cit.
24. The Christian Manifesto, Documents TSPM, op. cit., pp. 19-20.

25. Paton, David and Alison, private letter dated Fuzhou, 7 May 1949.
26. Message from Chinese Christians, Documents TSPM, op. cit., p. 14f.
27. Zhou Enlai, *Selected Writings on the United Front*, op. cit.
28. Documents TSPM, op. cit., p. 27.
29. Izzard, Ethel M., "Some Recollections of Life in China 1933-50", personal paper.
30. Pollio, Gaetan, *Le Calvaire de l'Église dans la Chine Nouvelle*, translated from the Italian by Marie Clemy, Libraire P. Tequi, Paris 1962, quoted in Bush, op. cit., p. 55.
31. Paton, *Christian Missions and the Judgement of God*, op. cit., p. 51.
32. Jones, Francis Price, *The Church in Communist China: A Protestant Appraisal*, Friendship Press, New York 1962.
33. *Tian Feng*, 332, 20 September 1952, pp. 541 and 382-3; 24 September 1952, p. 533.
34. See for example, Hunter, Edward, *The Story of Mary Liu*, Hodder & Stoughton, London 1956.
35. Wickeri, op. cit., p. 272.
36. Quoted in Jones, op. cit., pp. 78-9.
37. Wu Yaozong, *Tian Feng* 425-7, 3 September 1954, p. 435, quoted Wickeri, op. cit., p. 294.
38. Documents TSPM, op. cit., p. 97.
39. *Tian Feng*, 425-7, 3 September 1954, p. 469.
40. "Report on the China Christian Three Self Patriotic Movement, July 1954 to March 1956", Documents, op. cit., pp. 121-33.
41. Bates, Searle M., *Gleanings from the Manuscripts: The Protestant Endeavour in Chinese Society 1890-1950*, National Council of Churches of Christ, U.S.A., 1984, p. 69.
42. Hood, George A., *Mission Accomplished?*, pp. 275-6.
43. *China Bulletin*, National Council of Churches of Christ, U.S.A., Vol. 4, No. 10, 10 May 1954.
44. ibid., Vol. 5, No. 18, 24 October 1955.
45. ibid., Vol. 4, No. 8, 12 April 1954.
46. ibid., Vol. 7, No. 6, 18 March 1957.
47. ibid., Vol. 7, No. 18, 14 October 1957.
48. ibid., Vol. 7, No. 21, 25 November 1957.
49. ibid., Vol. 4, No. 13, 21 June 1954.
50. ibid., Vol. 7, No. 8, 15 April 1957.
51. ibid., Vol. 2, No. 19, 29 December 1952.
52. Wickeri, op. cit., pp. 436-7 for translation.
53. *China Bulletin*, Vol. 6, No. 13, 25 June; No. 20, 5 November; No. 22, 3 December; No. 23, 17 December 1956.
54. ibid., Vol. 7, No. 5, 4 March 1957.
55. Rees, Dr D. Vaughan, *The Jesus Family in Communist China*, The Paternoster Press, London 1959.
56. Documents TSPM, op. cit., pp. 60-5.
57. *Tian Feng*, April 1958, translated in MacInnis, Donald E. *Religious Policy and Practice in Communist China: A Documentary History*, Hodder & Stoughton, London 1972, Document 69.
58. See for example, Lyall, Leslie, *Three of China's Mighty Men*, Overseas Missionary Fellowship, 1973, and Kinnear, Angus I., *Against the Tide: The Story of Watchman Nee*, Victory Press, Eastbourne 1973.

59. Wickeri, op. cit., pp. 320-1.
60. Wang Mingdao, *We, Because of Faith*, translated Documents TSPM, pp. 99-14.
61. Quoted in Choy, Leona, *Floodtide*, Spring/Summer, 1980.
62. See Wickeri's discussion, op. cit., pp. 326-34.
63. Ting, K.H., "A Stern Warning to Wang Mingdao", *Tian Feng*, 477-8, 15 August 1955, p. 608.
64. Bush, op. cit., p. 107.
65. Hanson, Eric O., *Catholic Politics in China and Korea*, Orbis Books, New York 1980, p. 35.
66. *China Missionary Bulletin*, Hong Kong, III (IV) May 1951, p. 388.
67. Details in Bush, op. cit., pp. 122-5 and Hanson, op. cit., p. 73-82.
68. *People's Daily*, 29 July 1955.
69. *China Missionary Bulletin*, Vol. 7, May 1955, p. 463.
70. *China Bulletin*, Vol. 5, No. 21, December 1955.
71. Hanson, op. cit., pp. 113-14.

VII
The Years of Conflict
1957-1969

Angels on high strengthen me,
Walk us through this Dragon Hill.
This land toss and turn and roar;
Calm its brave heart, still our fear.[1]

The point is that in the latter half of 1955 the situation in China underwent a fundamental change.

Mao Zedong[2]

The Socialist High Tide

It was with supreme self-confidence that the leaders of the CCP viewed China's internal situation in 1955-56. Their optimism was not without justification. For the first time this century China was united, stable and free of foreign control. The First Five Year Plan had had some considerable success in bringing industrial growth, and the country's finances were on a firm footing. Internationally, the Korean War was over, and although still isolated from much of the world, China was emerging as a leading power in her own right, commanding considerable respect in what we would now term the "Third World". Internal opposition had been muted, and the general acceptance of the rule of the CCP amongst the people was based, at least in part, on their perception of the Party as the legitimate source of moral authority. The United Front had drawn in many minority groupings most of whom had come to terms with the leading role of the Party; hoping that in return their particular interests would receive a degree of toleration and protection. These two years did indeed see a general relaxation of pressure, a new opportunity for rebuilding after the intensive campaigns of the early years since Liberation. At the same time those who continued to resist the supervision of the CCP found that they were even more isolated and vulnerable. It was in this period that the Catholic opposition was overcome, as well as that of awkward individuals like Wang Mingdao. Taken overall, the CCP had good grounds for being pleased with itself, and the Chinese people seemed to be entering a period of stability which promised to improve the economic lot of the common people after at least two centuries of growing impoverishment.

Mao, however, was not referring to these achievements when he wrote the above words in December 1955. The "fundamental change" was the "socialist upsurge" in China's countryside during 1955, in which in a few months sixty per cent of China's 110 million peasant households had pooled their land, animals, farm tools and labour. Mao believed that within three years the socialist revolution would be achieved. Up to now, China was considered to be a New Democracy, an alliance of different political groupings, and not a socialist state. The unexpected speed of agricultural collectivization now convinced Mao that the next stage in the revolution could be pushed forward. Mao also believed that a socialist "high tide" would be accompanied by a surge in production, and he recognized that in order to achieve this it would be necessary to mobilize the enthusiasm of all sections of society, including even those most adversely affected by the revolution.

Mao had also achieved a personal victory over Party critics who had urged caution in rural policy. Now the CCP leadership was compelled to acknowledge that he had been right. The Eighth Party Congress that met in September 1956 gathered in an atmosphere of general confidence and with a leadership that was more or less united. Moderation prevailed. Mao himself had expressed his concern over the question of the Party's relationship to the people, in two major speeches in April and May 1956. It was a concern that had been heightened by Khrushchev's denunciation of Stalin in January 1956, at the Twentieth Congress of the Communist Party of the Soviet Union. In his major speech "On The Ten Great Relationships" Mao re-affirmed the central place of the United Front policy, and reinforced it by adding the need for "long-term coexistence and mutual supervision" in the relationship between the CCP and the eight "democratic" parties. A week later he made his famous speech, "Let a hundred flowers bloom, let a hundred schools contend". The over-all result of the Party's self-confidence and its increased awareness of the need to retain a wide spectrum of political support was that in 1956-57 intellectuals and non-Communist groups in the cities, and rich peasants and even "counter-revolutionaries" in the countryside, benefited.

Contradictions in Society

After the Hungarian Revolt in the autumn of 1956, Mao became even more preoccupied with the question of Party relations with the people – a preoccupation that resulted in his key speech on 27 February 1957 "On the Correct Handling of Contradictions among the People". In January there had been an important meeting of intellectuals convened by Zhou Enlai, and at the CPPCC national meeting at the end of the month, Guo Moruo, Chairperson of the Academy of Sciences, had urged the need to cultivate the intellectuals, only forty per cent of whom, he estimated, really upheld socialism. A twelve-year programme was announced, to educate the intellectuals in socialist values and to draw them closer to the masses. The CCP was gearing itself up for a period of economic consolidation and development, and the class struggle was to recede into the background.

The original text of Mao's speech had been frank in its admission of the Party's errors, and many non-Communists were impressed. Mao then announced to a national propaganda work conference on 12 March, the beginning of a "rectification" campaign in which criticism of the Party would be encouraged. Mao had in his mind the successful rectification in Yanan in 1942. However, potential critics were not keen to speak out after the experiences in the political movements of the early 1950s, and many cadres were not convinced of the wisdom of allowing such open criticism. In his speeches Mao went out of his way to stress the need for the movement and he tried to reassure critics:

> What if one dare not write? Some people say that they dare not write even when they have something to say, lest they should offend people and be criticized. I think such worries can be cast aside . . . If what you say is right, you need fear no criticism, and you can explain your correct views further throughout the debate. If what you say is wrong, then criticism can help you correct your mistakes, and there is nothing bad in that.[3]

We now know that there was considerable unease over Mao's proposal to extend the idea of Party rectification beyond intra-Party criticism into a general movement in society. The opposition was headed by no less a figure than Liu Shaoqi, number two in the Party hierarchy. Mao was supported by Zhou Enlai and Deng Xiaoping. They overcame objections, and the launch of the Hundred Flowers Movement was announced in a directive on 30 April. The campaign lasted for five weeks, from 1 May to 7 June. The storm of criticism unleashed in these brief weeks of "blooming and contending" took the Party by surprise. Mao's initial judgement of the need to rectify the Party was confirmed, but so was the view of Liu Shaoqi that "open-door" rectification was a mistake. On 8 June, *People's Daily* published an editorial, "Why This?" It was the beginning of the fateful Anti-Rightist Movement.

The Anti-Rightist Movement

The sudden end of the Hundred Flowers and the subsequent attack on the Party's critics marked a turning point in China's modern history. Mao's Party opponents sought to make the campaign even more severe. Mao himself seems to have been considerably disillusioned by the bourgeois intellectuals, but he tried to limit the severity of the campaign. The outspokenness of the attack on the Party by some critics in May had shaken the leadership, and the reaction was not really so surprising. Mao obviously did not expect the sort of attack that came, and there is no real evidence to support the often stated view that the Hundred Flowers was a deliberate attempt to draw out the critics in order to suppress them subsequently. Rather, the failure of the Hundred Flowers must be seen as, in part, the failure of the United Front policy to involve non-Communists in an effective way, and, in part, as the result of fundamental disagreements within the leadership of the CCP. At the Third Plenum of the Eighth Central Committee convened on 20 September, Deng Xiaoping outlined the compromise thrashed out between the opponents and supporters of rectification. The Hundred Flowers was now to be seen in relationship to socialist culture and not as a licence for the expression of anti-socialist opinions. At the same time Deng re-affirmed the need for the United Front:

> A new United Front which serves socialism is needed during the period of socialist revolution. The policy of long-term co-existence and mutual supervision among the parties should be carried out on the basis of the six standards [put forward by Mao]. The opinion that the democratic parties and groups no longer have a role is erroneous.[4]

We have dwelt in some detail on the political situation in China during 1956-57 because of its importance in understanding the dramatic change in the circumstances of religious believers after 1957. Mao's bold experiment in liberalism was over:

> It was Mao's first major mistake since the regime had come to power, and his miscalculation can be explained quite simply: because there had been no previous airing of views, Mao had no means of knowing how people really felt.[5]

The damage to his prestige within the CCP, the need to reach a compromise within the leadership, the rise to prominence of severe economic problems associated both with the "high tide" of 1956 and with the inappropriateness of the Soviet planning model adopted wholesale in industry after 1950: all helped to ensure a turning away from the concerns of early 1957. Mao and Liu Shaoqi now joined forces in the development of a new economic strategy that in the next year was to involve the whole country in an unprecedented mobilization that rapidly brought normal life to a halt. The failure of the planners was one reason for the choice of the mass mobilization model of development. Another was the need to bypass the intellectuals. Around 400,000 were labelled as "rightist" and many were sent to the countryside for manual labour. Deng Xiaoping in his speech to the Third Plenum therefore re-introduced a Twelve Year Programme for Agriculture, originally drawn up in 1956 but then shelved due to pressure from the planners, to bring about a "high tide" in rural production in the winter of 1957-58.

The Great Leap Forward

The movement into collective agricultural units had continued after 1955 with the creation of even bigger conglomerates. By 1957 there were 762,000 Advanced Agricultural Producers Co-operatives, containing almost ninety-four per cent of peasant households. As a result of the new emphasis of late 1957 the movement to form the People's Commune got under way in April 1958. It was accompanied by the Great Leap Forward, which has been described as "mainly a mental attitude", in which the whole nation engaged in a frenzy of militant activity in every sector of society: "The pressing need for economic construction had the urgency of a drive for national salvation".[6] Economically, the Great Leap was a failure. This failure was masked by the excellent harvest in 1958 and by the reporting of grossly exaggerated figures for grain production. The harvest in 1959 was badly affected by the disastrous weather that year and by the failure of the communes to provide an adequate structure for production. The following year's harvest was even worse and there were widespread food shortages. In some areas it seems to have reached famine levels, resulting in widespread malnutrition and some mortality. The withdrawal of all Soviet aid in the summer of the same year made matters even worse, especially in industry, which was already in considerable disarray after the failure of the Great Leap Forward.

Today's official CCP view is that in 1957 the "leftist line" took over. This would seem to be correct, as far as it goes. "Leftism" implies a number of things within the Chinese context. Most fundamentally it is the belief that socialism can be achieved through the mobilization of human beings to engage in a struggle against nature, against "class enemies" and against non-Communist elements in their own thinking. Mao was a great believer in voluntarism – the power of the human will over objective obstacles – and there is no doubt that it was Mao who forced the CCP to launch the Great Leap. Not only was China to "Overtake Britain in fifteen years!", she was to produce a new sort of person, both "red and expert". The drive for production was accompanied by the reorganization of people's lives within the "commune" – which for a short time meant the provision of communal kitchens, free distribution of food and the organization of life along military lines. It was accompanied by a massive attack on superstition, prejudice and fatalism.

It is obvious that the tumultuous events of these years must have had a serious effect on religious practice. Apart from anything else, the swing to the left meant the general abandonment of the organizational structures that had been so carefully nurtured in the preceding years. Despite Deng Xiaoping's assurances as to the continuing importance of the United Front, after the Anti-Rightist Movement there was no chance of the United Front policy having any real meaning during the Great Leap period. In any case, religious believers were caught up in the general frenzy, and normal life simply came to a halt for months on end. As the nation surged towards

Communism so old ways of thinking were to be discarded, and religion could have no role in this brave new world.

In August 1959 the internal divisions within the CCP surfaced into open conflict. At the Lushan Plenum of the Central Committee Mao had to fight hard to head off his critics. Peng Dehuai, the minister of defence, was replaced by Lin Biao, and Peng's supporters were removed. Nevertheless, despite the re-affirmation of the Leftist line, Mao was compelled to make a long self-criticism. Many of the more extreme aspects of the Great Leap had already been abandoned and this process continued through 1959-60. However, the Soviet withdrawal, and the near-famine in 1960, finally gave the Party moderates their opportunity and in 1961 a major "re-adjustment" began.

The Protestant Scene 1957-61

Christians and the Hundred Flowers

We have seen how for most Christians during 1955-56 life had become more relaxed. The CCP seemed to be satisfied that, in general, the United Front policy was working well. Religious policy had never received any systematic formulation, nor was it based on any detailed theoretical framework. Philip Wickeri has suggested that the CCP operated on the basis of a functional viewpoint developed as a working hypothesis about the nature and function of religion in China. The hypothesis was put forward most comprehensively by Li Weihan in his speech to the Seventh National Conference on United Front Work, on 4 April 1957. He proposes "five characteristics of religion": its protracted nature; its complexity; its mass character (thereby acknowledging that religion is not simply a reactionary tool); its ethnic character (this refers mainly to China's minority peoples, many of whom are Buddhist or Muslim, and a few Christian); and finally, its international connections.[7]

CCP policy was thus based on a recognition of some important characteristics of religion in China. It is hardly an adequate analysis of religion, but as Wickeri suggests, its framework is easily grasped by grass-roots cadres and it has played an important role in terms of the practical implementation of religious policy. It also offers a far less rigid interpretation than that later developed within academic circles within the Institute for World Religions in Beijing after it was established in 1963.

The Hundred Flowers provided an opportunity for many Christians to air their grievances. The most comprehensive critique was made by Marcus Cheng (Chen Chonggui) at the CPPCC meeting on 19 March 1957, which was reported in full in *People's Daily* and published in the 13 May issue of *Tian Feng*. He began by supporting some criticisms of the implementation of religious policy by Y.T. Wu made at the same meeting, but he then went on to plead for debate between believers and unbelievers "to discover the truth . . . calmly, without abuse or name-calling". He called attention to Chairman Mao's words on 22 November 1952, in Tibet:

> "The Communist Party protects religion. Believers and unbelievers, believers in this or that religion, all are protected and respected." We believers appreciated very much this word from Chairman Mao, and what especially impressed and comforted us was his statement that the Government would not only protect, but would also "respect". Now this means that you must not blaspheme the God whom we worship, nor defile the churches in which we worship him.[8]

Cheng's speech was moderate in its tone, yet he became one of the principal targets in the Anti-Rightist campaign when this was extended to the Church in November 1957.

As early as 11 June 1957 the head of Shanghai's Religious Affairs Bureau, Cheng Zhiming, speaking at a meeting with Christian leaders in the city, let it be known that "blooming and contending" was never intended for religious believers.[9] In July he told another meeting that the ideological understanding of many Christians was still "unclear" and open to manipulation by "imperialism, rightists and reactionary classes".[10] It came as no surprise therefore when on 12 August *Tian Feng* reproduced a report from the *Yangzi Daily* denouncing Francis Wei Zhuomin of Central China Normal College as the organizer of an anti-Communist conspiracy.[11] Other denunciations were also taking place in various cities. Pastor Sun Pengxi of Shenyang, and Yu Peizang of Zhengzhou, were both accused in August. Yu was said to have criticized the tight control exercised by the local RAB over the Three Self Movement, of which he was a Vice-Chairman.[12]

It was, however, the meeting of the Tenth (Enlarged) Plenum of the TSPM, which lasted from 28 October to 4 December 1957, that saw the intensification of the movement within the churches. As Wickeri comments, "the Tenth Plenum marks a decisive shift in the TSPM towards what became an increasingly leftist position".[13] The main task of the Plenum was the denunciation of a number of so-called Christian "rightists" on the basis of very tenuous charges. These included Marcus Cheng and the others were Liu Lingqiu, editor of the bi-weekly *Farmer*, who was accused of saying that while it had taken the Guomindang twenty-two years to become corrupt it had taken the CCP only eight; Zhou Qingze, pastor of the Church of Christ in China church on the island of Gulangyu in Xiamen, Fujian; Dong Hongwen and Zhou Fuqing, both pastors in Shanghai; Fan Aishi from Ningbo, and Sun Pengxi.

The tragedy of this whole episode was that it re-opened divisions that by 1956 were beginning to be overcome. The renewal of struggle and denunciation at this stage could only undermine the over-all objectives of the Three Self Movement. Leftism had manifested itself within the TSPM at various times in earlier years, but it had never been a dominant element. After 1957 it came to the fore, and the TSPM was diverted from its aim of unifying Protestant Christians within the United Front. This is not surprising in view of the fact that the United Front policy itself was in disarray. Marcus Cheng was cleared of "rightism", probably in 1961-62 when some "rightist" labels were removed, and he remained a leader of the TSPM until his death, aged 81, in 1963. The other six have been rehabilitated since 1978, along with many thousands of others denounced in 1957.

The Anti-Rightist struggle continued through 1958. Various "Study Institutes" were held, in which leading church people were denounced. In Shanghai, Jia Yuming, the prominent conservative principal of the Spiritual Cultivation Seminary, was attacked. In Hebei, Ma Xingge, the Chairman of Baoding City TSPM, was charged with usurping the leadership so as to oppose the CCP, and in Shanhaiguan the TSPM Chairman, Li Yanlin, was attacked. In Hunan three outstanding leaders were denounced, including the provincial TSPM Chairman, Li Changshu.[14] In the city of Wuhan, fifteen Christians were either arrested or denounced, including the Anglican Bishop Zhang Haisong. The fate of the individuals caught up in these accusations is unclear. Not all were imprisoned or sent to the countryside, but many were dismissed from their posts and suffered other penalties. One lay Christian in Sichuan worked in the iron mines and then in the countryside, but he continued to receive his former salary. According to his own account, life only became really hard with the outbreak of the Cultural Revolution, when his salary was removed, and he had to rely on charity from his neighbours and his relatives in the city in order to survive.[15]

The Great Leap Forward and the associated commune movement had serious effects on Christian life, but neither movement was directly concerned with the religious question. During 1958, however, the Anti-Rightist campaign shifted into a concern with "illegal activities" by Christians. Thus a Study Institute in Jiayu County, Hubei, launched an attack on the True Jesus Church. Of thirty-seven True Jesus pastors, thirteen were accused of being counter-revolutionaries. Charges against them included stressing exorcisms and faith healing, preaching against the government and obstructing socialist production:

In 1958 when the farm villages undertook the Great Leap

Forward in production, and everybody was very busy, the True Jesus churches of Jiayu County still continued to hold meetings with large congregations. For example, the church in Maan held a meeting on 4 April which lasted all night with 140 persons present, at which they took up a collection of over $30. Since so many Christians were so late in getting to sleep, their work the next day was very poor, and this not only gave the people a bad impression of the church, but was also a serious hindrance to the Great Leap Forward in production.[16]

The campaign against the True Jesus Church in the Wuhan area continued, and the *Yangzi Daily* of 5 November 1958 denounced Isaac Wei and other members of the Standing Committee of the National Headquarters of the church as "special agents, traitors, former Guomindang military officers and counter-revolutionaries".[17]

Christian leaders were also urged to engage in productive activities. In Shanghai 120 church workers were organized into a volunteer working corps packaging medicines.[18] It was expected that church workers should be self-supporting. The famous small iron furnaces of the Great Leap appeared on church premises. *Tian Feng* had a picture of one in the court-yard of the church in Dengshikou, Beijing being tended by Newton Chiang (Jiang Yizhen), Anglican priest and professor at the Yanjing Seminary.

Church Unification

Church life was so disrupted that attendances dropped dramatically, and the lack of personnel and resources was a major factor in the sudden movement that emerged in 1958, to unify churches through the closure of many and the amalgamation of congregations of different backgrounds. There can be little doubt that the process was not a truly voluntary one, especially as it was carried out within a short period throughout the nation. The TSPM supervised the unification process, and it is probable that the government did not intervene directly: the general "leftist" atmosphere creating its own pressures. In Beijing sixty-five churches were reduced to four; in Shanghai two hundred to twenty-three. Similar reports came from Fujian, Zhejiang, Yunnan, Shanxi and many other provinces. In Dali, Yunnan, each denomination surrendered its property to the TSPM and then voted itself out of existence. *Tian Feng* published in full the regulations from Taiyuan, provincial capital of Shanxi, and they are worth recording:

ON THE PLANS FOR UNIFICATION

Worship in the city of Taiyuan shall be unified with a ministerial staff of three or four. Except for the ministerial staff and fellow workers in the Three-self office, all other church workers shall throw themselves into the socialist construction of the motherland. The physically weak and the elderly may retire. All real and movable church property and church funds shall be turned over to the Three Self committee to be administered in common.

ON THE REFORM OF CHURCH ORGANIZATION

1. Church organization: All former church committees, governing committees and boards and all administrative organs shall cease operations. The administration of the churches shall be unified under the Three Self Patriotic Movement committee.

2. Ritual, regulations and church order:
   a. Worship shall be unified. No church shall stress its own religious ritual.
   b. Hymns used in worship shall be unified and a hymnal committee established to undertake reform of hymn content.
   c. Examination and criticism of all books and publications used by churches in interpreting the Bible shall be undertaken. Those containing poisonous material shall be rejected without exception. Teachings which promote co-operation and which accord with socialism should be encour-

aged. At the same time a critical approach shall be taken of all material received from abroad.

d. Negative and pessimistic doctrines such as the Last Days and the vanity of this world should no longer be stressed. Efforts should be made to bring into play the principle of the unity of faith and practice and to inspire in believers a consciousness which upholds the dignity of labour, the control of nature, a recognition of the division between ourselves and our enemies and of the distinction between right and wrong.

e. Belief and unbelief shall not be an issue in marriage.

3. Reform in individual churches:

a. The Little Flock shall abolish its women's meetings, its weekly breaking of the bread, and its outdated rule against women preaching. Members shall no longer be required to submit to an interview before the breaking of the bread.

b. The Salvation Army should no longer stress its military regulations.

c. The Seventh Day Adventists shall abolish their daily morning prayers. Beneficial good works and economic production may be done on the Sabbath. The clergy shall not be supported by the tithe system in Shanxi. The unification of accounts shall be abolished and local churches shall manage themselves.

d. YMCA secretaries shall temper themselves by taking part in productive labour or change jobs so as to effectively enter into socialist construction. The closing of the Taiyuan YMCA as a separate organization is presently under consideration.

The Taiyuan Christian Three Self Patriotic Movement Committee.[19]

Such a regulation was probably not untypical. Its whole tone is leftist, confusing political and religious categories. It also goes directly counter to the spirit of the principle of mutual respect. It must, however, be remembered that an ending of denominational differences was an aspiration of many educated Chinese Protestants in the past, and it is likely that in many places the process was carried through without major dissension. The main problem was the political climate in which the unification was carried out, and it must have been perceived as political interference in internal church affairs by many Christians, thus alienating many from the TSPM structures. The Campaign to sign "patriotic pledges" in early 1958 was a further sign of undue political pressure.

A Time of Transition

The general picture during the period from late 1957 to 1961 is of a steady decline in church activity. Yet, one must be cautious. The shaking of the foundations may in the long run have helped Christians to transform their attitudes. Manual labour; sharing in the frenzied activities of the Great Leap Forward: Christians were learning to be of the people. Some Chinese Christians understood what was happening. A letter from Suzhou dated 20 September 1959 puts it succinctly:

> At first glance it would seem that the church in China has no hope. But in fact the opposite is the case. We who believe in God also believe that all the vicissitudes of life are governed by God. He will fulfil his will and raise up a united church, which is what our Lord prayed for. Just as God long ago used Cyrus, so today he is using Chairman Mao to cleanse his Church. He will raise up a Church which will not be the Church of any one person (some pastor), but of all believing people.
>
> In this transitional period the Church is daily growing stronger. This is the work of the Holy Spirit, by whose influence the faith of believers is being united. At first (that is, after the unification of a year ago) Suzhou had only one place of worship (before that unification it must have had twenty-five or thirty), but recently because of

the increase in the number of worshippers it has been necessary to open a second place of worship . . . In the future still more places of worship may be opened as need arises.

We must remember that the Lord Jesus Christ is the true God, and that the human heart needs its faith. Our Lord has said that heaven and earth may pass away, but his word will never change. And so I believe that his church on earth will grow and prosper.[20]

Church life was learning to sustain itself in new and informal ways. The home meetings that were to be such a feature of church life in the future, now really began to take off, possibly stimulated by the influx of urban Christians into the country-side for manual labour. Bishop K.H. Ting, in an interview with Philip Wickeri on 29 June 1982, observed:

The major positive development after 1957 was the growth of Christian meetings in homes.

He went on to give the reasons for this: lack of churches, preference for informal worship and grievances against the TSPM:

Some wished to sow alienation, but others had real grievances. There were some in the Three-Self, for example, who thought Christians meeting in homes would be illegitimate. This was wrong, a result of the increasing ultra-leftism in society as a whole.[21]

A moving description of the changes in one small Christian community during these years was recorded by Raymond Fung in his telling collection of real life stories *Households of God on China's Soil*. A woman tells her story. In the late 1950s the town pastor, Pastor Pi "lost his church and asked my husband if he and others could use our home for prayers. That was how this home meeting began." She continues:

For three years, Pastor Pi conducted worship services each Thursday afternoon in this room. I understand he held similar services in two other Christian homes on

different days . . . In my case we began with about fourteen people, all housewives like me, all members of the
congregation. Soon, things became difficult: several had
to take regular street patrol duties; others were assigned
to work in canteens and workshops. What with the
twice weekly study class, there was not much time. So
attendance dropped . . .

Soon after this Pastor Pi stopped preaching and in 1963 he
died. The home meeting continued until the advent of the Red
Guards. Then it stopped.[22]

Apart from such personal recollections gathered many
years later, official statements by Church or Three Self leaders
and the reports in *Tian Feng* constitute virtually the sole source
of information at this period, and these became increasingly
formalistic and concerned with matters relating to socialist
development. Fewer and fewer reports on church affairs
appeared, and the picture we have of these years is extremely
hazy. There were a few ongoing international contacts.
Bishop Ting and three others were able to visit Hungary in early 1958, and in July 1959 a delegation of six Australian Free
Churchmen spent a week in China, but, in general, official
attitudes towards foreign churches were increasingly hostile.
There was a renewed emphasis on missionary imperialism,
and the tone of the discussion was generally over-dogmatic
and an obvious distortion of history. During 1960 *Tian Feng*
itself was no longer sent overseas, a situation that lasted into
1961.

The Second National Christian Conference

It was in this highly-charged and politically sensitive
atmosphere that an attempt was made to hold the Second
National Christian Conference. It was held in Shanghai from
12 November 1960 to 14 January 1961, with 319 delegates from
twenty-five provinces. Despite this wide representation and
the participation of a number of individuals previously
attacked as "rightists", such as Jia Yuming of Shanghai, the

mood was very different from the first conference. Most of the speeches appear to have been concerned with secular matters, and Wu Yifang's survey of the work of the TSPM since 1954 tells us little about the life of the Church. The Constitution adopted at the conference is noteworthy for its stress on patriotism and for the significant deletion of the previous article concerning mutual respect. The conference elected a committee of 145 and a Standing Committee of 49. The Chairman was Y.T. Wu and the Vice-chairmen were Chen Jianzhen (Bishop Robin Chen), Wu Yifang, Ding Guangxun (K.H. Ting), Deng Yuzhi (Cora Deng), Ding Yuzhang (Nanjing Seminary), Xie Yongjin (Shanghai) and Jia Yuming.

The conference may have been an attempt to move beyond the leftism of the past three years, but if so, it failed. Perhaps if it had taken place a few months later the tone and its results would have been very different. 1961 was, as we have already noted, the year when the moderate elements within the CCP regained the initiative, ushering in a second brief period of relaxation.

Theological Reflection Since 1949

There was little opportunity during the years since Liberation to engage in theological reflection. T.C. Chao had abandoned theology, and his contributions were limited to comments on Christianity and imperialism or the contribution of Christians to building socialism. The lack of published materials does not mean that the theological thinking of Chinese Christians was not changing. The impasse that faced Chinese theology in 1949 was a result of the problem of relating faith and culture. Either the association was rejected or Christianity tended to be subsumed within ethics. Liberation challenged Christians to re-think. What began in the 1950s was a process of re-appraisal in which many of the traditional Protestant assumptions began to be questioned. The Nanjing Seminary was the centre of this re-appraisal but it was reflecting the deeply felt concerns of many ordinary believers, such as the author of the Suzhou letter quoted above.

The central issue was the relationship of nature and grace. During the 1950s there was much criticism of Mrs Charles E. Cowman's devotional book *Streams in the Desert*, which had immense popularity with Chinese Christians. The heart of the criticism was the world-denying nature of the book. In the context of the New China it was important for Christians to discover ways of affirming the world and man's own creativity without thereby denying the sovereignty of God. So rather than a negative rejection of materialism, it should be evaluated from the perspective of "mutual respect" and of "seeking the common ground while reserving differences". It was Chen Zemin of the Nanjing Seminary who expounded this most cogently in his contribution to the *Nanjing Seminary Theological Review* of August 1957, "The Task of Theological Construction in the Chinese Church".[23] Chen develops the idea of mapping the theological locus (borrowed from Melanchthon). He suggests that in the history of theology the divine and the human are like the two foci of an ellipse, with the circumference sometimes closer to God and sometimes to man. God is always the active centre, but by preserving a certain relationship and a certain distance, the dangers of pantheism or humanism – if God is absorbed into man – are avoided. Equally, the denial of man implied in an infinite separation of God from man, and its opposite and consequent possibility of atheism, are also avoided. This model has been employed by Uchimura Kanzo to relate faith and patriotism. In his Neesima lecture at Doshisha University, Japan, in September 1984, Bishop Ting expressed his appreciation of Kanzo's development of the model, quoting his words:

> Jesus and Japan: my faith is not a circle with one centre; it is an ellipse with two centres. My heart and mind revolve around the two committed names. And I know that one strengthens the other.[24]

Extreme emphasis on the fallen nature of the world destroys the meaning of the Incarnation. On the other hand failure to give due weight to sin would result in a shallow humanism. As Chen wrote:

> We should clearly recognize that there are undoubtedly social factors in the root of evil, but in spiritual terms, it still represents humanity's incompleteness and pride before the face of God. Therefore the spiritual problem cannot be resolved by a change in the social system. Evil will never disappear because social morality has been raised.

He goes on to say, however:

> It was not humanity's utter depravity that caused God to seek us, but that humanity is the crown of creation, created in the image of God to help God oversee this world.[25]

Bishop K.H. Ting, in a remarkable address to the graduating students at the Nanjing Seminary on 12 June 1957 and published in the *Nanjing Theological Review*, deals with similar concerns. The address was given at the very end of the Hundred Flowers and is a forthright defence of Christian theism, rejecting the simplistic division between Christianity as "idealism" and Marxist materialism. He also disputes the idea that Christianity is in essence the "opium of the people". He then goes on to speak of the relationship of nature and revelation:

> Unless you come to know God through revelation, nature itself will only be space and mystery, and not much else. But if after receiving the revelation you again look at nature, all is now new. You now perceive that the whole of nature, and all the truth, beauty and goodness of the world, proclaim the glory and the working of God.
>
> In short, we Christians on the one hand recognize that the witness of nature is not enough, we cannot expect to know God from it, and therefore we are not disturbed or alarmed when a man says that he cannot find God in nature. On the other hand, we do not look upon nature with hostility or deny it, because it is after all the handiwork of God. St Thomas Aquinas summed it up very well,

"Grace does not deny nature, it fulfils it".[26]

In a less coherent form, these insights could be found amongst many conservative Christians, who were no longer happy with the all too common acceptance of a radical dichotomy between believers and unbelievers on the presupposition that the Church stands over against the "world". As Bishop Ting put it in 1983, "How does one assess the true, the good and the beautiful outside the realm of the Church?"[27]

To return to our critique, in Chapter Three, of the form of theology in nineteenth-century missionary thinking. We stressed then the need for an analogical understanding of the form of Christ in relation to all human forms. Ting's words, "Christ is not an intruder into the world alien to God",[28] are an essential corrective to the distortions of an extreme Protestantism. Indeed, it is remarkable how close this Chinese viewpoint is to that expounded by some of the foremost thinkers of Eastern Orthodoxy. The tradition is biblical, but its earliest exponent in the post-biblical Church was Irenaeus. Irenaeus spoke of the "art" of God drawing "out of himself the beautiful form of created things", and maintained that sin cannot disprove this art and "the light does not grow weak because of those who have blinded themselves . . . and do not wish to keep his art". The world is "capable of receiving the Father's glory". God "increased and expanded the things of nature which are free and common to all, making gifts to men without envy and without stint". As Hans Urs von Balthasar comments:

> Such a theology will have a tendency to find even the most elevated teachings of the Gospel traced somewhere in ordinary human nature . . . It will everywhere stress the congruence of grace and nature . . .[29]

It is very important to understand that Chinese Christians were not mere passive, reluctant spectators in the dramas of the 1950s and beyond. Whatever the problems and difficulties of adjustment, and of exposure to the criticisms and campaigns of those years, something new was in the making, changing the perspectives of the past and preparing the way for a more appropriate Christian form within the Chinese context. It has, however, to be admitted that a conscious search for this form was the concern of a minority. Yet it is probable that the majority sensed that something had to be done. It is only from the perspective of the 1980s that we can truly begin to appreciate what was happening, and why, in the end, the Three Self road can be vindicated in spite of its excesses and leftist errors. Of course, the process of adaptation is still in its early stages, even today. Many questions await treatment, many cannot be addressed without further developments in the general Chinese discussion of the relationship of traditional Chinese culture to contemporary culture. It is a subject to which we shall have to return when we look at the relationship of Christianity to the culture of post-Cultural Revolution China.

Chinese Catholics 1957-62

The end of overt Catholic resistance after 1955 was followed by a steady rise in the influence of the patriotic movement amongst Chinese Catholics during 1956-57. From 19 to 26 July 1956 thirty-eight Catholics attended a conference for the formation of a Preparatory Committee for a Catholic Patriotic Association. There were four bishops at the meeting, and the delegates were received by Zhou Enlai on 27 July. This meeting was followed by a further one 12-16 February 1957, with fifty-five delegates, including the Archbishop of Shenyang, Pi Shushi, and four bishops. It was decided to establish the Catholic Patriotic Association (CCPA) itself at a national conference to be held in March, although in the event the conference was delayed until June.

The general relaxation in early 1957 during the period of the Hundred Flowers led to some public criticism of government policy towards the Catholic Church at the National People's Congress in Beijing (27 February-1 March). Two of the speakers were Dong Wenlong, Vicar General of Jinan,

Shandong, and Bishop Gong's original successor in Shanghai, Zhang Shilang. Their criticisms were directed at local cadres obstructing implementation of religious policy rather than at over-all government policy towards the Catholic Church. Their caution was perhaps wise in view of what was to happen in the autumn, but the relaxed political atmosphere must have encouraged many of the 241 Catholic leaders who came together on 17 June at the start of the first National Catholic Conference.

The First National Catholic Conference

The Conference was designed to assert the right of the national church to order its own life, but despite a very critical attitude towards the Vatican, it sought to preserve the spiritual link with Rome. Bishop Li Boyu of Zhouzhi in Shaanxi explained the policy of "love country, love church" (*aiguo, aijiao*):

> The national Patriotic Association is an organization of the Catholic masses determined to love their country and their religion. It is not an organization of the Catholic Church. Since all the members . . . are Catholic, we have therefore to preserve, on the religious plane, the spirit of the Holy Catholic Church, and to obey the directives of the Pope in the matters touching on the religious doctrines to believe and the ecclesiastical rules to observe. But in political questions, the Vatican supports the capitalist system, follows American imperialism and continually opposes the Soviet Union, the Communist Party and socialism . . .

Archbishop Pi's closing address made similar points, and the final Resolution adopted on the closing day, 2 August, stated:

> The Catholic Church of China shall keep strictly religious relations with the Vatican and shall submit to the Pope in regard to religious doctrines to be believed and ecclesiastical regulations to be practised. However, the

independence, honour and interests of our country must not be violated.[30]

The conference took place at the very end of the Hundred Flowers, and in response to the call for criticism of "rightists" it seems that the mood of the conference shifted as it progressed. At the same time there is some evidence to suggest that the government acknowledged its "mistakes" in policy towards Catholics and offered concessions, including the right to publish Catholic journals and newspapers, to establish a national seminary and to restore confiscated properties.[31]

Relations with Rome

Despite the stress on maintaining relations with Rome, the seeds of the 1958 break were already being sown. The Vatican had been requested to ratify the appointment of Zhang Jiashu as the legitimate vicar capitular of Shanghai and had, not surprisingly, refused. The Conference protested at this refusal. What might have happened if the political climate in China had not swung decisively to the left in July is of course impossible to say, but the fact is that the Conference Resolution was not implemented. Indeed, in the follow-up provincial meetings not only was there no mention of the crucial issue of maintaining religious links with Rome, but the delegates were actually asked to agree to the severance of these links. It is, of course, possible that the inclusion at the National Conference of the words on submission to the authority of the Pope was a deliberate ruse, but it seems more likely that the change in emphasis at the provincial meetings was the result of the changed political situation.

Whatever the truth may have been, it is clear that by early 1958 the government was insisting on a severance of links with the Vatican. There was, without doubt, a serious crisis in the leadership of the Church with the departure of the foreign bishops and of six Chinese bishops including Yu Bin, Archbishop of Nanjing, who was now in Taiwan. Others were in prison, including Deng Yiming (Dominic Tang) of Guangzhou, arrested on 5 February 1958, allegedly for threatening to excommunicate Catholics who joined the CCPA, and the administrator of the Hankou Diocese, Father Odoric Liu Hede, who was sentenced on 31 January 1958 to twenty years' imprisonment as a counter-revolutionary. Altogether there were over one hundred vacancies by early 1958. The decision to consecrate Chinese bishops without Rome's approval was, in part at least, the product of the internal situation of the Church. Rome's opposition to the Catholic Patriotic Association should not in principle have prevented support for the local nomination of bishops, since the CCPA was a United Front oganization and did not claim to be the Catholic Church in China. The Vatican's willingness to allow General Franco in Spain the right to be involved in the appointment of Spanish bishops suggested that the strong anti-Communist feelings of Pope Pius XII were a major factor in the Vatican's refusal to make allowances for the particular circumstances in China. It must also be said that most discussions of these events have down-played the patriotic feelings of Chinese Catholics, even though the historical evidence suggests that many Chinese priests were deeply resentful of the foreign control of the Church. Moreover, seen from today's perspective, the desire to choose one's own bishops seems a not unreasonable assertion of the rights of the local church over against the monarchical claims of the papacy.

The Episcopal Elections

The Shanghai Catholic newspaper, *Xin Ge*, in an editorial on 28 February 1958, sounded the first public call for the local election of bishops:

> The Vatican, in order to sabotage our Church in China, has struck at patriotic priests and it continues its desire to control the nominations of personnel. We can now no longer have any illusion about the Vatican, and we ourselves must assume responsibility with regard to the problem of the bishops: we ourselves must elect and consecrate them. [32]

The first episcopal elections took place on 18-19 March 1958 in Hankou and Wuchang (Wuhan city), when Dong Guangqing and Yuan Wenhua were nominated. Rome was informed of the elections, but replied threatening excommunication to both nominees and those who proposed to consecrate them. The consecrations went ahead on 13 April with Bishop Li Daonan of Puqi as main consecrator, assisted by Wang Xueming of Hohhot, Inner Mongolia, Li Boyu, Yi Xuanhua of Xiangyang, Hubei and Chen Guangzu, administrator of Suixian, Hubei. It was the beginning of a process that continued up to the Second National Catholic Conference in 1962. Within three months of the Wuhan consecrations thirteen more consecrations took place, conducted by five bishops, including the Chairman of the Patriotic Association, Archbishop Pi Shushi, despite his previous opposition to such elections expressed publicly in the summer of 1957. Altogether at least forty-two bishops were consecrated in this way up to 1962, after which there were no further consecrations until the election of Fu Tieshan as Bishop of Beijing in December 1979.

Rome's reaction was swift. On 29 June 1958, Pope Pius XII issued the encyclical *Ad Apostolorum Principis* in which he asserted that the right to nominate bishops belongs solely to the Roman Pontiff, and warned that excommunication was "automatically incurred" by consecrators and consecrated. He also stated:

> Acts requiring the power of Holy Orders which are performed by ecclesiastics of this kind, though they are valid as long as the consecration conferred on them was valid, are yet gravely illicit, that is, criminal and sacrilegious . . .[33]

The nature of the consecrations and the status of the bishops so consecrated has been subject to considerable misunderstanding. Since the consecrators were themselves legally consecrated, the validity of the illicit consecrations has never been in question. Despite the threat of excommunication, none of the consecrating bishops were excommunicated, nor were their names removed from the official *Annuario Pontificio*, the annual list of Catholic bishops throughout the world. Nor is the Chinese Church considered to be schismatic, in spite of the use of the word "schism" by the new Pope, John XXIII, in late 1958. On 26 November 1962, at a meeting with fifty-nine bishops who had lived and worked in China, John XXIII promised not to use this term. As the former bishop of Ningxia, Bishop van Melckebecke, said in 1964, "schismatic" implies separation "knowingly, willingly and obstinately", and he was of the opinion that this was not the case.[34]

Like so many fateful decisions in church history, political factors played a major role. It is not for nothing that many both inside and outside China have seen a historical parallel with the course of the English Reformation under Henry VIII, although the analogy should not be pressed. It does, however, put into perspective both the attempt by leading Chinese Catholics to go along with the political demands, while at the same time seeking to preserve the organization of the Church, and the attitude and activities of those who felt compelled to refuse to co-operate. Under Pope John XXIII, the climate of opinion in the Catholic Church changed dramatically, expressed, of course, in the Second Vatican Council (1962-65). Paul VI continued this more open policy and made a number of overtures towards China in the mid-1960s. Yet Vatican policy towards China remained ambiguous. On the one hand Pope Paul sent a message of best wishes for peace to Chairman Mao on 31 December 1965, while on the other hand, on Christmas Eve 1966 Vatican Radio announced the elevation of the internuncio in Taiwan to the status of nuncio. The Pope's subsequent message to China on 6 January 1967, in which he stressed the desire for contact, could hardly be expected to be taken seriously by the Chinese government, even if China had not been in the throes of the Cultural Revolution.

Catholic Life

The "leftist" turn in Chinese politics meant that the life of ordinary Catholic believers became more difficult, with increased discrimination against believers in society and the closure of many churches, with priests and nuns sent to engage in manual labour. Pressure on recalcitrant Catholic leaders continued to mount. Thus in October 1958 the last remaining foreign bishop in China, Maryknoll's James E. Walsh, was arrested, after being allowed a relative degree of freedom while under house arrest in previous years. He was finally brought to trial in Shanghai in 1960, together with Bishop Gong Pinmei and thirteen other Chinese Catholics. The trial lasted for two days (16-17 March); Bishop Gong was sentenced to life imprisonment and Bishop Walsh to twenty years. Only now was the Catholic Patriotic Association established in Shanghai, on 6 May 1960, with Hu Wenyao as Chairman. It was followed by the election of Zhang Jiashu as Bishop of the Diocese.

The Second National Catholic Conference was held in Beijing 5-19 January 1962, and attended by 256 delegates. Few details of the proceedings were ever made public and the *Guangming Daily* report on 20 January concentrated on the political support for the CCP and its religious policy. One specifically religious matter referred to was the provision of a seminary in each diocese. The last episcopal consecrations took place two days after the conference closed, when Archbishop Pi consecrated seven new bishops. After the conference formal Catholic activity was minimal; believers were left to fare as best they could as China moved steadily to the left. The Cultural Revolution was in the making.

The Prelude to the Cultural Revolution

The retreat from the Great Leap Forward, confirmed at the Ninth Plenum in January 1961, continued throughout the next two years. In the countryside, the free market re-appeared and the commune system underwent major readjustment. "Spontaneous capitalist tendencies" emerged, together with a revival of rural "superstitions" and wedding and burial customs. In the political arena, the left was forced on to the defensive, and in February 1961 the performance of Wu Han's play *The Dismissal of Hai Rui from Office*, a thinly disguised plea for the re-habilitation of Peng Dehuai, represented a clear attack on Mao's leadership. China experienced something of a cultural revival, but its appeal was to the rising urban elite who were also benefiting from the more liberal economic policies. Accompanying the retreat from social engineering was an increasingly bureaucratic tendency, paralleled by a rise in petty corruption and nepotism. The experiences during the Great Leap had led to a more cynical attitude towards politics amongst many ordinary Chinese. There was a sober realization of the immensity of the development task facing China. Thus the early 1960s can be said to have produced a certain crisis of faith in the Revolution and a retreat to older, more traditional attitudes.

The Socialist Education Movement

It was in reaction to this that Mao Zedong made his famous appeal at the Tenth Plenum of the Central Committee in September 1962, "Never forget class struggle!" He spoke in the context of a general consensus amongst the leadership on the need for the launching of a Socialist Education Movement. It was to be the last united meeting of the CCP under Mao's leadership. Within a few months major disagreements as to the nature and scope of the Movement broke out amongst the leadership, and the lines of conflict that burst into the open in 1966 were laid. The story of the Movement and of the differences within the CCP cannot be told here.[35] For our purposes all we need to know is that by 1963 the brief "blooming" of 1961-62 was coming to an end as the different Party groupings sought to occupy key areas of policy for themselves. Mao and the left were able to take over the cultural world more easily than the economic, and many writers and artists were denounced as "rightists". The social sciences came in for particular attack, and the more creative Marxist philosophers such as Yang Xianzhen were denounced as "revisionists". Meanwhile, in the countryside in particular, the political struggle continued. The Left only managed to gain the upper hand in 1965 when the Socialist Education Movement turned into the Four Clean-ups Movement, aimed at the four areas of politics, economics, organization and ideology. The renewal of class struggle now began in earnest, and it was the continued resistance to Mao's over-all aim of socialist transformation through such struggle that led him to launch the Cultural Revolution in the following year.

Christian Life 1962-66

There is very little information about the day-to-day life of Chinese Christians in these years. In 1961 life returned to some sort of normalcy after the upheavals of the Great Leap Forward. The Nanjing Union Theological Seminary reopened its doors in April 1961 after several years of complete closure, with an intake of eighty-six students. It appears that at least in some places church workers were able to return from manual labour to take up church work again. In Ningbo, for example, where only one Protestant church was left by 1958, all church workers were sent to labour on the Hongguang farm and subsequently to work in factories. They were allowed to return in 1961 and most continued in church work until 1966, serving a remnant community of three hundred Christians.[36]

Tian Feng from 1961 was only produced on a monthly basis and with fewer pages per issue. Sources of news declined steadily in subsequent years, and while the general impression is of an ongoing decline in organized church life and the imposition of more and more restrictions, this impression may not be entirely accurate. *Tian Feng* itself stopped publication in 1964, reflecting the mounting political tensions as the struggle around the Socialist Education Movement intensified. The increasing attention to class struggle and ideological transformation must have had serious repercussions for rural Christians, Catholic and Protestant. In the cities life continued more normally, and a number of foreign visitors were able to witness ongoing activity. Professor Ralph Lapwood was able to talk with an old Tianjin friend, pastor Liu Qingfen, in September 1964, and learnt that in his church in Tianjin there were around eighty people attending each week, and a further three churches were also open in the city. In Nanjing, Lapwood visited the Seminary, where Bishop Ting informed him that Nanjing was now the only theological seminary in China, the others having closed in 1963. There was a total of eighty-five students, and Ting insisted that although half a day a week was spent in political study, Marxism-Leninism had no place on the curriculum.[37]

The Debate on the Nature of Religion

It was during this period that, for the first time, the theoretical basis of religious policy was discussed. Research on religion had been conducted by a few scholars, notably Ren Jiyu, who was later to emerge as the Director of the Institute for the Study of World Religions under the Chinese Academy of Social Sciences. According to Ren, Mao Zedong had urged him to study religion in 1959, and in 1963 issued a directive on criticizing theology and studying religion but the policy was never effectively implemented due to the Cultural Revolution.[38] In 1978, at a Forum on the Study of Religion, it was revealed that the Institute for the Study of World Religions had in fact been established in 1964, but "it functioned abnormally" and was more or less disbanded after 1966.[39]

The debate that went on between 1963 and 1965 had its origins in the renewed struggle against "superstition" that accompanied the rise of the Socialist Education Movement. Mao's concern, as expressed to Ren Jiyu, was to study religion in order to criticize it. The ensuing debate was really over methodology rather than a meaningful disagreement as to the nature of religion. Yet, for believers the debate was potentially of great importance. On the one side there were those, represented by Ya Hanzhang, who argued for the need to tolerate religion while stepping up atheist propaganda – in their opinion coercion was counter-productive. On the other hand there were those, led by Liu Junwang and Yu Xiang, who argued for class struggle against religion. Ya's position may be identified as akin to the perspective of the United Front policy, Liu and Yu's to the "leftist" line that was gaining the ascendancy in the late '50s and early '60s.[40]

The discussion was, ostensibly, an academic debate over the nature of religion. In an important article in *People's Daily* on 8 August 1963, Ya argued that one must distinguish between "man-made religions" which are the product of class society, and "spontaneous religion" which it gradually replaced. His analysis owed much to Engels, but he introduced a distinctive Chinese note by speaking of personal theistic belief as distinct from organized religion, and also by separating religion from "superstition". This threefold description has behind it the traditional Confucian standpoint on religion: a separation of private philosophy from public religion associated with a contempt for popular religion. The distinction of religion from superstition is, however, the fundamental one as far as religious policy is concerned. Man-made religion is highly organized, possesses scriptures and specialist terminology, whilst spontaneous religion tends towards "superstition" and is, therefore, an essentially negative social force. Neither type of religion can be eliminated by force but the policy of freedom of religious belief cannot be applied to those who use superstitions to exploit the people (what is termed "feudal superstition"). An inherent ambiguity of interpretation is introduced here, for it is not clear at what point "spontaneous religion" turns into "feudal superstition". Man-made religions can be permitted to exist as long as they do not interfere in society and politics. There is no necessary connection of religion to imperialism or hostility to socialism. Therefore, only ideological persuasion can be permitted, and believers must never be coerced through administrative means. While Ya's position is partly based on a conventional Marxist understanding of religion, its importation of traditional Chinese views on religion indicates a potential flexibility in application which, in the climate of the time, could have no immediate significance, but which was to become of crucial importance after 1979.

In the short term Ya Hanzhang's analysis was attacked as "unscientific" by Liu and Yu. They argued that the extinction of religion is inevitable, but it will not come about voluntarily. The struggle against religion is a struggle between the working class and the bourgeois class. They allow for the limited toleration of religion within the United Front but this is a temporary expedient aimed at isolating class enemies and transforming religious patriots through ideological struggle. The emphasis was very much on struggle, although they stopped short of advocating the use of force against religion. The debate continued through to 1965, with other, more radical, voices joining in as time went on. Ya's position was subjected to increasingly sharp criticisms, and he was eventually accused of undermining the Marxist perspective on religion. Finally, two months before the outbreak of the Cultural Revolution, two new writers, Liang Hao and Yang Zhen, accused him of "revisionism" and of not advocating forceful enough measures against religion. He was said to have "prettified religion"![41]

The course of the discussion must be directly linked to the progress of the Socialist Education Movement. As that Movement drifted towards the left, culminating in the Four-Clean-ups, so the attack on "feudal superstitions" mounted. In fact, 1963-65 saw a radicalization in the whole society that was reflected in the religious sphere by increasing pressure on church life. It was a more systematic process than during the Great Leap Forward, and is clearly related to the directive to criticize religion issued by Mao Zedong in 1963. Ya Hanzhang's moderate line could not survive the pressures, and he was forced to retreat from some of his positions, albeit to no avail. The debate in these years seems abstruse and muddled, and it certainly contributed nothing to the study of religion itself. It was, however, of crucial political importance for China's religious believers, and the rejection of Ya's position was reflected in increased suppression. By 1965 the United Front policy was finished, and events were moving inexorably towards the declaration of the Great Proletarian Cultural Revolution in early 1966. The most extreme statement of the new attitude towards religion was made in the foreword to a book on the history of Tang Buddhism published in 1965. The author of the foreword was a leading historian and an alternate member of the Eighth Central Committee, Fan Wenlan. He wrote:

> Religion . . . will not disappear of its own accord . . . [It] will rely on the force of custom to prolong its feeble existence and even plot to make a comeback. When a dying cobra bites a man, it can still wound or kill him. Therefore no matter how little of religion's vestigial poison remains, it is necessary to carry on a rigorous struggle against it on all fronts and to pull up and destroy all of its poisonous roots.[42]

The Great Proletarian Cultural Revolution

Leftist attitudes were reflected in many spheres of life as China moved towards the tragedy of the Cultural Revolution. Already attacks were mounting on writers and artists, and it was an article by Yao Wenyuan attacking Wu Han, the author of the play *Hai Rui Dismissed from Office*, on 10 November 1965, which can be seen as the opening salvo in the Cultural Revolution. Originally the Cultural Revolution was planned as an extension of the Socialist Education Movement, and in the autumn of 1965 the Mayor of Beijing, Peng Zhen, was asked by Mao to head up a small planning group. However, in February 1966 Peng refuted the criticism of Wu Han, thereby incurring the wrath of the leftist elements gathered around Mao's wife, Jiang Qing. The campaign against Peng began to turn the spotlight away from writers and "bourgeois elements" and towards what would later be called "top party elements taking the capitalist road". Mao, who until now had bided his time, in March sided with the left, and the outcome was the promulgation of the "May 16 Circular", in which the struggle against Peng Zhen was generalized to include many senior officials of the Party.

The events between May and the end of September witnessed a struggle for the control of the movement between what became known as the Cultural Revolution Small Group of Jiang Qing, Chen Boda, Kang Sheng, Yao Wenyuan, Zhang Qunqiao and later, Wang Hongwen, and the traditional Party hierarchy. Leftist pressure increased during June and Peng Zhen was dismissed. Mao's call to "Bombard the Headquarters" in his "big character" poster of May, and the Small Group's encouragement of student rebellion provoked a conservative response. The first Red Guard groups were formed from the children of senior officials, and their aim was to deflect the attack from their parents by choosing the traditionally vulnerable targets such as bourgeois intellectuals and religious believers. The resulting campaign against the "four olds" (old customs, old habits, old culture and old thinking) which continued until October was a reflection of the Party apparatus's attempt to control and deflect the growing leftist challenge. At the same time the left took the chance offered by the emergence of the Red Guards to create their own Red Guards, and Party control began to slip with the convening of the first of the huge Red Guard rallies in Beijing on 18 August. One million enthusiastic youngsters gathered to hail the "great helmsman" in the words of *The East is Red*:

> The East is red,
> The sun is rising,
> China has brought forth a Mao Zedong . . .

By October the initiative had passed to the Small Group and the radical Red Guard factions. In 1967 the "January Storm" saw the establishment of the Shanghai Commune and the assault on the Party's senior leadership. Party control broke;

the army vacillated; mass politics took to the streets, and chaos ensued. As one writer has expressed it:

> The net result of this type of politics was chaos and anarchy. After taking control from the hands of the élite, the Chinese masses were drawn directly and suddenly into the political process without the benefit of previous experience.[43]

The factional conflicts led to an eventual stalemate, and from September 1967 Mao adopted a policy of retrenchment. The search was now on for a means of harnessing the mass organizations behind the competing élites at the centre in a reconstructed Party. The solution that emerged in 1968, and which was enshrined in the Ninth Congress of the CCP in 1969, was the result of a compromise between the radicals of the Small Group, the Army, and the mass conservative groups. This uneasy coalition was probably led by the Army commander and designated successor to Mao, Lin Biao.

Overthrowing the Idols

The Red Guard assault on religion that began in August 1966 was, in one sense, merely the culmination of the process that had begun in 1957. The mass rally of 18 August was followed by several days of violence and terror on the streets of the capital as Red Guards went on the rampage. Their targets at this stage were the "four olds", and churches, temples and mosques came under attack alongside all symbols of traditional culture. Ornaments and furnishings were stripped from churches, and in the Protestant Rice Market Street Church a bust of Mao was placed in the middle of the sanctuary – an ironic comment on the religious fervour of the Red Guards' devotion to Chairman Mao. The following poster was stuck up on the walls of the Beijing YMCA:

> There is no God; there is no Spirit; there is no Jesus; there is no Mary; there is no Joseph. How can adults

believe in these things? . . . Priests live in luxury and
suck the blood of the workers . . . Like Islam and
Catholicism, Protestantism is a reactionary feudal
ideology, the opium of the people, with foreign origins
and contacts . . . We are atheists; we believe only in
Mao Zedong. We call on all people to burn Bibles,
destroy images, and disperse religious associations.[44]

Throughout the country the events in Beijing were imitated
by iconoclastic youngsters, believing that they were heralds
of the dawn of the Communist age. The very idea of the United
Front was an affront, and by the Spring of 1966 the cadres of
the United Front Work Department were under attack. Li
Weihan, its Director and the major architect of religious
policy, had been removed from all his posts. United Front
work cadres, including officials of the Religious Affairs
Bureaus throughout the country, were to be disgraced and
humiliated, accused of collaboration with reactionary
religious elements. Churches, mosques and temples were
forcibly closed from one end of the country to the other, with
only a few hundred mosques out of a total of 14,000 in Xinjiang
left open. Elsewhere, the destruction of public worship was
complete. Many buildings were used as Red Guard headquarters and were later to become factories, meeting halls,
offices and even residences. Others were destroyed. In Tibet
the Red Guards blew up the most prestigious and ancient
temples, and in China proper many historic religious sites
suffered varying degrees of damage. Simply from a cultural
point of view, it was a disaster of horrifying proportions. Some
things were saved through the intervention of Zhou Enlai,
who sent the Army to protect threatened sites, and many
ordinary citizens risked life and limb in order to hide relics
and scriptures. We have already had occasion to note how as
the Red Guards destroyed the Ricci tomb in Beijing, one
courageous person managed to rescue the gravestone (see
Chapter Two).

Trial by Fire

All religious personnel were forbidden to engage in religious activities and many were subjected to abuse and ill-treatment. Such abuse was conducted on an arbitrary basis, and it was much worse in some places than others. In the early stages many clergy and also lay believers had their homes ransacked, their religious books taken and burnt, and their movements and activities watched. As social chaos mounted so the tides of the factional struggles could sweep up people on a random basis. Priests, pastors, Buddhist monks, imams, found themselves sharing in manual labour with intellectuals, democrats, and disgraced Communist officials, including the former cadres of the Religious Affairs Bureaus. This shared suffering was to influence the future attitudes of many in more tranquil times. There is no doubt of the suffering experienced by Christians during these long years, but Christians were by no means the prime target of the persecutions. Zhao Fusan spoke on this matter in a lecture given in the Philippines in 1985:

> To the Christians, the Cultural Revolution served as a trial by fire – all the external things were taken away from them. One felt like being pushed against a wall and being asked about the very ultimate meaning of "being", not just one's work, not just of one's vocation, not just of the things that one loves. The question was raised directly at one's very existence, not only once in one's life but almost twenty-four hours a day for ten years. That is the period when every Christian learnt to ask these basic questions about himself and to remember what had been taught in the Bible; and he learnt to transcend personal gain or personal fame; he learnt to look at one's encounter and to look at the whole of the Cultural Revolution, then to understand the meaning of the prayers of Jesus Christ when he prayed "Lord forgive them for they know not what they do". Not to have a Bible at hand, but the

absence of which made the words and sentences of the Bible living messages. Not just for one or two or a few, but for a whole generation of Christians.

He also spoke of how, for the first time in Chinese history, Christians and non-Christians "all suffered alike" and so came into closer contact with one another.[45]

The little home meeting described in the story recorded by Raymond Fung stopped meeting, but:

One day, my neighbour's 14-15-year-old son with two friends wearing the Red Guard armbands, came to my door and quietly tipped me off about a "house confiscation" visit by Red Guards any time. I was so frightened I cried on the spot. The youngsters comforted me, told me it was routine, and that I should get rid of my Jesus things, although, as they hastened to add, "everyone on the block knows you are a Jesus believer". I prayed all night. My husband, who had never joined me in the meetings, also broke down and prayed. He told me to get rid of the ivory cross. So I hid it in the charcoal pile in the kitchen. Three days later they arrived, over forty of them, most standing outside, bearing small placards on which was painted a single character "loyalty". The leaders were nervous, but tried to be cool and firm. They announced their purpose was to eliminate the "four olds", but not "old mamas". They bowed in front of my Mao poster and searched the place. They found the ivory cross with ease. The leader took it right in front of me, moved his young head in mock pity, let the cross fall and crushed it with his foot. I was too scared to react . . . My Bibles and hymns and several other books were also confiscated. The leaders left. Then the others came in and took away all my valuables and furniture, leaving only two chairs and a table, saying: "You have too much, others have none". Several days later, two families moved into my house. One occupied the now empty second bedroom, and the other placed themselves in the corridor.[46]

This woman's experience was repeated time and again. Life would not return to normal until after 1978.

Others faced more severe difficulties, especially the leaders of the Three Self Movement – one wall poster described the Three Self as "a conspiracy between Liu Shaoqi and Y.T. Wu". The extent of the persecution depended on the pattern of local factional struggle. The Christians of Fuzhou City were unlucky, and in February 1967, or possibly even earlier, the Protestant leadership was imprisoned after being paraded through the streets. Those reported as being arrested included Bishop Michael Zhang Guangxu, his assistant bishops Moses Xue Pingxi and Liu Yucang, and his secretary Yang Weizhong, Dr James Ding Xiancheng, a leading Methodist and others.[47] Bishop Zhang died on 12 May 1973. Many people were able to attend the funeral on 14 May but official acknowledgement of the suffering he and others endured was not made until 1981, when on 3 April a memorial meeting was held to "commemorate the cruel and bitter death" during the Cultural Revolution of Bishop Zhang Guangxu and Mr Chen Zhimei, the former Chairman of the Fuzhou Three Self Committee. A service of remembrance at the Flower Lane Church was held for Michael Zhang, Bishop Liu Yucang, Pastor You Ruilin and Dr James Ding. There is no doubt that their deaths were the result of persecution, but it must not be forgotten that their story is only one of a countless number that could be told. The terrible deaths of senior Party leaders such as Liu Shaoqi and Tao Zhu have been told in detail in the Chinese press in recent years. Others, including Deng Xiaoping, survived after enduring immense hardship – Deng's son Deng Pufang was crippled for life, and has become the foremost advocate of welfare for the handicapped in the 1980s.

Bishop Zhang's story can be seen as symbolic of the transformation experienced by thousands of other Christians. He was the most outstanding Christian leader in North Fujian and, as David Paton remembers, in early 1947 when they first met, Michael Zhang seemed more interested in Anglican events outside China than with what was going on in Beijing.

But as political events speeded up, his attitude soon changed and with typical foresight he appointed as his Secretary Yang Weizhong, a young man who, unlike most Christians in Fuzhou, sensed the way the nation was going. Despite his earlier denunciation of David Paton, in 1956 he started writing to the Patons and it was very evident in the years since Liberation he had been changed and deepened, not only in his political understanding but in his Christian convictions. After his terrible experiences in the Cultural Revolution one Chinese friend told David Paton that he considered that Michael had become a saint. He was probably right.

There is some evidence that the Cultural Revolution saw the adoption of a more systematic campaign against religion. In 1981 the Director of the restored Religious Affairs Bureau, Xiao Xianfa, spoke of a campaign to destroy religion (*xiaomie zongjiao*), promoted by Xie Fuzhi, Deputy Premier and Minister of Public Security during the Cultural Revolution until his fall from power in early 1968. No further details are known, but it helps to account for the fact that after the initial Red Guard campaign against the "four olds" had come to an end, religion was not allowed to re-emerge throughout the period of the Cultural Revolution (1966-76).

The Church in our Hearts

In China there are always exceptions. In March 1967, in the radical stronghold of Shanghai, an Austrian journalist, Louis Barcata, was taken to the northern suburbs of the city to a Catholic church where around a hundred people were gathered to hear Mass celebrated by an elderly priest. The priest told him that he was permitted to say Mass once a week by the Anti-Religious Combat Office in Shanghai. He said that he knew of two similar congregations in the city.[48] It is a strange report, and certainly there can have been few such congregations in China at that time. How long it survived is a matter for conjecture. Yet, in some places, especially in the countryside, people never stopped meeting for quiet worship. One of the stories told to Raymond Fung recounts how the

Cultural Revolution never really affected the village and how the home meeting continued throughout with 100-150 people present each week. Nor were their Bibles ever taken away.[49] It is all too easy to generalize about China – there must have been many communities barely touched by the more extreme manifestations of the factional struggles of the mid-1960s. Nevertheless, it remains true that, at best, religion could only be expressed privately and that even those groups who managed to continue meeting did so in isolation, without access to books and teaching. As one Christian later expressed it "we had no Church but the Church in our hearts".

In Lingdong, Shantou, the Cultural Revolution led to the destruction or confiscation of church property, burning of Bibles, hymn books and church records and to personal attacks. In Shantou City church leaders were paraded with dunce's caps, forced to stand all day in the hot sun in front of the ransacked West City Church, and ridiculed. At the same time the Religious Affairs Bureau appears to have continued functioning and "thanks to the mutual trust which existed between the church leaders and the RAB, a factory was established within the old mission compound which provided employment for some ministers and preachers who might otherwise have become destitute".[50] As time went on this became a common method of providing employment for religious personnel. Sometimes such factories or farms were run by leaders from all the major religions, an invaluable ecumenical experience that has contributed to the new feeling of mutual respect to be found amongst the different faiths. It also helped to heal the traditional hostility between Catholics and Protestants.

Needless to say, not all Christians were able to survive the pressures of the Cultural Revolution. There are stories of courageous witness, like the old lady who prayed outside the closed gates of the Community Church in Shanghai every Christmas throughout the years until it re-opened in 1979, but there are also stories of denying the faith and of the betrayal of fellow Christians. As the churches re-opened after 1979 the question of the re-acceptance of those who had failed in these ways was an urgent one. This sensitive issue has been handled by recalling that in the New Testament there is the story of the betrayal of Judas, but also that of the denial by Peter and his acceptance of forgiveness. For the vast majority the Cultural Revolution was a time to bend with the storm, like the bamboo, and so survive. As one Beijing pastor told a visiting British Methodist in 1981:

> We were not good shepherds and during those ten years were like the apostles – we became afraid. Like Peter, we denied our Lord. So we have seen ourselves to be very weak. But we have discovered that Christ is True and Alive! We have discovered that he is in heaven praying for us.[51]

It was a quiet and hidden faithfulness through a time when Christians found themselves suffering with their neighbours; a time of purgation. In 1958 Zhao Fusan wrote in *Essays in Anglican Self-Criticism*:[52]

> We did not weep with them that wept in old China, neither do we rejoice with them who rejoice in the new. We seem to have become pitiful strangers in our own country and among our own people.

Now indeed Christians were able to share in the suffering, so that Bishop Ting could speak these words in the chapel of Lambeth Palace on 1 October 1982:

> How strongly many Chinese Christians feared at the time of the Liberation in 1949 that we were losing so many things dear to us, only to find later they were mostly just excess baggage. But it was during the Cultural Revolution, which turned out to be quite anti-cultural and not much of a revolution either, that the Chinese people suffered so much and we Christians suffered so much with them. We felt the Gospel to be something precious, but the Red Guards and the so-called rebels thought of it as nothing but a poisonous weed. We had no means of communicating it or of answering the

attacks in the big-character posters. Not a single church remained open. There was no government organ to protect us from lawlessness. We had no rebel group of our own to support us, nor any bandwagon to ride on. It would be fortunate if we could just worship in a small group in a home. We were very weak indeed, a little flock. By all human reckoning Christianity, perhaps for the fourth time in Chinese history, was again breathing its last breath. What we were blind to was that when we were weak and dying life was in the offing.[53]

A Sort of Calm

The year 1968 saw an end of the first storms of the Cultural Revolution. The CCP now sought to re-establish a degree of order and stability within society. The upshot was an uneasy compromise between the remaining members of the Party hierarchy; the powerful provincial army commanders; the central military group around Lin Biao; and the Cultural Revolution left. The rise of the "revolutionary committees" as temporary organs of local power was accompanied by the dissolution of the mass organizations and the "sending down" of huge numbers of young people to the countryside. The Twelfth Plenum of the Eighth Central Committee that opened on 11 October was enlarged with representatives from the provincial revolutionary committees and by the members of the Cultural Revolution Small Group. In fact, the Party had been almost destroyed, many of its most senior and experienced leaders eliminated or in disgrace, only nominally in command of the Army which was the only organization to remain intact, and with Party "leftists" in control of the organs of progaganda, education and culture. The Ninth Party Congress that met, eight years late, in April 1969, reflected the interests of these groups, with one quarter of the membership of the new Central Committee coming from the Army and with Lin Biao dominating the proceedings. The Congress nominated him as Mao's successor. The Standing Committee of the Political Bureau clearly had supreme power and its membership was reduced from seven to five: Mao Zedong, Lin Biao, Zhou Enlai, Chen Boda and Kang Sheng. Of these, only Zhou represented the moderates, surviving through his skilful riding of the storm and his administrative ability, which Mao recognized as indispensable.

The Ninth Congress marks an important stage in the Cultural Revolution. Mass politics was at an end. From now on the struggle was between factions at the top, supported by key provincial army and political leaders. A degree of stability returned to the country. As we shall see, the next few years were to see the coming of new life to the Church. There had been a profound change in people's consciousness during these years, a change that gathered momentum in the remaining years of the Cultural Revolution. The CCP had lost its authority: shattered as an effective organization, its rebuilding in 1969 was only at the top level. Its middle and local level officials were demoralized or caught up in factional struggles; the people disillusioned. The loss of authority was perhaps the most telling long-term result of the Cultural Revolution for it was not a mere loss of political authority. In a China still dominated by a traditional understanding of the nature of government, in which the State is seen as the mediator of moral values, the CCP up to 1966 was regarded by the majority of people as the legitimate and final arbiter of moral authority. This tradition reached its climax in the apotheosis of Mao and his Thought in the late 1960s.

The collapse of the mass rebellion, and the re-imposition of authority through the use of the Army and the revolutionary committees, accompanied by the dismissal of the Red Guards to the countryside, brought a rapid end to the cult of Mao and the beginning of the end of traditional attitudes towards government. When the CCP finally re-emerged as a viable organization – which in a sense did not really happen until

1978 – its relationship to the people of China was no longer, at root, a traditional one. From now on it would have to rule by consent, even though on the surface the structures bore a close resemblance to those of the 1950s. Its relationship to society was to become far closer to that of a Western government in the sense that it was contractual – based on a tacit agreement that in return for political loyalty it would guarantee the people's livelihood and seek to achieve certain long-term objectives. Of course, many traditional attitudes would persist, the existence and nature of the contract would not be acknowledged, and many in the CCP would seek to restore the former position and status of the Party. Nevertheless, the comparative freedom within post-Mao China, and, for example, the re-emergence of a revamped and revivified United Front as a central instrument of policy, are pointers to the fundamental change in social awareness that has resulted from the events of the Cultural Revolution.

For Christians the Cultural Revolution was also a turning point. The past, with its ambiguities, could begin to be put behind them. There was to be a new relationship to Chinese society, based on shared experiences, both of a real liberation from foreign control and the cycle of famine and disease with its accompanying social problems; and of a shared suffering. As Bishop Ting told Professor Lapwood in 1964:

> There is a spiritual hunger that no material achievement can satisfy. At present many people may not feel it. But man cannot in the end avoid thinking of his relationship with God. We have this essential and unique message, and it is our responsibility to witness to it. But that does not mean that we stand over against our national plans and spirit. We must communicate with our people from *within* our society. So we speak as patriots and Christians . . .[54]

The problem for Christians before 1966 was how to speak of their faith in such a way as to be listened to. After 1969 many were anxious to listen. Facing the Church once more, in a profound and urgent sense, was the question of how to speak the Word of God to a China both ancient and new; to a society looking to the future but deeply influenced by her past; to a culture searching for new forms of expression, yet uncertain of her relationship to the richness of her past cultural traditions.

In 1956 Bishop Ronald Hall of Hong Kong and his wife Nora visited Beijing. Bishop Timothy Lin Xianyang of Beijing took them to the Altar and Temple of Heaven. Bishop Hall tells of their experience:

> It was to the Altar of Heaven rather than to the Cathedral we all three needed first to go. My wife and I were amazed how much we had forgotten of its incredible beauty, dignity, simplicity and grandeur. For here in that simple arithmetic of all pure art and true religion is recorded how God's demand for obedience and self-naughting in national life, have been answered by his Chinese people.
>
> Here, the Bishop told us, he often comes to meditate on "the mysterious meaning of the ancient history of his people; and on God's demands today upon the Chinese people and the Chinese Church".
>
> He prayed for us and for his people as we stood together there on that Altar where the Emperor as the Father of his people made the annual offering to Heaven of the whole nation and all the varied pattern of its earthly life. The Bishop prayed for God's mercy, upon his people and upon the Chinese Church. As he prayed the soft rain, so much loved of farmers for its growing powers, began to fall upon us, reminding us of the quality of God's mercy which falls as the gentle dew from heaven.[55]

Timothy Lin was accused and denounced in 1966. He died some time in the Cultural Revolution. On 27 September 1980 the government sponsored a memorial meeting for him at the

Babaoshan cemetery where the heroes of the revolution are buried. His widow wrote to Bishop Baker of Hong Kong, "I think Timothy, who is now in heaven, must be very much delighted at this particular moment, and his soul at rest".

REFERENCES

1. Fung, Raymond, *Households of God on China's Soil*, World Council of Churches, Geneva 1982.
2. Mao Zedong, *Preface to Socialist Upsurge in China's Countryside*, Foreign Languages Press, Beijing 1957.
3. Mao Zedong, Speech at the CCP Conference on Progaganda Work, Foreign Languages Press, Beijing 1966.
4. Deng Xiaoping, text in *Communist China 1955-1959: Policy Documents with Analysis*, Harvard University Press, 1962, p. 349.
5. MacFarquhar, Roderick, *The Origins of the Cultural Revolution, Part I: Contradictions Among the People 1956-57*, Oxford University Press, 1974, p. 311.
6. Guillemaz, Jacques, *The Chinese Communist Party in Power 1949-76*, Westview Press, Boulder, Colorado 1976, p. 207.
7. Wickeri, *Seeking the Common Ground*, pp. 170-81, for the text of Li Weihan's speech and detailed analysis.
8. Chen Chonggui, Documents, pp. 151-1.
9. Shen Derong, "My Understanding of Blooming and Contending", *Tian Feng*, 531, 24 June 1957, which is based on Cheng Zhiming's views. Wickeri, op. cit., pp. 338-9.
10. *Tian Feng*, 29 July 1957, Wickeri, op. cit., p. 339.
11. *China Bulletin*, Vol. 7, No. 17, 30 September 1957.
12. *China Bulletin*, Vol. 7, No. 19, 28 October 1957.
13. Wickeri, op. cit., p. 340.
14. *China Bulletin*, Vol. 8, No. 13, July 1958, and No. 16, 22 September 1958.
15. Personal conversation in 1983.
16. *Tian Feng*, 5 May 1958, translated in *China Bulletin*, Vol. 8, No. 15, 8 September 1958.
17. *China Bulletin*, Vol. 9, No. 18, 12 October 1959.
18. ibid.
19. Translated *China Bulletin*, Vol. 9, No. 19, 26 October 1959.
20. *Tian Feng*, 22 September 1958, translated Wickeri, op. cit., pp. 425-6.
21. Wickeri, op. cit., p. 347.
22. Fung, op. cit., pp. 1-2.
23. Chen Zemin, "The Task of Theological Construction in the Chinese Church" (II), *Nanjing Theological Review*, August 1957.
24. Ting, K.H., "A Rationale for Three Self", September 1984, reproduced *CSP Bulletin*, No. 28, November 1985.
25. Chen Zemin, op. cit., translated in Wickeri, Philip L., *Theological Re-orientation in Chinese Protestantism 1949-84, Part I, Ching Feng*, Vol. 28, No. 1, March 1985.

26. Ting, K.H., "On Christian Theism", translation by Jones, F.P., as amended by Lutley, A.F., privately circulated paper 1957.
27. Ting, K.H., "Another Look at Three Self", *Tian Feng*, February 1983, p. 7.
28. Ting, K.H., "Religious Policy and Theological Re-orientation in China", address at Toronto School of Theology, October 1979. Reproduced in *CSP Bulletin*, No. 13, July 1980.
29. Balthasar, Hans Urs von, *The Glory of the Lord, A Theological Aesthetics:*, Vol. 2, *Studies in Theological Style: Clerical Styles*, T. & T. Clark, Edinburgh 1984, pp. 80-1.
30. Translated by Trivière, Leon, *China Missionary Bulletin* M.E.P., Hong Kong, Nos. 114, 115, 118 July-November 1958.
31. Bush, Richard C., Jr., *Religion in Communist China*, Abingdon Press, Nashville, Tennessee 1970.
32. *China Missionary Bulletin*, June 1958.
33. *Ad Apostolorum Principis, The Pope Speaks*, Vol. 5, No. 2, Spring 1959, pp. 195-7.
34. *Fides*, 5 September 1964, p. 525, quoted Bush, op. cit., p. 145.
35. Baum, Richard, *Prelude to Revolution: Mao, The Party and the Peasant Question, 1962-66*, Columbia, 1975.
36. "The Church in Ningbo: Recovery and Reconciliation", *Bridge* No. 7, September 1984, p. 14.
37. Lapwood, Ralph, China Diary, 1964, privately circulated.
38. Ren Jiyu, "Investigate Religion and Criticize Theology", *Guangming Ribao*, 27 September 1977, translated Ching Feng, Vol. 20, No. 3, 1977.
39. NCNA, in Chinese, 25 April 1978, BBC SWB FE 5800, 28 April 1978.
40. For details of the debate see the collection of key articles in MacInnis, Donald E., *Religious Policy and Practice in Communist China, A Documentary History*, Hodder and Stoughton, London 1972, Section 3. See also *China Notes*, Vol. 2, No. 5, October 1964, and Vol. 3, No. 4, October 1965.
41. Liang Hao and Yang Zhen, *Xinjianshe*, 20 December 1965, MacInnis, op. cit., p. 69f.
42. *Xinjianshe*, 20 October 1965, translated Welch, Holmes, *Buddhism Under Mao*, Harvard University Press, 1972, p. 360.
43. Lee, Hong Yung, *The Politics of the Chinese Cultural Revolution: A Case Study*, University of California Press, 1978, p. 8.
44. *Current Scene*, 31 May 1967, US Consulate, Hong Kong.
45. Zhao Fusan, *The Past Forty Years in Christianity in China*, Carino, Theresa C., ed., Three Lectures by Zhao Fusan, China Studies Program, De La Salle University, Manila 1986.
46. Fung, op. cit., pp. 3-4.
47. *China Notes*, Vol. 5, No. 2, April 1967, quoting *Ecumenical Press Service*, 23 February 1967.
48. Barcata, Louis, The Catholic Church in Shanghai, *China Notes*, Vol. 6, No. 3, July 1968.
49. Fung, op. cit., p. 44.
50. Hood, George, *Mission Accomplished?*, p. 277.
51. Kan Xueqing to the Rev. Geoffrey Senior, April 1981.
52. Zhao Fusan, "Penitence and Renewal in China", Paton, David M., ed., *Essays in Anglican Self-Criticism*, SCM Press, London 1958.

53. Ting, K.H., Address in Lambeth Palace Chapel, 1 October 1982, *The Church in China*, British Council of Churches, 1983.
54. As quoted by Lapwood, op. cit.
55. Quoted in Paton, David M., *"R.O.": The Life and Times of Bishop Ronald Hall of Hong Kong*, Diocese of Hong Kong & Macao and the Hong Kong Diocesan Association, Alan Sutton Publishing Ltd., Gloucester 1985, pp. 182-3.

VIII

A Hidden Seed
1970-1980

What is of all things most yielding can
overwhelm that which is most hard. Being
substanceless, it can enter in even where
there is no crevice. That is how I know the
value of action which is actionless. But that
there can be teaching without words, value
in action which is actionless, few indeed
can understand.[1]

Dao De Jing

The Hopeless Years 1970-76

A Moderate Interlude

The Ninth Congress had ended with an uneasy alliance of the
various factions within the leadership of the CCP and the
Army. A semblance of normality returned to the country, and
the laborious task of rebuilding the Party and government
organs began. Mao and Zhou were now pushing for the
rehabilitation of some of those attacked in the height of the
Cultural Revolution, and at the Second Plenum (23 August to
6 September 1970) the radicals led by Lin Biao and Chen Boda
came into conflict with Mao, enabling the more moderate
position of Zhou to gain ground. By April 1971 Chen Boda was
removed and later denounced as a Guomindang agent,
Trotskyist renegade and secret agent! The Cultural Revolution
Small Group was no more. The internal Party struggle
intensified in the next few months, leading to the still myster-

ious events of September 1971. Lin Biao, his wife and son, with six other people, were killed when their plane crashed in the Mongolian People's Republic on 13 September. It was only in 1973 at the Tenth Congress of the CCP that Zhou Enlai officially announced that Lin Biao had been plotting a coup d'état in which he planned to assassinate Chairman Mao.

The result of these events was the gradual re-assertion of more moderate policies, although leftism still dominated all areas of life. As important cadres were quietly rehabilitated so the left found itself under threat. Jiang Qing and her allies had not been directly associated with Lin Biao so they were able to distance themselves from him after his death, but despite their control of the media and of cultural and educational life, their actual power base was small. The next few years were to witness the rising conflict between them and the veterans around Zhou Enlai. However, for the time being, there was a lull, and in 1972 China experienced a period of relative calm. It was the year of the American President Richard Nixon's visit, an event that marked the beginning of a decisive shift in China's international role and status, that by the 1980s had significantly altered the terms of the world balance of power.

Public Religious Life

One looks in vain for any signs of relaxation on the religious front from 1969 to 1971. There were, however, a few small concessions to international feeling. On 28 February 1969 at the Dongsi Mosque in Beijing the festival of Corban (Id Al-adha) was celebrated with the participation of members of the diplomatic staff from Asian and African countries.[2] In 1971 a New China News Agency report stated that they "exchanged festival greetings with Chinese Muslims".[3] It was also reported that "leading members of the Islamic Association of China" attended a banquet in honour of Yahya Khan, President of Pakistan.[4] According to two Canadian visitors to the Dongsi Mosque in June 1971, Friday worship had been resumed for the Chinese Muslim community in the city, a major retreat from the attitudes of a year or two before.[5]

The Chinese government clearly wished to improve its international image. China was proclaiming herself as the natural leader of the Third World and was seeking entry into the United Nations. Moreover, the remarkable decision to seek the normalization of relations with the U.S.A. meant that religious policy, and in particular, policy towards Christianity, assumed considerable diplomatic importance. The freeing of Bishop James Walsh from prison in July 1970 was, with hindsight, an essential prelude to the process of normalization. This was followed by the release of a number of Chinese priests in April 1971, suggesting that diplomatic considerations were perhaps linked to the desire for some internal relaxation. The possible restoration of the Religious Affairs Bureau in January 1970 under Xiao Xianfa, its previous head since July 1961, also suggests that a limited amount of religious activity by Chinese was to be allowed.[6] The definite resumption of the Bureau's work was only reported in May 1973, but it can be assumed that its actual revival had indeed taken place earlier.

The resumption of Chinese Muslim worship in 1971 was followed by the re-opening of the Southern Cathedral (Nantang) in Beijing. A high-ranking Italian visitor, Vittorius Colombo, was able to attend Mass on Saturday 20 November in the company of about thirty Chinese worshippers. The celebrant was the Vicar-General of Beijing Diocease, Thomas Wang Jiting.[7] Subsequent visitors' reports indicated that the services were held on a regular basis in the cathedral, although Chinese attendance dropped to one woman in 1974 when the leftists launched the campaign against Confucius. The first Protestant service resumed at Easter 1972 at the Rice Market Street Church, but unlike the Catholic service, it appears to have been set up in response to a request from a British diplomat.[8] There were two pastors, Yin Jizeng and Kan Xueqing, accompanied by an official of the city TSPM, Ms Wang Yuhua, together with a handful of foreigners and two or three Chinese members of the congregation.

The next few months saw a number of foreign visitors to Beijing who were able to meet with a small number of Catholic and Protestant leaders in the capital. On 20 August the author and his wife spoke with a joint group at the Nantang, and in early September Dr John Fleming of St Andrew's, Scotland, attended the Rice Market Church, and also had a meeting at the Nantang. Little information emerged from any of these meetings beyond the fact that there were said to be around five hundred Protestants and five to six thousand Catholics in the city. There were references to another Catholic church being open, and to other services being held in the city on weekdays. It was obvious that none of the Chinese present had any clue as to the religious situation in the rest of the country. They were, however, anticipating the gradual restoration of religious activities, thereby helping to confirm that the opening of Beijing churches and mosques had been intended as the first stage in a more general relaxation.

There were other important, if inconclusive, pointers to this. In the same year one privileged foreign visitor, John Strong, grand-nephew to Anna Louise Strong, one of China's most well-known foreign residents, was able to visit ten Buddhist monasteries in various parts of China, as well as the offices of the Buddhist Associations in Beijing, Xi'an and Guangzhou. The Lama monastery in Beijing, the Yonghegong, was functioning, and he found signs of ongoing religious life elsewhere. Zhao Puchu, head of the Chinese Buddhist Association, had reappeared in public the previous year, and in his talk with John Strong expressed the hope that the situation might continue to improve.[9] In May 1973 a delegation of Japanese Buddhists actually arrived in China and toured eleven monasteries in eight cities, finding resident monks in all but one – but no lay people.[10] A similar visit took place in April 1974.

A further indication of the more relaxed atmosphere in 1972 was the re-establishment of contacts with senior Christian leaders. Until November 1972 it had proved impossible for any visitor to meet with Christians outside of Beijing, and visitors to Nanjing had failed to make contact with Bishop Ting. Then, on 6 September, it was reported that Bishop Ting and Wu Yifang had been present at the funeral of He Xiangning,

Honorary President of the National Women's Federation.[11] In mid-November Miss Maud Russell, former YWCA secretary in China, was able to meet the Tings and Wu Yifang. In Shanghai she met with Y.T. Wu and Liu Liangmo. Ting and Y.T. Wu both met with Doak Barnett, a leading American Sinologist and son of a former YMCA secretary, and he attended the first Christmas service at the Beijing Church since 1966.

James Endicott made a visit to China in January and February and was able to go to Sichuan, a province closed to foreigners in these years owing to the intense factional conflicts and consequent economic decline. Re-visiting his old haunts and talking with old friends convinced him that Christianity too was on the decline. He found no evidence of Christian worship, and his limited discussions made him "speculate that from now on there will be fewer and fewer young people who will feel the need to 'become Christian' in the usual meaning of that term". He felt this was due to a general acceptance of Marxism and commented:

> It can be argued that the prevailing standards and practices of the Cultural Revolution are those which are loosely called the principles of the Sermon on the Mount.[12]

The only future for Christianity might be as "a non-institutionalized religion" and more family- and lay-centred.

The Anti-Confucius Campaign

Endicott's perception of the situation in China was, of course, far off the reality. The period of relaxation following on the death of Lin Biao and the Nixon visit was marked by attacks on Lin Biao for his "leftism". However, in early 1973 the criticism suddenly changed tack, and he was accused of being a rightist and a follower of Confucius. In August a full-scale campaign was launched against Confucius, a thinly-veiled attack on Premier Zhou Enlai. The absurdities of the anti-Confucius campaign need not detain us. The Tenth CCP Congress, which met from 24 to 28 August 1973, marked another swing to the left. The appointments to key Party positions represented the usual attempt to straddle the differences within the leadership, but the continued rise to prominence of the Shanghai radicals around Jiang Qing, Zhang Qunqiao, Yao Wenyuan and Wang Hongwen (who was abruptly promoted from ordinary membership to be a Party vice-chairman), was an indication of the continued leftist strength. The Congress also, however, saw the re-appearance of distinguished victims of the Cultural Revolution such as Deng Xiaoping – thereby preparing the ground for the major conflict that broke out in late 1975. Behind the scenes throughout the rather uneventful year of 1974, the moderates were preparing a series of policies designed to shift China away from the leftist line. As the administrators returned to office they noted with consternation the problems in the economy, in education and cultural life, in provincial and local government. The convening of the Fourth National People's Congress, ten years late, in January 1975, was a triumph for Zhou, and he was able to use the Congress to promote an ambitious new economic programme, the Four Modernizations (agriculture, industry, national defence and science and technology). Thus by early 1975 the political pendulum appeared to be swinging once more towards moderation. The Chinese people had had enough of leftist slogans, and longed for greater prosperity and an end to political tension, and the suppression of criticism.

Christian China-Watchers

Endicott was not alone, however, in his romantic but mistaken understanding of the Cultural Revolution. His views were shared to a greater or lesser extent by a good number of radical Western Christians who were impressed by the image of Cultural Revolution China. In 1974 a major ecumenical seminar was held at Båstad, Sweden on the "Theological Implications of the New China", and it was followed in September 1974 by a Colloquium in Louvain attended by ninety people from twenty-two countries.[13] Both meetings reflected a wide range of opinion, but there was considerable emphasis on such questions as "the new man in China". Much scorn has been poured upon the concerns of these meetings in recent years, and it must be acknowledged that, in the light of what we now know, the preoccupation with the theological implications of Mao's China seems to have been founded on a profound mis-perception. And yet . . . in another sense these and similar discussions represented a stage in the changing understanding of China amongst churches that until then had not even begun to come to terms with Chinese Marxism or the implications of the Chinese Revolution for their own theology of mission. David Paton's radical challenge to the Western Church in *Christian Missions and the Judgement of God*[14] had not been faced. Too many of those who criticised the naïvety of the views of Endicott and others had themselves never felt the real challenge of Marxism to Christian faith and could not, therefore, begin to understand the attitudes and activities of the majority of Christian leaders in China since Liberation. The acceptance that Chinese Marxism could challenge one's own Christian faith, even though there was a great deal of fantasy involved, was a first step in the new beginning that began to emerge in relationships between Chinese Christians and the non-Catholic churches in the rest of the world after 1979.

Endicott's belief that the future of Christianity in China was one of decline was also widely shared both within China and outside. It was, of course, an argument based on ignorance for no one really knew what was happening in different parts of the country. The Chinese media were dominated by leftists, and the propaganda maintained that the new Maoist person had no need of "superstition". Moreover, the rhetoric about the death of religion was all the more credible in view of the steady decline in public religious life before the Cultural Revolution and the apparent failure to attract young people. It would not be the first time, after all, that Christianity had simply faded from the Chinese scene.

Bishop Ting Meets Foreign Christians

Bishop Ting became the major Christian figure to meet with visiting foreign Christians in the next few years. In April 1973 and again in the same month two years later he met with the Rev. Ted Johnson of the Presbyterian Church of Canada,[15] and in August 1975 he had a second meeting with John Fleming. His own opinions were not dissimilar to Endicott's with regard to the future of the Church in China. He stressed the informality of Christian life; its emphasis on lay leadership; its suspicion of church buildings as symbols of Western domination; and of clerical control. Christianity is now "a world view of those who adhere to a biblical faith".[16] The family has become the main locus for religious teaching. Ting himself believed throughout this period that Christianity was declining, and in an interview with Eugene Stockwell on 22 October 1976, just after the arrest of the "Gang of Four", he responded to a question about whether Christianity would die out of China:

> I would not be too surprised if that were to be the case, but I think there are bound to be people, if in small numbers, who with all their political enthusiasm will still believe that it is Christian faith and teaching that will give them answers about ultimate questions . . . But such people will be few.[17]

The Nanjing Theological Seminary had been used as a Red Guard headquarters at the height of the Cultural Revolution. Half the faculty stayed to tend the seminary buildings while the other half were sent to work on a commune near the city. In 1973 Ting was hopeful that some sort of work could re-start in 1974, but in 1975 it was evident that little had happened, although some faculty members were involved in exploring training possibilities amongst home meetings.[18] The Church in Nanjing consisted of around two hundred and fifty members meeting informally, but quite openly, in homes or schools.

It is important to place all these foreign visitors' reports into perspective. At the time the reports were seized on in the West by people anxious for some news about the Church in China, and this has given them a greater significance than they warrant. In fact they impart a very limited amount of information. They tell us that in 1972 there was some relaxation internally and that this had a limited positive effect on public religious expression. However, expectations that 1973-74 might see a more sustained relaxation were not realized. International factors played a key role in the 1972 opening up and in the contacts made by foreigners until after 1976. While these were probably not the only reasons for the limited degree of freedom given to a small number of religious leaders to meet with foreign church people, they played a considerable role.

The reports also tell us that whatever Christian activity was continuing, it took an informal and low-key form. Outside of the Beijing churches (for the foreign diplomatic and student community) the home meeting was the only possible type of gathering for worship. Bishop Ting was quite clear that the two churches had been re-opened for foreigners.[19] Ting's personal experience was limited to Nanjing, and here he was able to report on the existence of on-going home meetings, which, at least in 1975, met openly. His more general impressions of church decline were understandable but, in the event, wrong. On the other hand, his emphasis on a lay, non-institutional, form of Christianity was obviously true to his Nanjing experience, and even today, after the revival of church structures, remains an important dimension of Protestant life. Outside of Beijing and Nanjing, we simply have no information from these reports, other than the negative information that there were no indications of church life elsewhere. It is no wonder that the outside world concluded that Christiananity in China was on the way out!

Deng Xiaoping's "Right Deviationist Wind"

After the Fourth National People's Congress in January 1975 Deng Xiaoping, working closely with Zhou Enlai, now a sick man, gradually took over the work of government. He soon appointed his supporters to the top positions in seven provinces, and he convened a series of national meetings to deal with the problems of the economy and defence. In the autumn he prepared three outspoken policy documents. The most important, "On the General Programme of All Work for the Party and the Country" was, according to one astute diplomatic observer, "a clear signal that Deng was preparing an assault on the legion of left-wing dogmatists who had prospered because of the Cultural Revolution".[20] The document was dated 7 October 1975 but the leftist counter-attack had already started in March with an attack by Yao Wenyuan on "empiricism".

The Tiananmen Incident

Throughout the autumn of 1975 the counter-attack on what was termed the "right deviationist wind" mounted, with Mao's support, but it might have come to nothing if it had not been for Zhou Enlai's death in January 1976. During February and March the leftist campaign grew, but so did the frustration of the people. When on 25 March a Shanghai newspaper dared to refer to Zhou as a "capitalist-roader" the tide of discontent swelled and burst into a series of demonstrations that began in Nanjing and reached their peak in the famous Tiananmen incident in the great square in the very centre of Beijing. It was the time of the Qing Ming Festival when Chinese people traditionally honour their dead, and in at least fourteen provinces the festival was used as an opportunity both to mourn Zhou and to demonstrate dislike of the leftists. Foreign eye-witnesses to the Tiananmen events have testified to their dignity and courage in the face of almost certain suppression. From 30 March to 4 April the mourners came in their thousands, carrying wreaths, pledging themselves to defend Zhou and his ideas. Spokesmen of the groups or organizations who came gave eulogies, frequently in the form of a poem. One of these read:

> Devils howl as we pour out our grief,
> We weep but the wolves laugh,

We shed our blood in memory of the hero,
Raising our heads, we unsheath our swords.[21]

The targets of the crowds were very clear: Jiang Qing, Yao Wenyuan and Zhang Qunqiao, and Mao himself. As Roger Garside has written:

The political heart of China had been occupied by forces fighting for a vision that rivalled Mao's. The essential message of the flowers was simple: the Mandate of Heaven had been removed from Mao.[22]

In the early hours of 5 April the wreaths were removed by the municipal authorities. In the course of the day the tension mounted and there were various violent incidents, until in the evening the Workers Militia were set on the crowd, beating the unarmed protestors. As many as one hundred may have died; thousands were arrested. Two days later Deng Xiaoping was stripped of all his posts and the Tiananmen incident condemned as "counter-revolutionary". It was a signal for chaos. Mao's own health was rapidly declining, there were strikes in industry, peasants restored individual farming, the Cultural Revolution "fighting groups" re-emerged, and provincial officials were attacked and even kidnapped. Mao died on 9 September and an uncanny calm descended as the nation waited. At the funeral on 16 September the eulogy was delivered by Hua Guofeng, Mao's chosen successor, in the presence of all the senior leadership, including the leftists. On 6 October Wang Hongwen, Zhang Qunqiao, Yao Wenyuan and Jiang Qing were arrested. On 12 October the world knew of the arrests, and by 14 October of the existence of the "Gang of Four".

Roger Garside tells of his visit to the Rice Market Church in Beijing on Sunday 17 October. He noticed that the English version of the service-sheet had a different reading from the Chinese. He writes:

My religious sentiments were overwhelmed by my China-watcher's habits. This was most obviously a last-minute change, unique in my experience of that most meticulously planned church . . . I could hardly contain my curiosity to know which passage the Chinese minister would read . . . It was from Romans 3, "None is righteous, no, not one; no one understands, no one seeks for God. All have turned aside, together they have gone wrong; no one does good, not even one. Their throat is an open grave, they use their tongues to deceive. The venom of asps is under their lips. Their mouth is full of curses and bitterness. Their feet are swift to shed blood, in their paths are ruin and misery, and the way of peace they do not know. There is no fear of God before their eyes".[23]

Within a month the threat of civil war had evaporated. The nation was exultant. Yet, much remained to be sorted out, not least the status and role of Deng Xiaoping. It was to take another two years for true political stability to be achieved. In the meantime the nation took stock of the situation, and was appalled by the mess that long years of leftist policies had brought about.

The Rebirth of Christianity

"What we were blind to was that when we were weak and dying life was in the offing", as Ting said in his Lambeth address in 1982. The story of the rebirth of Christian life is still not fully known, but it would appear that the turning point came in 1972. Up until then some Christians were able to meet quietly in their homes, but most dared not expose themselves to attack by leftist cadres in an atmosphere where very often even the trust within families had broken down. In 1972, with the relative political relaxation, it became possible for many more to meet quietly, especially in the countryside. So began one of the most remarkable and compelling stories in the history of the Church in modern times – a story hidden from view and at the time not even understood by its participants. While it particularly concerned Protestants, Catholics were also involved, although even less is known about their situation.

The few available sources of information are not altogether satisfactory. Some reports were published at the time but their isolated nature and use of unverifiable information meant that they could not be placed in any over-all context. Today, knowing from many sources within China that the growth that any interested visitors can now see for themselves began in this period of the Cultural Revolution, these earlier reports are of great help in filling out the picture. What follows is drawn from a few reports from overseas Chinese who were able to visit their native places; from three Chinese Christians who left China during the Cultural Revolution; from correspondence; and from some post-Cultural Revolution sources within China.

Zhejiang Province

Zhejiang, of all Chinese provinces, has the greatest number of Protestant Christians, and the neighbouring provinces of Fujian and Guangdong are also areas with a considerable Protestant presence. These South-eastern coastal provinces are areas of traditional migration overseas, and are therefore most influenced by the outside world and most visited by overseas Chinese. Looking first at Zhejiang, it is apparent that some sort of active Christian life was being restored after 1970, but that the real period of growth probably began from 1976; a pattern reflected in other parts of the country. In the city of Ningbo, one of the very first centres of Protestant missionary work in the last century, home meetings began to expand from groups of two or three to more sizeable gatherings, so that by the end of 1970 there were forty such groups served by lay leaders and elders who even administered the sacraments of baptism and communion.[24] In the area around Wenzhou City by 1976 it is evident that Christian activity was fairly uninhibited. One report, citing a young Christian man recently arrived in Hong Kong from the city, mentioned 50,000 Christians out of a total population of 400,000, with only one elderly but still active pastor.[25] In one county in the area there were said to be 117 home meetings with 6,500 people receiving communion. The presence of large-scale Christian activity in the Wenzhou municipality has been confirmed by more recent reports. In Yongjia County in the township of Wuniu by 1984 there were eighteen villages and 1600 Christian families (about 8,000 people) and a total of fifty, mostly new, churches. Many houses displayed prominent red crosses painted on their doors.[26] In Pingyang County in late 1981 thirty churches were reported as re-opened and thirty-six as newly built.[27]

As early as the autumn of 1974 it was possible to hold a Christian funeral in public in at least one village in the province, although it may have been exceptional in that the deceased was a returned overseas Chinese.[28] Again in Zhejiang, one young girl, who had been a Red Guard and then became a Christian through the influence of her grandmother, reported – after her emigration to the U.S.A. in 1973 – on Christian life in her own and neighbouring villages. The church in the area was closed in 1962, and in 1966 all worship stopped and Christians were "struggled" against. However, home meetings resumed after the high tide of the Cultural Revolution passed, with leadership assumed by elders who travelled from village to village. One pastor's daughter travelled widely, including visits to Shanghai for preaching. The girl mentioned a number of interesting points. First, the emphasis on faith healing and exorcism which seems to be a marked characteristic of rural Christianity in China. Second, in a neighbouring village, the Christians could worship openly because the mother of the CCP secretary was a Christian. Third, the importance at this time of class origin – those classified in the course of land reform as poor and lower-middle peasants were all right, even if they engaged in preaching (when you "will be lectured of course"), and those in the "black categories" such as landlords, rich peasants, rightists and counter-revolutionaries, who would be in real trouble. Fourth, she indicates the importance of family influence in the propagation of the faith.[29]

It is risky to attempt to generalize on the basis of one report, but the picture that emerges from the above interview rings true. While political circumstances obviously varied widely from place to place, county to county, and province to province, the mixture of political constraints imposed from above and mitigating local circumstances suggest that even in the darkest days it was possible for some Christians to worship together, and to sustain informal networks within, for example, the natural marketing areas surrounding ancient towns and cities. The report gives us a most helpful insight into the reality of rural Christian life, and all but the third point remain relevant today.

Other Parts of South-east China

That this resumption of a relatively public expression of Christian belief was not possible in all parts of the South-east is suggested by an interview conducted by Jonathan Chao with a Chinese businessman from Europe who visited his family home in the spring of 1974. Here, because of the matter of trust, ordinary Christians in one town or village would not know who the Christians were in neighbouring towns and villages. This, however, did not necessarily mean a total isolation, for there was an organized network of itinerant lay preachers, with a number of people engaged in a full-time ministry, cared for by the congregations. Unfortunately, the report has no reference as to location beyond indicating South-east China, but the impression is of more intensive activity than in the area of Zhejiang from which the young girl came. Thus, the home meetings in his family village of 300-350 families held three seasonal retreats a year on a mountain attended by young people. Each lasted for one week and was attended by sixty to seventy people. Once a year a week's training was held by neighbouring Christian groups, again in remote locations. Such networks would be unusual and could only function where there were sufficient concentrations of Christians and a degree of connivance from officials. The report, in fact, indicates that most local cadres were friendly, that not a few were themselves Christians, and when:

pressures from above come to the local cadres to implement a certain nationally promoted movement . . . then
they tell Christians to play down their activities. After the
movement is over, the cadres return to their "opening one
eye and closing one eye" policy.[30]

Christians were also respected by many officials for their
honesty and hardworking spirit – this is a point that emerges
time and again in the more relaxed times after 1979, and it is
interesting to find this early reference.

The signs of a growing amount of Christian activity and the
involvement of many young people are evident from these
reports. Another interview, conducted in Hong Kong in 1976
with a young Chinese Christian, probably from Fujian, refers
to the baptism of a hundred people, including the elderly and
small children. Her background is likely to have been the True
Jesus Church, as the worship was on the seventh day and she
refers to the fact that "our church is indigenous and was
never related to any foreigners". Worship continued throughout the Cultural Revolution and no one in the village
experienced any problems as a result. Some local cadres are
Christian. Some members

> travel around our county visiting other house churches
> and shepherding members and recent converts. As far as
> I know they experience no difficulty in doing that. They
> receive a monthly stipend from us. This money comes
> from our regular offerings.

This report is of particular interest because reference is made
to her attitude towards her country. Her answer demonstrates
her awareness of the overall context of her faith and her
understanding of the fundamental meaning of Three Self:

> I'm a Chinese and of course I love my country. I am not a
> member of the Party but I support my nation. We have a
> saying in our church, "Love country, love the Lord and
> love peace". I see no contradiction in this, do you?[31]

A number of other reports were received from Fujian in these
years. In the provincial capital of Fuzhou some Christian

meetings were said to started in 1969, and by late 1973 between 1,000 and 1,500 people were meeting secretly in three different locations. However, in February 1974 the lay leaders were paraded through the streets wearing dunce's caps, and one man was imprisoned. This report has not been verified, but there seems no reason to reject its over-all authenticity, even if some of the details are incorrect.[32] According to one source Christian activity in the Fuzhou region (probably not in the city proper) re-started in 1974, with 300-400 openly attending large services, but closed again in late 1975 or early 1976. In South Fujian in Quanzhou, Xiamen and Shima secret worship continued after 1966, and from 1972 in some places more openly.[33]

The difficulties of continuing Christian life in the large cities were much greater than in the countryside. Yet in Guangzhou, for example, from 1971 or 1972 small home meetings began, each with from eight to ten members.[34] In Shanghai, the leftist stronghold, one woman who visited her relatives in the city was able to attend secret home meetings in 1973. The report suggests that most believers were elderly and that they were waiting for the Second Coming of Christ, although at the same time, "they are longing for the churches to re-open so that they can preach the Gospel freely".[35]

To these reports on Protestant life one must add a report from a Chinese Catholic businessman from Indonesia, who visited Fujian in April 1973. According to his report, despite an absence of priests whole villages were being converted in the areas around Fuzhou, with many miracles of healing and the exorcism of demons.[36] The information is remarkably similar to that contained in some of the more enthusiastic reports emanating from Protestant circles, and while one must doubt the scale of the conversions, there is no reason to assume that some sort of revival was not under way. Catholic conversions have been reported from Shantou, Wenzhou, and from the inland provinces of Shanxi and Hebei. Details are scanty but the reports do suggest that the Catholic Church was also able to respond to the changing attitudes amongst the people of China, at least in areas of its traditional strength.

This last proviso is an important one. Almost every report of Protestant activity we have discussed has come from one region of China, an area with a history of a relatively strong Christian presence. To this one can add a brief report from Shandong, also a Christian stronghold in the past, about the existence of home meetings in 1973,[37] and the existence of the Nanjing home meetings. That leaves most of China out of account, and there is no reason to think that in the majority of the remaining provinces, Christian activity existed, except on the most limited scale. It may be that in Henan things were already different, for after 1978 this was one of the areas that witnessed the greatest growth, but we have to say that for the present we simply do not have sufficient information to draw any conclusions as to the situation away from the coast.

Chinese Politics and Culture 1976-80

Before discussing the post-1976 story of the Church and the re-establishment of the public life of the Church in 1979-80, it is necessary to look with some care at the secular context in which the Church found itself, and in particular at the movement of thought that took place at this period. Here it is important to distinguish rural from urban attitudes. The township, (which has now replaced the commune), and the village may contain eighty per cent of the Chinese population, but it is the city and its intellectuals that have moulded the politics and culture of China through the centuries. Before discussing the events and attitudes within this urban world of the élite, it is important to understand the wider rural context over which this élite presides.

Change and Continuity in the Countryside

It has been a matter of intense debate amongst foreign sinologists as to the impact of the Revolution on the society and social values of the rural people. The matter is complex, but in essence the debate hinges on the question of whether the political and economic changes introduced on an overwhelming scale by the CCP have been accompanied by a change in consciousness amongst the rural inhabitants. The CCP at various times has claimed a total transformation – the land reform was seen as far more than an economic affair for it was *fanshen*, a turning over of the body or in other words a total liberation of the person. Western observers have been more sceptical, suggesting the persistence of traditional values and a dislike of change which has constantly frustrated the aims of Communist mobilization campaigns. The return to farming by individual households since 1978, albeit on collective land contracted out to the household, has confirmed many in the belief that the Chinese countryside is reverting to its past patterns of organization.

There is little objective material available to test these various viewpoints, but in recent years a number of limited sociological investigations have been carried out by Western scholars, with some interesting results. In a major study William L. Parish and Martin King Whyte have analysed the patterns of change in rural Guangdong, and have come to certain important conclusions. They conclude that "the extent of change does not correspond in any clear and simple way with government priorities and pressure". The major structural changes of the 1950s had the greatest impact but, since then, peasant response has been much more selective. In the early campaigns the CCP built on existing solidarities and interest groups while eliminating others, but subsequently, the actual extent of social transformation has been limited. Government priorities in health care, birth control, educational provision, and in the improvement of agricultural methods, have been accepted, as has the suppression of clan and lineage linkages and their accompanying temple cults. On the other hand, none of the post-1957 attempts to "communize" rural life have been accepted, and family celebrations, marriage and burial customs persist despite government attempts to reform them. In other areas of life there has been a partial change, for example in the ancestor rites, freedom of choice in marriage and the position of women. (We may note at this point that the changing role and status of women has been an important component of many of the other changes.) They conclude that successful change usually takes place where the government proposals reinforce changes already under way due to alterations in rural social structure and where peasant solidarities and interests are not threatened.[38]

The Chinese countryside today is not therefore the same as in the past, nor do the most recent changes imply a return to that past. There is a dynamic within the countryside which results from the interaction of different forces. You will neither find the socialist "new man" nor the traditional peasant supposedly motivated by purely selfish interests. Increased prosperity as the result of the gradual adoption of modern agricultural techniques, together with the release of individual and family initiative through the new organization of production and the abolition of the commune, is producing a momentum for social change and a concomitant transformation in values, which in the long term may well lead to a more fundamental re-orientation in traditional patterns of social and political organization than has occurred through attempted social engineering by the CCP. Inevitably, this process is also bringing its problems. There can, for example, be little doubt that there is complete disillusionment with leftist politics, and that this has produced a crisis in the thinking of many local officials with a consequent upsurge of petty corruption and nepotism. There is also a tendency to downplay social co-operation in favour of the individual family, at the expense of the more deprived members of the community.

It is within this context that we must look at the attitude towards religion in rural society. There is plenty of evidence to suggest the persistence of popular religion in many places but, outside of the family cult, it seems unlikely that such religion has the same power as in the past. However, it is the rituals with the family that persist, but in a simplified form. This is so in spite of government attempts to suppress them or to introduce "political" substitutes for the religious elements. One must presume therefore, that most peasants retain the traditional values of the Chinese family and that it is these that provide them with basic security. To make an impact on rural society Christianity would have to appeal on this level at the very least. The family nature of Christianity in the countryside has already been noted above. Moreover, the disappearance of much of the religious ritual at village level and of the religious personnel such as geomancers, chanting fellows and the like, has left the way open for Christianity to present itself as a desireable alternative. In the midst of a collapse of political values and the demoralization of the cadre élite, the appeal of Christianity is apparent. The authorities have opposed "superstition" on the grounds that it represents a conservative force inhibiting change, whereas Christianity with its social ethic can be seen as a progressive force by officials anxious to encourage honesty and hard work. We have already noted the positive attitudes towards Christians by some local officials, and it is an attitude that would appear to become more common in the 1980s. This is not to play down the persistence of anti-religious attitudes amongst many cadres and the continuing problems caused as a result, but it indicates that, provided leftist influence declines still further, there are objective reasons why Christianity may be treated with increasing toleration.

The Return of Deng Xiaoping

We turn now to look at the political development in post-Mao China. Hua Guofeng may have been Mao's chosen successor, but he was incapable of exercising supreme office. The supporters of Deng Xiaoping were determined to rehabilitate him, and in January 1977, on the anniversary of Zhou Enlai's death, posters appeared in Tiananmen demanding Deng's return and also the "reversal of verdicts" on the Tiananmen incident, the dismissal of Wu De, the Mayor of Beijing and other leaders. Throughout the spring the matter remained unresolved, but at last, in July, at the Third Plenum of the Tenth Central Committee, Deng was rehabilitated. In August the Eleventh Party Congress was held and Deng was restored to all his former posts, although this did not mean that the struggle within the Party was over. Nevertheless, there were many policy changes and the adoption of the "four modernizations" strategy first put forward by Zhou Enlai and developed in detail in Deng's 1975 reports, now "fragrant flowers" rather than "poisonous weeds", indicated the steady shift towards more pragmatic policies. The economic programme put forward in 1978 under Hua's direction proved to be far too ambitious, and the resulting over-extension of the economy helped to contribute to his failure to consolidate his political position. Underlying this failure were his associations with the left in the past and his consequent inability to move far enough in Deng's direction. In an attempt to gain credibility he invoked Mao's supposed deathbed words, "With you in charge I am at ease", and attempted to create a minor personality cult around himself. In a bid to seize the ideological initiative he advocated the "two whatevers": whatever policies Mao devised we will resolutely support, and whatever directives he laid down we will forever observe".

In the spring of 1978 an article by Hu Fuming of Nanjing University was published in *Guangming Daily*, "Practice is the sole criterion of truth". It was the beginning of a public and private offensive against what the West has called "Maoism". Twenty years of policies were called into deep question, and the remaining leftists found themselves on the defensive. In the autumn both Wu De and Wang Dongxing, the commander of the élite 8341 Unit that had guarded Mao and other top leaders and which had arrested the Gang of Four, were removed. There were calls for greater democracy by the media; the cult of Mao was condemned; the victims of leftist movements exonerated. On 15 November it was announced that 100,000 of the victims of the 1957-58 Anti-Rightist movement were to be rehabilitated. The Tiananmen demonstrations were now hailed as acts of revolutionary heroism. For four months over the winter of 1978-79 Democracy Wall flourished, and scores of unofficial journals and newspapers were published. It was an extraordinary phenomenon, reflecting the hopes and fears of ordinary Chinese people. It should not be forgotten however, that it could only have happened with official approval, and that it was allowed to happen at the very moment when Deng finally set his mark on the direction of China. On 10 November a Central Work Conference began its meeting, which continued until the middle of December, and it was followed in the same month by the now famous Third Plenum of the Eleventh Central Committee. 1980 was to see the consolidation of the reformers' position, with major changes in the political leadership of the country. Hua Guofeng was compelled to resign as Premier and CCP General Secretary, being replaced respectively by Zhao Ziyang and Hu Yaobang, both protegés of Deng Xiaoping. In November the trial of the "Gang of Four" and other "Leftists" started. Now, at last, the Cultural Revolution was truly over!

The Democracy Movement

"Democracy Wall" with its outspoken calls for sweeping re-form of the political system and for the "Fifth Modernization" – democracy – was the work of a relatively small group of urban intellectuals, most of whom were now workers in industry where they had been sent during the Cultural Revolution. It was not a student movement and its most active members were already in their thirties. They voiced the feel-ings of many young people, but their outspokenness and use of wall posters also frightened older intellectuals who feared a backlash. In the event these fears were well-founded, for Deng had no intention of allowing the free debate to continue beyond the limits or the time he deemed useful. Deng is no liberal democrat and it is misleading to suggest that he is a pragmatist rather than a Marxist. He is, however, a realist who understands the need for stability and unity within society, and perceives that a degree of freedom of expression is essen-tial in order to achieve this goal; but he is also a firm upholder of "democratic centralism", and anything that challenges the fundamental prerogatives of the Party is unacceptable. There seems no reason to doubt that Deng Xiaoping truly desired more freedom of expression, but he obviously felt that the movement was going too far. There was also considerable pressure from within conservative sources in the Party and government to curb the tide of dissent, and Deng could not afford to jeopardize the carefully constructed balance of forces within the CCP. Thus in March 1979 the first regulations to control the movement were issued, and on 29 March the most famous of the democracy movement's leaders, Wei Jingsheng, was arrested, subsequently to be sentenced to fifteen years in prison. In spite of the seemingly dramatic and sorry end of this movement, which – contrary to the impression created by the Western focus on events in Beijing – extended to all China's major cities, the China of 1979-80 was a far freer place than at any time since 1949, and probably before.

It was abundantly clear that Marxism no longer appealed to the more daring young thinkers amongst the urban élite. Beginning from the Tiananmen incident a whole generation turned their backs on the ideology that had inspired their parents. The Cultural Revolution had delivered the *coup de grâce*. The erstwhile Red Guards had overthrown the idols they once adored. There came a realization that the democratic revolution had never been properly carried through, and that the cult of Mao was a remnant of "feudal" culture. In the words of Sun Jingxuan's poem, "A spectre wanders in the land of China":

> With our blood and sweat, with our hard work,
> We thought we were building the edifice of socialism,
> But it turned out to be another frightening church.
>
> We pushed the three big mountains off our backs,
> Is it for the purpose of erecting another temple?
> We burned the images of the god of prosperity and
>   Buddha,
> Is it for the purpose of hanging the portrait of a new
>   deity?[39]

It was as a result of the disillusionment brought about by the Cultural Revolution that the Party no longer commanded the ideological loyalty of thoughtful Chinese. Since the Cultural

Revolution it has seemed unable to offer a compelling vision of life, and its authority in post-Mao China is now based on political and not ideological criteria. The emancipation of thinking and the exhilaration that accompanied the blooming and contending in those heady months in the winter of 1979-80 are not to be belittled, despite the suppression of the Democracy Movement itself and the periodic re-imposition of restrictions. There was a liberation of thought that has continued to this day. At the same time there is, one feels, a task unfinished. Time and again since 1980 recognition of this has surfaced into public debate. The Party itself has raised the question in terms of "spiritual civilization", although there remains a basic ambiguity as to the meaning of this phrase. It was first mentioned by Ye Jianying in a speech on 29 September 1979, but it was Deng who gave it authority, in a speech at a Central Work Conference in December 1980. The leadership was acknowledging the problem of ideology even if its immediate solution was to offer more of the same. In 1981 the Party sought to safeguard orthodoxy through the promulgation of the "four basic principles" (Marxism-Leninism Mao Zedong Thought, socialism, the proletarian dictatorship and Party leadership), but in so doing has left the question of the fifth modernization unanswered. It is a question that will not so easily go away.

In 1982 Hu Yaobang suggested that one reason for the ideological crisis was "the decade of domestic turmoil" in which the criteria of right and wrong, good and evil, and beauty and ugliness were confounded. "It is much more difficult to undo its grave spiritual consequences than its material ones.[40] Hu went on to suggest that a further reason for the problem was the result of the opening to the outside, bringing "corrosion" by capitalist ideas. This is a frequently used excuse, but there is a degree of truth in it. Fascination with the West and with China's developed neighbour Japan, is all too apparent amongst urban young people. The new willingness to explore alternative understandings of social and political reality has, at times, produced a somewhat naïve and simplistic belief in "democracy" and in the virtues of the developed capitalist nations. The critique of the "democracy movement" is devastating, its prescriptions for the future vague and in-effectual. This is, of course, hardly surprising after so many "closed" years and in the light of years of leftist propaganda and the suppression of creative expression.

Marxism and the Spirit of May Fourth

Sun Jingxuan's poem raises some fascinating and perplexing questions. On one level it is a valid critique of the personality cult of Mao. At a deeper level it indicates the persistence of ancient cultural values in which meaning is discovered through the art of living rather than through adherence to religious doctrines. Sun is a fine example of the Chinese intel-lectual's dislike for "superstition". At the same time he is heir to the iconoclastic spirit of the May Fourth Movement of 1919, with its anti-traditional orientation towards the world of science and technology: the world of the West. How far, one wonders, has the May Fourth spirit persisted in its original ethos, and how far has the fact that Chinese Marxism was itself a product of May Fourth affected the modern generation of intellectuals? The twentieth century has seen a paradig-matic shift in Chinese thought, and it remains true that the old paradigms cannot be restored – this has been the fruitless endeavour in Taiwan since 1949. But Marxism in its turn has become a new orthodoxy and so far the efforts of the CCP to regenerate Marxist theory have stumbled over the political unwillingness to concede that the Leninist model of the Party is outmoded. In fact Chinese Marxism also has within it elements of populist tradition drawn from the heterodox tradi-tions within Chinese history that could provide a means of self-renewal. These traditions have manifested themselves at various points in the history of the CCP, but have in general been quickly submerged, both by the Leninist model, and by the dominant Chinese tradition of political élitism. As Chinese Marxist thinkers have themselves admitted, the spirit of Chinese "feudal" thinking is not dead.

So long as Chinese Marxism fails to deal with the question of democracy, to that extent the May Fourth spirit is being denied. This is what the democracy movement rightly drew attention to. Chinese Marxism will need to break through the procrustean bed of Leninist dogma if it is to be a creative force in the future; otherwise the CCP's political credibility will be lost. In general the radicals of 1980 were calling for the Party to reform itself, not for its overthrow. The years 1978-80 did indeed see the beginnings of such a creative discussion, but the demise of "Democracy Wall" revealed the still "forbidden zones" which in 1986 were to receive a far more extended and widespread critique, before a conservative backlash in 1987 led to the dismissal of Hu Yaobang himself and new restrictions on cultural and intellectual debate. In so far as the democracy movement called for the reform of the present system it was acknowledging that Chinese democracy cannot be a mere imitation of Western social democracy, and that it must draw on the resources of Chinese tradition to adumbrate an appropriate form for the Chinese world. This is an insight which the more thoughtful members of the CCP have themselves retained, and it legitimizes a degree of concern over the extent of Western influences. Such a concern need not necessarily be linked to the perennial attempt to deny that social alienation can arise from within a socialist society by blaming the infiltration of foreign ideas. In fact, a debate over "socialist humanism" and the existence of alienation in society was to become a major issue after 1981.

Marxism and the Meaning of Life

Sun's poem also raises the question of how far it is appropriate to speak of a "spiritual vacuum" in China today. The question was brought up publicly in 1980 when there was an extensive discussion on the "meaning of life". A letter in *China Youth News* in 1980, by a girl named Pan Xiao, provoked a huge response. Thirty thousand people wrote to the magazine, and it had obviously struck a chord in many people's hearts. In her letter she wrote:

I am now twenty-three years old. It should be said that I have just begun to experience life. Yet for me life has lost all its mystery and attraction. I have come almost to the end. I have travelled the path from hope to disappointment and despair. What began with selflessness now ends with egoism.[41]

Without doubt she voiced the feelings of a generation. Her search for meaning took her to a Catholic church, and she considered becoming a Buddhist nun. For her, and for many other young people, the simple formulas of Maoist rhetoric no longer rang true. At the same time their knowledge of their own cultural heritage was limited. In this sense there is a crisis of belief and a new openness to alternative ways of thought, including the insights offered by the major religions. There is also, however, as in Pan Xiao's case, a retreat into "egoism" which is more common amongst the generation that is too young to remember the early years of the Cultural Revolution, and which represents a more profound threat to socialist values than the political ideas of "bourgeois liberalism".

Christianity, in particular, has found itself a subject of curious interest among many of the young. In seeking to account for this one writer from the Shanghai Society for the Study of Religion, Xiao Zhitian, said:

Among the number of new religious believers in Shanghai, Protestants account for the greatest number and Buddhists are second, while Catholics are less evident. Most of these new believers are retired workers and youth (18-35), and their reasons for adopting religion are varied. Indeed there are "some people turning to religion for spiritual nourishment", and this is most striking among the youth. Many people carry spiritual wounds from the ten years of chaos, or they turn to religion for spiritual sustenance because they fail in studies or career or these things have not gone according to their wishes, or because, in their view, present political or economic conditions are wrong, and their political thinking is wavering. Among some youthful new believers, the influence of Western culture has had a definite role . . . [42]

Whether or not this analysis is adequate, it does reveal that the climate of opinion concerning the place of religion in modern society had changed dramatically from the mood that prevailed in the 1950s and 1960s. This is not to say that the official view of religion had changed, although as we shall see, a major debate over the nature of religion did get under way in the 1980s, but clearly the popular view had moved from one of cynical indifference to "superstition" to one of either a tolerant curiosity or, with a minority, active sympathy. For Christians the Cultural Revolution had brought Christianity nearer to being accepted as a Chinese religion, and many now did so, but its associations with the West also helped to make it an object of respect amongst young people attracted by Western culture. Wisely, the leadership of the Church has refused to capitalize on this, and they are rightly cautious of too many contacts with the Western churches.

Intellectuals and Tradition

Sun's views, however, reveal another side to the question. The vitality of Chinese humanism and its ability to renew itself without recourse to metaphysics should not be easily dismissed. That this cannot bypass May Fourth should be obvious. May Fourth's slogans were "science" and "democracy". We have looked at the continuing need to introduce more democracy into Chinese society. Marxism claims to be "scientific" and Chinese Marxism has inherited from the West the positivistic view of science universally in vogue until recently. The fact that this mechanistic understanding of science is gradually giving way to a non-reductionist and holistic perspective which, while profoundly humanistic, does not preclude the religious dimension, is posing a fundamental challenge to traditional Marxism. Chinese humanism, as argued in earlier chapters, was not lacking in a spiritual understanding of the world, even if it showed little overt interest in metaphysics. There are many parallels between the insight of modern theoretical physics and the insights of ancient Chinese thought, in particular in Taoism and Chan Buddhism.[43] A renewal of Chinese philosophical thinking will need to take up these insights. Many educated Chinese, including many who espouse Marxism, continue to express themselves through poetry, painting, calligraphy, the art of bonsai and the cultivation of flowers, as well as through the art of friendship. Even in times of social breakdown Chinese have found meaning for their lives in these activities. Christians have, in general, failed to understand this, and this failure suggests that it would be wise to exercise a degree of caution before speaking too glibly of "spiritual vacuums". It is all too likely that foreign Christians, seeking for evidence that at last the tide has turned in favour of Christianity, will once again mis-read the complex reality of China.

That there is an awareness of this dimension within contemporary China is evidenced by the recent publication of a study of Zhuang Zi and Chan Buddhism by Li Zehou, a research fellow in the Institute of Philosophy of the Academy of Social Sciences. The lengthy article was first published in *Chinese Social Sciences* in early 1985, and in 1987 it appeared in the English language *Social Sciences in China*.[44] The subject would have been anathema before 1985, especially as Li's treatment of Taoism and Chan Buddhism is, at root, sympathetic in spite of his criticism of Zhuang Zi's "pessimism" and Chan's "mysticism". He rightly points out that these two schools never replaced Confucianism as the dominant influence in Chinese life, as happened in Japan, but he suggests that, nevertheless, they did strongly influence cultural life, and their influence has not been entirely negative. "Detachment" can lull one into passivity, but it has also produced a spirit of non-co-operation with adverse circumstances and corrupt politics, as well as the valuing of intuition, perception and personal experience, thereby inspiring great art. He writes:

> Zhuang Zi, Neo-Taoism and the Chan School may mould, cultivate and enrich man's spiritual world and state of mind, and may teach man to forget worries about personal success or failure, free himself from considerations of gain or loss by transcending vulgar and silly calculations about reality as well as of human bondage, or teach man to cherish high aspirations or live happily and contentedly by becoming one with a lively and vivacious nature wherefrom man may draw strength and vitality. These philosophies may replace religion to provide balm and consolation for wounds in the heart and afflictions in life. This explains why the Chinese literati of all times did not actually destroy themselves or convert to religion after suffering colossal failure or catastrophe. Instead, they mostly preserved their lives, adhered to integrity, led a hermit's life, delighted in scenic beauty and retained their personal purity.[45]

Li goes on to discuss the intuitive mode of thinking in contrast to what he sees as the Western mode, with its stress on analysis and formal reasoning. Creative intuition is an essential mode of thought within the writings of Zhuang Zi and Chan Buddhism. He suggests a parallel with the mode of scientific discovery in which increasingly amongst physicists:

> aesthetic sense seems to be [the] guide among abstract symbols: if a choice is to be made between two theories – one being more beautiful while the other is more in conformity with experiments – the choice of the former seems preferable.

This is "revealing truth by beauty", precisely the question that "aethetics today should explore".[46]

There is a direct challenge here to Christian theology. Li himself concludes his article with a reference to this (incidentally revealing in the process his own mis-understanding of the biblical view of man):

> In short, although Zhuang Zi and the Chan school detest, reject and negate the actual world and are in pursuit of emptiness and extinction, they still reveal an interest in and an affirmation of human life, living beings, nature and perception and show the characteristics that intuitive comprehension is higher than reasoning thought. Perhaps this is the important point where the Chinese tradition differs from the Western (either the Hebraic separation of soul and flesh or the Greek juxtaposition of perception and reason).[47]

There is only one modern Western theologian who has addressed himself systematically to the question of aesthetics, and that is Hans Urs von Balthasar. He asked whether Christianity has not lost itself in its retreat from aesthetics, and poses the question of the future direction of theology. He suggests that theologians have an:

> inescapable obligation to probe the possibility of there being a genuine relationship between theological beauty and the beauty of the world and – in spite of all the dangers inherent in such an undertaking – to prove the feasibility of a genuine encounter between divine revelation and antiquity.[48]

Balthasar is concerned to discuss this encounter in terms of the Greek understanding of the beauty of forms and Christian faith, but in the light of the above, it is an encounter that might with more difficulty, but with equal validity, take place between faith and the Chinese tradition. The logic of a theology that denies the possibility of an analogy between worldly beauty and the beauty of the divine is a denial of the Incarnation. The encounter with the Chinese world-view as expressed so admirably by Li Zehou, by no means implies the denial of the Christian revelation. The integrity of each of the forms must be respected or there can be no encounter – this is precisely the problem of the early Jesuits and the missionaries of later times, as well as of most Chinese Christian theologians. It is also why T.C. Chao is of such importance for in his profound appreciation for the poetry of Tao Yuanming he, almost alone of Chinese theologians until very recently, had tried to take this encounter seriously. It is a sign of hope for that encounter that in China today there is the beginning of a rediscovery of their own heritage, and as we shall see in our last chapter, it is a concern that is now becoming central to the thinking of the small group of theologians based at the Nanjing Seminary.

The Growth of the Church 1976-80

Growth and Renewal

The great growth in the numbers of Christians after 1976 must, in part, be explained by the changes outlined above. Of course, a great deal more investigation would be needed in order to test out this tentative hypothesis, but it appears to fit the known facts. We will need to look more closely at the nature of rural Christianity in the next chapter before a final evaluation of the future prospects for Christianity in China can be made. For the present it is necessary to outline what we know of the story of the Church between 1976 and the reopening of the first church building in April 1979. It is unfortunate that little detailed information is in fact available as yet. The major growth points would appear to be the same places as had experienced some sort of revival in the early 1970s, although the manner in which the growth got underway must have differed from place to place and area to area.

Probably not untypical is the story told in Raymond Fung's collection:

Around about 1975 or 1976, Christians were meeting in homes again. Pastor Chung of what used to be the Presbyterian Church reappeared and word soon circulated of Christians meeting with him. We took heart and revived our meeting. Pastor Chung paid us a visit and gave us his New Testament. We held hands and prayed aloud, thanking the Lord for his word.

There is as yet no public worship in our town. Pastor Chung is working on it . . . As of now, there are over fifty people in our service, about half over sixty, the rest young people in their teens and twenties. We have many needs. But the main thing is that we have survived and have not dishonoured the name of Jesus.[49]

It was from such small and humble beginnings that the Church began to grow in this three-year period. One overseas Chinese who returned to his home town in Fujian in March 1980 found Christian home meeting points (often termed "house churches" in English), in the towns in the district with anything from one hundred to four hundred attending, with over a thousand on special occasions. Until 1976 these were all "underground" but since 1977 they have met openly, albeit not without some interference by local officials. Since early 1979 they have met freely. One pastor's wife spoke of the meeting points as "like flowers blooming everywhere". There are many young people, and the majority of people are new converts.[50] A report from a Shanghai Christian who visited rural Zhejiang spoke of the large numbers of Christians meeting in homes, and their hope for the return of church buildings before too long. He found great enthusiasm and saw over eight hundred people baptized in two places. He also found a shortage of church workers, few Bibles, the development of heretical beliefs, and controversy over such things as covering the head in worship (Little Flock), meeting on Saturday or Sunday (Seventh Day Adventist, True Jesus Church), and over baptism.[51]

One factor in the growth of church activity was the release of pastors, evangelists and others from prison or labour camp, as well as the return of others from places of exile. Both Bishop Moses Xue Pingxi in Fuzhou and Zheng Shaohuai in Shantou were able to return home from the North, the one in 1980, the other in 1978. As we have already noted, it was in 1980 that Wang Mingdao was finally released from prison. Many Catholic priests were released during 1978-80, including Bishop Dominic Deng Yiming of Guangzhou on 9 June 1980. He was, in fact, allowed to resume his episcopal role, and this rehabilitation was seen at the time as a good omen for an improvement in Vatican-China relations. In the event the hopes proved to be premature.

The persistence of Catholic communities in the rural areas has been noted already. They do not seem to have experienced the same explosion in numbers as the Protestants, but there was a degree of growth and, more importantly perhaps, a shift of focus from the cities to the villages. Edmund Tang of Pro Mundi Vita has suggested that "these rural communities are tightly knit by a bond of unity, served by a few priests, sometimes itinerant".[52] This impression has been confirmed by reports from overseas Chinese priests who have been able to visit their home areas. In one Catholic village near Changchun in Liaoning religious life began to return to normal in 1978, but there were still restrictions, and one woman was arrested for overtly engaging in religious propaganda. At this stage people were unsure of the religious policy of the government and the situation differed from place to place. Many Christians, Catholics especially, continued to meet in secret, waiting to see what would happen.

One must not under-estimate the effect of isolation on both Protestant and Catholic rural communities. Extreme emphasis on healing miracles, on the casting out of devils, on the cult of Mary amongst Catholics; these can soon lead to questionable beliefs and practices. Heresy is an ever-present threat in such a situation, as is the manipulation of new believers by self-seeking and self-styled leaders and evangelists. This negative side of the "house churches" must not be forgotten when one admires the undoubted strength of faith and the zeal of these Christians. It is an admiration shared by many church leaders in China itself. One pastor in Hangzhou was reported as saying that the Cultural Revolution:

was like the apostolic age all over again. People gathered in "families" for worship – prayer, singing, bible study and sharing experiences. Some even reported miracles, faith healings and the like. The power of God's spirit was keenly felt . . . People learnt that Christian theology is not a theoretical set of ideas but that it is what emerges out of the experience of living as the people of God under pressure. In Hangzhou we had thirty such "house groups". Some of them grew to be as large as five hundred people. People tore walls out of houses, joined courtyards, built roof extensions, to accommodate the growing numbers.[53]

This then was the situation at the end of 1978. No churches were open apart from the two exceptional instances in Beijing. Religious policy was, however, being relaxed and people were hopefully expectant, even if apprehensive of a future clampdown. Many Protestants were confident enough to meet openly, Catholics were more cautious. Both communities had experienced growth; both remained in relatively isolated circumstances with few trained leaders, few if any religious books, and with many of the characteristics of religious sects. It was this that gave them strength and had enabled them to endure: belonging to a natural environment, tightly knit, with indigenous leaders, and experiencing spontaneous growth. As Edmond Tang suggests, this sectarian tendency also had its weakness: often socially backward and inward-looking, and dependent on a strong leader.[54] The danger would be that such communities would be unable to respond in an altered situation and that their theology would, in the long run, keep the Church on the margin of Chinese society despite their indigenous nature. It is for this reason that "indigenization" is not in itself an adequate goal for a national Church, even if it is an essential aspect of the life of a Christian community within a particular historical and cultural setting. In our subsequent study of the development of the Church in the 1980s this is a point we will need to keep very much in our minds. Growth in numbers is also an inadequate yardstick by which to measure the true depth of church life, and this too we must be careful not to forget as we discuss a situation of obvious growth in numbers. It is perhaps salutary that we cannot give precise figures and are compelled, in the end, to stop playing the numbers game.

Having reached this point we should retrace our steps a little and follow the changes in religious policy after the death of Mao, and the formal reappearance of religion within the People's Republic of China.

Back to the United Front

The first signs of a shift in the official attitude to religion came with the appearance of sixteen people from religious circles at the meeting of the Fifth CPPCC which began on 24 February 1978, just prior to the convening of the Fifth National People's Congress. K.H. Ting, Archbishop Pi Shushi of Shenyang, Chairman of the CCPA (he died on 16 May, aged 81), Bishop Zhang Jiashu of Shanghai, Liu Liangmo, Luo Guangzong and Yan Jiale were the Christian representatives. A CPPCC Religion Group was established at the subsequent meeting of the Standing Committee 14-15 April. Ting, Liu Liangmo and Wu Yifang were Standing Committee members. At the National People's Congress there were thirty-four religious representatives. The convening of the CPPCC was a major signal that the policy of the United Front was to be restored; its last meeting had been in January 1964. It was some months before the results of this restoration worked through in terms of a major shift in the policy on religion, but the Buddhist and Muslim associations were now functioning properly. A group of Chinese Buddhists visited Japan in April 1978, and there were a number of reports of the relaxation of religious policy in areas inhabited by minority peoples. On 23 May it was made known that Yang Gaojian had replaced Archbishop Pi as Chairman of the Catholic Patriotic Association,[55] thus indicating that the Christian patriotic committees were expected to function again. Wu Yaozong (Y.T. Wu) was appointed to the executive committee of the China Welfare Institute, and the official report referred to him as Chairman of the Three Self Movement.[56]

The Question of the Constitution

Meanwhile religious leaders within the National People's Congress were expressing their concern over the wording of the 1976 Constitution article on religion. It was being proposed that the wording of the first Constitution of 1954 be restored, "Citizens have the freedom to believe in religion". Evidence of a serious attempt by the authorities to implement the Constitutional provision was contained in the Criminal Law adopted at the People's Congress on 1 July 1979. Article 147 read:

A State functionary who unlawfully deprives others of their freedom of religious belief or violates the customs and habits of minority nationalities to a serious extent will be sentenced to detention or imprisonment for not more than two years.[57]

At the Fifth Session of the Fifth National People's Congress meeting in late 1982 the new Constitution, adopted on 4 December, did indeed restore the 1954 clause but it also expanded the article considerably, so that Article 36 reads:

Citizens of the People's Republic of China enjoy freedom of religious belief.

No state organ, public organization or individual may compel citizens to believe in, or not to believe in, any religion; nor may they discriminate against citizens who believe in, or do not believe in, any religion.

The State protects normal religious activities. No one may make use of religion to engage in activities that disrupt public order, impair the health of citizens or interfere with the educational system of the State.

Religious bodies and religious affairs are not subject to any foreign domination.[58]

At the same time the CPPCC adopted a new Constitution. Article 13 states:

The national committee and the local committees of the CPPCC shall propagate and help implement the State's policy on religion and unify the patriots in the field of religion and religious believers in offering their share to the building and reunification of the motherland.[59]

Thus by 1982 the United Front policy of the CCP was fully implemented in terms of law and in terms of the creation of the relevant structures to implement the policy on religion, although a legal formulation of a detailed religious policy is still awaited.

The clauses in the Constitution were founded on the premise that religion would remain an essentially private matter, and that religious organizations would be run from within the country. The references to health and education were included, according to Ren Jiyu, because "in some localities there were people who tried to substitute religious education for primary education and witchcraft for medical care". On the inclusion of the phrase concerning discrimination against non-believers Ren commented that in some of the areas "where religious people live in compact community, there are cases in which people who do not believe in religion were despised and discriminated against".[60] In the main such problems have occurred in national minority areas such as Qinghai, Ningxia and Xinjiang, and, of course, Tibet, but a letter to *Nongmin Daily* (the peasant newspaper) on 20 October 1983 complained of Boddhisattvas being put into school buildings in other parts of the country.[61] As far as Christians are concerned, undue emphasis on faith healing and exorcism could cause problems. The last clause has particular reference to the Catholic situation, although as Bishop Ting has pointed out, it relates more generally to the need to support the Three Self principles.[62] A letter published in *Tian Feng*, in the period when comments on the proposed new Constitution were being solicited, gave a general welcome to the new article but asked whether this particular clause might not eliminate the spontaneity of Chinese Christian patriotism.[63] In response Ting accepted that there was some validity to this criticism but felt that in general the reference was to interference from outside, especially by Catholics.[64]

The Implementation of Religious Policy

These discussions over the Constitution were going on at the same time as a major shift in religious policy took place. The signal was given to the rest of the country on 2 January 1979, through the convening of a meeting in Shanghai for more than eight hundred people in religious circles. In its report Shanghai Radio stated the purpose of the meeting as one of criticizing the undermining of religious policy and the "ruthless persecution" of believers by Lin Biao and the Gang of Four. It was announced at the meeting that "all false charges and slanders forced on patriotic personages in religious circles must be redressed" and that, through the restoration of the municipal Religious Affairs Bureau, "normal" religious activities would be restored.[65]

It was not long before these reforms were under way throughout the country. Bishop Yang Gaojian of the CCPA told a visting Italian in April 1979 that churches were soon to re-open in Shanghai, Tianjin, Taiyuan, Wuhan and Guangzhou.[66] On Easter Sunday around five hundred Chinese and foreign Catholics attended High Mass in Beijing. A group of Chinese Protestant ministers from Hong Kong was able to tour China in March and April, and in Hangzhou they saw the Drum Tower Church in the process of restoration.[67] In nearby Ningbo the very first church to be restored to Chinese Christians after the Cultural Revolution opened at Easter on 15 April. Shanghai's first church, the Moore Memorial Church, opened on 2 September with twelve hundred worshippers. It was followed the next Sunday by Purity of Heart (Qingxin) Church, and on 23 September by a church in the north of the city. Already around five thousand were attending each Sunday, including many young people. Some of these may have been just curious, but the numbers were to increase steadily in the next few years as even more churches re-opened. Even as these events were happening Y.T. Wu, the architect of the Three Self Movement, died in the city on 17 September, aged 88. Two months later, on 21 November, T.C. Chao died.

The re-opening of churches was to continue apace and is discussed in the next chapter. The key point about this process was that the revival of the Church began at the local level. For Protestants this was to be of vital significance, as it meant that there was to be no attempt to impose a national structure from above, or to enforce uniformity in worship or belief. The principle of "seeking the common ground" and of "mutual respect" was to become central to the life of the Church. For Catholics, it meant that the deep divisions between "patriotic" Catholics and those loyal to Rome, need not become an insuperable barrier. Much would depend on local circumstances. The return of priests and pastors, the sorting out of problems relating to the payment of compensation or rent by the organizations that had occupied the churches, and the detailed negotiations to get them out, could all go on at a local level. Of course there was a negative side to this, in that policy was not implemented uniformly, and even today in some places there are considerable problems over the return of property. In the circumstances, however, such things could only be sorted out locally.

The restoration of public worship naturally posed a problem for both Catholics and Protestants. The Catholics did not face the Protestant problem of a multiplicity of traditions and patterns of worship, but they had to decide to restore the Latin Mass rather than to introduce the Chinese vernacular. In practice this was the natural thing to do, for both priests and laity were accustomed to Latin but it was an indication that Chinese Catholics had little knowledge of or desire to come to terms with the changes in the Roman Catholic Church after Vatican II. All Christians returned to the models of the past in the absence of an alternative, and many a foreign visitor has been somewhat perplexed at the conservative nature of Christian worship in China, and indeed, at its essentially Western form. Protestants had to compromise between the different local traditions, and the methods adopted have varied from place to place. In some smaller cities, and quite widely in the countryside, there is little problem since in the past one tradition dominated. In larger places different solutions have been adopted. We will say more about this later but at this point need only note that the intention has always been to preserve unity. There is to be no going back to the denominational divisions of the past as far as the overwhelming majority are concerned. Sectarian divisions are not absent, but they are generally in the background.

The Catholic Church Reorganized

The Catholics obviously felt the need for a national Church, and the thorny question of the native hierarchy immediately came to the fore. Of the forty-five Catholic bishops who were around up to 1962, thirty were said to be still alive in 1979.[68] On 25 July Michael Fu Tieshan was elected to be Bishop of Beijing, replacing Joseph Yao Guangyu who had died in 1964. In August the Vatican let it be known that it did not consider the election valid, and the Chinese responded by attacking Rome for arrogant interference in internal Chinese affairs. On 19 August Pope John Paul II endeavoured to be conciliatory, expressing cautious hope in the recent growth in religious freedom. The presence in China at this time of a senior Chinese Jesuit, Father Michael Chu, facilitated contacts, although there was no public change in the position of either party. It was, however, a time of hopefulness amongst Catholics outside China, and probably within. There were misleading reports about the possible re-establishment of the Jesuit Aurora University in Shanghai, which in the event amounted to no more than the possibility of some Jesuit teachers being invited to teach in the city.

Nevertheless, the liberal climate within China encouraged speculation, and it was reinforced by the release of Bishop Dominic Deng Yiming, and the visit to China of a number of senior ecclesiastics. Bishop Georg Möser was the first such visitor, a member of an official state delegation from Baden-

Württemberg in October/November. He was able to meet Fu Tieshan and the delegation was received by Hua Guofeng. Far more significant was the arrival on 27 February 1980 of Cardinal Roger Etchegaray of Marseilles. He was quickly followed by Cardinal König, President of the Secretariat for Non-Believers, on 10 March. Both had extensive contacts with United Front officials, but their contacts with the Catholic Patriotic Association were more limited. The status of both visits was deliberately left ambiguous, and in the event neither achieved more than a useful exchange of opinions. On 14 September the Pope remembered Bishop Deng in his prayers, praised Catholics loyal to the Holy See, and stated that he saw no contradiction between love of Church and love of country. It soon became clear that the Vatican was not prepared to concede over episcopal elections, and that the CCPA and the Chinese government were not prepared to make concessions from their side. The Vatican's continued diplomatic recognition of Taiwan as the legitimate government of China has remained a further political obstacle, even though the Vatican downgraded its representation in Taibei after the departure of the Nuncio in 1971.

The reorganization of the Catholic Patriotic Association was formally ratified at the Third National Congress, which was held from 22 to 30 May 1980. Present were some two hundred representatives. Apart from defending the record of the CCPA, plans were made for rebuilding the structures of church life. The Third National Committee was elected, with 118 members, with Bishop Zong Huaide of Jinan as Chairman and six more bishops, one priest and one layman as Vice-Chairmen. A most significant moment in the history of the Catholic Church in post-1949 China then took place. A separate All China Catholic Representative Conference was held from 31 May to 2 June, and this established a new National Administrative Commission and a Chinese Bishops' College. In a comment on the CCPA meeting, New China News Agency had stated on 22 May that "the CCPA is a political body . . . religious activities are conducted in dioceses through the Church and various cathedrals".[69] On paper at least, the Church was now recognized as distinct from the Patriotic Association, and it should therefore be logically possible for a Catholic bishop or priest to be active within the public structures of the Church without being a member of the CCPA.

The task of the Bishops' College was the supervision of doctrinal matters, but it also had as a secondary aim the expansion of friendly contacts with foreign Catholics. Zhang Jiashu of Shanghai was head of the College and Director of the National Commission. There were said to be thirty-three members of the Bishops' College. These meetings seemed to re-affirm the hard line against Rome, although there is reason to think that some delegates argued strongly for unity with the Holy See. If so, then their expression of this opinion in such a forum may have contributed to the restoration of a degree of trust, at least in some circles and in some places. The restoration of Deng Yiming in Guangzhou must be seen as a part of this process, for he himself did not join the CCPA on his release.

These national meetings were quickly followed by a succession of provincial and city-level meetings during the second half of the year and in 1981. Chinese Catholics were facing many problems. In an Open Letter issued by the CCPA national meeting, reference was made to the implementation of religious policy which "still meets with much difficulty and faces many obstacles".[70] It also referred to internal difficulties within the Church, accusing bad elements who "invent miracles, spread rumours, create division and undertake illegal activities". According to Bishop Yang Gaojian, in a BBC interview in February 1981, there were about a thousand priests left in China, with a total of over three million Catholics. How accurate these figures were it is impossible to say, but the number of priests is probably about right. We do not know how many of these were members of the CCPA, nor how many were willing to serve in churches opened by the CCPA, but it is likely that few were CCPA members whilst a good number were willing to serve in local churches. By the end of 1980 around forty churches had re-opened, but as yet diocesan structures were not functioning. On 26 October

1980 the Beijing Diocese ordained a new priest, the first in the country after the Cultural Revolution.

Sources close to Rome suggest that only twenty per cent of priests "support" the CCPA, but this begs the question as to what constitutes "support". It would seem likely that only a minority is in active opposition to the CCPA. One overseas Chinese visitor to North-east China reported that even remote villages were aware of the change in religious policy, although the authorities enforced restrictions on those below eighteen attending Mass. Five priests were serving the Catholics in the diocese where there had been thirty in 1949. All five had been released recently, and the youngest was aged sixty. In such places the issue of the CCPA may seem remote compared to the scale of pastoral need.

Meanwhile, grass-roots pressures to allow greater freedom were mounting. An excellent illustration of this was the un-official celebrations at the Marian shrine on Sheshan, near to Shanghai, in May 1980. Sheshan is the only hill in Shanghai, about an hour's journey into the lush countryside, with its network of canals connecting to the great waterways of the Yangzi Basin. Approaching one sees in the distance a huge basilica perched on the hill, like a piece of southern Europe transplanted to the rice paddies of China. Traditionally it had been the site of pilgrimage by Chinese Catholics, especially in May, Mary's month. Thousands of fishing folk would come in their small boats to worship at the shrine. But the last such festival was in 1962, and in 1980 the hill was still surrounded by barbed wire: the two churches, the second and earlier one mid-way up the hill, were closed. In the previous October Shanghai Catholics reported seeing shining lights and of being told that in the following March the "Shining Blessed Mother" would appear. On the day of the expected apparition (15 March) up to ten thousand pilgrims had gathered, and although there was no miracle, the atmosphere was one of intense devotion. Groups of fishermen stormed the hill and opened the churches. The next day even more people were present, and the authorities chose to keep a low profile. In fact the Shanghai Bus Company put on extra buses! In May 1981 the site was given back to the Catholics, and the Shanghai church held the first official festival, with many thousand attending.

It was allegedly as a result of this event that on 5 May Father Stanislaus Shen was arrested and sent back to labour camp in Anhui, from where he had been released in 1978. It was the first case of re-arrest. Another priest was reported as being re-arrested later in May, and in December 1980 and January 1981 two more priests received similar treatment.[71] It is uncertain how far these arrests were related to the events of March 1980, but the status of the priests was provisional in any case, as they had never received residents' permits for Shanghai. The real reasons probably related to their active contacts with the Jesuit Order and with the Vatican.

Protestant Reorganization

Protestant reorganization began at a meeting of the TSPM Standing Committee, which met in Shanghai from 25 February to 1 March 1980, and was attended by twenty-four members. It issued "An Open Letter to Brothers and Sisters in Christ of All China", and announced the convening later in the year of the Third National Christian Conference. Its tone was concilia-tory, seeking unity on the basis of mutual respect. It was a return to the mood of 1956 before the swing to the left, and it announced a programme of work to strengthen the Church. It declared:

> We have seen that the Church has not let her light be put out but has gone through trials and been strengthened, and that our witness to Christ also has not been dimmed but has in quietude borne fruit.[72]

The Third National Christian Conference met in Nanjing from 6 to 13 October 1980, with 176 delegates. Out of the con-ference there emerged a new church structure, the China Christian Council. According to its Constitution it is:

> the national organization in charge of Church affairs for

Chinese (Protestant) Christianity . . .

The objective . . . is to unite all Christians who believe in the one Heavenly Father and confess Jesus Christ as Lord, and who, under the guidance of the one Holy Spirit and abiding by the common Bible, with one mind and in co-operative efforts, seek to further the cause of a self-governing, self-supporting and self-propagating Church in our country.

This Council seeks to serve all the churches and all the Christians throughout the country in their ministry, and advocates mutual respect in matters of belief. As to relations among members of the Body, it heeds the call to "forbearing one another in love, eager to maintain the unity of the Spirit in the bond of peace".

The articles go on to explain that the relationship with the TSPM is one of division of labour. The Constitution of the TSPM makes it clear that the TSPM is a movement of Christians committed to the principles of the United Front and to fostering the Three Selfs within the Church.

The China Christian Council was not intended as a national Church. Bishop Zheng Jianye, in his statement to the conference, made this very clear:

The church affairs organ we envisage would certainly not be a national Church, nor would it be a superstructure imposed upon local churches . . . It will handle those matters which local churches cannot easily do by themselves, such as the translation and publication of the Bible, the production of literature of Christian nurture, the opening of a seminary for the training of pastoral workers and theological researchers, and so forth. At the invitations of local churches it may also send people to undertake visitations . . . When necessary, it can also organize discussions and study of questions which are of our common concern.[73]

The President of the Council and Chairman of the TSPM was Bishop Ting (Ding Guangxun). Wu Yifang was elected

Honorary Chairperson of the TSPM. The Council's nine Vice-Presidents included the former General Secretary of the National Christian Council, George Wu Gaozi. The General Secretary was Bishop Zheng Jianye, with Han Wenzao and Ms Cao Shengjie as Associates. Shen Derong became General Secretary of the TSPM, assisted by Han Wenzao and the editor of *Tian Feng* (which re-appeared in late 1980), Shen Chengen.

By the end of the year the structures were in place to begin the gradual process of rehabilitation. By the time of the Conference between fifty and sixty churches had re-opened, all in cities.[74] Opinions about the home meetings seemed to be divided. Some Christians from main-line churches felt that they had served their purpose and should revert to being adjuncts of church worship. Others, including Bishop Ting, were convinced of their continuing importance. Official attitudes remained suspicious, and at the CPPCC meeting in September 1980 Ting had to plead for recognition. His comments were published in *People's Daily* on 9 September, along with comments by other members, the first time that excerpts from the small group discussions at the CPPCC had been made public. He was reported as stating:

> There are great obstructions to irplementing religious policy. During the Cultural Revolution all Christian churches were closed down and few are now open. The great majority of believers hold worship in homes. It is the duty of the TSPM to unite all Christians in the country. We cannot let those who take part in house meetings be labelled a group apart. As one of the leaders of the TSPM, I cannot bring myself to say that they are illegal. In interpreting the Constitution, we cannot say that there is religious freedom in church buildings but not in homes. We cannot carry on a Three Self Patriotic Movement among a small minority of people, but we should bring the more than one million Christians together into it.[75]

The leadership of the Council were also very anxious to renew international contacts. Bishop Ting had made an extended private visit to North America in the autumn of 1979, and

Zhao Fusan had visited the U.S.A. and Britain in 1979/80. The first delegation to travel overseas was a general religious one, consisting of eight religious leaders, which attended the Third World Conference on Religion and Peace, held in Princeton, New Jersey, from 28 August to 8 September 1979. The delegation was led by the Buddhist leader Zhao Puchu and Ting was the deputy leader. Li Shoubao of the YMCA was General Secretary, Chen Zemin of Nanjing, Secretary, and Han Wenzao was one of the members. After the Conference the four Christians made a tour of the U.S.A. at the invitation of the National Council of Churches. The principle of sending religious delegations had been established, and during 1980 discussions were being held privately with the Canadians, Americans and British about the exchange of delegations.

In December 1980 Bishop Ting issued "A Call for Clarity: Fourteen Points from Christians in the People's Republic of China to Christians Abroad". It was a careful response to the interest being shown in the Church in China, a warning to those who sought to intervene directly or indirectly, an explanation of the nature of Chinese Christianity, and a caution as to the limited possibilities for exchange due to the internal tasks facing them. It did, however, reveal a new willingness for contact and even to receiving contributions from friendly sources abroad:

> We are pondering over the wisdom of accepting certain contributions from friendly church groups and persons overseas, with no strings attached and with due respect for the independent stance of our Church, simply as an expression of the universality of our Christian fellowship.[76]

At the same time Ting drew a clear line between friends and those who oppose the Three Self, especially those seeking to do evangelistic work or to restore denominational organizations in China. Opening the doors certainly was to bring its own problems, and Ting and others rightly feared that some foreign Christians would have no sensitivity to their situation, having failed to understand the significance of the Chinese Christian experience since 1949.

Research Into Religion

The changing policy on religion also meant that religion once more became the subject of debate amongst academics and policy-makers. In this chapter we will look at the academic discussion, and then in the next chapter at the formulation of religious policy. It will be convenient to look at the whole ten-year period from 1977 to 1987.

The first public analysis of religion appeared in an article in *Guangming Daily* on 27 September 1977, entitled "Investigate Religion and Criticize Theology", written by none other than Ren Jiyu.[77] Essentially it repeated his opinions of the early 1960s and took an extremely narrow view of the study of religion. Nevertheless, it was the first article on the subject to appear since the debates of 1963-65, and in March 1978 it was followed by the re-establishment of the Institute of World Religions within the Chinese Academy of Social Sciences and under the direction of Ren. A National Forum for planning scientific research in the study of religion was held in Beijing in April. Zhou Yang, adviser to the Academy of Social Sciences at the time, and previously the CCP's principal spokesperson on cultural affairs, before he became one of the main targets of the Cultural Revolution, stated:

> In studying religion, it is necessary resolutely to safeguard Marxist atheism and adopt a clear-cut stand. Efforts should be made to study conscientiously the history of world religions with a Marxist view and write in detail the history of Buddhism, the history of Christianity and the history of Islam with correct views and abundant reference materials. To write works of scientific value, it is also necessary to do a great deal of work in compiling reference materials and translate and explain with footnotes all kinds of classical religious documents.[78]

It was perhaps an inadequate understanding of academic research in so far as it assumed without question the correctness of the Marxist critique of religion, but it represented quite a step forward. A draft programme for research into religion was drawn up at the meeting. Twenty-two post-graduate researchers were enrolled.

A number of provincial Institutes appear to have been set up at the same time, although there has not been much information about their work. In Xinjiang an Institute under the Xinjiang Academy of Social Sciences was established to study Islam. A special Society for the Study of Tibetan Buddhism was also established in Beijing, and a journal started. Part of the work of the Beijing Institute concerns the study of atheism, and a Chinese Association of Atheism was set up in 1978. A Society for the Study of Religion was established at a meeting in Kunming 12-22 February 1979. Ren Jiyu was made Honorary President, but the President was the Buddhist leader, Zhao Puchu. A number of Christians were on the fifty-six-strong Executive, including Bishop Ting and Jiang Wenhan of Shanghai, who under the auspices of the Shanghai Academy was writing on the history of Christianity, Islam and Judaism in China, a work that was only partially completed at the time of his death in 7 September 1984. T.C. Chao was made an Honorary Co-Chairman.

The Debate on the Nature of Religious Studies

Ren Jiyu has been one of the principal exponents of the conservative Marxist approach to religious research. In a major article in 1979 he called for the criticism of "fideism and obscurantism" in order to foster the four modernizations – in other words, religion is to be seen as an essentially negative force that impedes modernization:

> Not only will our enemies oppose [modernization] but various conservative forces coming from the people internally will put up obstacles. Among these, religious

ideas and various forms of fideism will seriously hinder the realization of the four modernizations.[79]

He then goes on to accuse Lin Biao and the Gang of Four of turning Marxism and Mao Zedong Thought into "lifeless religious dogmas". Despite this negative standpoint, Ren is careful to stress the need for mutual respect and for the abolition of "forbidden zones" in religious research. Ren's article is more careful and balanced than his 1977 piece, but it still begs many questions.

A great deal of the work appearing in the publications of the Beijing Institute has been vitiated by the same failure to overcome a dogmatic approach that sees all religion as a negative force. It is interesting, therefore, to consider the first issue of the journal *Research on World Religions* which appeared in August 1979.[80] The foreword offers a number of reasons for studying religion. First, it is an objective fact of world history and it must be recognized that while "our faith and worldview is different" from that of "not a small number of religious believers" who have taken positive political positions, yet it is important "to understand how to co-operate with progressive religious people in the world struggle". Secondly, domestically it is important because of the remnants of feudal thinking and habits, but also because of "the re-emergence of religion in reaction to Lin Biao and the Gang of Four". It went on to accuse the leftists of having turned Marxism into a covert religion. Of the essays in the journal several are quite free of ideological clutter, but Yang Zhen's "A Glimpse of Contemporary Christian Theology" is a rather tendentious survey which, taken together with the publication in 1979 of Volume 1 of the same author's *A General History of Christianity* demonstrated that he too had not changed his ideas since he had contributed to the debate with Ya Hanzhang in the early 1960s. It is perhaps significant that no more volumes of this work have been published. Overall, however, the journal's approach does suggest a way forward, and its understanding of religion is not entirely negative. The appointment of Zhao Fusan as one of the two deputy directors of the Institute, was an indication that Ren's understanding was not the only one. In June 1980 Zhao Fusan, also of course a well-known Christian leader, stated at an international seminar on the social sciences that:

> By acknowledging Marxism as the theoretical basis of all social sciences research, Chinese scholars mean that they take the research of Marx, Engels and Lenin as their starting point, but never as consummate truth.[81]

He added that Marxism is an "open system".

Zhao's views appear to have had little immediate effect on the Beijing Institute, and with his appointment to wider work within the Academy it would appear that his involvement was minimal. However, in 1985 he became a Vice-President of the Academy, giving him considerable over-all influence. His appointment was made soon after he had made some surprisingly outspoken remarks on the place of religion within socialist society, and he followed this with an in-depth critique of the classical Marxist-Leninist understanding of religion, both of which are discussed in detail below.

The establishment of the Nanjing Centre for Religious Studies under the auspices of Nanjing University, with Bishop Ting as the director from 1 January 1979, marked an important new departure. It represented a very different view of religious studies, and in conversations with the author in October 1979 Bishop Ting implied that Marxist scholars had a lot to learn about religion. He confirmed that the original intention of the Beijing Institute was to criticize religion, but that as a result of discussions with believers the Centre had moved towards a more purely academic role. He was also very critical of the linking of the cult of Mao to religion, and indicated that this had stopped after the protests from believers. It was considered particularly unfair in view of the fact that religious people had been in the forefront of the criticism of the cult of Mao. One has to say, however, that "Maoism" certainly took on many semi-religious features, and that it functioned for a while as a surrogate religion, as Sun Jingxian's poem incisively indicates.

The Centre planned to take a number of graduate students to study Christianity. "They can be Christians or Marxists or those uncommitted but eager to sort things out".[82] The staff of twenty-four were all Christians, the former members of the Nanjing Seminary faculty, although the students would not necessarily be believers. This link to a secular university was quite unprecedented. In May 1979 the first lecture to staff and students of the university, "On Christian Theism", was delivered. A year later over a thousand students attended a series of lectures on Christianity. The Centre had three post-graduate students before its work was superseded in 1981 with the re-opening of the seminary itself. Since then the work appears to have been integrated into the life of the seminary, and research students are generally graduates of the seminary, but the close links with the university have been maintained.

Religion and Superstition

A key statement on religious policy that appeared in the *People's Daily* on 15 March 1979 re-affirmed Ya Hanzhang's arguments in 1963-64 concerning the nature of religion and its relationship to "superstition". It represents the first detailed statement of religious policy after the Cultural Revolution, and clearly reflects the viewpoint of Ren Jiyu. Thus it re-affirms the view that all religion is illusory, "an opiate paralysing the people's will". Religious policy has as its ultimate objective the elimination of religion when social conditions are right. Its current task is the patient education of believers so that they can "come to correct conclusions". It repeats the clause of the 1978 Constitution which had been taken over directly from the Constitution of 1975, which as we have seen, was already under attack as "leftist" and which it has been strongly rumoured Ren was endeavouring to defend:

> citizens enjoy freedom to believe in religion and freedom not to believe in religion and freedom to propagate atheism.

Religion, it argues, must be differentiated from "feudal superstition", and it defines religion in terms of world religions with "scriptures, doctrines, religious rites, and organizations", while "feudal superstition" refers to witchcraft, divination, divine healing, exorcism, geomancy and related practices. On the other hand, ancestor worship and the belief in souls, ghosts and immortals, while "also a sort of superstition", should not be forbidden by force.[83]

In terms of our present discussion this viewpoint represents no significant theoretical advance. As Philip Wickeri points out in his assessment of the re-emergence of religious studies:

> The very fact that religious subjects are again being discussed is a positive sign, as is the re-affirmation of the moderate position which was associated with people like Ya Hanzhang in the past. But leaving aside the practical implications of the "Marxist science of religion" and focussing on the actual study which is going on, one encounters a fundamental problem. The difficulty is not that religious studies in China has been critical of theology – that has been the situation in the West for at least one hundred years – but that it has not been critical of itself.[84]

In the 1980s this uncritical position was questioned both by Christian and non-Christian scholars. It was in the Shanghai Institute of Religious Studies that a forum for a more open discussion of religion developed. Their objective appears to be very different from the Beijing Institute, namely the study of religion in the field rather than the development of a "Marxist science of religion". By 1984 the Institute was engaged in three major areas of research: the sources of religious belief in a socialist society, the changes in religion under socialism, and developing a more satisfactory policy on religion. This more open approach could allow for a positive role for religion under socialism, and understands religious policy as the development of genuine mutual respect.

A matter of considerable argument has been the description of religion as "opium". Bishop Ting raised the question in discussion with Marxist philosophers in Nanjing, and it has been pursued in detail by Zhao Fusan. It is not possible to enter into a very detailed discussion of the ongoing debate, but it does have considerable implications for religious policy. In fact, the most important directive on religious policy issued in 1983 by the CCP Central Committee omits any reference to religion as an opiate, although it does speak of religion being used by the oppressors to "benumb and control the masses" – a formula that leaves some room for a more positive evaluation of religion in a socialist society, in which it can be presumed that the oppressing class is no longer considered to exist.[85] A reassertion of the Marxist science of religion viewpoint appeared in *Research on World Religions* in 1983.[86] It concedes that in a socialist society religious believers are good citizens but "this does not mean that the nature of religion has changed". It persists because socialism has not yet eliminated all difficulties. Believers' profession that they oppose social evils is the result of the increasing crisis of religion in the face of human progress:

> the propagating of goodness and the promoting of virtue are one of the trends religions follow in order to "modernize" themselves. If this is the case with religion, can we use it to supplement socialist spiritual civilization? No, definitely not.

This question takes us to the heart of the matter. We have noticed a fundamental ambiguity in the United Front policy with regard to religion. This ambiguity stems from the Marxist premise that religion is a negative social force, and has meant that religious policy is based on the assumption that religion will eventually disappear. Therefore, the debate over policy within the Party is a debate over methodology, ranging from the moderate line of Zhou Enlai, with its stress on both supervision and toleration, to the extreme line of Xie Fuzhi in the Cultural Revolution, of "exterminating religion". In practice, of course, the predominance of one line over another is of vital importance to religious believers, but on either view in the end religion cannot make a genuine contribution to the values of a socialist society, even though on the moderate view it is accepted that religious people may be able to contribute to the modernization of the country. This latter perspective has prevailed since 1978, but the fundamental issue has not been resolved.

Religion and Socialist Spiritual Culture

In the August of 1984 Zhao Fusan accompanied a National CPPCC delegation which visited Xinjiang. As a result of the insights he gained into Muslim attitudes he prepared a short statement, "Religion, Spiritual Culture and National Unity". In March 1985 he delivered a revised version of this statement to the National CPPCC meeting in Beijing, and it was subsequently published in the July issue of *Tian Feng*. As the Editor commented:

> We need not point out that such a statement could not have been issued during the Cultural Revolution, and could hardly have been uttered even in 1983 [during the anti-spiritual pollution campaign]. This statement will be effective in clearing away misunderstanding concerning "leftist" influences affecting the implemention of religious policy. This "leftist" influence still maintains its ground, but more and more people, including some Marxist-Leninsts in academic circles, are taking a more objective and impartial attitude towards religion, and are no longer dismissing it as mere "opium".[87]

Zhao Fusan begins by pointing out the influences of religion on the history, culture and social order of all nations. He argues that this heritage must be handed down "whenever a nation shapes anew its spiritual culture". To reject this heritage would be an act of folly. Moreover,

> If we regard religion as nothing but the opium by which the exploiting classes control and poison the labouring people, and at the same time advocate the restoration of Buddhist temples, the protection of religious relics and the printing of the Chinese Tri-pitaka, would this not be self-contradictory?

He goes on to call for a more scientific understanding of religion. He admits that religion has often been used as a political tool in class society, and that in the midst of a revolution it is understandable if the revolutionaries stress this aspect of it. In a socialist society this aspect has been greatly weakened, and religion can have a positive role in assisting internal cohesion and in the Four Modernizations. He then comes to the crux of his argument, based on his awareness of the multi-national nature of modern Chinese society:

> But how should one regard the connection between religion and the building up of a spiritual culture on the part of the various races of our country? If religious people can take part only in the building up of the material culture of socialism, and if they are pushed aside when it comes to spiritual culture, or are simply criticized, the religious people will only be able to proceed half-heartedly along the road to socialism.

He then states his understanding of the United Front as existing to unite people in the establishment of both cultures, by "seeking the common ground and accepting minor differences".

It is a remarkable statement and it did not go without retort from the hard-liners. Initial reaction was, however, positive. *People's Daily* on 7 November 1985 reported the statement in some detail, but significantly omitted the key section on spiritual culture. *Beijing Review*, the foreign language weekly, re-published a survey of differing academic views on religion.[88] One view is negative, seeing religion as a narcotic. "The people with this viewpoint say education on atheism should be emphasized in order to eliminate religion as quickly as possible". Another view maintains that under socialism religion is not a tool of the ruling class and can be co-ordinated with socialism. Yet another view suggests that the great religions began as positive forces, and although later used to exploit the masses have made a great contribution to cultural development. This last viewpoint appears to be a somewhat inadequate reference to Zhao Fusan's standpoint.

The critical reaction came in an article by Jiang Ping, deputy Director of the United Front Work Department of the CCP, in *Red Flag* published in May 1986, although Zhao Fusan was not mentioned.[89] It is a lengthy justification of the thesis that religion is the "opium of the people", refuting "some comrades" who have negated the idea. It re-states the arguments of the 1983 article discussed above, on the role of religion in a socialist society. The "poisonous role of religion in ideology should be negated". In a pointed reference he writes:

> Although some people apply Marxism to the study of religion, they adapt Marxism haphazardly to the religious belief of their religious followers in order to satisfy their demands. Some people use religious points of view to explain Marxism . . . Academic circles should respect the ideological beliefs of religious circles, whereas religious circles should also respect academic circles' Marxist study of the religious theory and propaganda activities.

After this somewhat strange definition of what constitutes the academic study of religion, he goes on to repeat the general line of religious policy as stated since 1979, and which we will need to look at in more detail in the next chapter.

A Reconsideration of Religion

Zhao Fusan's next major contribution was published in the *Chinese Journal of Social Sciences*, in the autumn 1986 number, and was translated in the English edition.[90] It is argued from the standpoint of an open Marxist framework and not on the basis of Zhao Fusan's personal faith in Christianity, the intention, presumably, being to present an argument for the radical "reconsideration of religion" within the terms acceptable to those responsible for China's religious policy. An argument on the basis of faith would be self-defeating. It is not easy to summarize a complex and closely argued paper, where each stage of the argument ought to be followed through, but its over-all importance necessitates a brief outline of the most significant points of his argument.

He begins by suggesting that the changes in religion in China since Liberation have been of a qualitative nature. The important question today is not to investigate the class nature of religion within a feudal or capitalist society, but from within a socialist context to seek to understand what are the commonalities which constitute the essence of religion. The usual Marxist answer that it is the "opium of the people" is far from adequate although, as he attempts to show, Marx's own understanding of the meaning of this phrase was very different from the later interpretation by Lenin, made within the context of Russian society, in which Lenin argued that as "opium" religion was a tool used by the reactionary class with the intention to "befuddle" the working class. The Chinese translation of Lenin is incorrect and reads "religion is the opium which befuddles the people", which strongly reinforces the idea of religion as nothing more than a tool. Zhao then seeks to demonstrate that, contrary to Lenin, the essence of religion in Marx's understanding is the "self-consciousness and self-esteem of those who feel unable to master their own fates". Religion is not primarily a "tool", an "opium *for* the people" but something possessed by the people themselves, an "opium *of* the people", and it is this which constitutes its continued survival within a socialist society:

> religion is the self-consciousness and self-esteem of those who feel unable to master their own fates.

Zhao then argues for a far subtler understanding of the relationship between social existence and consciousness, in which the economic base can be, to some extent, modified by ideas. It is inappropriate to isolate religion from the human subject for the believer's

> emotional and perceptual experience of religion are frequently ignored in social practice, and it is not realized that religion is the believer's self-consciousness of the perceived totality of social relations providing the bedrock upon which he has built his life.

This is the origin of "leftist" views of religion, which ignore its complex social role. Zhao returns here to his concern with the historic link between religion and human culture and suggests that at certain historical epochs "religion adds to the impetus for progress of that epoch". He suggests, therefore, that the fact that religion has been used to "befuddle" people does not necessarily tell us anything about the nature of religion itself. Examination of the "befuddling" effect of religion reveals that this occurs when religion is used by reactionary ruling classes, but there are many examples of religion playing a different role.

He then draws certain conclusions as to the effect of religion on human thought and action. Religious ideas "are not without significance for man's understanding of the objective world or of himself". This is not negative, but rather "represents an awakening of social consciousness in the persons concerned, who are thus one step ahead of those who live without bothering to think". Religious ideas have not always had a negative impact on believers' social practice. Religion as an escape from reality is not uncommon, but there are people "whose understanding of social contradictions [has] been deepened because of religion's critical attitude towards them". He cites examples from Chinese history and suggests that "the realities of China today tell the same story". So he can deal with his concern with the positive contribution of religion to socialist culture. He discusses this in terms of ethics and morality and even argues that religious morality

makes it possible for believers to be independent of the constraints exercised by external forces (i.e. law, public opinion, etc) and rely on self-control instead.

Religion can, therefore, have a "positive effect on the construction of a socialist spiritual culture today". He concludes with a plea for mutual toleration, and suggests that the prevailing understanding of religion in China distorts religious policy into "a sort of expediency", opening the way to "leftism" which damages the United Front and the cause of socialism.

He ends with a statement of his understanding of the United Front:

> In hoping to harmonize religion and socialism, China's aim is to harmonize relations between believers and socialism. Religious people are requested to be patriotic and law-abiding, but not to give up their faith; Marxists are required to be politically united with religious believers, but not to give up any of their ideological principles.

How far have any of these ideas influenced the application of religious policy? In as much as Zhao Fusan is on the frontiers of the discussion, one would expect to find that their impact has been limited. It may be, however, that Zhao's viewpoint has had more impact on the policy-makers than one might have expected, even though it takes time for the effect to work through the system. In an interview in *Liaowang* on 9 June 1986, Zhang Chunting and Han Hua, two officials of the Religious Affairs Bureau, revealed a partial acceptance of Zhao's viewpoint. In reply to a question about whether religion can play a positive role in socialist society their reply included the following:

> The negative role of religion is being restricted and the good traditions of religion are being developed and have begun to develop along the orientation which conforms and co-ordinates with socialism. For example, the rational parts of some religious moral standards still conform to the building of socialist spiritual civilization, so they can play an auxiliary role.[91]

They conclude with the observation that religion "is playing a positive role in society". On a question about religion as "opium" their answer is rather circumspect but essentially rejects Zhao's understanding.

The remarks made by Xi Zhongxun at the Fourth National Christian Conference in August 1986 were even more explicit, and as a member of the CCP Political Bureau, his endorsement of Zhao Fusan's position is of major significance:

> During the new historical period, China's Christians may

also make contributions to promoting socialist materials and spiritual civilization. It is wrong to think of promoting civilization as conflicting with citizens' believing in religion.[92]

Such a declaration is a landmark in the development of United Front policy.

The long-term impact of this discussion remains unknown. The removal of Hu Yaobang as CCP General Secretary on 16 January 1987, and the subsequent campaign against "bourgeois liberalization" may have affected the situation, but by early July the initiative appeared to be passing back to the reformers. Such ups and downs are a reminder of the comparative precariousness of the political situation in China, even after almost ten years of the reform process. However, assuming that there will be no drastic alteration in the over-all reform programme, if Zhao Fusan's plea for a more open Marxist understanding of religion can penetrate further into the academic study of religion, this will continue to have a significant impact on the making of religious policy. But Zhao's arguments also have wide-ranging implications for the self-understanding of Chinese Marxism itself. To admit that religion can make a positive contribution to "socialist spiritual civilization" is to alter the fundamental premises upon which Marxist orthodoxy has been built. That such a standpoint can be put forward by a senior Party leader is an indication of how far China has come in the past ten years. In this context a Christian theology that can draw on the inner strengths and beauty of Chinese tradition may be able to share with open Marxist thinkers in the renewal of China's cultural life, to the profound enrichment of us all.

REFERENCES

1. Lao Zi, *Dao De Jing*, Section 43.
2. NCNA, 28 February 1969, *China Notes*, Vol. 9, No. 1, Winter 1970-71.
3. NCNA 6 February 1971, *China Notes*, Vol. 9, No 2, Spring 1971.
4. NCNA, 11 November 1971, ibid.
5. Whitehead, Rhea M. and Raymond L., "A Visit to a Peking Mosque",

China Notes, Vol. 9, No. 3, Summer 1971.

6. This report has not been confirmed but the timing is appropriate in view of the restoration of public worship in Beijing. See Trivière, Leon, "The Church: China and the Believers", *China Notes*, Vol. 9, No. 4, Fall 1971.

7. *Information Catholiques Internationales*, 15 December 1971.

8. Private memo, 1972.

9. Strong, John, "Buddhism in China", *China Notes*, Vol. 9, No. 1, Winter 1972-73.

10. NCNA, 15 May 1973.

11. NCNA, 6 September 1972.

12. Endicott, James G., "The Future of the Christian Religion in China, Notes of a China Visit, 1973", *China Notes*, Vol. 11, No. 3, Summer 1973.

13. *Christianity and the New China, Vol. 1: Theological Implications of the New China. Vol, 2: Christian Faith and the Chinese Experience*, Lutheran World Federation and Pro Mundi Vita, Ecclesia Publications, William Carey Library, South Pasadena, California 1976.

14. Paton, David M., *Christian Missions and the Judgement of God*, SCM Press, London 1953.

15. Johnson, the Rev. Dr E.H., Notes on the Church in China, private paper, 1973, and "Christian Voices from the Church in China, April 1975", *China Notes*, Vol. 13, No. 3, Summer 1975.

16. Fleming, the Rev. Dr John, private report, dated 5 August 1975.

17. Stockwell, Eugene L., "The Life of Christians in China", *The Christian Century*, 23 February 1977.

18. Bishop Ting told E.H. Johnson of his hopes in 1973, op. cit. In 1975 he told John Fleming that some staff were visiting different parts of the country to investigate what sort of training might be appropriate, op. cit.

19. Johnson, "Christian Voices', op. cit.

20. Garside, Roger, *Coming Alive: China After Mao*, Andrew Deutsch, London 1981. p. 75.

21. Quoted ibid., p. 120.

22. ibid., p. 128.

23. ibid., p. 151-2.

24. "The Church in Ningbo, Recovery and Reconciliation", *Bridge*, No. 7, September 1984.

25. *Asian Outreach Report*, No. 84, Hong Kong, March 1977, and Chinese Church Research Centre, Hong Kong, October-December 1980.

26. British Council of Churches Small Group report on visit to Hangzhou, December 1981.

27. *Bridge*, No. 7 September 1984.

28. "A Christian Funeral in Zhejiang", *Pray for China*, China Research Centre, Christian Communications Ltd., Hong Kong, No. 4, November 1974, which carries a picture of the coffin being carried.

29. Chao, Jonathan ed., *The Spirit of God at Work in China*, China Graduate School of Theology, Hong Kong 1975.

30. Chao, Jonathan, *A Glimpse of Christian Community Life in a Chinese Village*, China Graduate School of Theology, Hong Kong 1974.

31. Carroll, Ewing. V., Jr., ed., "Christian Worship in Rural China", *China Talk*, Vol. 2, Nos. 4/5, December 1977, United Methodist Church of the U.S.A., China Liaison Office, Hong Kong.

32. Report to "Love China 1975", China Study Seminar, Manila, 7-11 September 1975. Another source suggests the arrests were in late 1971, *Pray for China*, China Research Centre, Hong Kong, No. 1, May 1974.
33. Chao, Jonathan, ed., Interview with Christian doctor from Xiamen in 1976, "Christians in Fukien Today", China and the Church Today, Chinese Church Research Centre, China Graduate School of Theology, Hong Kong, No. 1, 1979.
34. Li, Stephen, Memoir, Chinese Church Research Centre, China Graduate School of Theology, Hong Kong October 1979.
35. *Pray for China*, No. 3, September 1974.
36. Private Source, China Program, National Council of Churches of Christ, U.S.A., 12 November 1973.
37. ibid., 10 December 1973.
38. Parish, William L. and Whyte, Martin King, *Village and Family in Contemporary China*, University of Chicago Press, 1976.
39. Sun Jingxuan, *Chang'an* No. 1, 1981 pp. 8-9, quoted in Yu Shao-ling, "Voice of Protest: Political Poetry in the Post-Mao Era", *China Quarterly*, 96, December 1983, p. 713.
40. Hu Yaobang, *Beijing Review*, No. 37, 1982, quoting *Renmin Ribao* 8 September 1982.
41. Pan Xiao, *China Youth News*, translation of this paragraph from NCNA, 29 July 1980. See *Monsoon Magazine*, Hong Kong, November 1980 for full translation. Reproduced *CSP Bulletin*, No. 14., December 1980.
42. Xiao Zhitian, *Some Opinions on Recent Religious Phenomena, Collected Essays on Research in Religion*, Shanghai, September 1982, translated by Janice Wickeri, *Ching Feng*, Vol. 26, No. 4, 1983.
43. See for example, Capra, Fritjof. *The Tao of Physics*, Fontana, London 1975, and *The Turning Point: Society and the Rising Culture*, Wildwood House, London 1982.
44. Li Zehou, "Zhuang Zi and Chan Buddhism", *Social Sciences in China*, No. 1, 1987, pp. 61-102.
45. ibid., p. 99.
46. ibid.
47. ibid., p. 100.
48. Balthasar, Hans Urs von, *The Glory of the Lord: A Theological Aesthetics, I: Seeing the Form*, T. & T. Clark, Edinburgh 1982, p. 80.
49. Fung, Raymond ed., *Households of God on China's Soil*, World Council of Churches, Geneva 1982. p. 78.
50. Private paper dated 29 May 1980.
51. Morris C., ed. and translator. *Christians in Rural Zhejiang*, Chinese Church Research Centre, Hong Kong, May 1980.
52. Tang, Edmond, "The Catholic Church in China Today: A Preliminary Interpretation", unpublished paper, Pro Mundi Vita, Brussels, December 1980.
53. Quoted in Karsen, Wendell, "A New Chapter in the Book of Acts: The Church in China Emerges", unpublished report, June 1980.
54. Tang, op. cit.
55. Ta Kung Pao, Hong Kong, 23 May 1978.
56. NCNA, in Chinese, 14 June 1978, BBC SWB FE 5845, 22 June 1978.
57. Text in *Renmin Ribao*, 7 July 1979.

Unfinished Encounter

58. Text in *Beijing Review*, No. 52, 27 December 1982, see *CSP Documentation*, No 10, March 1983. p. 7.
59. NCNA, 11 December 1982, BBC SWB FE 7209, 15 December 1982, see *CSP Documentation*, No. 10, March 1983, p. 7.
60. Ren Jiyu, NCNA, in English 28 November 1982, *CSP Documentation*, No. 10, March 1983, p. 6.
61. Li Wen, "How Can the Buddha Re-enter Schools?" *Zhongguo Nongmin Bao*, 20 October 1983, see *CSP Documentation*, No. 15, October, 1984. p. 53.
62. Ting, K.H., *China Daily*, 9 December 1982.
63. Jiang Ping, *Tian Feng*, No. 4, July 1982.
64. Ting, K.H., Interview, *China Notes*, Vol. 20 No. 2/3, Summer/Fall 1982.
65. Shanghai City Radio, 11 January 1979, BBC SWB FE 6017, 16 January 1979.
66. *Le Monde*, 4 April 1979.
67. Lee, Peter, K.H., "Meeting with Protestant Leaders in China", *Ching Feng* Vol. 22, No. 2, 1979.
68. Wei, Father Louis, "Le Chinois de Jesus", *Le Nouvel Observateur*, 9 April, 1979.
69. NCNA, 22 May 1980, BBC SWB FE 6435, 3 June 1980.
70. Letter to All Catholic Clergy and Laity of China, unofficial translation by Pro Mundi Vita, Brussels, *CSP Documentation*, No. 4, February 1981, p. 22-24.
71. *Sunday Examiner*, Hong Kong, 30 May 1980 and 23 January 1981. *Tablet*, London, 17 January 1981.
72. Text in *CSP Documentation*, No. 2/3, July 1980, pp. 51-4.
73. Zheng Jianye, "On the Question of a Church Affairs Organization", October 1980, see *CSP Documentation* No. 5, May 1981.
74. Yap Kim Hao, Report on Visit to China, Christian Conference of Asia, October 1980.
75. *Renmin Ribao*, 9 September 1980, translation by Janice Wickeri.
76. Ting, K.H., "A Call for Clarity; Fourteen Points from Christians in China to Christians Abroad", *Ching Feng*, Vol. 24, No. 1, March 1981.
77. Ren Jiyu, "Investigate Religion and Criticize Theology", *Guangming Ribao*, 27 September 1977, translated in *Ching Feng*, Vol. 20, No. 3, 1977.
78. NCNA, in Chinese, 25 April 1978, BBC SWB FE 5800, 28 April 1978.
79. Ren Jiyu, "The Struggle to Develop a Marxist Science of Religion", *Zhexueyanjiu*, No. 4, 1979, translated, *Ching Feng*, Vol. 22, No. 2, 1979.
80. *Research on World Religions*, No. 1, August 1979, reviewed by Wickeri, Philip L., in *China Notes*, Vol. 18, No. 3 Summer 1980.
81. Zhao Fusan, quoted NCNA, 11 June 1980, BBC SWB FE 6451, 21 June 1980.
82. Ting, K.H., quoted in Johnson, the Rev. Dr E.H., "Christian Theologians in the Changing China Scene", unpublished paper.
83. *Renmin Ribao*, Editor's Column, 15 March 1979.
84. Wickeri, Philip L., *Seeking the Common Ground*, pp. 162-3.
85. Document No. 19 (classified), CCP Central Committee March, 1982. The Document became available overseas and is reproduced in full in Wickeri, op. cit., pp. 549-64.
86. Kong Fan and Li Shen, "A Realistic Approach to Religious Problems Through the Reading of Deng Xiaoping's Selected Works", *Shijie Zongjiao Yanjiu*, No. 4, 1983, pp. 1-3, translated Barry, Peter, *Bridge*, No. 4, March 1984.

87. *Tian Feng*, July 1985, translated *CSP Bulletin*, No. 28, November 1985, and included in *Chinese Theological Review*, 1985, Nanjing.
88. *Beijing Review*, No. 47, 25 November 1985, quoting *Xueshujie Dongtai*.
89. Jiang Ping, "Study Conscientiously Marxist Theory on Religion and the Party Policy on Religion". *Hong Qi (Red Flag)*, 1 May 1986, BBC SWB FE 8264, 21 May 1986, also *CSP Journal*, No. 2, 1986.
90. Zhao Fusan, "A Reconsideration of Religion", *Zhongguo Shehui Kexue*, No. 3, 1986, translated by Feng Shize in *Social Sciences in China*, Autumn 1986.
91. Zhang Chunting and Han Hua, Interview, *Liaowang* Overseas Edition, 9 June 1986, *CSP Journal*, No. 3 1986.
92. *Xinhua* in Chinese, 22 August 1986, BBC SWB FE 8348, 27 August 1986, see also *CSP Journal*, No. 3, November 1986, p. 48.

IX

Out of the Shadows
1981-1987

With mountains and waters all around
We wondered whether there was a way out.
Flowers brightened us up in the dark shades of willows,
And we soon found ourselves reaching another village.[1]

The mood amongst Christians in China at the beginning of
1981 was buoyant. The national conferences in 1980 had
demonstrated the reality of a new orientation in religious
policy. The fact that churches were overflowing, that many
youngsters were showing interest, and that more and more
restrictions were being removed, contributed to this feeling of
optimism. The continuing difficulties experienced in some
places, the ambiguities of government policy, the challenge of
rebuilding the public life of the Church with insufficient
human or material resources, were recognized, but were seen
as secondary. The story of the Church from 1981 to the early
months of 1987 is the subject of this chapter. It is a story of
revival and consolidation, of laying the foundations for the
future, but above all it is a story that is told in the joy of
people's faces, the fervour of their prayers, in the hands extended in greeting towards fellow Christians from across the
world. As we seek to portray this Church we shall have to deal
with its difficulties and problems, but these should never be
allowed to mask the vibrant reality. Here indeed is a Church
rooted in Chinese culture, able at last to offer something from
within that culture and not from the outside – except in so far
as the Gospel is alien to every culture. The forms are often still
taken from the past – still Western in origin – but the spirit that
makes these forms live is definitely an indigenous one.

It is unfortunate that the only way to communicate this wonderful story is by a mass of detailed information. The detail is necessary if we are to understand the situation, for a great national revival (always remembering that Christians are a tiny proportion of the total population of China) is itself the sum total of a mass of happenings that to an outsider sometimes appear irrelevant. This chapter will seek to trace the over-all patterns discernible through the details, in the hope that we can arrive at a reasonably coherent view of the state of Chinese Christianity by mid-1987. This, hopefully, will enable some more general conclusions to be drawn. In the final chapter we shall attempt an over-all theological evaluation of the "unfinished encounter" between Christian faith and Chinese culture.

By 1987 many things had been achieved, but a great deal of practical consolidation remained to be done, and the more fundamental theological and ecclesiological issues had hardly been articulated. There was, however, a growing awareness that Christians could no longer be content with theological forms that produce separation and exclusiveness. The encounter with the society around presented a theological challenge to thoughtful Christians, aware that Christianity had failed in the past to take Chinese culture and society seriously. Today such an encounter must engage with the full complexity of contemporary Chinese reality, which as we have already seen, is itself in a state of rapid change and uncertainty. It is precisely in such an open situation that Christians can hope to make a positive and creative contribution. No longer facing a self-confident and self-sufficient Confucian or Marxist social consensus, there is a new opportunity for Christianity.

It would be misleading to pretend that the process of inculturation is complete, or that the change in consciousness has affected all Christians. The new opportunity could easily be lost, for there are also forces within Chinese Christianity that have never come to terms with the challenge of Marxism, and for whom the experience of the past almost forty years has been one of mere survival against the odds. For such people their faith has helped to sustain them in troubled times, and there are still many factors in society which will continue to reinforce this way of believing. This tradition of a church in the ghetto is easily explained in the light of Christian history in China, and those who have chosen this way of survival in a hostile environment can hardly be blamed. Such groups are indigenous, living according to the principles of self-government, self-support and self-propagation, but they are exclusivist and negative in their view of society. One need only think back to the teachings of Watchman Nee and Wang Mingdao to understand their perspective. Although indigenous they have been unable to adapt to their context, not necessarily through any fault of their own. The mentality is essentially escapist, and in this sense Marx's critique of religion as the "heart of a heartless world" may legitimately be applied to them. There are also many foreign groups who seek to encourage the growth of this type of fundamentalist faith amongst both Protestants and Catholics, and Christians of this sort are very vulnerable to such external influences.

One of the major debates over the past few years in China has been on the question of whether a socialist society can itself produce "alienation". An important body of opinion within Marxist circles now basically accepts that this can happen. It is in response to such alienation that some of the growth of the Church has taken place, and it is likely to be proven to be a house built on sand. The insights of the leaders of the Three Self Movement, gained so painfully during and after the 1920s, are still valid, even if they must be adapted in a new situation and in the light of experience. The rise of leftism in the Church as well as in society, the collapse of the United Front policy after 1957, the follies and mistakes of individuals, none of these must be allowed to obscure the fundamental achievement of the Three Self Movement in preparing Christians to live within a socialist society and to leave the ghetto. The fruits of this endeavour are only now being harvested.

Any commentator should be aware that balanced interpretation is elusive: personal preconceptions, theological and political, are bound to influence one's selection of material in a situation in which, despite far more information being available than ever before, much remains still obscure and uncertain. We shall find that this is most true of the Catholic situation. The conflict with Rome has not been resolved at the time of writing, and the view taken as to the nature of this conflict profoundly affects any interpretation of the Catholic scene in China. On the Protestant side the greatest area of dispute is over the nature, size and importance of the groups who still espouse the sort of conservative perspective mentioned above. It is our contention that ultimately a marginal existence on the sidelines of a civilization, whether this takes the form of Protestant sectarianism or of the closed world of Tridentine Catholicism, is a denial of the central thrust of Christian outreach. It is a return to the pre-Pauline outlook of Jewish Christianity, a tendency constantly to be found in Christian history and as constantly resisted by the mainstream of Christianity. For an incarnational faith there can be only a road to nowhere in the choice of the ghetto, even though the other way leads into the ambiguities of the world of politics and human society. Here indeed we have to choose between Y.T. Wu and Wang Mingdao, to put it starkly!

The Political Context 1981-87

The last chapter ended with a detailed discussion of the ongoing debate over the nature of religion and its position within a socialist milieu. It will be necessary to pursue this matter a little further, by looking at the evolution of the religious policy of the CCP after 1981, for this defines in good measure the extent of public religious expression – always bearing in mind the local circumstances that can radically influence policy application. In previous chapters we have traced the course of secular history, without which the situation of religion would have been inexplicable. In this chapter we shall not need to do more than paint in the outlines of the secular context, as the lines of policy laid down at the Third Plenum in late 1978 have not been significantly modified. Of course, from 1981 to 1986 there were major changes in economic and administrative structures, but the changes were a working out of the policy guidelines set between 1978 and 1980. China's social and economic problems are immense: population, land, resources – these three define the limits within which a government must operate, and they leave little scope for manoeuvre. Add to this the problems left over from history, the problems of finding a way through the outdated political and administrative forms, and the problem of people's rising expectations, and one becomes aware of the awesome task that faces China's present rulers.

Deng Xiaoping had already demonstrated his willingness to face many of these problems head-on, and it was under his leadership that a series of innovative policies were introduced. The most notable and far-reaching of these were the new rural policies which freed the countryside from the shackles of bureaucratic controls. The rural revolution, in which within a short period of time the countryside moved from a collective form of organization to one based on farming by individual households, had happened spontaneously, moving ahead of Party policy and taking everyone by surprise. What had taken place was a dismantling of the structures erected after 1956 in the countryside, as well as a reversal of the values of egalitarianism that had accompanied the creation of the communes. Conservative critics in the Party could point to some definitely undesirable results of this change, such as the demise of many co-operative medical schemes, the increase in the disparities between rich and poor areas, the growth in corruption, the rise in "feudal super-stitions" and in the crime rate, but the rise in rural productivity and incomes made it difficult to attack.

China also entered into uncharted international waters in this period, and found herself exposed as never before to powerful forces from outside, both for good and ill. Many in the Party expressed fears of "spiritual pollution" from over-seas, and their fears were not without foundation. One famous example was the attempt by Open Doors to smuggle into

China, on 18 June 1981, a claimed one million Bibles. It was a blatant act of provocation that had serious repercussions for the group of Chinese Christians who had foolishly got caught up in the affair, and it is just one example of how insensitive foreign agencies can confirm the suspicions of officials, if not play into the hands of those seeking an excuse to curtail the implementation of more liberal policies.

The power of the more conservative elements in the CCP was exerted briefly in 1983, in the movement against "spiritual pollution". While the campaign was largely conducted within the ideological sphere, the conservatives' objective was to curb the most radical of the economic reforms – which they rightly saw as leading in the direction of political reform. It was for this reason that the immediate cause of the backlash was the call for a socialist humanism, and the assertion by Wang Ruoshui and Zhou Yang of the existence of alienation within socialist society. The conservatives considered that the authority of the CCP was being undermined, and the ground prepared for the reform of the political system. However, they miscalculated and attempted too much, with the result that in early 1984 the backlash was essentially contained, but the defeat of the conservatives was certainly not decisive, and they bided their time. The next stage in the economic reform entailed the tackling of the more intractable problems of industry and commerce. Considerable resistance to the reorganization was soon encountered, both from the labour force and the manager. The labour force were threatened with the end to their "iron rice bowls" through the introduction of incentives, and productivity-related rewards and penalties – including possible dismissal. The managers were open to dismissal for incompetence. Further, the dismantling of the Soviet-style planning and administrative structures that began in this period proved to be a difficult and controversial task. In all areas of life there were dramatic changes. Many benefited, but some suffered loss of status and personal income as well as insecurity. Those who found the threat of change too much either opted out of their responsibilities or set about feathering their own nests. Many officials were forced to re-think the habits of a lifetime and, as might be expected, a good number resisted.

Economic changes, all in the direction of freeing individuals and institutions from central controls, are bound to have implications for what Marxists term the "superstructure" of society. This logic appeared to receive the endorsement of Deng Xiaoping in 1986, and to pave the way for political restructuring. The freedom of debate in 1986 was both surprising and stimulating – this time the concerns of the "democratic movement" were being voiced by senior officials themselves. At last, perhaps, the underlying question of the "fifth modernization" – democracy – was being taken seriously at the highest level. But such discussions were too much for the old guard, and in a dramatic reaction to student demonstrations in late 1986, in January 1987 the CCP dismissed Hu Yaobang as General Secretary of the Party. The long-term implications of this development are unclear, but the reformers were put on the defensive for the second time since 1980. At the time of writing the reformers appeared to be regaining the initiative as the CCP prepared for its Thirteenth Congress.

It is within this context of rapid change, intellectual ferment, material growth and the rise of accompanying social problems that the story of Chinese Christianity must be set. In the previous chapter we have suggested that Christians may be able to contribute positively within this environment, and that some, at least, within the CCP recognize this. It is also within this changing situation that government officials have sought to define religious policy. The conservative reaction in 1987 does not appear to have caused immediate problems for religious believers, but continuation of such a mood would seem to curtail opportunities for a creative contribution to socialist culture.

Religious Policy

The acceptance of Ya Hanzhang's views on the question of the relationship between religion and superstition was accompanied by a revival of Li Weihan's "five characteristics of religion", first expounded in the early 1950s. The CCP undoubtedly saw itself as returning to the correct policies of the past. In fact, the nature of the religious "problem" had changed in the intervening years, with the result that many of the former assumptions were no longer adequate to the situation. The result has been, on the one hand, an attempt to contain the situation within the bounds of the 1950s, and on the other hand, a gradual shift towards more realistic policies. In the 1980s the CCP found itself facing a religious revival which contradicted the glib assumption that religion would inevitably decline under socialism. In the face of this it sought to limit the sphere of influence by religion while acknowledging the rights of believers. Xiao Xianfa, head of the Religious Affairs Bureau until his death in August 1981, did on a number of occasions stress the need for the proper "management" of religious activities. In a *People's Daily* article on 14 June 1980,[2] he drew a distinction between "management" and "interference", treading a delicate path towards a definition of what was meant by the oft-repeated phrase "normal religious activities". Xiao's understanding relates back to the 1950s United Front policy, in which there is over-all supervision by the government but with a limited, but defined, sphere of "toleration". It was a policy that was never fully implemented in the 1950s, but it has obviously remained as a model in the minds of cadres responsible for religious affairs.

Throughout 1981 and 1982 there were references to the need to ensure that religion remained within certain limits. On one level this took the form of stressing the need for education in atheism, especially amongst young people. *China Youth News* carried items on why religious faith was increasing, and on the need to propagate atheism while not despising young people with religious faith.[3] *Wen Hui Bao* on 11 October 1982 stressed that the new Constitution did not mean that members of the CCP or the Communist Youth League were now free to believe in religion.[4] Concern over this surfaced time and again, it being stressed that Party members with religious beliefs should resign from the Party if they refused to give them up. As *Fujian Daily* put it in October 1981:

> We uphold atheism, oppose theism and do away with superstitions . . . CCP and CYL members must not believe in religion or join a church . . . As for the small number who believe in religion and participate in religious activities, we should do painstaking educational work among them and persuade them to give up their religious belief and to quit church activities. Those who refuse to do so should be persuaded to withdraw from the Party or the CYL.[5]

Concern with the growth of religious influence was also reflected in the publication in *Party Life* of a report from Shanghai of the return of an old Party member to the CCP after she had started to attend one of the newly opened churches in the city.[6]

The adoption of the "four fundamental principles", with their stress on the leading role of the Party and the propagation of Marxism-Leninism Mao Zedong Thought, could have caused difficulties for religious policy. In fact, the "Resolution on Certain Questions in the History of Our Party", adopted at the Sixth Plenum of the 11th Central Committee on 27 June 1981, explicitly dealt with this issue:

> It is imperative to continue to implement the policy of freedom of religious belief. To uphold the four fundamental principles does not mean that religious believers should renounce their faith, but that they must not engage in propaganda against Marxism-Leninism and Mao Zedong Thought and that they must not interfere with politics and education in their religious activities.[7]

A further aim of religious policy was the remoulding of the thinking of believers. The basic assumption was still that believers could be patriotic but that their faith could make no contribution to socialist culture. Formal statements of religious policy stuck to this position until 1986 when, as we have seen, Zhao Fusan's viewpoint was espoused by Party spokesmen. The negative evaluation of religion inevitably tends to lead to restrictions. The nature of the restrictions has been a matter of intense speculation outside China, with much misleading and inaccurate information being spread around. One reason for this is the lack of publicly available regulations. Another reason is the variation in provincial and local policies.

Religious Regulations

A number of external reports at this time mentioned the existence of guidelines relating to the re-opening of churches. These have been variously referred to as the "Eight Bans" or the "Ten Don'ts", and there can be little doubt that more often than not such guidelines were the product of provincial and not national officials – indeed the existence of such local regulations has been acknowledged nationally and criticized as "leftist". The prohibitions invariably refer to not propagating religion to those under eighteen or to members of the Party; to limiting religious activities to designated places – therefore no public evangelism or home meetings; no contact with foreign religious organizations, and no publications without prior approval.[8] The "Ten Don'ts" were reported from Henan and Zhejiang. These appear to have included additional items dealing with interference in politics, education and marriage, not raising funds through offerings, not praying for the sick or engaging in exorcism, not posing as a pastor or elder and conducting ordination, or baptism, and not praying every day, but only on Sundays.

It has to be said that the "Ten Don'ts" are considerably more restrictive than the "Eight Bans" and must be taken as reflecting the persistence of strong "leftist" attitudes in these provinces in 1981-83, the period of the reports. The "Eight Bans" are likely to have had a wider provenance, for a number of the prohibitions would tend to fit in with known policies, and it can be assumed that local Religious Affairs officials were simply reviving the guidelines originally issued in the 1950s.

It is, therefore, necessary to exercise caution when discussing these prohibitions. They seem likely to have been transitory phenomena, in the sense that they were adopted in a situation in which officials had to react speedily to what local officials in Henan dubbed "Christianity fever".[9] Another set of regulations entitled the "Eight-Point Internal Policy on Religion", which was accompanied by a "Six-Point External Policy on Religion", are of wider interest, assuming them to be genuine. The origin of these regulations can only be guessed at, but their tone is decidedly more moderate than the others and may originate nationally. It is possible that the "Eight Bans" and "Ten Don'ts" were local interpretations of this national set of guidelines, leaving out the nuances. Despite the uncertainty as to their status and authenticity, it will be useful to look at them in more detail as they cast light on a number of perplexing aspects of religious policy.

Time and again the question of the status of those below the age of eighteen has been raised by foreign visitors to churches in China, without any uniform or coherent answer being forthcoming. In general there is no formal Christian work amongst young people under this age – only one Sunday school in China is known to the author – and the attendance of children at church varies from place to place. Infant baptism amongst Protestants has been all but abandoned in most places, not only, one presumes, on theological grounds. One is forced to the conclusion that at the very least there is a general understanding that religious teaching will not be given to those under eighteen except within the family setting, but that there is a degree of confusion within China itself over the scope of restriction. The fact that a similar answer tends to be received from any part of the country implies the existence of some sort of regulation, but the confusion suggests that it is open to varying interpretations. The first two of the "Eight Points" would help to explain the ambiguity:

> Citizens above the age of eighteen have the freedom of religious belief. That is, believers and non-believers will

not interfere with one another's business and will respect one another without any discrimination.

Adolescents under the age of eighteen shall not be instilled with religious faith. But if they want to believe in God of their own will, that is an exception.[10]

Such a wording could explain why, with regard to adolescents, many officials have interpreted national policy as meaning a ban on religious activity by those under eighteen. Thus on 19 July 1980 Lanzhou Radio quoted a cadre in Hezheng county, Gansu, as saying that such activities were illegal on the basis that, "This is definitely stipulated in the Constitution of our country".[11] It would appear that the leadership of the Church is unhappy with this restrictive view, for Bishop Ting used the opportunity given him by the reception of the Archbishop of Canterbury and the British Council of Churches Delegation in December 1983, by Deng Yingchao, Zhou Enlai's widow, to raise the matter directly. In response she made it clear that "There is no regulation in the Constitution about the age of belief".[12] Deng's view is strictly correct, and the "Eight-Point Policy" does not contradict this, although its prohibition of religious instruction of the young opens the way to more discriminatory policies by less discerning officials.

The remainder of the "Eight Points" need not detain us. They repeat the over-all lines of religious policy as explained in published documents since 1979, and they do not include the more restrictive aspects of either the "Eight Bans" or the "Ten Don'ts", nor do they attempt to legislate on home meetings, prayer, or other matters relating to the internal life of the Church. The "Six Points" are of some interest, however, for they flatly contradict the ban on foreign contacts found in the other sets of regulations, and even talk of limited financial contributions from foreign religious organizations. They stress autonomy and the Three Selfs, but open the way to the exchange of delegations and attendance at international conferences that did in fact begin in 1980.

Document Nineteen

A number of statements of religious policy were published in 1981 and 1982, but these were all superseded by the promulgation of Central Committee Document Number 19, dated March 1982. The main contents of the Document were published in the form of a major article in *Red Flag* on 16 June, but the text of Document 19 itself has since become available, and our analysis is based on that since this will have formed the basis of the application of policy throughout the country. The preamble calls on all responsible organs to "undertake conscientious investigation and discussion of the religious question" and to "increase supervision and prompt inspection as regards the implementation of each item related to this policy".[13]

The Document begins with a re-statement of the classical Marxist view of religion, couched in moderate terms and, as already noted in the last chapter, avoiding all reference to religion as "opium". It concludes its first section with the words:

> All Party members must have a sober-minded recognition of the protracted nature of the religious question under socialist conditions. Those who think that with the establishment of the socialist system and with a certain degree of economic and cultural progress, religion will die out within a short period, are not being realistic. Those who expect to rely upon administrative decrees or other coercive measures to wipe out religious thinking and practices with one blow, are even further from the basic viewpoint Marxism takes towards the religious question. They are entirely wrong and will do no small harm.

Section Two states that the absolute number of religious believers has increased since 1949, but the proportion in relation to the population has declined. It is an assertion that it is impossible to check out, but the figures given for Protestants are 700,000 in 1949 and three million in 1982, an absolute and proportional increase. Prior to 1949 "all religions were manipulated and controlled by the ruling classes" but since

Liberation "the status of religion has already undergone a fundamental change". Religious questions now belong primarily to the category of contradictions among the people. Section Three discusses past religious policy, affirming the work up to 1957 but admitting that "since 1957 . . . leftist errors gradually grew up in our religious work". In the Cultural Revolution the violent measures against religion "forced it to go underground". Since the Third Plenum, matters have been corrected but opposing "leftism" remains the main task. On the other hand, matters must not be allowed to drift. Once again one detects the dual concern with both freedom and supervision.

The next Section is a key one. It elaborates on the meaning of freedom of religious belief in terms of the right to believe or not believe, indicating that people are free to change their beliefs in whatever direction they choose. In opposing coercion it makes a most important statement:

> We must further understand that, at the present historical stage, the difference that exists between the mass of believers and non-believers in matters of ideology and belief is of relatively secondary importance. If we one-sidedly emphasize this difference . . . then we forget that the Party's basic task is to unite all the people . . . in order to construct a modern powerful socialist state.

It then reiterates some of the known policies, such as not allowing religion to interfere in "administrative or juridical affairs of state, nor to intervene in the schools or public education". On the question of age limits it takes a clear line that it is "absolutely forbidden to force anyone, particularly young people under eighteen years of age, to become a member of a church, to become a Buddhist monk or nun, or to go to temples or monasteries to study Buddhist scripture".

Section Five deals with the role of religious professionals, seen mainly as key figures in ensuring a patriotic orientation amongst believers. Only a very few are opposed to socialism. The Party's task is to "unrelentingly yet patiently forward their education in patriotism, upholding the law, supporting socialism and upholding national and ethnic unity", and in the case of Christians to "strengthen their education in independence and self-government of their churches". Redressing of grievances, proper arrangements for their livelihood, ensuring they can contribute to society and to the academic study of religion, are all means of mobilizing positive elements in religious circles to serve modernization within a broad United Front. Section Six calls for effective measures to re-open places of worship, but makes it clear that in principle the goal is for all public religious activities to take place in "designated places", although considerable scope for private observances in homes is given:

> All normal religious activities held in places so designated, as well as those which, according to religious custom, take place in believers' homes – Buddha worship, scripture chanting, incense burning, worship, prayer, Bible exposition, preaching, Mass, baptism, initiation of a monk or nun, fasting, celebration of religious festivals, extreme unction, commemoration, etc. – are all to be conducted by religious organizations and religious believers themselves, under the protection of law and without interference from any quarter . . . As for Protestants gathering in homes for religious activities, in principle this should not be allowed, yet these activities should not be harshly prohibited. Rather, persons in the patriotic religious organizations should make efforts to persuade the mass of religious believers to make more appropriate arrangements.

This last proviso has been much attacked from outside China, yet its significance should not be overstated. The earlier part of the paragraph concedes the right to engage in religious activity within homes, and the pointed reference to Protestants must therefore be taken to refer to situations where such meetings are organized over against an alternative "designated" place of worship, whether this be in a church building or a home. The continued and large-scale existence of home meetings since 1982 suggests that this interpretation is correct. Whether or not one approves of such interference is another matter, but it is important to understand the specific objective of this clause. It must also be remembered that family rites such as Christian marriage and burial services are increasingly common.

The next two Sections relate to the role of the patriotic religious organizations and the training of young religious personnel. The underlying assumption in both sections is that the over-all aim is the fostering of patriotic sentiment amongst believers. Section Nine deals with the prohibition on Party members believing in religion, but makes an important exception in the case of national minorities, recognizing that some minority Party members will find it difficult to shake off all religious influence. Section Ten deals with the use of religion by anti-revolutionary elements, with particular reference to "superstitious practices". Section Eleven deals with international relations, taking a generally positive view except in the case of

> reactionary religious groups abroad, especially imperialistic ones such as the Vatican and Protestant foreign mission societies, who strive to use all possible occasions to carry on their efforts at infiltration "to return to the China mainland".

The last Section calls for strengthening government organs dealing with religion, developing the academic critique of religion, and aiming for the building of a highly developed civilization in which the role of religion in providing "an illusory world of the gods to seek spiritual solace" will simply disappear.

As we have already discussed the question of the Marxist view of religion, and have looked with some care at the underlying assumptions behind the policy of the United Front in the 1950s, we need not dwell on the implications of this Document. Its characteristically patronizing standpoint flows naturally from the belief that all religion is an illusion. The assumption that it is the duty of believers to support the goals of the state is both Marxist and Confucian. The Document represents a decisive re-statement of the moderate under-standing of religious policy, but with a number of important new emphases. Perhaps the key one is the statement that religion is a secondary difference. As Bishop Ting has pointed out, it would be inappropriate for a believer to say this, but for the Central Committee to make this statement is a most significant step forward.

Document Nineteen has remained the basis of religious policy since its promulgation. It also hinted as to the pro-mulgation of a religious law, and in a speech to the Catholic Patriotic Association on 23 April 1983 the new head of the Religious Affairs Bureau, Qiao Liansheng, indicated that such a law would be formulated within a year or two, and would greatly assist in the implementation of religious policy in a consistent way throughout the country. In the meantime some areas will go their own way, and locally produced regulations can easily infringe believers' rights without much possibility of redress. The continued references in some areas to such phenomena as the "Patriotic Pledge" is an indication of the persistence of this problem. Nevertheless between 1982 and 1987 there has been a steady improvement in the position of religious believers in all parts of the country. Bishop Ting, meeting with Shanghai pastors on 8 January 1987, indicated that a new, more liberal statement of Party religious policy was under discussion. It may be, therefore, that the more restrictive aspects of Document Nineteen are about to be removed.

The campaign against spiritual pollution that hit China in the autumn of 1983 saw a temporary reversal, especially in areas still under strong leftist influence. At the national level the leadership was clear that the campaign had nothing to do with religion. As Li Xiannian, President of China, told the Archbishop of Canterbury in the very middle of the move-ment, "Religion and the effort to clear away cultural con-tamination are two entirely different things".[14] However, the media carried a number of reports implying such a link, notably in regard to certain cultural works which "enthusia-stically preach religion",[15] and a *Guangming Daily* report highlighted the problem of spiritual pollution amongst students in Beijing, some of whom have "even pinned their hopes on religion".[16] In such an atmosphere it was inevitable that some places put curbs on religion, although according to one informed source in Hong Kong the adverse effects were only felt in places where the religious affairs cadres were of low quality and were seeking to obstruct the implementation of religious policy.[17]

The Religious Affairs Bureau

The RAB is the government organ that supervises religious affairs. Its personnel were subjected to mistreatment during the Cultural Revolution, as the "black backstage" of religion and the structures of the RAB below national level had also to be rebuilt after 1978. Moreover, in recent years the Bureau has suffered from frequent changes of Director. Xiao Xianfa died on 28 August 1981, and his successor, Qiao Liansheng, died on 15 January 1984. He was succeeded by Ren Wuzhi, former First Party Secretary in Tibet. The RAB is a government and not a Party organ. Policy is made by the Party and supervised by the United Front Work Department. The powers of the RAB are therefore limited, and as we have seen in the 1950s, the work of the Bureau is easily undermined through the activities of the public security organs. According to Wang Hongkui, deputy director of Shanghai's RAB, the UFD itself does not have cadres assigned to religious work as such, and in principle the RAB is the body that implements religious policy. However, the separation of Party work from government work, one of the major reforms now underway, is incomplete, and in some counties or urban districts the RAB does not yet exist.[18] At the lower levels the Bureau is staffed by many of the cadres who were there in the 1950s and who suffered greatly in the Cultural Revolution. Their relationship with religious leaders is now often amicable, and it is mistaken to assume that the RAB necessarily adopts an obstructive attitude towards implementing a policy of greater freedom. Indeed, without the RAB many of the achievements of the past few years would have been impossible. As Deng Zhaoming comments in a *Bridge* Editorial:

> At present, close links between the United Front Work/Religious Affairs Bureau of the government and bodies of believers are necessary. For in China, every aspect of life is bound up with the government, at whatever level. Looked down upon as something poisonous and passive for such a long time, religious freedom and practices cannot make much headway unless the stigma from the past is removed by word and action from the higher authorities. The UFD/RAB, therefore, have a vital and constructive role in this transitional period of modernizing China and bringing about a more free and open society.[19]

An example of positive government intervention was detailed in *Tian Feng* in 1984. The city of Zhengzhou in Henan set up a special office, and issued a document concerning the restoration of property belonging to religious organizations. The document stipulated that if a property had been sold or demolished then compensation or rent or removal expenses should be paid by the occupant. A standard rental was fixed and a two-year limit set for payment. Fifty per cent was to be paid within three months, the remainder by the end of 1985 – failing which, interest would be charged according to the bank rate. Enterprises could use depreciation funds or enterprise funds, and government bodies could use either available funds or could pay through the City Finance Department.[20] An interesting case in Lanxi, Zhejiang involved the prosecution of an individual who refused to abide by an agreement to move out of property belonging to the local church.[21] The problems involved in regaining property are well illustrated by the difficulties encountered by the Xiangchun Street Church in Changsha, Hunan. The UFD Department decided in 1980 that the property ought to be returned, and a committee of inspection issued a directive to the occupying unit, the Changsha Motor Accessories Workshop. At 11 p.m. on Christmas Eve 1980 two-thirds of the upper floor was handed over, but the remainder was only returned after lengthy negotiations at Christmas 1983. Thereafter the managers of the workshop simply ignored a directive of the City Government, despite an offer of 80,000 yuan compensation, and in April 1984 they ignored a further directive from the provincial authorities. At the time of the report the matter was pending in the local People's Court as a result of action by the Changsha Three Self Committee.[22] It is also possible for the RAB to seek to monopolize religious work. A report from the provincial religious work conference in Heilongjiang on 6 May 1986 clearly stated the supervisory role of the RAB. Religious sites "should be subject to the management of religious organizations and professional religious personnel under the administrative leadership of the religious affairs departments". However, it also called attention to the fact that "cadres should not monopolize everything of the religious organizations".[23]

The Return of Churches

The number of churches either returned, rebuilt or newly opened since 1979 has now reached a total of over five thousand of which around one thousand are Catholic. In Fujian in 1987 there were seven hundred open churches, a hundred and twenty of which have been newly built. In Zhejiang the figure had reached over a thousand by Christmas 1985. It goes without saying that the attitude of the local authorities is all-important. No place of worship could open without approval from the local government, and without such help it is very unlikely that occupying units would be prepared to move out or pay back rents, compensation, etc. As Wang Hongkui commented, "No unit which occupies church property can easily be convinced to move".[24] The issue of government approval has sometimes been criticized from outside, but in a society where strict control of neighbourhood life is the norm it is not a matter for surprise and is not so different from the planning controls operating in many societies. There appear to be three main conditions relating to the re-opening of a church. First there have to be a sufficient number of Christians; secondly, adequate leadership; and thirdly, a building. Where these conditions are absent it is possible to register as a home meeting, linking with the local Christian structures. Bishop Ting suggested that there were around thirty thousand such registered meeting points by early 1986. The question of the relationship of home meetings to the church organizations will need to be looked at further below.

In 1984 the National CPPCC sent inspection teams to each main region of the country, to investigate how far United Front policy had been implemented, and the Religious Affairs Section sent out special teams to investigate the situation in Shaanxi, Sichuan and Hubei. In Shanghai the investigation was carried out in each relevant organ, with the result that a number of "old, great and difficult" problems were resolved. In Hangzhou the return of the YMCA was obstructed by the leader of the municipal sports committee, on the grounds that "I'm a Marxist-Leninist. What's Christianity to me!" As a result of the problems discovered by the teams the CPPCC determined to redouble its efforts to oppose leftism.[25] The problem of "leftism" continues to obstruct the proper implementation of policy in all sorts of ways. Bishop Ting, in an interview with *Beijing Review* in 1984, referred to "ultra-leftism" as the greatest problem.[26] Hunan is one of the areas still badly affected, with its own regulations, its "patriotic covenant", and continuing problems over the return of church properties, so that in 1985 only fourteen were open.[27] In Guangxi pastors' travel is restricted.[28]

However, problems can arise even in places with a strong Christian community. In June 1985 *China Daily* reported that an official from a factory in Wenzhou, Zhejiang, had led an assault on the local Catholic Church during Sunday Mass on 19 May, as the result of a dispute over the ownership of the church house.[29] He was promptly arrested, but the incident reveals the sensitivities which remain, and which Wang Hongkui mentions as a problem for the RAB, with religious people accusing them of tardiness and others "asking us whose side we are on".[30]

Social Discrimination

One of the hardest tasks is to change people's assumptions about religion and religious policy after long years of discrimination. Misunderstandings can readily arise, and it is not always easy to get redress, especially where proper channels of communication are lacking. There is a great deal of simple ignorance about religion. Thus in one place in northern Jiangxi the local officials put Christians and Buddhists together in the same house of worship, to the great embarrassment of both groups.[31] Much of the petty discrimination against Christians arises out of the same lack of knowledge. However, there does not appear to be a systematic policy of excluding believers from work in spheres such as education and health, and where it exists it is a local problem. A letter published in *Tian Feng* in July 1985 illustrated this:

> I am a supply teacher, and I am a Christian. But the leader of our commune says, "Teachers should not be religious believers". So just now I am a covert believer, though I am aware that continuing in this way is not a practical policy – Yao Yunchang.

In reply the Editor indicated that there are a great many Christians in educational work and many of these have been commended as model teachers. He suggests proving that a Christian can be a good teacher through actions and behaviour – possibly a piece of ineffectual advice but also a shrewd perception of the only way ultimately to overcome prejudice in the community.[32] The prohibition on Party members believing in a religion means that Christians are unable to assume senior political posts, but the gradual reversal of the previous tendency to make the Party conterminous with government should allow an increasing number of non-Party people to take part in government. It is already reflected in the growing number of religious representatives being elected both to the local CPPCC and the local People's Congresses. At the same time old attitudes persist, and are more likely to be found in sensitive areas such as higher education. The number of people entering higher education is small, and becoming a student is considered a great privilege and responsibility. There would appear to be some discrimination against believers seeking admission to university, but this is not universal and is probably less common lower down the scale of institutions. There are Christians graduating from college, and it must be assumed that there is no over-all policy of discrimination.

The Life of the Protestant Church

Church Organization

The situation in South-east China, with its large numbers of Christians, many living in compact Christian communities, is very different from that in areas such as Hunan and Guangxi where Christians are few and live in more scattered groups. Logistically, it is far more difficult to develop effective structures, and elderly pastors or priests may find it impossible to travel to outlying villages. There also seem to be more restrictions in these provinces. Thus, for example, pastors' travel was restricted in Guangxi by RAB officials. Guangxi has only small numbers of Christians – there were, perhaps, as few as twelve thousand Protestants although probably significantly greater numbers of Catholics in 1984, and until the First Representative Assembly held 13-17 June 1985 no Protestant Christian Council existed in the region. Without doubt the lack of an over-all provincial organization has contributed to the difficulties encountered by the fifteen or so pastors. There is an urgent need to move beyond the informal home meetings towards more formal structures, not least because of the protection such an organization can provide to believers. It is naïve to imagine that the home meetings or even local churches can be self-sufficient.

By the Fourth National Christian Conference in August 1986

the three autonomous municipalities, and all provinces and autonomous regions, with the exception of Tibet, had established both Three Self Movement and Christian Council structures for the first time. Organizationally the formation of this new structure has represented an important step forward, but in point of fact many increasingly urgent issues relating to church order are pressing. The question of establishing an effective national church organization that moves beyond the limited nature of the present structure of Christian Councils is now a matter of some concern to many in the present leadership. In an extremely interesting article in the *Nanjing Theological Review* in June 1985 Su Deci discusses the question of "self-government" in the context of the establishment of a national church organization, "the most important problem confronting Chinese Christians today":

> Denominational structures ceased to exist not long after Liberation, and then in 1958, the Church began to follow the path of unity and has continued to do so for twenty-six years. This was, without a doubt, a positive development, and we often thank God that through the circumstances of the times he enabled us to eliminate differences and undertake the miraculous work of "uniting under the head, Jesus". But we must also admit that in terms of church organization, church management benefited from the original denominations which fulfilled an administrative function the united church could not entirely inherit or replace. Following the Cultural Revolution, in October 1980, a nationwide association was established, and at the same time many localities started their own associations or church affairs committees. Still, no matter what the name or constitution of these organizations implied, nor what their accomplishments, they did not assume total administrative responsibility. Recently, liberalizing tendencies in Christianity have appeared at the grass-roots level and I think this is not without some connection to the emergence of these organizations. Different areas have experienced meddling by the

Religious Affairs Bureau, and in addition to faults within the Religious Affairs Bureau itself, I think the absence of an organizational structure in the church as a whole similarly encourages government interference in its affairs.[33]

It was such concern, together with an underlying issue of ecclesiology in the minds of people coming from non-congregational type churches, that led in 1985 to the establishment of a small sub-group to prepare recommendations on church order for the Fourth National Conference. Opinions were solicited from local churches and provincial leaders, and it became very clear that to move ahead with any proposal at this stage would result in division. In particular, members of the Little Flock, many of whom were now co-operating in the local churches and Christian Councils, had strong objections relating to their belief in one church for each locality and their objection to any form of ordained leadership. In the event the matter was dropped for the time being, presumably on the basis of considerations such as those referred to by the Vice-Principal of Nanjing Seminary, Chen Zemin, in an address to his students in 1985:

This is not a question to be hastily resolved, but should be decided on the basis of our historical conditions, the actual situation in our society and our cultural traditions. We must try to find a new road, one which has a theological foundation. In the past China was a mission field for foreign mission boards; all the different denominations came to proselytize in China. But the period of development for these denominations and organizations was relatively brief, their roots shallow, so we cannot choose one to be the model for our church structure without careful consideration . . . We must not be anxious to realize our goals, doing things carelessly as a result. What is even more important is that we safeguard unity and maintain mutual respect. We should manage our church ourselves. As for the method employed, we can explore this slowly.[34]

The issues are indeed complex. Su Deci is surely right to see this issue as central to the question of moving beyond this present period of transition towards a situation in which the Church assumes a far greater degree of autonomy from government organs. On the other hand Chen Zemin's caution is also correct, in so far as the building of mutual trust between believers from very different backgrounds is a process that is still very much unfinished. The Protestant Church in China is certainly post-denominational, but it is not yet in a position to create one Church. The establishment of a viable and comprehensive church network is a process that is still under way. National leaders recognize the seriousness of the Little Flock objections: to give up their "local church" principle would mean denying their very *raison d'être*. The creation of such a network has also been impeded by a number of purely practical things: lack of trained personnel, the age and health of surviving pastors and elders, lack of Bibles and other Christian materials, the time needed to negotiate for the return of properties, problems in transport and communications. Many of these problems had become less acute by the time of the Fourth Conference, but time is still needed, especially as the practical problems are linked to the more intractable difficulties caused by continuing leftist influence; by China's outdated and inefficient administrative system that consumes so much time and energy; and by the disparate traditions within the Christian community itself.

It is this last problem which continues to frustrate the formation of a proper administrative structure, as Su Deci has indicated. The origins of a significant section of the present Protestant community in China lie within indigenous sects. Even many Christians from main-line churches have inherited an exclusivist and narrow biblicism that can easily move towards sectarian attitudes. The characteristics of Chinese Christianity in the past have been one of the themes of this book. It has been our contention that, for a variety of reasons, both Catholic and Protestant Christianity in China has tended to be inward-looking, narrow in its theology, existing on the margins of society, and hostile to the society around. These characteristics have enabled it to survive in troubled times, but in the long term are unlikely to sustain Christianity within a modern, secular context in which Christian witness is no longer a question of survival as an opposition group but of discovering a meaningful role within an increasingly pluralistic society. Such groups as the Little Flock, the True Jesus Church and the Seventh Day Adventists were hostile to both Liberation and to other Christians. The experiences of the Cultural Revolution in particular helped to perpetuate the hostility to the political world, but tended to break down the hostility towards other Christians, with the result that many former members of these sects are now working with Christians from other backgrounds. Slowly, in the new political circumstances, attitudes towards society are also changing. It is most important to sustain this process, and this accounts for the extreme care with which the question of "church order" is being tackled. Inevitably, there are also many people who continue to maintain former attitudes, especially in areas where such groups live in compact communities. Isolation has re-inforced their sectarianism. Such groups remain opposed to co-operation with the formal structures, and pose a continuing problem calling for great sensitivity and patience. In Zhejiang the Little Flock is most numerous and most intractable, and initially the TSPM leadership in the province failed to get to grips with the problem. It is the increased awareness of the sensitivities of the situation in parts of Zhejiang and elsewhere that has led to the extreme caution with which the question of church organization is being tackled.

The experience of ecumenical discussions in the rest of the world suggests that the Chinese are right to build on the foundation of local ecumenical co-operation towards a national Church order, rather than to seek unity from the top down. The administration of a local church is carried out by a Church Committee with the pastors and representatives from the different former denominations. Thus even where there are different services for groups such as the Little Flock and Seventh Day Adventists, all decisions are collective ones. The peculiar circumstances in China have provided the Chinese evolution of Chinese forms of worship has hardly begun. The most significant step towards this has been the publication in 1983 of a new Chinese hymnal, with a quarter of the total of four hundred hymns being newly composed and using Chinese tunes. However, there is considerable resistance to the use of traditional musical instruments in place of the harmonium or piano.

Home Meetings

The history of the Three Self Movement since the 1950 Christian Manifesto has obviously been a controversial one. The unpreparedness of most Christians for the Communist take-over; the narrow theological perspective fostered since Morrison's arrival in 1807; the failure of Christian social reform in the 1930s; all these, combined with a militant Chinese nationalism in Marxist guise, contributed to the traumas of the 1950s. Under intense pressure Christians were forced to respond to the unfamiliar as best they could, and the pressure was most strongly felt by full-time church workers. In our study of this period we have tried to show how the Three Self Patriotic Movement, for all its mistakes, represented the one real hope that the Church could not only survive the storm but emerge from it in a form appropriate to a constructive existence within a post-revolutionary society. In the short term the strategy appeared to have foundered but, from the perspective of today, we can see that the task of establishing a Church rooted within contemporary Chinese culture, now in the process of being realized, is a result of these earlier, painful, choices. The political option chosen by the leaders of the Three Self Movement may, with hindsight, seem somewhat naïve, but it was surely the right choice to have made. To see the "three-selfs" as no more than a question of indigenization is to ignore the crucial question of its nature. The indigenization associated with Watchman Nee was founded on a theology whose eschatology encouraged a wilful unconcern with the sufferings of the common people. Marxism's critique of religion as an opiate finds its mark here, and theology cannot presume to move beyond Marxism without first acknowledging that while the Marxist view is partial, it is also a prophetic judgement on what human beings have done to religion.

The same sort of questions have to be asked of the present Christian scene in China, both Catholic and Protestant, especially as we seek to evaluate the relationship between the public structures of Three Self or Catholic Patriotic Association and those who choose to keep themselves apart from these structures. We shall have to deal with the Catholic situation later. Here we shall be discussing what many outside China choose to term the "house-church movement", a description that we have deliberately chosen to avoid, both because it is not a correct translation of the Chinese term *jiatinghui* and because of its particular associations within Britain and North America. The term "home meeting" is both more accurate and neutral.

Looking back over Protestant history in China we find that meetings in homes were always a common form of meeting for prayer and Bible study. The lack of church buildings in some rural areas, which we have noted during the 1920s and 1930s, meant that many Christians have always gathered in homes for Sunday worship. In the same period the growth of indigenous movements such as the Little Flock and True Jesus Church also meant an increase in "house churches". After 1949 the closure of rural churches during Land Reform led to many new home meetings, some of which were discontinued when churches re-opened later. In many places, however, churches did not re-open, either because of the political situation or through lack of funds and personnel. During the 1950s the home meeting became increasingly central to Christian life, a process that was speeded up after 1957 and which also affected the towns and cities. In the Cultural Revolution the home meeting was the only possible form of Christian worship, a situation that only began to change in 1979.

Such gatherings have a variety of origins, as noted in Chapter Six. For some Christians they have been the norm. For others they were originally a supplement to Sunday worship in a church. For yet others they resulted from the closure of churches after 1949 and represented a strategy for survival. The opening of over four thousand churches since 1979 is an impressive achievement, but the majority of Christians still have no choice – the home meeting remains the only option. The ethos of most of these meetings is a world apart from the modern Western "house church". As Jack Weir commented when returning to his native Manchuria in December 1983, they seemed more like Irish cottage meetings than the modern House Church Movement.[35] Others might think of Methodist home meetings, and indeed it is possible to trace such meetings back into the last century. For the majority of Protestants the hope would always have been to build a church, and there was never any question as to whether or not they would relate to non-local church structures. No wonder that with the gradual re-establishment of a church network, reaching out from the main cities into the surrounding countryside, there has been a steady increase in the number of home meetings coming into contact with the structures of the Three Self and the Christian Council.

Quite apart from the natural desire of Christians originating from main-line Protestant denominations, such contact brings a number of advantages – access to books, training of local lay leaders, and access to pastors who are able to baptize and celebrate Holy Communion. A further important advantage is the registration of the group, providing legitimacy as a home meeting. The perennial suspicion of Chinese governments towards informal religious networks, reflected also in Document Nineteen, suggests that survival outside of a legally constituted network will be fraught with difficulties. Such groups may retain in their own eyes a spiritual purity unsullied by compromise with the world, but there is a different price to pay for any group that chooses to separate itself from both society and Church, claiming that it alone is truly the Body of Christ. There are still situations where Christians may have no choice but to remain on the margin, but the longer this continues the more problems are likely to arise. Lack of contact has brought many problems relating to the quality of local leadership, false teaching, influence from folk religion, etc. Registration brings contact, and it also brings protection. Given the ongoing political realities of China a failure to register brings a very real possibility of proscription.

The great changes over the past forty years, the political upheavals and the experience of persecution with its accompanying isolation, have left their mark on the attitudes of many Christians. Suspicion of government intentions, fear of the consequences of an open declaration of belief, are natural and have made many people cautious over making contact with formal church structures. The wounds caused by experiences of being denounced by fellow Christians, experiences of imprisonment or being sent to the countryside, all these things have had their effect.

It would be foolish to deny that there are home meetings that refuse all collaboration with the Three Self Movement and the China Christian Council. Such positive refusal almost certainly includes only a comparatively small minority of such groups, and most of these are sectarian in their origins. However, there are a much larger number who are reluctant to get involved for quite understandable reasons. There is always the fear of control. Groups that have been meeting without obvious obstruction from local officials may well feel that becoming part of a wider network will bring restrictions; they may also simply be content with what they have. One tends to forget how restricted is the outlook of the majority of Chinese village people, most of whom will never move outside their home area, and who are naturally suspicious of city people. The urban/rural divide is probably as great as in the past. Related in part to this there is suspicion of theological liberalism – it usually being assumed that many church leaders are theologically unsound. China is no different in this respect from any other place! Finally, there is in some areas a well-founded dislike of local Three Self officials, who may have pushed ultra-leftist policies in the past and whose present attitudes are based on an over-political understanding of the role of the TSPM. A legitimate concern over such leftist influence is not always easy to distinguish from an unjusti-

Protestant Church with a unique opportunity. The survival of this experiment must depend upon forbearance and the fostering of unity on the basis of a genuine respect for differences as well as on the elimination of "leftist" vestiges within the Three Self Movement itself.

In the long run the most appropriate form of organization would probably be based on some sort of episcopal order, but with the bishops functioning in a spiritual rather than an administrative capacity – as a kind of available gurus. The monarchical type of episcopate would seem quite inappropriate, and the actual organization of the church might better follow a congregational/presbyterian pattern. This form of episcopacy would seem to suit the Chinese tradition of respect for the wisdom of the old while allowing the local congregation to retain considerable importance. Some of the present leaders are known to be thinking along these lines, and its implementation cannot be postponed indefinitely.

Minority forms of worship are offered on a Saturday, or at a different time on a Sunday from the main service. That service is usually an amalgam of the forms of worship used by the main traditions in the locality. Sometimes different forms are used on different Sundays. More often than not the main Sunday worship consists of hymns, readings, prayer and a long sermon (up to an hour). Communion is usually held on a monthly basis, sometimes only every three months, and different rites are used according to the predominant traditions within the locality. Baptism is offered in most places to adults only, although infant baptism has continued in a few areas. Adults are generally offered the choice of sprinkling or immersion. The overwhelming ethos is non-sacramental, and with few exceptions liturgy is of little concern either to pastors or congregation. The Nanjing Rite Number One, produced at the Seminary, is the old Anglican rite following the Book of Common Prayer, and this is used in places with Anglican background. In Zhengzhou, Henan, a locally produced prayer book is modelled on Anglican services, but is used only when the duty pastor is a former Anglican. Fujian has also produced its own form of communion service. The fiable criticism of local pastors and religious leaders for being prepared to seek accommodation with the political authorities at all. It is all too easy for Christians without positions of responsibility to accuse others of getting their hands dirty.

In 1980 there must have been many home meetings who shared some or all of these attitudes. As time has passed so more and more have had their fears and suspicions allayed. Moreover, a process of mutual forgiveness and reconciliation has been taking place. Gradually, also, leftism amongst government officials and within some Three Self organizations has been overcome. Pastor Liu Qingfen of the Binjiang Road Church in Tianjin has described the process within a city context:

> We have studied and analysed why some of our Christian brothers and sisters fail to come to church, and tried to find solutions to the problem . . . As we know, the reason why so many Christian believers are not willing to go to church lies in the fact that they were, to some degree, criticized or punished in the various political movements after Liberation in 1949, and they were persecuted particularly in the Cultural Revolution. So they fear that those unhappy things could happen to them again some day. They are afraid that the Government's policy on religion is apt to change. They think that any connection with the Church would incur trouble and danger. They feel they can worship and pray to God for mercy in their home instead of going to church.
>
> Other Christian brothers and sisters would not like to go to church only because they themselves were forced, during the Cultural Revolution, to criticize and make inappropriate comments on religious belief. Now they feel ashamed and guilty . . .
>
> We should show sympathy with that part of our fellow believers. Everyone has his own weakness and failure, but we can depend upon God for compassion and pardon . . .
>
> There are still other Christian brothers and sisters who

do not come to church because they have different views from ours about "Three Self" or they misunderstand it. We must admit that we had shortcomings and made mistakes in carrying out "Three-Self", for our thinking was influenced and disturbed by the then prevailing "Left" line. So now we must make earnest self-criticism and explain to them why that happened and how it can be avoided in days to come.

With regard to the question of relationships with sectarian groups, Liu Qingfen suggests the need to adhere to the principle of "seeking common ground while reserving differences", and deciding on church rites and activities only after repeated consultation. He suggests that in the past too much attention was paid to "seeking common ground on major issues" and not enough was given to "reserving differences on minor ones", with the result that:

we did not do a good job in respecting and making allowances for the customs that are peculiar to some Christian religious sects, and they strongly objected to that approach of ours, by refusing to go to Church.[36]

It should be obvious by now that the reconstruction of a public life for the Church, that began in 1979, was a formidable task after years of official hostility and isolation. The Christian leadership itself inherited its own set of problems, and was faced with the task of rebuilding trust within the Christian community and between that community and the non-Christian society around. The legacy of leftism still powerfully affects many aspects of life in China, and it has taken years for some provinces to be weaned from leftist attitudes. Between 1980 and 1984 there were instances of continued harassment of Christians, including arbitrary arrest and imprisonment. While such abuses were frequently the result of leftism, there were also problems caused by Christians themselves, and the situation in Henan has exemplified them all.

Continuing Problems

In 1949 Henan had around 100,000 Protesants. By mid-1986 there were at least 600,000 with a further 100,000 "enquirers". The reaction of the provincial authorities to this unprecedented growth appears to have been one of attempted suppression, through the use of the "Ten Don'ts" and by the harassment of active lay leaders. Reports of arrests in 1983 came from the counties of Lushan and Nanyang, although most people were said to have been released after two to four weeks' detention. It should, of course, be borne in mind that these arrests took place during the height of the brief anti-spiritual pollution campaign.[37] One issue that disturbed the authorities was itinerant evangelism. Another concerned the spread of unorthodox teachings.

Bishop Wang Shenyin of Shandong wrote about some of these aberrations. A man named Li Baocheng in Henan styled himself "the Living Jesus" and called his son "Little Jesus". He acquired seven houses and persuaded a number of young women to serve him. In another area a sect known as "Love not the World" forced people to cut themselves off from their families.[38] The sort of confusion that existed is well illustrated by a report from Fangcheng County in Nanyang Prefecture. A certain Brother Chang sent out thirteen teams to preach, with one team of fourteen being sent to neighbouring Biyang County, where the believers refused to receive them. The team then started to preach in the streets, gathering a crowd of five thousand. They were soon arrested and, according to the report, badly maltreated and returned to their home places.[39] In another county an elder who was released from prison after thirteen years ordained more elders and deacons, but lack of proper preparation led to some of these new leaders abusing their position. Two visiting pastors then ordained a separate group of elders. Both groups sought support from the Three Self Movement.[40]

A report from a leader of a Henan home meeting listed five heretical groups in the province, including the group that Chinese sources have dubbed the "Yellers" or "Shouters" because of their method of praying. The arrests in Henan in 1983 were in part of Yeller activists, but many non-Yellers were caught up in the purge. It is difficult to be sure of the reasons for this, but it seems unlikely that local public security officials were well informed as to what separated Yellers from other Christians, especially in a situation where no formal church structures existed. The position of the Three Self Movement in Henan has not been easy. Henan appears to have been under leftist influence well into the 1980s, and it may be that the Three Self Movement also tended towards leftist attitudes. But apart from this the remnant Christian leadership was faced with a more daunting task in the province. With few pastors available it was only possible to open churches in main centres, despite the sudden increase in numbers of Christians. By 1986 seventy had been opened, but in the countryside the task facing the leadership was still enormous. There have been ordinations of some new pastors, and Bible Study and lay training courses are being held each year. More and more home meetings have been brought within the organized church network. Slowly the problems of 1981-83 are being resolved. At a Henan Provincial Conference on Religious Work on 27 March 1986, the problem of overcoming continuing leftist attitudes amongst some cadres was mentioned.[41] Obviously there is still much to be done, but provided present trends continue, there is every expectation that an orderly Church life can be established.

Outside Influences

The interference of outside religious organizations during the present time of transition has caused a number of problems. Attempts to infiltrate surrogate missionaries in the form of English teachers are being made by some groups, although the influence of such individuals is negligible. The most serious example has been the activities of the Children of God, who are said to have entered China in 1985 from their base in Hong Kong. According to the *South China Morning Post* on 4 July 1986, about a hundred members of the cult had succeeded in getting teaching posts in China.[42] On 28 August 1986 four members of the cult were expelled from China for recruiting local youngsters.[43] The most serious aspect of all these activities is the possible effect they might have on the situation of Christians in China. They also, of course, reveal a total lack of sensitivity towards the local Church and an arrogance that presumes to make critical judgements as to the authenticity of the faith of the Christian leadership in China. It is not difficult to deprecate the activities of Christian cults, but there are also more respectable Christian bodies who are engaged in similar activities.

Far more dangerous than attempts by Westerners to evangelize in China have been the activities of certain overseas Chinese Christians. It was in this way that the "Yellers" movement started. In 1982 Witness Lee's Local Church, a breakaway from the Little Flock, entered China. In a situation still unorganized and with many Christians lacking in sound teaching, considerable numbers of rural Christians were recruited. The movement began in Wenzhou on the Zhejiang coast but spread rapidly through the province and into neighbouring Fujian by means of the dissemination of tapes and literature. It then seemed to spread to inland provinces through the use of itinerant preachers, and it soon took hold in parts of Henan. The confrontational methods adopted by the "Yellers", which included the forcible occupation of church premises, led to violence in Dongyang and Yiwu counties in Zhejiang in early 1982.[44] The authorities eventually declared it an illegal organization, and arrests of members of the sect occurred in a number of provinces. In Dongyang the majority left the "Yellers", but about a thousand are said to have persisted in their beliefs, albeit somewhat toned down. Gradually, their influence has been reduced but the rapid spread of such a heterodox movement shows the vulnerability of the home meetings when these are not a part of a wider church structure. Sudden and speedy growth without effective organization is bound to lead to problems. Untrained and often self-selected leaders can lead to the espousal of a whole range of heresies and to the domination of groups by people with their own hidden agendas.

The Case of Lin Xiangao

There have been occasional reports of arrests of itinerant evangelists and leaders of home meetings in other parts of China. The background is seldom clear and it is hard to comment on the wider implications of such reports, even assuming that they are accurate. However, the detention of Lin Xiangao in Guangzhou in December 1982, was widely reported in Hong Kong and elsewhere. Lin Xiangao had been released from prison in 1978 but deprived of political rights for a further five years. He proceeded to establish a home meeting at his home in Damazhan, and he refused to be associated with the local Three Self Movement. His arrest was on the grounds that he was not permitted to run such a meeting since he had no political rights, but the charges against him included allowing foreigners to carry out religious activities in his home. The RAB in the city was almost certainly acting out of line with national policy, for when Lin's civil rights were restored on 16 June 1983 he was allowed to resume his meeting.[45] Since then his work has continued to expand without interference from the authorities.

To conclude this discussion of home meetings we should remind ourselves of the continuing ambiguity of government policy in this regard. As church structures extend and consolidate it is possible that those who wish to remain aloof from them will come under pressure from the authorities, although Lin's case suggests that greater self-confidence may lead to greater toleration of dissentient minorities. In one Zhejiang county it is reported that the RAB ordered the closure of home meetings in one area as soon as the church re-opened,[46] but such intolerant attitudes were more common in the early stages of implementing policy. The difficulty of drawing the Little Flock into fellowship with other Christians was compounded in Zhejiang through the application of the "Patriotic Covenant" and the "Ten Don'ts". In more recent times the removal of such restrictions has led to a gradual breaking down of fear and prejudices. The general picture that emerges in Zhejiang and elsewhere is one of restraint – a desire to foster mutual understanding. This is very noticeable in a province like Fujian, where groups such as the Little Flock continue with their own services of worship, Bible study, etc., but increasingly from within the network being established by the provincial Christian Council. Liu Qingfen's remarks indicate how much many in the national leadership are acutely aware of the need for diversity and toleration of differences. Local problems and difficulties will no doubt persist, but the over-all situation seems likely to continue to develop in the direction of a greater unity and a steady reduction of suspicion and hostility.

The Numbers of Christians

How many Christians are there in China? It is a common question. It is also unanswerable and ultimately irrelevant. It is an issue that all too easily diverts attention from the more important things that we should seek to know and understand – what matters is not how many people call themselves Christians but the quality of their witness. Some have suggested that while there may be four million linked to the China Christian Council, there are millions more in unregistered home meetings. In our view this is unlikely, but even if it were true, this by no means implies that the majority represent the future course for Christianity in China. The latest official figure is four million Protestants, given by Bishop Ting in an interview with *Beijing Review* on 1 June 1987.[47] These are baptized members. The actual figure of believers will be higher if one takes into account "enquirers", unbaptized believers and those not as yet linked to the China Christian Council. The problem here is how to define "Christian" – and this is one reason why some sources have quoted much higher numbers. A figure around five to six million would not seem impossible, but in the absence of reliable statistics it would be unjustified to claim a figure of fifteen to twenty million, let alone fifty million. (See Appendix Seven.)

Christianity and Folk Religion

One aspect concerning the nature of rural Christianity that needs to be mentioned is the tendency in a few village groups towards syncretism. In one remote mountainous area in Henan Buddhist and Confucian elements have been incorporated into Christianity.[48] A similar report from Jiangsu spoke of Buddhist scriptures circulating as Christian.[49] One is reminded of the ambiguous relationship of Christianity to the White Lotus in the last century and the development of the Taiping movement. The world of the secret society is not altogether dead even today. There are even known to be at least two White Lotus communities still extant in China. It is entirely possible for some Christians to move in the direction of traditional patterns of rural dissent or, more likely, to incorporate aspects of Chinese folk religion into their religious practice.

There is little doubt that faith healing and exorcism are two areas in which Chinese Christianity, especially in the countryside, relates directly to traditional concerns within Chinese folk religion. However, this relationship is more complex than is often thought. It is certainly true that government officials are likely to view faith healing and exorcism as verging on "superstitious" practices, but in fact in the context of a society in which possession by spirits is widely accepted as a valid understanding of mental and even physical sickness, a Christian approach can be truly liberating, removing the fear that can dominate the daily routine of people's lives. Inadequate medical facilities also mean that many face chronic illness, disability, and a lack of treatment for common complaints. The general state of health in the countryside is remarkably high for what are still poor communities, but the extent of provision is still uneven and limited. It is also the experience of highly developed societies that medical provision is only one aspect of creating a healthy society. The need for a holistic medical approach is increasingly recognized, and faith healing is no longer scorned by many members of the medical profession in the West as "unscientific". Faith healing in the West has little or nothing of this folk religious element, and has rather more to do with medical professionals but it is not so far removed from the concern of responsible Christians in China. Chinese traditional medicine is itself holistic and, freed from the elements of fear and exploitation, is able to make an invaluable contribution to world medicine. The crucial question, therefore, with regard to Christian healing, is whether it is seen as complementary to medical science or as opposed to modern medicine. As a complementary force it can draw on ancient Chinese insights into health and healing while freeing people from exploitation by unscrupulous practitioners and from the fear of spirits and ghosts that is so much a feature of traditional Chinese folk religion.

It is certainly true that faith healing and exorcism formed an important aspect of Christian life in the past amongst both Catholics and Protestants. Margaret Budd who once worked in Ningbo, Zhejiang, reported in 1948-49 that all Christians believed in devils and spirits. However, it would seem that such healing was very much taken for granted as a normal part of church life, without it assuming an undue importance. Mass healing services, the sort of emotional scenes that manifested themselves amongst some extreme groups in Shandong and elsewhere, were avoided. The usual practice was for local congregations to pray for people, sometimes with them present, and for the sick person and a relative to live in the church for several months.[50] Lin Xiangao, the leader of the independent home meeting in Guangzhou, is reported as saying that "signs and wonders in the house churches are a key factor in the rapid spread of Christianity today".[51] He also accuses the Three Self Movement of opposing faith healing. Such statements must be treated with extreme caution. It is known that one of the results of isolation and poor teaching has been the emergence of groups stressing healing and exorcism almost to the exclusion of all else. An extreme example was cited by Peng Shengyong of the Community Church in Shanghai, quoting the *New People's Evening News* of 22 March 1986. According to the report from Sanmenxia in Henan, a man whose daughter was ill refused to seek medical help and relied on prayer. When she died, for a whole year he "knelt every day before a crucifix and prayed that God would restore his daughter to life".[52] Pastor Peng cited the story to attack those who rely solely on prayer for healing. Other articles in *Tian Feng* have reinforced this line and have suggested that to refuse medical attention is to "degrade our precious faith to the level of feudal superstition".[53]

The concern expressed in *Tian Feng* is then with those who see faith healing as an alternative to modern medicine, and whose faith becomes dominated by a concern with "signs and wonders". It may well be that for many rural people their first experience of the Church will be as a result of a desire for healing or exorcism. In itself this should not be disparaged. *China Daily* in 1984 carried a report from Yanling County in Henan which was very revealing. It showed, first, that faith healing has played an important part in the growth in the number of Christians to ten thousand out of a population of five hundred thousand, triple the number in 1949. The report quoted the local elder as saying, "Unless there's illness, nobody wants to become a Christian". One woman whose husband was a member of the Party, decided to go to church to seek a cure for her son's congenital heart condition. She was opposed by her husband on ideological grounds, and by her parents-in-law because they feared that if she became a Christian they would no longer be able to offer sacrifices to their ancestors.[54] Faith healing may be regarded by Party members as a part of "superstition", but at the same time belief in Christianity may be seen as a threat to rural folk religion. This is confirmed by a fascinating report in *Bridge* on Meixian, Guangdong.[55] Here folk religion exercises a profound influence and demon possession is felt to be a reality. In this situation Christianity offers freedom of mind and body to people seeking to escape from the financial and spiritual burdens imposed by much of the practices of Chinese popular religion. One woman's story of possession after contact with a sorceress resulted in her attempting to beat herself to death:

Hearing of this situation, some Christian sisters came to see Liuti. They knelt to pray and taught her daughter to recite the Lord's prayer sentence by sentence. At this moment Liuti's husband, who worked far away in Shenzhen, came home. He saw the love of the Christians and was deeply moved.

The demon left Liuti completely. Since then the whole family has come to believe in the Lord. Liuti is now an active member in the Shuizhai Church.[56]

A number of factors must be taken into account in attempting to assess the significance of such phenomena. There is no reason to question the validity of such events, even though such things are no longer common in our own culture. Christianity can also be seen as a progressive force in traditional rural communities in a situation of rapid social and economic change. Faith healing and exorcism in themselves tell us little about the quality of Christian life. The mistake made by Lin Xiangao and many who support his line outside China is to assume that "signs and wonders" are in themselves signs of grace, even though Lin may be correct in saying that healing is one of the main factors in church growth. Christian communities that are dominated by a concern with healing may succeed in converting many people, but their faith will be distorted so that ultimately there is a real danger of being absorbed back into the traditional rural culture from which they emerged. Stories of faith healing and exorcism can also be found in Catholic sources, and these must be evaluated by the same criteria. The concern expressed in *Tian Feng* is fully justified, provided that it allows a legitimate place for healing prayer. A true ministry of healing and reconciliation within rural society can indeed be a powerful force for good, and in its own way may open up another channel through which Christianity can deepen its encounter with the riches and wisdom of Chinese tradition.

The Meaning of Indigenization

We return to one of our key questions: What is the meaning of indigenization in a Chinese context? Faith healing poses this question in a dramatic form. It can be a stage in freeing people's minds from traditions that are less and less relevant to a society that in the next few years is likely to see further secularization – not in the sense of an acceptance of the Marxist critique of religion, but in the sense in which the West is now secular. Or it can itself be a manifestation of backward looking forces. In so far as Christianity in China is of the latter type, it may succeed in winning over many people in a situation of continuing need and insecurity in values, but it is likely to be a short-term phenomenon. In so far as it is of the former type, it can be a creative force which faces the challenge of the future. This creative response to the context in which Christians find themselves might be better termed "contextualization". Put in this way it is those groups who, for whatever reasons, cannot come to terms with the new situation and who persist in exclusivist attitudes who will ultimately become irrelevant. The future lies with those who are being gathered into the public structures of Christian life, who are prepared to take the risk of moving out from their traditional attitudes for the sake of the whole.

Ge Jingqing from Xi'an has put the issue well:

Discussing the problem of indigenization serves merely as a prologue, which provides a lead, an inspiration, an association of ideas. What is to be discussed is the problem of our common investigation of the way forward for the Chinese Church, how it can cope with a situation in which the Four Modernizations are being pursued in a socialist society; the problem of the way in which the Chinese Church is going to develop so as to bring about the display of its "golden lampstand".

"Indigenization" is an inappropriate formula. If we were to alter it to "How is the Church to grow and develop here in China, in this corner of the world?", so that we could be discussing the Church's historic destiny, the scope of the discussion would be much wider. Moreoever, the limitations of the problem of indigenization are severe. It involves exclusiveness, it is unfavourable to the absorption of anything from outside, and it lends itself to needless misunderstanding.[57]

Christian Witness in Contemporary China

Overarching the issue of indigenization is the far deeper one of "inculturation", a theme we will need to discuss more fully when we have looked at the situation of Chinese Catholics. One aspect which should be dealt with at this point concerns the position of the church within society. The search for a positive role within contemporary society is a critical aspect of the contextualization of Christianity. However, "incultura-tion" implies far more than this, not least the development of a dialectical relationship to society and culture. In a colonial or semi-colonial situation this is impossible, and the immediate need is for the development of Christian patriotism. In China this has meant accepting the limitations of the United Front policy, in which religion is expected to be a private affair.

How then is the Church addressing itself to the issue of a way forward in socialist society? Bishop Ting has perceptively commented that in the 1950s:

> The survival of Christianity depended mainly on the state's policy of religious freedom. Only survival was possible; bearing witness was out of the question.[58]

The Chinese Christian witness must begin with an identifi-cation with the hopes and aspirations of the society around. It was this lack of identification that so crippled Christian witness in the past. "Evangelism takes place only in love. Evangelists must first of all be lovers. Thus, we guard against the unloving Jonah mentality with all its jealousy and ill-wish and lack of identification with the people to whom he or she is sent."[59] There is considerable misunderstanding of the stress by Christian leaders in China on "patriotism". It may have appeared at times in the 1950s that the stress on being "patriotic" was somewhat frenetic, but this arose from a basic insecurity. Today, "patriotism" is no blind allegiance, "My country right or wrong", but a real commitment to the future of the country. As Ting indicates:

> We Christians should be filled with gladness at the reconstruction of the motherland, and rejoice with those who rejoice. However, the work of liberation is of long duration. China is still far from ideal, and there are vast areas of underdevelopment and darkness. People are now working very hard in every field to expand the bright side and overcome the dark side . . . Naturally, Chinese Christians do not stand aloof from all this activity. In the life of the nation, the Church should make a clear distinction between right and wrong. She ought to protect, learn from and promote the good, and bring about the accomplishment of the good quickly. At the same time, the Church ought to criticize and oppose evil things, and hasten their demise. This is real patriotism in today's situation.[60]

For a small Church living in a cultural milieu so different from that in the West, the question of identification with the experience of the majority in their society must be a priority. The increasing involvement of Chinese Christians in social concerns is the most telling confirmation that Bishop Ting is articulating the actual experience of the Christian community in China. At the most basic level Christians are honest and hardworking, and the impact of becoming a Christian has been noticed and remarked on by Party officials. A deputy Party secretary in the Hongmentang Rural District in Xiangxiang, Hunan testified to the change in his community. In disputes over land Christians were reticent over making claims, thinking of the common good. Young Christians are quite ready to break with old customs such as lavish expenditure on weddings. Christians oppose "feudal superstitions", and the "conduct of Christians is upright, open and above-board, and they do not defraud others".[61]

Christians are frequently cited as "model workers". On 13 March 1985 seventy Christians belonging to "Five Excellencies Households" in Dalian, Liaoning attended a special conference.[62] Many other examples could be cited. A considerable number of local churches have become involved in local economic activities through the establishment of small workshops or factories, or through running Christian restaurants and hotels. As well as contributing to society such undertakings help finance the Church and provide employment to young Christians. The Church has also been encouraged by the government to re-start welfare work in what is a quite remarkable reversal of past policy. Many places have started kindergartens and arranged evening classes in English, typing skills, and even marriage bureaus! In Longquan County, Zhejiang the Church has opened a Middle School; in Wenling County, a Centre for the Handicapped; in Linqu County, Shandong, a Three Self Clinic. Amongst Catholics similar developments are under way in Beijing, where the local CCPA has established the Xiangbo School. In Longjiang County in the Yanbian Korean Autonomous zone in Jilin province the Catholic Church has started a restaurant and a rice-processing plant.[63] The Protestant Church in Guangzhou has set up the most elaborate programme. On 28 January 1985 the Guangzhou Benevolence Social Service Centre was established, to provide services in occupational training, adult education and also a hostel and travel service.[64]

The revival of the life of the YMCA and YWCA has been a major sign of the ability of the Church to serve society. As a constituent part of the All China Youth Federation the "Y"s have an exceptional status, and they have been able to use this to develop an extensive programme in those cities where they have re-opened. The headquarters is still in Shanghai on Tibet Road, where a new building has been completed, linked to the old building and the over-all complex providing hotel accommodation, national and local "Y" offices, and meeting rooms. In a combined programme evening courses are offered in computer studies, foreign languages, and a range of other subjects. Similar programmes are developing in Tianjin,

Guangzhou, Wuhan, Hangzhou, Xiamen and Beijing. Since 1982 the Tianjin "Y" has run a preliminary nursing class, for which it received special commendation at local and national levels. Exchanges with foreign "Y"s have taken place, and in 1985-86 two young staff of the Shanghai YMCA spent a year at the YMCA College in London. The work of the "Y"s is proving to be one of the most significant aspects of Christian outreach in the cities.

All these developments are indications of the changing status of Christians in society. A simple but delightful story in *Tian Feng* perhaps sums this up:

> For business reasons I had to travel to Nanjing on 26 January. At 9.57 I boarded the train bound for Nanjing from Qiqihar. I had nothing else to occupy me on the journey, so I opened my Bible and began to read.
>
> "Comrade!" said a woman's voice near where I was sitting. I looked up to see the woman who had been occupying the next seat. I asked her what she wanted, and she said, "I want to take the child along to the lavatory for a few minutes, so could I trouble you to keep an eye on my luggage?"
>
> A few minutes later, along came a man aged about thirty. "What do you think you are doing?" he asked the woman in a stern tone of voice.
>
> "I'm taking the child to the lavatory," she calmly replied.
>
> "Couldn't you have waited until I came? How could you just go off and leave all this luggage here? Suppose someone were to steal it!"
>
> "I got someone to look after it."
>
> "Who?"
>
> The woman pointed to me and said, "This comrade. He believes in Jesus."
>
> "How do you know that?"
>
> "You can see he's holding a Bible."
>
> The man gave her an embarrassed smile.
>
> From this little incident, my fellow Christians, you can

see the kind of reputation Christians have in the eyes of the general public. This is the outcome of the words and deeds of all of us who are Christians. Still, it must be said that what we have done so far is still not enough. We must continue to use every effort as we strive to bring glory to God and benefit mankind.[65]

The Amity Foundation

The spirit of service to society so evident in the activities of Christians at the local level is reflected most dramatically in the work of the Amity Foundation. The Foundation was established in early 1985 on the initiative of Bishop Ting and others, both concerned Christians and sympathetic non-Christians, mostly from Jiangsu province, as a contribution towards the development of educational, health and welfare work. The Foundation decided to concentrate its energies on areas of special need such as the handicapped, the mentally sick child, child nutrition, support for a new anti-pollution device, etc. It also decided to invite friendly church agencies overseas to participate through grants, the supply of equipment, and through the recruitment of foreign language teachers.

It was this international involvement which astonished the world. A variety of overseas church organizations had become involved in aspects of educational, medical and cultural work, working through government channels. There had been a few direct links with local churches – notably links were being established between Hong Kong and Guangzhou – but this was the first time that foreign Christians had been invited to co-operate with Chinese Christians in a major programme.

Reaction outside China was generally enthusiastic and involved a wide range of Christian agencies, including those more conservative agencies more accustomed to doing their own thing. Some were more cautious and a few even declared that this was the end of the "Three Selfs"; others that this was a bid to control all foreign church agencies' work in China by forcing them to go through one officially recognized channel.

There was also amongst more sympathetic circles some initial worry that the work might be concentrated within the comparatively wealthy province of Jiangsu. Amity was able to satisfy most of these initial fears. In fact, it was not part of the TSPM or the China Christian Council; it was not asking for direct support of church work; it also intended gradually to extend its work to other parts of China when requested to do so by local churches and when adequate personnel and resources were available. It certainly had no intention of seeking to monopolize and control links overseas, and in any case as an organization of Chinese Christians its primary objective was the service of society rather than relating abroad. All Christians, Chinese and foreign, were being invited to share in the work of Amity, but foreign Christians would have no control over the work. Amity was seen as a part of the witness of the Church in China, showing its concern for the welfare of the people and its commitment to the "Four Modernizations". It would help to give Christians a higher profile in society, breaking down ignorance and prejudice. As a recent statement by Amity has put it:

> As a non-governmental and non-church organization, Amity represents a new form of Christian involvement in Chinese society. There are at least two distinctive features of such newness. First, the initiative for the Amity Foundation came from within China; all projects are identified, designed, studied and evaluated in consultation with Chinese specialists according to local needs and conditions. Second, Amity represents a form of co-operation between Christians and non-Christians, including Chinese Communists, to work together for the good of the people. By making contributions to the humanitarian welfare of the Chinese people without religious discrimination, the Amity Foundation also makes Christian involvement and participation in China's social development more widely known to the Chinese people and to people the world over.[66]

Such a new undertaking needed the political good-will of the provincial authorities before it could begin work. Jiangsu gave enthusiastic support from the beginning, and other provinces were to follow, notably Fujian and Zhejiang. By 1987 over fifty foreign teachers were working for Amity in a whole variety of institutions of higher education in the three provinces. It was planned to receive up to ninety teachers in September 1987, and it was hoped to extend the work to Jiangxi and Shandong, and possibly even to Urumqi in Xinjiang. Although recruited by churches in Hong Kong, Britain, the United States, Canada, West Germany and Japan, they were employed by Amity – paid through block grants from overseas and in part by the receiving institutions. The response from overseas has been immediate, and it has forced some radical rethinking by denominational agencies who came to realize that a denominational response would be entirely inappropriate. In Britain the involved church mission boards or societies got together to establish an ecumenical way of relating to Amity, involving some sacrifice of conventions and a waiving of denominational procedures. The response to the Amity initiative is an excellent example of how the Chinese Christian experience is forcing Christians elsewhere to rethink their priorities.

One partial exception to Amity's non-church role concerns the agreement with the United Bible Societies to establish an up-to-date "Amity" Printing Press in Nanjing. The logistical problems involved in establishing an ultra-modern press led to the realistic decision to involve overseas Christians in this particular programme. The plant was due for completion in 1987, and a major priority was to be the printing of Bibles and other Christian literature, as requested by local church authorities. The press is, however, a joint venture with a Jiangsu company and it will print other materials of general service to society. It will also print material for Catholics, Muslims and Buddhists.

Overseas Relations

Amity would not have been possible without the steady progress in relationships between the China Christian Council and overseas churches since 1981. It would be tedious to list the numerous visits by Christian delegations from National Councils of Churches and confessional groupings or individual denominations, as well as by prominent church leaders, that have taken place up to 1987. Each has been important for the renewal of links and the development of trust and friendship. Many of these visits have been returned from China. Taking Britain as an example, in Autumn 1982 seven Chinese Christians led by Bishop Ting visited the United Kingdom and Ireland, and then went on to West Germany, Sweden and Finland. Part of the group also went for a brief visit to Kenya for the meeting of the All-Africa Conference of Churches. Then in December 1983 the Archbishop of Canterbury, Dr Robert Runcie, led a delegation from the British Council of Churches on a return visit. Former antagonisms were forgotten and bridges of friendship repaired. Thus, for example, the damage done in 1956 by Fisher's failure to welcome Ting was repaired in early 1982 when the Archibishop made a private visit to Nanjing, and this was consolidated in the 1983 visit.

The formation of the Friends of the Church in China in Britain in late 1985 represented a different style of relationship, with its stress on developing support amongst individual Christians and local congregations. Notable in the process of its development was the fact that the China Christian Council was consulted about the name and its objectives, and that the two joint patrons are Bishop K.H. Ting, as President of the Chinese Christian Council, and Dr Robert Runcie in his capacity as President of the British Council of Churches.

It was fitting that the name given to a major international conference held in Montreal in late 1981, and attended by a delegation of Chinese Catholics and Protestants, was "God's Call to a New Beginning".[67] It was a unique occasion – the first such conference to be held since 1949, and the first time that Chinese Catholics and Protestants had participated together in an ecumenical conference. Appropriately, the purpose was not to discuss "the Church in China" but to begin a dialogue with Chinese Christians. There is little doubt that the major achievement of the conference was that it gave an opportunity for Chinese Christian leaders to define the terms of their future overseas relationships in an atmosphere of acceptance. The long legacy of suspicion could not simply be wished away, especially on the Catholic side. The convening of a major international conference in Nanjing in May 1986, under the title of "Ecumenical Sharing: A New Agenda", was an attempt to take Montreal a stage further, in the direction of partnership with the Church in China. Once again it was a gathering of Protestants and Catholics but this time it also included some Orthodox Christians. It demonstrated a commitment by the participants, coming from twenty-two countries, to think through the implications of the Chinese Christian experience for their own missiology. From the meeting in Montreal to the meeting in Nanjing represents two key stages in the development of the international relations of the Church in China.

Critics of Montreal and Nanjing have complained that the conferences were not representative enough of the world-wide structures of the Church. While this is true, and both events were too dominated by North Atlantic participants – despite a considerable input from noted Third World theologians, especially at Nanjing – it would have been impossible to make the meetings representative in view of the history of Christianity in China. The World Council of Churches has discovered this to its cost, as the Korean resolution of 1951 has stood in the way of the WCC taking a more direct role in developing relationships with China. By 1987 it was more a question of the Chinese having neither the personnel nor the time to become too closely involved in international organizations, although as a matter of principle the China Christian Council has been most concerned to foster bi-lateral relations in the first stages of building new relationships. More recently, with the foundations securely laid, it has been concerned to develop friendly relations with major confessional groupings and it has showed a willingness to enter into discussions with the WCC. There is a parallel here with the question of internal church relationships: start locally and then move upwards rather than starting at the top.

In the early 1980s most exchanges were with Western countries, but as time has gone on this has gradually changed. In March 1985 a delegation visited India, and in May a small group from North Korea visited China before going on to the Soviet Union, a most exceptional event. Bridges have begun to be mended with the churches in Eastern Europe. Bishop Ting and Han Wenzao shared in the Luther celebrations in East Germany in November 1983. Then, in September 1985 Shen Derong and Chen Zemin attended the Christian Peace Conference in Prague as observers, and in October a Hungarian Church delegation led by Bishop Karoly Toth went to China. A most important visit was that by Bishop Desmond Tutu in August 1986. Plans for Bishop Ting to attend his enthronement as Archbishop of Cape Town were cancelled at the last moment, after South Africa withdrew permission for a visa.

Chinese Protestants have re-established themselves as respected members of the international Christian community in a remarkably short period of time. It would be misleading, however, to imply that tensions do not still exist. The representative nature of the TSPM and the China Christian Council is questioned by some overseas church organizations and quite a few individual Christians, especially those on the more conservative and evangelical wing of the Church. It would be wrong to say that this suspicion is shared by all evangelicals, and, indeed, an increasing number are coming to realize that the situation is far more complex than they had previously assumed. The easy assumption that the leadership are all "theological liberals" does not stand up to analysis, and the attitude that considers all co-operation with a Marxist state as a betrayal of the Gospel is being questioned by many within evangelical circles. As time goes on more people are prepared to accept that the Chinese government is serious in its intention to allow a degree of religious freedom, and that the existence of two "churches" in China is a distortion of the real situation. Thus, while there is still disagreement over the nature and importance of the "house churches" in China, there is a moderation in the tone of many evangelicals that was certainly absent a few years ago.

Nevertheless, there are still organizations and groups who promote an entirely negative view of the so-called "official" church in China, in the name of the "real" Christians who are said to be under constant attack from the government and the TSPM. There are many more who, while accepting that this is a distortion, still seek to find ways of conducting missionary work in China. The underlying significance of the Christian experience in China is lost to them as they blindly seek to re-establish the patterns and relationships of the past. This intervention is sometimes justified on the grounds that some Chinese Christians have requested assistance. This is surely to miss the point! The issue at stake is the nature and quality of Christian witness in China in the light of the history of Christian missions to China. It may be that at some point a limited foreign Christian contribution to the work of the Church in China will become appropriate, but to bypass the Three Self experience as well as the public structures of the Church, would be an act of folly and arrogance.

A Brief Survey of Protestant Activity in China

We have looked at some provincial situations such as Henan and Guangxi, and have noted how very different they were both in terms of the over-all situation and in terms of the numbers of Christians. It remains to make a brief survey of other provinces in order to see the over-all situation more clearly. South-east China hardly needs discussion. We have seen the strength of Christian life in Zhejiang, Fujian and Guangdong as well as in Shanghai. Zhejiang has perhaps as many as one million Christians (eight hundred thousand was quoted in 1986) and over a thousand churches and at least twice that number of home meetings linked with the provincial Christian Council. Zhejiang also, however, has the largest number refusing to work with the TSPM, perhaps as many as 120,000, almost all of whom are associated in some way or another with the Little Flock, including the "Yellers".[68] Fujian has a minimum of 350,000 Christians with seven hundred churches. The situation in many areas as far as church buildings are concerned is as good as, or better than, in the past. In Quanzhou district, for example, there used to be eighteen churches, but by 1983 there were twenty-four with five new ones under construction. Guangdong had at least 110,000 Christians by 1984, sixty-six churches and three hundred home meetings. In Shantou, where George Hood once worked, in 1982 there were ten thousand Christians. In the city itself 2,700 families are organized into groups of fifty-six, led by a "liaison officer" who is responsible for ensuring that pastoral needs are met and who organizes a regular prayer meeting.[69] Shanghai has around twenty churches and 30,000 Protestants (compared to over 100,000 Catholics and twenty churches).

South Central China presents a very different picture. We have noted the problems in Jiangxi resulting from ignorance amongst government officials. Until recently Jiangxi was still hampered by leftist attitudes. The situation improved after 1984, and in 1985 there were sixteen churches open and around five hundred home meetings. Problems between Little Flock and Seventh Day Adventists on the one hand and other Christians were serious in some places, especially Yiyang County, but these were being overcome. Neighbouring Hunan has also suffered from leftism. In 1984 Changsha Radio reported on factionalism within the Public Security Bureau in the province.[70] Leftism in this home province of Mao Zedong has been endemic over many years, and the Church has suffered as a result. The RAB tends to be "leftist" in its interpretation of policy, and by 1985 only fourteen churches had been re-opened, and there were reported to be 141 home meetings with 23,000 Christians.[71] In 1986 the situation was improving, with a number of newly-built churches opening in places such as Yiyang and Shaoyang cities, reflecting a more positive attitude by the provincial authorities.[72] Hubei province has many more Catholics than Protestants, the number of the latter was reported in 1983 to be around 30,000. The city of Wuhan has an active Protestant community and is of course the theological training centre for the region. The numbers of Christians in these three provinces are probably greater than the reported figures, but there is little doubt that the numbers are tiny when compared to the coastal provinces or to neighbouring Henan.

Anhui has around 300,000 Christians and forty-one churches open. Considerable growth is evident from available reports. Thus in Ningguo a few Christians have grown to a thousand with 250 baptisms at one of the four churches in 1985 and 1986.[73] In Hekou Town there are ten churches and twenty-one "preaching stations". In Sixian County there are fifty home meetings and five thousand people worship in the home meetings in Yingshang County.[74] In Jiangsu province there has been a great growth in numbers, from 50,000 in 1949 to over 200,000 by 1984.[75] By late 1985 fifty-five churches had opened and there were over a thousand home meetings. Jiangyin, for example, has about six thousand Christians, twenty per cent recently converted. In Huiyin district, in the north of the province, in 1985 there were seven counties out of thirteen having churches and four more planned; six hundred registered home meetings and an equal number waiting to register. In Yangcheng district, with two cities and seven counties, there were 50,000 members, five churches and 154 home meetings.[76] Jiangsu has progressed a considerable way in its organization of church life, with carefully designed rules for ordination and financial administration together with regulations on worship and baptism which have laid the foundations for mutual respect and greater unity.[77] Shandong has many Christians, but reports on the situation have been rather few, perhaps partly because leftist policies have affected United Front Work until mid-1984, according to *Dazhong Daily*.[78] *Bridge* has reported three churches open in Jinan and two under renovation, together with forty home meetings. Qingdao had four churches open and two were open in Laoshan.[79] In Shouguang County the rebuilt church has added five hundred new members during the period August 1985 to spring 1986.[80] Bishop Wang Shenyin in 1986 indicated that over sixty churches had opened, together with two thousand home meetings, with a total of 250,000 Christians.

Northern China has traditionally been an area of major Catholic activity and this is reflected in the comparatively small number of Protestants in Hebei, Shanxi, Inner Mongolia and the municipalities of Beijing and Tianjin. Shijiazhuang in Hebei has quite a few Protestants, and nearby Zhaoxian County opened three provisional places of worship in 1985. Both Handan and Tangshan cities have churches.[81] Shanxi has many thousands of Catholics, but the Protestant church is small in comparison, although it too is growing. The Taiyuan church in 1982 had three hundred or so members, compared to a hundred in 1949, and many more people travelled in from surrounding villages.[82] Beijing has three churches open and Tianjin two churches. There are perhaps several thousand Protestant Christians in each city, compared to 10,000 Catholics in Tianjin (100,000 in the diocese) and 30,000 in the Beijing diocese. The Protestant presence in Inner Mongolia is more significant than in the past. The church in Hohhot is open, and in Baotou the church re-opened in 1983 but soon proved to be too small – with the result that two new churches were built, each seating three hundred. In the nearby village of Maoqilai there were no Christians in the past, but today a church has been erected for two hundred people. In the country known as Tumd Right Banner (the old Manchu tribal term is still used) the church has grown to 1,500 members, and in Salaqi when the church was restored in December 1985 there were 435 baptisms. A new church was built at Yingpawan in Urad Front Banner in 1986.[83]

North-east China has most Christians in Liaoning, where in 1983 there were said to be 50,000 with 110 pastors. In 1984 around fifty churches were open and there were many home meetings; of these eight were Korean churches and eighteen Korean home meetings.[84] It is the Korean church that accounts for many of the Christians in Jilin, concentrated in Yanbian Autonomous Prefecture. In 1984 six churches were open here.[85] Churches are open in most of the large cities in both Jilin and Heilongjiang. In Harbin there were three thousand Protestant Christians in 1984, and the Orthodox church re-opened in October of that year, serving a community of three hundred, including forty Russians. The Chinese priest is Zhu Shipu.[86]

The Church in the North-west is strongest in Shaanxi. Here, while there are not large numbers of Christians, there is a steady development of church life. In Xi'an in 1983 there were twice the number of Christians than in 1949, attending two churches and fourteen home meetings. In Tongchuan City, a mining area, the local pastor re-started worship in 1975 in one of the typical cave-homes in the area, and in 1982 a church was built. About five thousand Christians attend twenty home meetings.[87] The village of Lijiacun near Pucheng has a church for five hundred people as eighty per cent of the population are Christians.[88] No over-all figure for the number of Christians in Shaanxi is available, but on the basis of this report it must be quite considerable. Gansu is reported to have had 26,000 Christians in 1986, with up to 3,000 in Lanzhou City – where between 1981 and 1985 there were 1,543 baptisms and a further 200 in July 1986.[89] The minority nationality areas of Ningxia, Xinjiang and Qinghai are predominantly Muslim or Buddhist, and Christians are few in number and mainly to be found amongst Han Chinese who have settled in the area. The TSPM/Council structures had only been established in the regional capitals by the time of the Fourth National Christian Conference. In 1985 there were six centres of Christian activity in Ningxia and over a thousand Christians, but no pastor. One student went to the Nanjing Seminary in 1982, and in late 1984 he was responsible for organizing a training class. On 13 December 1984 several elders and deacons were ordained.[90] In 1986 Xinjiang had 11,000 Protestants with churches open in ten places and fourteen home meetings. The meeting in Shihezi had six hundred members and a church was desperately needed. Meetings also exist on Army farms, but there were not even evangelists to serve them.[91] A Russian Orthodox church opened in Urumqi in September 1985 serving a Russian community in the city of 640 (there are 2,600 in Xinjiang).[92] Qinghai has a number of churches, with 1,500 members of the church in Xining and 436 baptisms over four years.[93] Outside of the

Xining area the number of Christians must be tiny.

So, finally we come to the South-west. Sichuan, which has up to 300,000 Catholics, also has many Protestants, but no figure is available. The Church is active in all major cities and is also strong amongst some national minorities such as the Qiang people in the area around Wenchuan County. In Guizhou in Liupanshui there are 20,000 Christians, mostly belonging to the Miao or Yi peoples.[94] In Yunnan there are thousands of Miao, Yi and Lisu Christians around Wuding County, and in Luquan County 5,000 attended the church opening in August 1984.[95] Luquan is reported to have 40,000 Christians. In Simao Prefecture there are 10,000 Lahu and 10,000 Va Christians, and about a hundred delegates attended a training class in Kunming in 1986. Yunnan is said to have 300,000 Christians altogether.[96] Figures for Guizhou are not available but are likely to be considerable.

Our somewhat hasty survey is concluded. It is obvious that there are many gaps in our knowledge, especially with regard to certain provinces, yet the picture that emerges is of enormous growth and vitality. The provinces of Zhejiang, Fujian, Jiangsu, Anhui, Henan, Yunnan and Shandong stand out as the places with the greatest numbers and fastest expansion, but others may well be not far behind – Sichuan, Shaanxi, Guangdong. Other provinces have few Christians, including it would seem some large and populous provinces. Of course, our discussion so far has been limited to Protestant Christians, but as occasionally noted, Catholic strength may be in areas where there are few Protestants – Hebei, Inner Mongolia and Shanxi. We must now look at the way in which Christian leaders are seeking to train new pastors and to raise the quality of leadership amongst lay voluntary workers, for clearly an effective training programme is a key factor in the consolidation of church life.

Leadership Training

The Nanjing Union Theological Seminary re-opened its doors on 28 February 1981, with an initial intake of forty-seven students, eighteen of them women. Almost seven hundred people had applied, of whom three hundred and eight had sat the entrance exam. Few of the new students had any grounding in the fundamentals of Christian belief, and indeed many had never had access to a Bible. Applicants had to be active members of their local church, under twenty-five, graduates of senior middle school and recommended by their local church. The first graduation of students took place on 29 June 1985. Ninety-five graduated, fifty-one of whom had entered a shorter two-year course introduced in 1983. Five went on to post-graduate research at the Seminary.[97]

Nanjing has become the pivot of a network of theological seminaries that have been opening steadily over the past few years. On 6 October 1982 a one-year course opened in Fuzhou, with an intake of forty-two, and in the following year this became a two-year course. Also in 1982 a seminary opened in Shenyang, serving the three North-eastern provinces with an intake of over fifty students. 1983 saw the start of two more seminaries, one in Chengdu Sichuan, serving Sichuan, Yunnan and Guizhou, and one in Beijing. The Beijing seminary later joined forces with the even smaller seminary that opened in Tianjin in 1984, and at a meeting in March 1986 representatives from the churches in the two municipalities and from Hebei, Shanxi, Shaanxi, Inner Mongolia, Gansu, Qinghai, Ningxia and Xinjiang agreed to re-establish the Yanjing Theological Seminary, offering one- two- and four-year courses. The Wuhan Seminary, which opened in May 1985, was originally planned to serve South and Central China, (Guangdong, Guangxi, Hubei, Hunan and Henan), but Christian leaders in Guangzhou were anxious to have their own training facilities. In September 1986 a two-year course began there, while Wuhan offered a four-year course. Zhejiang had been able to start a two-year course in Hangzhou in September 1984, and the Huadong Seminary in Shanghai opened its doors on 11 September 1985 offering a three-year course. Finally, to complete the picture, a Theological Training Centre opened in Hefei, Anhui province, on 20 April 1986 with twenty-seven students on a two-year course.

The pattern that has been emerging is of one national seminary in Nanjing; several regional seminaries such as Shenyang, Beijing, Wuhan and Shanghai and Chengdu offering three- or four-year courses, although also in some cases offering a shorter course; these are fed by provincial seminaries such as Fuzhou, Hangzhou, Guangzhou, Hefei offering two-year courses. It is an impressive achievement, especially bearing in mind the problem of finding suitable buildings, the serious lack of qualified teachers and the lack of textbooks. Until recently there was little national co-ordination, and the quality of the courses varied considerably. In August 1985 the first national planning meeting for theological education was held, and in May 1987 the first meeting of a Theological Education Committee took place in Nanjing. As a result of the discussions that have been taking place since 1985, the Committee has been able to begin the rationalization of structures and the unification of curricula. Nanjing is to stress the training of theological teachers for other seminaries, and will train graduates as theologians. It will also specialize in religious art, music and writing. The regional seminaries will focus on training pastors for the urban churches, and the provincial seminaries will concentrate on training rural church workers. Of course, the best graduates from junior or intermediate seminaries will be able to go on to further training. Ordination will not usually follow immediately after graduation but will take place after two or three years of work in a local church.

Students are sent from their home churches and are generally expected to return to them. Inevitably, in the absence of a national church administrative structure, this causes problems in the over-all allocation of church workers since it is the stronger and wealthier churches that can most readily send students for training. However, it is possible to re-assign some people after negotiation, and at Nanjing, at least, special bursaries are available for students from national minority areas. Overseas contacts are also being developed. A number of foreign theologians have been invited to lecture to the students at Nanjing, and in 1983 Zhang Jinglong became the first student to study abroad, going to Toronto for a three-year theological course. In the summer of 1985 six students from Nanjing spent several weeks in the United States and a further six in Canada. In 1987 nine students from Nanjing and some of the other seminaries spent six weeks in Britain. The visits were aimed at improving English and at learning about the churches in the West.

By late 1986 around six hundred students were in training. Meanwhile, since 1981 over three hundred new pastors have been ordained as pastors, elders and evangelists. The ordination of a pastor can only happen when the person is considered to have had sufficient previous training and has been active in church work for some considerable time. A further criterion relates to social attitudes – candidates being expected to be good neighbours and loyal to the nation. Many of those ordained have been over sixty years old. Ordination involves the laying on of hands by local pastors, but the doctrinal question as to the nature of ministry is left for future consideration. The number of church workers has certainly increased in the past six or so years, but local churches and home meetings still depend very heavily on voluntary workers. Alongside the full-time training schemes there has therefore arisen an extensive programme of part-time training. Since 1981 a special syllabus has been sent out from Nanjing, mainly to leaders of home meetings. By 1985 36,000 copies were sent out four times a year. Provincial Christian Councils have sought to organize short training courses and Bible Refresher courses for pastors and full-time workers. Many of these courses last for several weeks, and students must obtain leave of absence from their places of work to attend. Factory workers must take unpaid leave, while rural people are supported by their families. In the countryside, the new agricultural responsibility system has enabled people to engage in extensive church activities where there is family support. In one county near Fuzhou, for example, voluntary workers meet for a two- or three-day retreat every month.[98] In provinces such as Zhejiang and Fujian courses have been held in many counties, and an annual course is the norm in some places. In Ningxia, on the other hand, it was necessary for the national leadership to send people to the region in order to run the first such course from 8 November to 20 December 1984.[99]

Christian Literature

The destruction of Bibles in the Cultural Revolution was extensive, although some people managed to keep them hidden. Most other Christian books were destroyed, and the extent of the loss can be gauged from a visit to the libraries in any of the seminaries. Many of the losses of foreign language books have been made up in Nanjing since 1982, through the supply of new books by overseas churches, but there is a complete lack of older out-of-print materials. But the greatest need is of course for Bibles. In 1981 and 1982 one million copies of the Bible, including a small number of New Testaments and Psalms, had been printed using the old plates of the 1919 Union Version. The term for God used was *shen*. In 1983 a futher 300,000 were printed using the term *shangdi*. The problem with this old version was its use of the unsimplified Chinese characters which most young people found difficult to read. By August 1986 the total had surpassed two million. In 1986 alone 250,000 New Testaments and half a million Bibles were printed, using specially thin Bible paper supplied by the United Bible Societies. Until 1985 it was necessary to wait for paper allocated by the government in a situation of chronic paper shortage. The Amity Printing Press will speed up the process of publication, for up until now it has been necessary to rely on government-owned presses. It was expected to be operating by mid-1987, and a planned 100,000 copies of a cross-reference Bible were to be produced by the end of the year.

It was after considerable effort that in 1986 a simplified character edition of the New Testament was published, which also adopted horizontal lines and modern punctuation, and work on the Old Testament was under way. In 1982 10,000 copies of the Korean Bible were printed in Shenyang, and in 1984 Bibles and hymnbooks in the Miao and Lisu tongues.

These were followed in 1985 by Bibles and hymnbooks in Lahu and Va. Jingpo language editions were under preparation.

The most important other pubications were a series of sermon collections, a devotional book *Manna for the Spirit* (designed to replace *Streams in the Desert*), and the Chinese Catechism. The Catechism represents the only formal doctrinal statement to have been produced, and must be taken as representing what is accepted as the minimum definition of orthodoxy. However, it relegates the historic Creeds to the Appendix out of respect for those who reject credal statements.[100] Bishop Ting's booklet *How to Study the Bible*, first produced in the 1950s, was reprinted in 1980 in the first issue of *Tian Feng (New Series)*.[101] It remains to note that a number of provincial and local churches are in the process of searching for, assembling, and publishing remaining archives, many of which were lost in the Cultural Revolution and earlier.

The Fourth National Christian Conference

The Fourth National Christian Conference was held in Beijing from 16 to 23 August 1986. There were 266 delegates, and representatives from Xinjiang, Ningxia and Qinghai attended for the first time. Bishop Ting was re-elected as Chairman of the TSPM and President of the China Christian Council. Three elderly former Vice-Chairmen of the TSPM Standing Committee, Liu Liangmo, Sun Pengxi and Tang Shoulin, were nominated as "Advisers" to both bodies. Nine Vice-Chairmen were elected for the TSPM and nine Vice-Presidents of the China Christian Council. None of these now served in a dual capacity, a development that reflects the increasing separation in secular life between Party and government. Shen Derong remained as General Secretary of the TSPM, assisted by Shen Cheng'en. Bishop Zheng Jianye remained as General Secretary of the Council, assisted by Cao Shengjie. Han Wenzao, former joint assistant General Secretary, appeared to have been released for full-time work with the Amity Foundation. (See Appendix for name lists.)

The Fourth Conference marked a new stage in the life of

China's Protestant churches. While the work of consolidation that began in 1979 had not been fully completed, much of the groundwork had been done. The conditions had been created for the long-term solution of the crisis in leadership, publications and church buildings caused by the years of leftism. International contacts were re-established and promised to move forward even more rapidly. Above all, the fostering of mutual respect amongst believers was bringing reconciliation and a sense of common purpose, and problems caused by years of isolation and lack of teaching were being overcome. Of course, not all outstanding matters could be solved in a few years; mutual respect was a principle not shared by all; leftism still created difficulties in some places, as did the existence of sectarian groups in others. The solution to the question of a national church organization had eluded them, and this problem was bound to create its own difficulties. Taken all in all, however, Protestant Christianity in China was stronger and healthier than ever before.

The Catholic Church 1981-87

Catholics and the Catholic Patriotic Association (CCPA)

It has been suggested in the last chapter that the majority of Catholic priests and believers were prepared to live within the publicly available structures provided by the Catholic Patriotic Association. The establishment of the Bishops' College and of a National Administrative Commission in 1980 had enabled many Catholics, who in the past had refused to join the CCPA, to move beyond some of the more confrontational positions assumed in the 1950s. The CCPA is not the Church; its role is within the United Front – acting as a bridge between Church and government. It was born out of a situation in which the Church was inextricably mixed up in the politics of the day as a result of its own manner of involvement in China and as a result of the pressures of political circumstances. The

CCPA removed the Church from political involvement, but until 1980 the domination of the CCPA over internal church life meant that the CCPA in reality tended to make the Church subservient to politics. The ambiguities of United Front policy discussed in Chapter Six emerged most clearly in relation to Chinese Catholics, and we have seen how this led to the problems in Shanghai and elsewhere. Unlike the TSPM the CCPA had no roots in past history. It received support from those who realized that the total opposition to the Communist government promoted by many Catholics was in itself a political option that would only deepen the separation of Christianity from Chinese culture, but this was not based on a coherent understanding of the need for the establishment of an indigenous Church. The issue of relationship to the universal Church, and in particular to the Holy See, was not thought through. The CCPA certainly had never meant to deny the spiritual authority of the Pope, as is clear from the requests sent to Rome concerning acceptance of episcopal nominations, but it produced no clear way forward and it was, perforce, in the general "leftist" climate after mid-1957, driven into a more extreme position than was acceptable to many. There is little doubt that most CCPA members retained their loyalty to the Pope as the spiritual father of the Church.

It, therefore, makes more sense to speak of the Catholic Church in China as one and not two churches. The testimony of Bishop Gong Pinmei and those like him is paralleled by the testimony of those who chose to express their "patriotism" by joining the CCPA. Both witnessed to a part of the truth; both failed to express the whole truth. This seems a far more helpful way to look at the situation than either an affirmation of the anti-Communist Ultramontanism that must share responsibility for the events of the late 1940s and 1950s, or a defence of the CCPA in terms of the "three-self" principles which in fact its supporters hardly understood. It is important to relativize the conflict if we are to move beyond the stereotyped viewpoints that have been all too common until now. Pierfilippo Guglieminetti S.J. has suggested that in spite of the conflicts and contradictions within the situation of the Catholic Church in China:

> the community of Chinese Catholics has continued, even after the establishment of the Patriotic Association, to be one church. It is one church giving two testimonies. Both types of Catholics in this one ecclesiastical community love their country and are faithful to the pastor of the universal church, even though they follow different paths of witness.[102]

The Cultural Revolution marked a decisive transition. All Catholics experienced a common suffering. In what precise ways this experience altered the terms of the discussion within the Catholic Church is hard to say, but in 1966 the implications of the CCPA position had not had time to be worked out and it must be doubted if organizationally speaking the Catholic Church had even begun to come to terms with the situation in which it found itself after 1949. Certainly, many attitudes were different in 1980 resulting, as Gugliemi-netti writes, in "practical and existential co-operation" between the two sectors of the Catholic community as, for the first time, the Catholic Church found itself in a position to rebuild itself as an indigenous institution.

Chinese Catholics and Rome

All the signs were that in 1980 Catholics were hoping for a resolution of the conflict with Rome. Yet, the hopes of 1980 were dashed in 1981. Bishop Deng Yiming, the visible sign of reconciliation within the Catholic community, and a potential bridge between Rome and Beijing, went to Rome on his *ad limina* visit in April 1981, apparently with the consent of the Chinese authorities. In February Pope John Paul II had spoken in Manila to the Chinese Catholic communities of Asia, in words that seemed to affirm the "patriotism" of Chinese Catholics. Cardinal Agostino Casaroli, Vatican Secretary of State, was cautiously optimistic at a joint press conference with Deng Yiming held in Hong Kong on 28 February. Then on 6 June the Pope appointed Deng as Archbishop of the

Guangzhou Diocese, in a move that was hailed at the time as opening the way for a papal visit to China and the end of the conflict. On 11 June Bishop Yang Gaojian, on behalf of the CCPA, denounced the appointment as illegal, and accused the Vatican of interference in the "sovereign affairs of the Chinese Church".[103] On 15 June the Religious Affairs Bureau expressed "full support for the statement", stating that Deng Yiming's acceptance was "a private move behind the back of China's Catholic Church".[104] On 22 June a meeting of the Guangzhou CCPA and Diocese removed Deng as Bishop. Deng himself expressed surprise and disappointment, and ultimately opted for remaining in Hong Kong. So ended the great hopes of the past months.

It was a perplexing episode. It may be that the Vatican misjudged the situation, seeing the appointment as a genuine gesture of good-will. It has been suggested that since it was the Chinese Church that made him Bishop of the Diocese (he was in fact made a titular bishop in February 1951 and was appointed only as the apostolic administrator of Guangzhou Diocese), Rome was merely confirming the choice by making Deng Archbishop of Guangzhou, the title of Archbishop being regarded as a formality in that the diocese had always had the status of an archbishopric. If this was the case then it is extraordinary that private discussions with Beijing had not taken place in advance, and indeed sources close to the Vatican at the time implied that this had happened. It might be that the rejection of the appointment by China reversed a private indication to the contrary. The time gaps between the appointment and Yang's rejection, and between his statement and that of the RAB, could suggest this. On the other hand, not everyone in Rome was anxious for a resolution of the conflict, and it may be that the Pope was badly advised. It perplexed a good number of notable Catholic leaders outside Rome also. What is not in doubt is that the episode put an end to all hopes of reconciliation, and led to both sides falling back to former positions.

The arrests of Jesuits and other priests, already mentioned in the last chapter, must be related to this heightened tension.

On 19 November 1981 four priests were arrested: Zhu Hongsheng, Zhen Wentang, Shen Baishun (all Jesuits) and Fu Hezhou, on charges of maintaining contacts with Rome. Subsequently a pamphlet produced by the Vatican in Latin and Chinese giving guidelines on how to conduct Masses in homes was produced in evidence. Others were also arrested in Shanghai at the time, and eventually in May 1983 Zhu Hongshen was tried and sentenced to fifteen years, Zhen Wentang to eleven years, Shen Baishun to ten years and another priest, Stephen Chen, to two and a half years.[105] Such incidents reveal that former attitudes persisted amongst some Catholics loyal to Rome and some government officials. According to Hong Kong sources, Bishop Fan Xueyan of Baoding, Hebei, was arrested in 1983 and sentenced to ten years for privately ordaining priests, receiving outside funds and colluding with the Vatican. A spokeswoman for the RAB confirmed the arrest in January 1984.[106] The existence of these "prisoners of conscience" is certainly a cause for major concern and an indication that religious policy is still too restrictive, but our concern must not prevent a recognition that these were exceptions. In general a healing process was under way, but it was a process that these events, and the international climate, impeded.

The next attempted *rapprochement* came in 1984, but it is difficult to know what substance there was to the rumours that the Vatican intended to downgrade its diplomatic relations with Taiwan and was preparing to recognize China. Premier Zhao Ziyang indirectly confirmed that something was in the air, at a press conference on 23 May 1984, in which he said that he had noticed that the Pope's recent remarks during his ten-day Asian tour in May had shown some change in position.[107] In the event nothing came of these rumours, although the tension may have been reduced as a result. Certainly something changed in the atmosphere during 1984, and this was reflected in the sudden surge in international exchanges from late 1984.

A group of Asian bishops visited China 24-29 September 1984, and this was followed on 27 October by the start of a private eleven-day visit by Cardinal Jaime Sin, Archbishop of Manila. Such visits could only have taken place with the knowledge and approval of Rome, and Cardinal Sin stated on his return that "China's rulers would not object to the country's Roman Catholic Church . . . realigning itself to the Vatican . . ."[108] The visit of Mother Teresa in January 1985 was symbolically important, especially as she met with Deng Pufang, Deng Xiaoping's crippled son, to discuss work with the handicapped. Her visit was followed by the visit of Bishop Wu of Hong Kong in March, obviously important because of Hong Kong's change of status in 1997, but also a significant move forward on the more general problem of relationships with the Vatican.

In July a CCPA delegation visited Hong Kong, led by Bishop Jin Luxian, assistant Bishop of Shanghai. Bishop Jin had led a return visit to the Philippines in the previous month, and his leadership and comments on these two occasions have led to much speculation as to his role as a "bridge". Jin himself has said that he is not a member of the CCPA, and his own Jesuit background combined with his intellectual rigour and openness make him the most suitable candidate for this role. Meanwhile, a delegation led by the Bishop of Beijing, Fu Tieshan, visited Belgium in November 1985. In February 1986 Bishop Wu made his second visit to China – a visit that was marred by the refusal of the RAB in Guangdong to allow him to say Mass in two localities near to his mother's home. In April and May of 1986 Bishop Jin Luxian spent three weeks in Germany, where he had contact with three cardinals, as well as discussions on social service agreements with Catholic aid agencies such as Caritas and Misereor – a clear parallel to the development of the Amity Foundation. Jin also visited the U.S.A. in September 1986, as part of a Catholic delegation which included four bishops (the others were Fu Tieshan, Tu Shihua, Director of the National Seminary, and Dong Guang-qing of Wuhan).

It is unclear what these unprecedented contacts are designed to achieve. They do reflect the increased confidence of the leaders of the "patriotic" part of the Church, and

there can be no doubt that Catholic life has been restored to a
far greater degree of normality than many foreign observers
had thought possible. It is, therefore, from a genuine base that
the CCPA can now address the Catholic community inside
and outside China. The opening of ten seminaries and of six
hundred churches and over a thousand chapels is an indication of this new strength. At the same time there remains a
section of the Church in active opposition to the CCPA and
those who work with it. Organized opposition is perhaps
limited to a few places, but the division and personal hurt
caused by such mutual antagonism needs to be healed for the
sake of the Church and of China. There is some evidence to
suggest that in Hebei, for example, the conflict has increased
in the past year or two, in part as a result of the greater
isolation of the Roman loyalists. The reported closure in May
1986 of an illegal seminary in Qiaozhai village, Xinlue County,
near Shijiazhuang City in Hebei, with the arrest of two aged
priests, is one part of the evidence.[109] The seminary was said
to have been formed for one year and it had almost forty
students. The students were held for a time but then sent
home. Hebei contains nearly a quarter of China's Catholics,
perhaps 800,000 people, and is served by 150 priests and 300
nuns. There are five bishops and a minor seminary in Shijiazhuang. Three of the bishops have been consecrated since 1981
(Liu Jinghe of Tangshan, Fan Wenxing of Hengshui and Liu
Dinghan of Cangzhou). It is an area of considerable activity,
and consequently the contradictions within the Catholic
community are likely to be more strongly felt.

The gradually changing situation amongst Catholic
believers in China should be greatly assisted by the new openness to outside contacts. The CCPA has tended to react to
developments on the basis of perceptions formed in the 1950s.
Undoubtedly, the Catholic Church has come a long way
since then, and Chinese Catholics of all shades of opinion are
only just becoming aware of the extent and significance of
these changes. For a Church still Tridentine at heart the discussions of Vatican II take a lot of getting used to. Moreover,
the CCPA rightly feels that Rome has been unwilling to listen

to a Chinese critique that stretches back to the Emperor Kangxi. One is reminded that at the height of the Rites Controversy the Emperor asked whether the Pope had enough Chinese to understand the issues at stake! Today the way out of the dilemma is available within the theology of the "local" church and the necessity for "inculturation" now espoused by the post-Vatican II Church. The particular problem of the appointment of bishops is not insoluble, for Rome has the discretion to authorize nomination, election or ratification, according to local circumstances. The election of Chinese bishops is, after all, not considered invalid, merely irregular. A major obstacle to normalization was removed on 3 July 1985, when Gong Pinmei of Shanghai was released from prison after thirty years. Ecclesiastically speaking, there seems no good reason for the conflict to continue. Politically, normalization must be in the interests of China as she seeks to improve her international relationships throughout the world, and a united community of Catholics must also serve her internal interest in stability and unity. What then prevents a *rapprochement*? Taiwan is the most frequently used excuse, but it is unlikely to be a real obstacle despite its symbolic importance to the Chinese government. Perhaps the explanation is to be found in the force of inertia and in the problem of trust. It is, in the end, a very personal matter, affecting those who have felt rejected and despised by the international Catholic community for making a choice which they felt was the right one. It would then be a pastoral problem rather than a political or ecclesiastical one.

In the light of the above understanding of the situation it is not helpful to compare the situation of the Catholic Church in China with that of the Church in England at the time of the Reformation, although some Catholic leaders in China have themselves drawn this parallel. Bishop Jin has clearly stated the situation as it is understood by him and, one can be sure, by almost all the Catholic leadership.

Each local Church [i.e. in this context, national] should be allowed to determine its own fate. The Church in

China has had its own personal experiences. At the same time, it knows very well that the Roman Curia has a world-wide strategy and it must attempt to balance the interests of many different peoples and powers, which is not always a simple task. We Chinese Catholics are Catholics who want to remain Catholics; we have no wish to become Protestants or Orthodox Christians. We basically accept the First and Second Vatican Councils, and we are trying now to implement the Second Vatican Council directives in China. With the help of God, we ourselves are able to administer and develop our Church in our own region.[110]

This is a most significant statement. The acceptance of Vatican II demonstrates beyond all doubt that, for Jin at least, the 1957 break was not decisive. It reveals a commitment to the Roman Catholic Church in spite of everything.

We have in the course of our discussion had cause to be critical at times of the CCPA and of the continued persecution of priests and bishops loyal to Rome, but we are also mindful of the fact that the CCPA symbolizes a concern about the attitudes and characteristics of the Vatican and of Western missionary bodies, to which we have drawn attention time and again through the pages of this book. The Rites Controversy, the re-imposition of French clerical control in the nineteenth century, the failure to create a native hierarchy until it was too late, the identification with the Guomindang, the Catholic policy towards land, the anti-Communism of Ultramontanist clergy in China prior to 1949 – all these have been noted with concern. Add to this the theological failure to deal with the issue of "inculturation", and one feels with some strength the appropriateness of a greater spirit of humility and penitence on the part of the Holy See than has as yet been evident. Few Catholic commentators have given sufficient recognition to this need for a clear sign to the Catholics of China that Rome itself was in part responsible for the divisions that occurred in the 1950s. Joseph Spae calls for the invention of a "new point of encounter" with the Church in China and the acceptance of a totally indigenous church. He continues:

> The inculturation which this presupposes should not be undertaken by antiquarian enthusiasts trying to construct a local Chinese Church which would display the classical features of the missionary past. Instead, the Church must express its national identity in contemporary terms, using an idiom which develops alongside the idiom of the times. Such an inculturation must be left to the Chinese themselves. Specifically, it must be left to the church leadership how best to lead the faithful in patriotic collaboration with the modernization of their country, as well as in pastoral and liturgical renewal based on Vatican II.[111]

Catholic Life 1981-87

The controversy with Rome has affected the internal development of church life but it would be quite wrong to draw the conclusion that the issue has dominated the lives of ordinary believers. The national Catholic journal *Zhongguo Tianzhujiao* which re-started in 1981 is less informative than *Tian Feng*, but reports over the years from many different parts of China make it clear that Catholic life is flourishing in spite of shortages of priests, lack of buildings and religious materials. An urgent task has been the restructuring of the 147 previous diocesan units, many of which were established in relationship to former missionary patterns of work and, in any case, frequently no longer conform to administrative boundaries. The triple city of Wuhan contained three separate dioceses in the past – this has now been unified under Bishop Dong Guangqing. Reports from Sichuan make it clear that the whole province had its diocesan boundaries redrawn according to civil boundaries by June 1984. The number of dioceses was reduced from eight to seven. Six of these are known to have active bishops. The diocese of Wanxian had eleven new towns added, so that the diocese now covers twenty-one county towns under the jurisdiction of Bishop

Duan Yinming. There were only ten priests, aged between sixty and eighty, and one student was training at the seminary in Chengdu.[112] A similar redrawing of boundaries was carried out in Yibin Diocese, and on 14 June 1985 Chen Shizhong was consecrated Bishop. Nanchong Diocese under Bishop Fan Daojiang now consists of twenty-two counties, with ten churches and eight priests, three nuns and 30,000 lay Catholics (compared to 19,442 and fifteen churches in 1949).[113] Sichuan as we noted above was reported as having had 300,000 Catholics in 1985 compared to fewer than 200,000 in 1949.[114]

Sichuan's growth and re-ordering is but one example of the process of renewal that has been under way since 1980. As we have seen, Hebei has the most Catholics, followed by Shandong and Shanxi. Anhui is an example of a province with a much smaller Catholic presence, reportedly with 70,000 Catholics compared to over 130,000 in 1949, although this apparent decline should be regarded with some suspicion. Three dioceses (Wuhu, Anqing and Bengbu) still exist but with only one bishop, Zhu Huayu, consecrated on 30 November 1986. Inner Mongolia, formerly with five dioceses, now has one under Bishop Wang Xueming, which in 1983 had ninety-six priests, thirty churches and 160,000 Catholics. The revival of Catholic life is well reflected in this huge and sparsely populated Autonomous Region. In Qahar Right Wing Front Banner in Meigui Cathedral during Bishop Wang's visit in May 1983 five thousand people attended; in nearby Liancheng three thousand attended. Altogether 3,477 people were confirmed from the area.[115] At the re-opening of the church in Siziwang over five thousand people were present.[116] On a visit to Tuquan County, in the far east of the Region, Father Tian Weiyun married twelve couples, gave extreme unction to 208 people, received 113 converts into the church, confirmed 1,284, and gave first communion to 1,167. Altogether he said ninety-six masses attended by a total of 46,984 people.[117] Similar reports came from Chifeng City in Zhaomeng, an area incorporated into Liaoning during the Cultural Revolution but restored to Inner Mongolia after 1978.

It would be tedious to go on listing figures and details of

similar reports, but enough has been said to demonstrate the vitality of local church life. The vast majority of Catholics still live in rural communities, and because of the foreign missionaries' policy of settling converts in Catholic villages there are many villages where the overwhelming majority of the population are Catholic believers. We have noted the phenomenon of the strong Catholic tradition amongst the fishing people of the Yangzi Delta who flocked to Sheshan. The non-urban nature of much Catholic life is reflected in the fact that the Cathedral in Suzhou Diocese is far from the centre of the city. Of the 40,000 Catholics in the diocese, half are fishing people. Jiangsu has at least 170,000 Catholics, four dioceses each with an active bishop. The life of small, compact Catholic villages is deeply traditional, but, as with Protestant home meetings, there have been problems in some places because of isolation and an absence of priests. On the other hand, the Catholic community in parts of China has had a long tradition of survival against the odds, and consequently of lay leadership. One wonders whether the "holy virgins" of yesteryear have resumed their role!

Lack of guidance has led to some extreme theological positions, and as one Hong Kong priest, closely in touch with some Catholic villages in South China from 1978, commented, "Their theology is very questionable but their faith is unshaken". He indicated that in one village a statue of the Virgin circulates from family to family. In another groups of two to three would gather to recite morning and evening prayer together, in yet another two or three young people taught the catechism, baptized and called people to prayer.[118] Such groups have gradually been drawn into the new structures of the Church, and in most cases are served by the few remaining priests in the area released from prison or manual labour in 1978. A vivid picture of life in a Shandong village was given by a visiting priest who returned to his family village for a five-month stay in 1981. While the report was in the early period of Catholic re-organization there is no reason to think that attitudes and customs will have changed very much since then.

The village of Weijia is about 150 km east of Jinan, the provincial capital. The population is 4,000 of whom 3,750 are Catholics. According to the visitor, relations with local officials are relaxed and the village is known throughout the province as a model, with productivity twenty per cent higher than the average. The reasons are similar to those we have already found amongst Protestant Christians – hard work, honesty, community spirit and commitment to the Four Modernizations. The one area of potential conflict with the authorities was attitudes towards family planning. Reports from other Catholic villages have suggested strong opposition to the policy, and Catholic leaders have been guarded in their comments on the issue. Bishop Fu Tieshan stated in an interview in 1984, with regard to the one child per family policy, that this was a matter for the couple, "From a theological point of view we advocate the safety period method of birth control. But some members of our congregation don't accept our idea."[119] Bishop Li Panshi of the Jiangmen Diocese in Guangdong indicated in 1984 that he supported contraception, but spoke out against abortion.[120] In Weijia village women have not taken the Pill since the end of the Cultural Revolution, but they observe the policy through other methods. Sterilization and abortion were unknown.

Since January 1980 a priest comes to the village to say Mass, and four Sisters lived in the village. All were loyal to the Pope but no one would be drawn about the CCPA, and when three Catholics were appointed by the local cadres to represent the village at CCPA meetings they accepted without protest. As the visiting priest comments:

> They intend to behave as conscience dictates: in non-essentials they feel free to comply; in matters of importance, such as allegiance to the Pope, they are inflexible. Such a spirit of compromise, we all know, is quite Chinese, and every official appreciates it.[121]

It is this spirit of compromise that explains so much about the situation, in which a strongly stated public policy concerning Rome is in practice ignored by most priests and laity and by not a few bishops. The CCPA guarantees the separation of religious life from political life, and while this may lead to an ultimate question as to the theological validity of such a separation, the history of China has to be taken into account, and the CCPA can be accepted as a means to an end. In the present situation it allows religious life to develop without undue interference always provided that the initial compromise is accepted.

Theological Training

The advanced age of most priests has meant that the training of new priests has become an urgent matter. A limited number of priests have been ordained, mostly people who had received some previous theological training, but in general the Church is having to wait until the young seminarians have graduated from the newly established seminaries. Six seminaries opened before 1984. The National Catholic Seminary opened in 1983, located in Beijing, and offers a six-year course. In 1984 it had fifty-six students. A Beijing Diocesan Seminary had opened on church land in Xibeiwang village in 1982. A Shenyang Seminary serving the three North-eastern provinces opened in 1983, offering a four-year course and with fifty students. The Sichuan Seminary, which also opened in 1983 with thirty-four students doing a four-year course, is in Chengdu, serving also Guizhou and Yunnan. In October 1983 forty students began their five years of study at the seminary in Wuhan, which serves Hubei, Henan, Hunan, Guangxi and Guangdong. The Sheshan Seminary in Shanghai opened in October 1982 serving six provinces (Jiangsu, Zhejiang, Anhui, Shandong, Fujian, Jiangxi and Shanghai) and offering a six-year course. Bishop Jin Luxian is the Rector, and with the opening of new buildings in 1986 the numbers expanded to two hundred. In 1985 a further regional seminary opened in Xi'an, serving the North-western provinces of Gansu, Ningxia, Qinghai, Xinjiang and Shaanxi, again with a four-year course, and with a planned intake of eighty students. A forum of the seven major seminaries took place on 4

September 1986 to discuss teaching materials, methods and staff training.[122]

Meanwhile in addition to the local seminary in Beijing other dioceses have opened minor seminaries. The Shijiazhuang Minor Seminary opened in December 1984, to serve the Hebei dioceses. The Jinan Minor Seminary opened its doors in February 1984, and the Taiyuan Minor Seminary in Shanxi in April 1985, serving the province and its large Catholic population and many churches (more than ninety are open around Taiyuan City alone). Xi'an also has a minor seminary, and plans were in hand during 1986 to open seminaries in Guangzhou and Hohhot. The re-opening of convents should also be noted in this context. By November 1986 ten convents were said to be in operation.[123]

Fourth National Catholic Conference

The Fourth Conference of the Catholic Patriotic Association was held in Beijing 18-29 November 1986, with three hundred delegates from twenty-eight provincial units. The National Administrative Commission and the Bishops' College also met during this period. On 30 November four bishops were consecrated, bringing the total number of bishops consecrated since 1981 to twenty-two (see Appendix Five).

Doctrine is the special concern of the Bishops' College, and there has been little sign of any major change in the theological thinking of the hierarchy. The Catechism was republished in Beijing in 1981, with a few changes. Thus in answer to the question, "What is the Church?" it responds:

The Church was established by Christ himself; everywhere it believes the doctrine of Jesus; it obeys the community that links the representatives of Jesus, as one body.

So all references to the Pope and infallibility are omitted. Also excluded are references to infant baptism; the ban on divorce and marriage dispensations. Infant baptism is in fact still widely practised. In 1983 Bishop Zong Huaide, Chairman of

451

the CCPA, told Sister Theresa Chu of the Canada China Programme that in rural areas it is the norm. On the other hand, in Shanghai a priest told Father Joseph Spae that only babies in danger of death are baptized. Once more we are reminded of the diversity of China and of the danger of generalizing from one particular situation.[124]

The Catholic version of the Bible has been printed in small numbers (75,000 according to Bishop Zong Huaide), and in 1985 the Shanghai Diocese was reported to be planning to publish 300,000 New Testaments in a modern version. Completion of the Old Testament will take considerably longer.[125]

The use of the Latin Mass is under discussion, and Chinese is said to be used on some occasions in a number of dioceses. The form of Catholic worship is deeply traditional, and during the Eucharist both prayers and songs are led from the congregation in forms well adapted to Chinese tradition. Indeed, Catholic worship has similarities to Chinese Buddhist worship, and is in many ways less alien than the usual pattern of Protestant worship, with its heavy stress on extempore prayer and lengthy sermons. Out of the spirituality of Catholic worship a new theology may indeed develop.

Indications of an increasing concern with theological questions emerged during 1986. The formation of the Association of Catholic Intellectuals in Shanghai on 27 June 1986, with an initial three hundred members, represented a most important step forward. Its aims include rendering service to society through offering lectures and seminars on science, medicine, education, the arts and religion and philosophy, as well as organizing service programmes to assist the Four Modernizations. Significantly it also aims at developing contacts with foreign Catholics, and two of its members attended a meeting on the "inculturation" of theology convened in October 1986 in Hong Kong. Another most important event took place in Changsha in November 1986, under the auspices of the Shanghai Catholics but attended by representatives from all over the country. The meeting was concerned with developing theological research, and two of the major topics singled out for study were Vatican II and Liberation Theology.

A theological review is expected to be published in Shanghai in 1987.

The Catholic community in China is a community still in transition. Its future development does not depend on the resolution of the conflict with Rome, but failure to resolve this problem will seriously hinder the move beyond the time of transition. The healing of the division is desired by most Chinese Catholics and is in the interests of both the Vatican and China. The consolidation of church life will probably assist the process, but what is most needed is an imaginative and generous gesture on the part of Rome. The Chinese Catholic community is now a truly indigenous Church, but as we have suggested with Chinese Protestants, indigenization does not go far enough.

"Inculturation" involves both the indigenization of leadership and the incarnation of the Church within the context of present social realities – in other words, it implies facing the political situation creatively. However, "inculturation" also implies the reformulation of theology in terms of the thought forms of the surrounding culture. Such an encounter can only begin when a church is both indigenous and related to the context of contemporary society in a manner that transcends mere accommodation. The question facing the Catholic Church in China is how to relate to contemporary society in an active and not passive manner. The discussion in academic circles over the possibility of religion making a positive contribution to socialist spiritual culture contains within it the implicit rejection of the traditional policy of limiting religion to the private sphere and, therefore, offers a new theological opportunity. Theology, in any case, is not condemned to be the preserve of academics and bishops, and the insights of the "people's theology" in Latin America, in South Korea and elsewhere, have shown that there can be a theology from below. Hopefully, the experience of Chinese Christians will feed the development of a theology rooted in Chinese culture. After all, an authentic theology must come out of listening to the questions being asked in the surrounding society. David Paton suggests that Christians have all too often not listened to the questions that men and women, nurtured with Confucius and Lao Zi in their bones, ask of Christianity. Only out of the answers given to their questions will come an authentic Chinese theology.

REFERENCES

1. Quoted by Ting, K.H., "Theological Mass Movements in China", Lecture at Rikkyo University, Tokyo, 23 September 1984, *Chinese Theological Review* 1985, p. 76.
2. Xiao Xianfa, "Correctly Understand and Implement the Party's Policy on Freedom of Religious Belief", *Renmin Ribao*, 14 June 1980, BBC SWB FE 6455, 26 June 1980 and *CSP Documentation*, No. 4, February 1981.
3. *China Youth News*, 11 March 1980 and 6 June 1982.
4. *Wen Hui Bao*, Shanghai 11 October 1982, BBC SWB FE 7161, 20 October 1982, *CSP Documentation*, No. 10, March 1983.
5. Article by Ye Shuangyu, *Fujian Ribao*, 23 October 1981, BBC SWB FE 6871, 4 November 1981, *CSP Documentation*, No. 7, March 1982.
6. "She Finally Came Back From The Church", *Party Life*, Vol. 2, Shanghai 1981, *CSP Documentation*, No. 7, March 1982.
7. NCNA in English, 30 June 1981, *CSP Documentation*, No. 6, October 1981.
8. The existence of the "Eight Bans" was reported by Wendell Karsen in a private report, June 1980, and by *Free China Weekly*, Taibei, 16 August 1981. The "Ten Don'ts" were mentioned in a report from Henan, 1 February 1980.
9. *China Daily*, 4 September 1984, *CSP Documentation*, No. 16, April 1984.
10. Originally published in *Asian Report* No. 128, Vol. 14, No. 8, 1981, Asian Outreach, Hong Kong, and reproduced *CSP Documentation*, No. 7, March 1982.
11. Lanzhou Radio, 19 July 1980, BBC SWB FE 6487, 2 August 1980.
12. Statement recorded by British Council of Churches Delegation. Text in *CSP Documentation*, No. 13, March 1984.
13. "The Basic Viewpoint and Policy on the Question of Religion During Our Country's Socialist Period", Document No. 19, 1982, Central Committee of the Chinese Communist Party, translated in full, Wickeri, *Seeking The Common Ground*, op. cit.
14. NCNA, 16 December 1983, *CSP Documentation*, No. 13, March 1984.
15. Report on Literary and Art Forum on 28 October 1983, Xinjiang Radio, 2 November 1983, BBC SWB FE 7483, 5 November 1983, *CSP Documentation*, No. 13, March 1984.
16. *Guangming Ribao*, 21 November 1983, BBC SWB FE 7512, 9 December 1983, *CSP Documentation*, No. 13, March 1984.
17. Deng Zhaoming, *Diocesan Echo*, Hong Kong, November 1984.
18. Interview with Wang Hongkui, "A Period of Transition is Needed", *Bridge*, No. 20, November/December 1986.
19. Deng Zhaoming, *Bridge*, No. 10, March/April 1985.
20. *Tian Feng*, No. 5, September 1984, *CSP Documentation*, No. 16, April 1985.

21. *Tian Feng*, No. 4, July 1984, *CSP Documentation*, No. 16, April 1985.
22. Statement by Liu Jun'an to Joint Standing Committees of National Christian organizations, *Tian Feng*, No. 5, September 1984, *CSP Documentation*, No. 16, April 1984.
23. Heilongjiang Religious Affairs Conference, Harbin Radio, 6 May 1986, BBC SWB FE 8255, 10 May 1986, *CSP Journal*, Vol. 1, No. 3, November 1986.
24. Wang Hongkui Interview, op. cit.
25. Report by Shen Derong to National CPPCC, *Tian Feng*, July 1985, *CSP Documentation*, No. 18, December 1985.
26. Ting, K.H., Interview in *Beijing Review*, No. 24, 11 June 1984.
27. "Difficulties in Hunan Province", *Bridge*, No. 10, March/April 1985.
28. "The Church in Guangxi", *Bridge*, No. 9, January/February 1985.
29. *China Daily*, 24 June 1985, *CSP Journal*, Vol. 1, No. 1, April 1986.
30. Wang Hongkui Interview, op. cit.
31. "The Church in Jiangxi Province", *Bridge*, No. 12, July/August 1985.
32. *Tian Feng*, July 1985, *CSP Documentation*, No. 18, December 1985.
33. Sun Deci, "Three Tasks in Chinese Theological Work Today", *Nanjing Theological Review*, June 1985, reproduced in *Chinese Theological Review* 1986.
34. Chen Zemin, "Self-Propagation in the Light of the History of Christian Thought", *Nanjing Theological Review*, June 1985, reproduced in *Chinese Theological Review* 1986.
35. Weir, the Rev. Dr A.J., British Council of Churches Delegation Report, December 1983.
36. Liu Qingfen, "Three Self in Tianjin", *Tian Feng*, March 1985, *CSP Bulletin*, No. 28, November 1985.
37. See *Pray For China*, No. 58, January/February 1984, Christian Communications Limited, Hong Kong.
38. Wang Shenyin, *Tian Feng*, No. 2, 1983, *CSP Documentation*, No. 12, October 1983.
39. *China and the Church Today*, Vol. 4, Nos. 4-5, 1982, Chinese Church Research Centre, Hong Kong.
40. ibid.
41. Report by Liu Zhengwei to Henan Provincial Religious Work Conference, Zhengzhou Radio, 27 March 1986, BBC SWB FE 8223, 3 April 1986, *CSP Journal*, Vol. 1, No. 3, November 1986.
42. *South China Morning Post*, 4 July 1986.
43. Xinhua in English, 28 August 1986.
44. For details see Deng Fucun, "The Truth About the So-called Dongyang and Yiwu Affair", *Tian Feng*, No. 2, 1983, *CSP Documentation*, No. 12, October 1983.
45. *China News and Church Report*, No. 16, 5 August 1983, Chinese Church Research Centre, Hong Kong.
46. Report from Cixi County, Zhejiang, *China News and Church Report*, No. 95, 8 March 1985.
47. "New Mission for Chinese Christians", *Beijing Review*, No. 22, 1 June 1987.
48. *China and The Church Today*, Vol. 4, No. 4, 1982, Chinese Church Research Centre, Hong Kong.

49. *Bridge*, No. 2, November 1983.
50. Budd, Margaret, personal papers, 1949.
51. Quoted in *Asian Report 137*, No. 7, 1982, Asian Outreach, Hong Kong.
52. *Tian Feng*, July 1986, *CSP Journal*, Vol. 1, No. 3, November 1986.
53. Deng Yueming of Shanghai in *Tian Feng*, No. 5, 1982.
54. *China Daily*, 4 September 1984, *CSP Documentation*, No. 16, April 1984.
55. The Hakka Churches in Meixian, *Bridge*, No. 5, May 1984.
56. Zhou Liuti–story told by Li Shuying, ibid.
57. Ge Jingqing, Prologue, *Tian Feng*, December 1985, *CSP Journal*, Vol. 1, No. 3, November 1986.
58. Ting, K.H., "Another Look at Three Self", *Ching Feng*, Vol. 25, No. 4, December 1982.
59. Ting, K.H., "Evangelism as a Chinese Christian Sees It", Lecture at Uppsala University, Sweden, 2 November 1982, *Missiology*, Vol. 11, No. 3, July 1983.
60. Ting, K.H., "Another Look at Three Self", op. cit.
61. Zhao Qixian, "An Educative Visit", *Tian Feng*, March 1985, *CSP Documentation*, No. 17, 1985.
62. *Tian Feng*, June 1985.
63. For details see report on Longquan County, *Tian Feng*, October 1985; on Wenling County, *Tian Feng*, October 1985; on Linqu County, *Tian Feng*, November 1985; *CSP Journal*, Vol. 1, No. 1, April 1986.
64. *Tian Feng*, June 1985, *CSP Documentation*, No. 18, December 1985.
65. Peng Ming, "He Believes in Jesus", *Tian Feng*, June 1986, *CSP Journal*, Vol. 1, No. 3, November 1986.
66. Amity Newsletter, No. 4, Spring 1987.
67. Chu, Sister Theresa and Lind, Christopher, eds., *A New Beginning: An International Dialogue with the Chinese Church*, Canada China Programme, 1983.
68. "Accounting for Differences: the Little Flock in Zhejiang", *Bridge*, No. 16, March/April 1986.
69. *Tian Feng*, May 1986, *CSP Journal*, Vol. 1, No. 3, November 1986.
70. Changsha Radio, 14 July 1984, BBC SWB FE 7698, 18 July 1984.
71. "Difficulties in Hunan Province", *Bridge*, No. 10, March/April 1985.
72. *Tian Feng*, July and August 1986.
73. *Tian Feng*, April 1986, *CSP Journal*, Vol. 1, No. 3, November 1986.
74. *Tian Feng*, November 1985 for Hekou and *Tian Feng*, June 1986 for Sixian and Yingshang; see *CSP Journal*, Vol. 1, No. 3, November 1986 for latter report.
75. See *Bridge*, No. 6, July 1984 and Xinhua in English, 14 January 1986, *CSP Journal*, Vol. 1, No. 1, April 1986.
76. For further details see *Bridge*, No. 14, November/December 1985.
77. Report by Peter Han, *Tian Feng*, October 1986, *CSP Journal*, Vol. 2, No. 1, April 1987.
78. *Dazhong Ribao*, 7 July 1984, BBC SWB FE 7715, 7 August 1984.
79. *Bridge*, No. 19, September/October 1986.
80. *Tian Feng*, October 1986.
81. Reports in *Tian Feng*, July and September 1985.
82. Chu, Sister Theresa, "Visit to Seven Dioceses in China", mimeographed report, December 1982.

83. Reports in *Tian Feng*, November 1985, *CSP Journal*, Vol. 1, No. 1, April 1986, and *Tian Feng*, July 1986, *CSP Journal*, Vol. 1, No. 3, November 1986.
84. *Bridge*, No. 4, March 1984 and British Council of Churches Delegation Report, December 1983.
85. ibid.
86. Xinhua in English, 17 October 1984 and *Bridge*, No. 4, March 1984.
87. *Bridge*, No. 18, July/August 1986.
88. *Tian Feng*, August 1986, *CSP Journal*, Vol. 1, No. 3, November 1986.
89. Overseas Missionary Fellowship China Prayer, October 1986.
90. *Tian Feng*, April 1985, *CSP Documentation*, No. 17, August 1985.
91. Report by Huang Qingzhi, *Bridge*, No. 20, November/December 1986.
92. *China Daily*, 1 October 1985 and Xinhua in English, 29 September 1985, *CSP Documentation*, No. 18, December 1985.
93. OMF China Prayer, July/August 1986.
94. Tang Rongtao, "Childlike Patriotism and Mature Love of God", *Tian Feng*, January 1986, *CSP Journal*, Vol. 1, No. 2, April 1986.
95. *Tian Feng*, No. 3 and No. 6 1984.
96. OMF China Prayer, June 1987.
97. Details in *Bridge*, No. 6, July 1984 and No. 10, July/August 1985.
98. Verbal report Lianjiang County, Fujian, BCC Delegation, December 1983.
99. *Tian Feng*, April 1985, *CSP Documentation*, No. 17, August 1985.
100. *Yao Dao Wen Da*, translation in *Chinese Theological Review* 1985.
101. Ting, K.H., "How To Study The Bible", *Tian Feng*, No. 1, 10 October 1980. Translation Tao Fong Shan Ecumenical Centre, Hong Kong, 1981.
102. Guglieminetti, Pierfilippo, S.J., "The Catholic Church in China: One Church, Two Testimonies", *Tripod*, No. 37, 1987.
103. NCNA in English, 11 June 1981, *CSP Documentation*, No. 5, October 1981.
104. NCNA in English, 15 June 1981, ibid.
105. Details in *Kung Kao Po*, 4 December 1981, Hong Kong Standard, 3 May 1983 and NCNA in English, 19 March 1982, *CSP Documentation*, No. 8, May 1982.
106. *Kung Kao Po*, 16 December 1983 and *South China Morning Post*, 11 January 1984.
107. NCNA in English, 23 May 1984, *CSP Documentation*, No. 14, July 1984.
108. *Zhonglian* (China Catholic Communication) Singapore, No. 8, January 1985.
109. *South China Morning Post*, 23 September 1986.
110. Jin Luxian, "The Church in China Past and Present", *Tripod*, No. 36, 1986.
111. Spae, Joseph J., "The Catholic Church in China", *Religion in Communist Lands*, Vol. 15, No. 1, Spring 1987.
112. Li I Te, Paul, "Redistricting of Wanxian Diocese in Sichuan", *Tripod*, No. 29, 1984.
113. Li I Te, Paul, "Consecration of Bishop Chen Shizhong", *Tripod*, No. 29, 1985.
114. *Bridge*, May/June 1985.
115. *Zhongguo Tianzhujiao*, No. 7, 1983, *CSP Documentation*, No. 13, March 1984.

Unfinished Encounter

116. *Zhongguo Tianzhujiao*, No. 8, 1984, *CSP Documentation*, No. 14, July 1984.
117. *Zhongguo Tianzhujiao*, No. 6, 1983, *CSP Documentation*, No. 12, October 1983.
118. "Voyage en Chine", *Echo de la Rue Bac*, No. 129, May 1979.
119. Fu Tieshan Interview, *South China Morning Post*, 30 June 1984.
120. *Bridge*, No. 8, November 1984.
121. Spae, Joseph J., ed., *Catholic Life in a Chinese Village*, December 1981.
122. For details see *Tripod*, No. 23, 1984; No. 32, 1986; *China Update*, No. 15, Spring 1986, Oud-Heverlee, Belgium.
123. *Hong Kong Standard*, 20 November 1986.
124. Chu, Sister Theresa, "Report on China Trip, 5 August to 8 September 1983", mimeographed paper, and *China Update*, No. 7, Spring 1984.
125. *South China Morning Post*, 8 April 1985.

X

Unfinished Encounter

God can be known to us in the same way as
a man can see an endless ocean by standing
at the shore at night with a dimly lit candle.
Do you think he can see much? Not much,
almost nothing. And nevertheless, he sees
the water well. He knows that there is an
ocean in front of him, that this ocean is
huge and that he cannot see it all at once.
The same is true of our knowledge of God.
St Simeon the New Theologian, Oration 61.

There is a small church not far from Fuzhou City at a place
known as Mawei. In the past it was familiar to many missionaries, and was known to them as Pagoda Anchorage. In
1983 when we visited it it was a somewhat rundown place; the
church had just been recovered, and a few of the families who
had moved in during the Cultural Revolution were still in
occupation of part of the building. The church was crowded
for the weekly lunchtime prayer meeting, and as it came to
an end we were overwhelmed by the church members as they
sought to clasp our hands, smiles of welcome on their faces.
As we so fleetingly touched each other's lives the bond of our
common faith linked us powerfully together, so that there was
no need for words. Today Mawei is in the midst of industrial
development as a new port is created to serve the modernization of China. No doubt the church is still full, many of the
same humble people kneel for their prayers, part of a rapidly
changing world, a world that we encountered for a few brief
moments but which we can never forget.

This book is meant as a tribute to the Christians in Mawei and in a host of other large and small places in every part of China. It is fitting to begin this last chapter with this simple image of ordinary people at prayer in their church, because that is what underlies all that is written here. In the end the story we have tried to tell is only given point when it is rooted in the spiritual experience of the Christians of China. Prayer is the hidden reality that has formed the heart of the Christian presence in China over the long centuries, whether expressed in the language of Nestorian hymns or in the Latin of the Mass or the vocal prayers of Protestant Christians, or in the silence of men and women's hearts. Missionaries have come and gone, and many gave their lives for the sake of China and her people, but it is the faith of Chinese Christians that has endured. We all stand on the edge of a vast ocean seeking to discern the immensity before us, and each of us sees only in part. If we have been critical of some aspects of Christianity in China in the past, this criticism has not been intended to deny the validity of the faith of missionary or convert. It is indeed true that the encounter between Christianity and Chinese culture has, for the most part, been superficial, but in making this assertion we must never forget that in the hearts and minds of many individuals a genuine encounter has taken place, albeit at a largely unconscious level. Instinctively, Chinese Christians have taken the Christianity of the missionary and have moulded it into a distinctive form. The transforming power of the Spirit has not been absent, and the survival and coming to maturity of Chinese Christianity over the past forty years is the most telling witness to this.

Our telling of this story must cease in mid-1987 at what is, inevitably, a somewhat arbitrary point in history, and yet it has a certain appropriateness, almost one year since the Fourth National Christian Conferences. 1986 marked a stage in the restoration of religious life, and 1987 has seen the beginnings of the next stage. We have no more to say of the particular circumstances of the Church in China, nor of the political and social context. Hopefully, time will fill in some of the gaps in our present knowledge. Some of the unanswered questions will be answered and some of the unresolved issues will be resolved. But not all. New questions and issues will arise, and we can surely expect that in the next century Chinese civilization will move to the centre of the world stage, and at the same time Chinese Christianity will enter into a new maturity out of which it will be able to bring its own gifts of theological wisdom and spiritual insight to the world-wide Church. Already, perhaps, we can detect something of what this might be like in the writings of a few gifted men and women. At various points in our narrative we have attempted to reflect on some theological issues. Our final task must be to attempt some more general theological reflections, seeking to draw together the threads of our discussion, always bearing in mind that our reflection is from the outside. Nevertheless certain themes seem to emerge, challenging us to re-assess our own theological presuppositions. It has been a source of some surprise that the concerns being expressed by theo-logical writings in China today, small in volume as they may be, seem to relate to some of the most fundamental theological issues of our time. We should not, perhaps be so surprised. For Chinese Christians are well placed to tackle these issues, many of which arise out of the position of Marxism in our world, the encounter between faiths, the contribution of non-Western cultures to the formation of new theological para-digms, and the place of religion within modern culture.

Faith and Culture in China

The personal resolution of the relationship of faith to culture has usually been achieved at the expense of theological coherence, with the contradictions between the form of Christianity and the form of Chinese tradition remaining unrecognized. Xu Guangqi, Ricci's first convert, is a key example of this. He achieved a personally satisfying synthesis between his Confucian and Christian commitments, accept-ing Ricci's thesis of an "original" Confucianism, but his

personal synthesis appears from the outside as a somewhat
unsatisfactory juxtaposition of disparate elements. One can
say the same for Liang A-fa in the early nineteenth century,
and so on down through to our own time. Perhaps T.C. Chao
was the one theologian before 1949 who recognized the contradiction, but despite many important insights, he was
unable to carry the encounter through. His last letter shows
that to the end he was acutely aware of the problem. Is indeed
the boundless universe under the governance of God or is it
simply a natural process? Chao realized that Marxism directly
challenged his faith. It was a challenge that most Christians
have sought to avoid. Whether it liked it or not Chinese
Christianity in 1949 found itself facing the challenge of
Marxism. The Marxist critique of religion as "the heart of the
heartless world" and as the "opium of the people" could not
be lightly dismissed. There was good reason why many
Christians found themselves attracted by Marxism – why T.C.
Chao "surrendered theology to his context",[1] and others
joined the CCP. In such a time of reckoning it was the
achievement of Y.T. Wu, K.H. Ting, Chen Zemin and others
that they recognized and accepted this challenge. We must
look more closely at the nature of their theology, rooted as it is
in an engagement with Marxism at both the ideological and
practical level, an encounter that enabled it to begin the
journey beyond the forms of theology that failed China in the
past. There could be no simple way back to a revival of the old
ways of speaking of God – the way had to be forward, and it
had to be a way that encountered the Marxist critique before it
could go beyond it. That is why we have suggested that the
path chosen by Wang Mingdao and Gong Pinmei, courageous
as it was, could take Chinese Christianity no further. T.C.
Chao, in his brokenness, points to the way beyond.

Why can this be so? Here we must ask a hard question of
spirituality. For many believers faith is a quest for certainty
where, by definition, faith is in things unseen. As Alan
Ecclestone writes:

To live with our uncertainties is not simply a necessary

facet of our education at all levels: it is the very truth of faith. To endure the sifting process of interrogation is the hallmark of discipleship.[2]

And as Kenneth Leech adds:

Only such a spirituality of questioning and of enhanced vision can survive the Marxist critique of religion as an opiate. Thus a test of our spirituality must be whether it makes us more aware of the realities of the world, and therefore more ready to respond to them, or not.[3]

True Christian prayer and spirituality cannot be an opiate. So, of course, both Bishop Ting and Zhao Fusan have argued in China. Prayer must be related to living and contemplation to action. To dissolve either side of the equation produces an unbalanced Christian life. For this reason, if for no other, Christians do well to heed the Marxist criticism.

The Form of Western Theology

One of our themes in the early part of this book was the emergence over the centuries of a form of Western Christianity which ceased to be open to adaptation to new cultural contexts, "haunted by the vision of a takeover", as Hickley has said. Nestorian Christianity remains important as a reminder of a different approach. John Robinson, in his outstanding book *Truth Is Two-Eyed*, testifies to this approach:

How little would Europe have made of Christ if the understanding of him had been limited to the messianic categories of Palestinian Judaism. Beginning with Paul, and continuing through the work of men like Clement of Alexandria and Origen, the wisdom of Greece, albeit from an alien culture, was boldly drawn upon to fashion the worth of Christ for us, the children of that Western world. We think of Christianity now as being a Western religion, but this is only because it became that through men who

463

took great risks in theology, spirituality and art, that we might know through the medium of our own cultural conditioning the wonderful works of God.[4]

Western theology, both Catholic and Protestant, has been dominated by a positivism which has manifested itself in a demand for carefully defined propositions, and a literalism in which the metaphorical and open language of the Bible has been replaced by a stress on the facticity of the biblical terms. Both tendencies can be traced back to the early period of the Western Church, but up to the time of the Reformation and Counter-Reformation an alternative strand of thinking, associated with the Greek Fathers, was never absent. Elements of this alternative tradition were certainly present in the Reformers, but it seemed to disappear from view in the doctrinal struggles that enveloped post-Reformation Europe. This positivistic theology that emerged from these struggles was to develop into Catholic and Protestant fundamentalist theologies in reaction to the Enlightenment challenge. An alternative way of coping with the rationalism of the enlightenment was the Romantic surrender of the outer world in favour of inwardness and the world of feeling. Theological liberalism, "modernism" and "social gospel" followed quite naturally and logically. A further and very different theological emphasis was developed in the thinking of Frederick Denison Maurice, whose work was rooted in St John and the theology of the Greek Fathers, and who in the mid-nineteenth century reopened access to this tradition for many people. Maurice may also be thought of as the father of Christian socialism. In his thought neither fundamentalism nor liberalism sufficed, and it was his form of open catholicism that T.C. Chao eventually discovered.

It is not far from the truth to say that fundamentalist theologies are the creation of post-Enlightenment Europe and are directly related to the process of secularization. In other words, the modern belief in the primacy of fact, expressed in the rationalistic approach to science in which, in principle, everything can be explained, is reflected in the interpretation of the Bible in which pseudo-scientific explanations are looked for. The language of myth, of metaphor and image, is no longer accepted as a valid method of discourse, and is dismissed. The essential ambiguity of all language is forgotten in the search for definitive propositions. Liberal theology is merely the obverse side of fundamentalism – it sees the absurdity of the literal interpretation of the Bible – but seeks in its stead a purely rationalistic explanation of the language of the Bible in terms of the positivistic sciences. It is, like these sciences, reductionist. From what we might call a post-modern perspective, both forms of theology are vitiated by their acceptance of the Enlightenment understanding of reality.

Chinese traditional thinking is far removed from this positivist form of theology. The spirit pervading Chinese culture is the spirit of the *Dao*, the primordial source of creativity, that interfuses all things and unites them. In both Taoist and Chinese Buddhist forms "The *Dao* that can be named is not the eternal *Dao*".[5] Western positive theology either dismissed Chinese modes of thought or looked for the Western concept of the divine hidden beneath the surface. This was, of course, the motive for Ricci's quest for an "original" Confucianism. Positive theology simply turned its back on the tradition of the great mystics, the tradition of the Desert Fathers and Mothers, whose greatest theological exponent was Pseudo-Dionysius, or Denys, who wrote most probably between 480 and 510. Hans Urs von Balthasar calls his work "perhaps the most important evidence of the presence of Asia in the heart of Western theology . . ."[6] Denys speaks of the "mystery" of God, using the term a little differently from its modern reference to detective stories! He means something that is infinitely true and impossible in this life for us to define. For this reason God is ultimately beyond all our categories of knowing, his mysteries "dazzle with a light of the utmost clarity in deepest darkness, and – in a way completely beyond our grasp and utterly invisible – overpower blinded minds with a splendour surpassing beauty".[7] God is, in the end, beyond all affirmations and all negations too. Such a theology begins and ends in prayer and in the silence before God that is contemplation.

It is not easy to grasp the meaning of this difficult theology, and for those unfamiliar with its themes the best way into it is probably through the fourteenth-century English mystics. Thus, for example, the unknown author of *The Cloud of Unknowing* speaks of the darkness and the cloud lying between us and God, but bids us "smite upon that thick cloud of unknowing with a sharp dart of longing love".[8] It is, however, Mother Julian of Norwich who provides the easiest way into this tradition, with her careful balance of grace and nature.[9]

Hans Küng, in his outstanding book *Christianity and the World Religions*,[10] suggests that Christians should take seriously the work of Nicolaus Cusanus who, drawing on Denys, believed that God is defined in identity with and difference from all other beings and therefore cannot be known save through "learned ignorance". In God all opposites hold together, but "in theology negative statements are true and positive statements are insufficient".[11] Japanese Buddhists have shown great interest in Cusanus, and we are immediately reminded of the failure of Christianity from Ricci onwards to take Buddhism seriously. Küng comments:

> Let me take a brief melancholy glance at the course of history since Nicholas of Cusa died, in 1464. It is strange to think what might have happened if Christian theologians had not always buried their own tradition of negative theology beneath their prolix tomes . . . How much more deepened understanding might have been applied to foreign religions just when new continents and peoples were beginning to be discovered! And how might the conversations with Japanese Buddhists have gone, if the first Jesuit missionaries had cited, not Scholastic proofs for the existence of God, but the penetrating analysis of the experience of God as detailed by Cusanus, whose writings they could have been familiar with?[12]

There is at present little sign of discussions on religious questions taking place between Christians and Buddhists in

China. But the old antagonism has gone, sometimes replaced by a real friendship between pastors and monks, as anyone who has been taken to a Buddhist monastery by a local Christian pastor can testify. A group of monks regularly visit the Nanjing Seminary. Friendship and trust are the prerequisite of dialogue, and circumstances are propitious for this to begin in China for the first time in history. Küng's book suggests important areas for discussion. He suggests, for example, that Buddhism can challenge the Christian tendency to define God in a series of propositions, while Christianity can perhaps challenge Buddhism to see the Absolute in terms of "spirit in creative freedom", a partner who embraces human inter-personality. There is room here for a richly creative encounter, an encounter that assumes considerable importance in the context of the breakdown of the mechanistic assumptions of Cartesian-Newtonian science, a subject to which we will return below.

Dualism and Materialism

Western theology, indeed in this instance almost all Christian theology, was also pervaded by an anti-materialism that was perhaps the most unfortunate result of the adaptation of Christian faith to Greek culture. Dualism in terms of a division between soul and body is without foundation in the Bible, and its results in terms of Christian attitudes towards human relationships have been disastrous. In China, missionaries, although they did not know it, were preaching a doctrine that was in fact not biblical and that was certainly profoundly antipathetic to Chinese tradition. It was one area where Chinese were most resistant to Buddhist teaching, and in some senses the development of Pure Land Buddhism was a response to this. An organic and dynamic view of the universe was common to the Taoist and Neo-Confucian, and pervaded Chinese poetry and painting. Most of Ricci's critics found his doctrine of the immortality of a disembodied soul unacceptable.

In order to find a rounded and fully biblical understanding we have to bypass much of Eastern and medieval theology before our own time and go back to Irenaeus. As Balthasar comments about Irenaeus' understanding:

> The true man is soul in body and grace in both (the Holy Spirit who lives in soul and body as in a temple), and therefore the eschatologically whole man is also not the disembodied soul after death, but emphatically the risen flesh . . .[13]

Denys, despite the seemingly Platonic background to his thought, actually retains a profound sense of the dialectical relation between the manifestation of God the unmanifest within the external splendour of the beautiful and the ever greater hiddenness of God. He neither denies Scripture nor devalues the images of nature but holds the two together in a sacramental understanding. His is the eye of the artist and he is able to capture "the whole spiritual energy of the Alexandrines and the Cappadocians in his work and at the same time to have banished definitely their tendency to threaten the Incarnation, the visible church and the resurrection of the flesh."[14]

Here indeed is a richness of insight that can resonate with some aspects of Chinese thought, and not only thought, but the artistic dimension of Chinese life, which Bishop R.O. Hall has so rightly insisted is one of the primary manners in which the Chinese people have sought to respond to the mystery of being. We have here that vision of a world transfused with the love of God that is most gloriously portrayed in the great iconographic tradition that culminated in the work of Andrei Rublev, in which the hidden structure of the composition holds the subject matter in a harmonious and balanced wholeness, conveying a sense of stillness and inner recollection, and often suffused with a light and colour that "create a sense that we are looking into a world illuminated not by an external light that casts shadows, but the light of divine grace . . ."[15] One is reminded of Gerard Manley Hopkins' words, "The world is charged with the grandeur of God".

We find then one part of the tradition of Western Christianity that is akin to the enduring insights of Eastern Orthodoxy and which presents us with a theology that recognizes with Gregory of Nyssa that "there is only one manner of knowing – to reach out ceaselessly beyond the known". A theology inspired by the contemplation of the beauty of God and which finds within his creation an analogy, not of *Being*, but of the *beautiful*. Dualism in its starkest sense can have no real place here, even if it is not always explicitly denied. It comes as no surprise to find Mother Julian speaking simply and beautifully of the body's digestion and evacuation of food for "so are we, soul and body, clad and enclosed in the goodness of God".[16] It is at its roots an artistic vision.

How much then it must be a matter of regret that Ricci and his fellow Jesuits, dominated as they were by a positivistic theology, failed to convey these insights! How serious a mistake it proved to be not to take Buddhism or Taoism seriously, and to see Neo-Confucianism as atheistical! The Jesuits in Japan also failed to take Buddhism seriously, but Ricci succeeded and they did not. Ricci's achievement seems all the more remarkable. It was an achievement that cannot be related to his understanding of Chinese philosophy, for he misunderstood the dynamic of Confucian development in his eagerness to find traces of a creator God in early Chinese thought. Intellectually speaking, despite the incredible achievements reflected in his translations and his writings in Chinese, Ricci's attempt at dialogue failed. But having said that, we have not said everything – far from everything. Ricci succeeded where many missionaries in the following centuries were to fail (and in so far as they were not a failure it was for the same reasons), and this success may be more important than his intellectual failure. He succeeded in the art of friendship, and in his own person witnessed to the love of Christ – surely it was this that drew to his side some of the greatest scholars of the day! And not only Ricci. Why else did the Emperor Kangxi feel so drawn to the Jesuits at his court, if not through the warmth and depth of their friendship? The sort of friendship that we speak of is not a superficial *bonhomie* but a true art, founded on a deep appreciation of the other and the worth of the gifts he brings. It is an art central to the experience of the Chinese people, and it is why it is not easily available to the outsider. It was the total commitment of the Jesuits that in part explains their success, in spite of the inadequacy of their theology.

Yet, it was the theological weakness that in the end betrayed them. The Rites Controversy stands as a fitting symbol of all that was ventured and all that was lost. What was gained was the foundation of the Church on Chinese soil, what was lost was the chance for Christianity to be enriched by the wealth of Chinese culture. Throughout the remaining years of the eighteenth century and during the nineteenth century, through to the May Fourth Movement of 1919, Christians were to be on the margin, both of society and culture. The Church defined itself in opposition to that culture, and endeavoured to impose Western theological norms on Chinese Christians – always, thankfully, with only partial success. Not that the nineteenth-century was a propitious time for Chinese culture itself as the familiar forms sank into decadence – ultimately to be rejected in the early twentieth century. To that extent the missionaries can be forgiven! Nevertheless we have to say that the influence of fundamentalist Protestantism in the early years of the growth of the non-Catholic Church in China was detrimental to the development of an appropriate Chinese theology, and led to the rise of indigenous sectarian groupings whose theology remained firmly in a nineteenth-century Western mould.

A Time of Reckoning

The twentieth century has seen the revival of Chinese nationalism, and this has brought Christianity to a historical reckoning. It is unfortunate that the North Atlantic churches have not yet digested the immense negative importance of their implication in Western imperialism. It is clear from our study of Christian history in China that in reality there was never any chance of Christianity becoming the religion of the majority, or of even providing the vehicle for the revival of China. The missionaries had been too involved in the humiliation of Chinese national pride for that to happen. Besides, Chinese intellectuals came to understand that Christianity was no longer respected amongst the intellectual community in the West. Fundamentalism could be dismissed, as indeed was happening in the West itself. In Edwardian times in a hidden way, and then openly in the 1920s, religious belief became intellectually inadmissible. That, at least, was the consensus of opinion, drawing on Darwin, Marx, Nietzsche, Freud and Durkheim. The young Chinese students who studied in Europe or America imbibed the agnosticism around them, and returned with a belief in "science and democracy" and an iconoclasm towards traditional beliefs that would inform the spirit of May Fourth and sustain the secular vision of that and the succeeding generation through to 1966.

Liberal theology may have been the vogue around the turn of the century, and allied to it was the "Social Gospel". Its charms were to prove shortlived. Sherwood Eddy could preach to thousands in China, but most of them were listening to his political message and not to his Christian one. Theological liberalism was to persist down to our own day, drawing on the strength of scientific rationalism and yet being drained of all meaning by that same rationalistic perspective. In the West it could continue to provide a refuge for those too nostalgic to abandon the Christian claims altogether, and it reached its all too obvious, and absurd, conclusion in the 1960s' "Death of God" theology. But in another context, such as China, theological liberalism could not provide a satisfactory way of believing, and it was rejected by non-Christians. By the 1930s Chinese Christians found themselves facing a formidable challenge to their faith, and the various forms of Western theology which they had inherited seemed unable to offer them a creative way forward. The sense of crisis that pervaded China from the mid-1930s gave a great impetus to those groups who preached millenarian or dispensational views, but the balance between prayer and living, contemplation and action was missing from most of these groups, perhaps with the exception of the Jesus Family, although this was unbalanced in other ways. Yet, in the faith of Y.T. Wu, in the sometimes grossly inadequate theology of the "Christian Movement", the ground was being prepared for the abandonment of both the fundamentalist and liberal perspectives in a search for new ways of expression, not only by intellectuals, but by many ordinary believers, in response to Liberation.

Roman Catholicism in Europe had set itself against the tide of modernism by the vigorous assertion of Tridentine values linked to the Ultramontanist view of the supremacy of all things Roman. The European missionaries shared this blinkered perspective. Not even Vincent Lebbe expressed discontent with the Ultramontanist views of the missionary community, which in other ways he so bitterly criticized. Intellectually speaking this was disaster enough, but politically speaking it was one of the supreme failures of the Church to address itself to the realities of the human situation. The triumph of Fascism, first in Italy and then in Germany, Portugal and Spain, was assured by the Vatican's failure to distance the Catholic Church from the anti-democratic forces. Support for Chiang Kai-shek through and beyond 1949 was quite logical, as was the strong anti-Communist line.

The hostile reaction of Christians to the rise of Marxist-controlled states is understandable, in the sense that the Church has frequently been the object of severe persecution, and human freedom has too often been denied on a massive scale in Soviet Russia and elsewhere. In the 1950s anti-Communism was pretty universal in both Western Europe and North America. The Soviet Union was, after all, in control of the major countries of eastern Europe as a result of the War and not through popular revolution. It was generally assumed that China was no different. It was different, and it is well to remind ourselves that the traditional anti-Communist viewpoint obscures more than it elucidates by seeking to describe all countries under Communist control in the same way.

We have already indicated that Christianity cannot so easily be rid of Marxism. Marxism must be understood in its aspect of prophetic witness against what the world of the Enlightenment had become, and as a radical critique of the churches and their theological failure. The missionary movement started at the very moment when Western theology was found wanting. It did not possess the internal resources to open itself to the cultures of the world, and Legge's act of homage before the Temple of Heaven must have seemed an act of sheer folly. On the one hand, liberal theology failed to deal with the social question that Marxism addressed directly, and on the other hand fundamentalist theology never even faced the social challenge and offered only a means of escape and consolation. It is true that in the 1930s we see the beginnings of a new theological approach in both Europe and America: an approach that at last took the challenge of secularism, and in particular that of Marxism, seriously. By the 1930s the dialectical theology associated with Karl Barth was beginning to make an impact in Europe and America. In a different way Reinhold Niebuhr opened up theology to the questions posed by contemporary social concerns. But only a few missionaries were aware of what these thinkers were saying, and their influence on Chinese Christianity was minimal. It was too late, and the implications of the new thinking would take years to sink into the thinking of Western Christians.

Karl Barth, however, saw to the heart of the matter, but his reflections were only published in German in 1948 and in English in 1960. Thus in Volume III Part 2 of *Church Dogmatics* Barth tackles the question of the relationship of soul and body, and therefore he also faces head on the issue of materialism. Karl Barth's dialectical theology cannot take us very far along the road towards an authentic encounter with non-Christian traditions, but Barth's contribution to theology far surpasses the immediate limitations of his dogmatic position, and nowhere is this more the case than in his discussion in this section of *Church Dogmatics*. Monistic materialism rests on "a certain honesty and sobriety" which rejects abstract dualism in the face of the "actual course of individual and social life".[17]

Such materialism is, he argues, not the product of biological and physiological science but of the rise of modern industrial man, "The figure of the human robot, who neither asks nor is asked about his soul":

> The real foundation of modern materialism, and the explanation of the validity and expansion which it has enjoyed in and in spite of its scientific weakness, are not to be found in the researches and results of modern biology and physiology, but in the rise of this form of humanity, in which every one who lives with open eyes in and with his time must willingly or unwillingly recognize a little of himself. "And so I solve the problem: only he who lives in prosperity lives agreeably" – so thinks the big man contentedly and the little man discontentedly, except that the big man is perhaps seldom honest enough to admit to himself that this is how he thinks.[18]

Marxism, Barth argues, has bound itself to this so-called scientific materialism, but we quite misunderstand Marxism if we think that it is grounded in this materialism. Marx's historical materialism arises out of the soullessness of modern culture as a protest and a summons to put an end to the inhumanity of this culture. It found in pseudo-scientific materialism an ally in so far as Marx's view of the relationship of economics to ideology was a parallel to crude materialism's view of body and soul. Barth is profoundly critical of Marxism's reduction of life to economics, for it is this very presupposition which leads to orthodox Marxism taking on itself "more and more of the spirit, or lack of spirit of that robot man". But, he argues, the whole modern community points unmistakably in this direction. Barth is saying what few Christians have cared to admit, for he then links the rise of this figure of "soulless man" to the Christian failure to do anything positive to prevent his emergence. The Church has always stood on the side of the "ruling classes"! Christian teaching on the separation of soul and body has "shown a culpable indifference towards the problem of matter, of bodily life, and therefore of contemporary economics". As man "fell victim first to economic and then to the related pseudo-scientific materialism" the Church "could do little more than complain and scold".[19]

Here we may say Barth identifies the crucial failure of Western theology. Theology will have nothing more to say in the future:

> But will always have a bad conscience in the face of both materialisms and therefore of the so-called "Marxist view of the world", so long as it does not undertake an energetic revision of its anthropology at this point in the light of its eschatology . . .[20]

We must follow Barth here. Certainly, as we have discovered, we can find within Christian history a tradition that is at least implicitly faithful to the biblical understanding of man, but Barth is surely correct to censure the Church for its over-all failure to safeguard the biblical anthropology. To follow is to accept that there is no way forward save through Marxism. Only where the Western churches have taken Marxism seriously have they truly been able to start anew in their relationships with Chinese Christians. The attractiveness of Marxism, its appeal to what is best in man, must be recognized before it is possible to question Marxist anthropology. Moreover, Marxism in China cannot be dismissed as no more than another totalitarian aberration. It was espoused by many of the most thoughtful young Chinese in 1918-19, a process that was to continue throughout the next three decades. It provided them with both an ideology and a way forward out of the social and political chaos that followed the demise of the imperial system. However understandable may have been the failure of the missionaries to see the significance of Chinese Marxism, it sealed the fate of the missionary movement in China. David Paton's words must be recalled once again. "Our mandate had been withdrawn . . . the time for missions as we had known them had passed . . . the end of the missionary era was the will of God".[21] Those words were written in 1952, and how truly prophetic they were. The Church we have described in the preceding pages is a Church that has come of age, a Church that is able to turn its back on its colonial past and to bear authentic witness within its own context, but it has only won through to this position in so far as it has faced Marxism as a challenge.

Contemporary Chinese Theological Thought

K.H. Ting has claimed that the theological reorientation that began in the 1950s was a mass movement amongst rank and file Christians, resulting from the fact they they were "situated at the boundary between the Church and the world" and were driven to formulate questions, think them through and attempt to answer them.[22] In its early stages the discussion focused on questions about the world and about human beings. The fundamental Christian insight remains that only God can remove the state of spiritual poverty, and that in Augustine's words, "Lord, you have made us for yourself so that we can find no rest until we find it in you", but the revolution has forced Christians to look again at the understanding of sin. In Chinese tradition "there has been no idea of an inborn perversity in human nature", and Christians now find it impossible to ignore "the latent image of God in man and the indwelling of the Holy Spirit in the world". Thus many Christians from a "social gospel" background found, as if for the first time, the Christ of St John's gospel and Ephesians and Colossians, and claimed him as their own. He is "the pre-existent Logos, the crown or the fulfilment of all creation, the revealer in all its fullness of its nature and meaning." It is a "divine yes to creation". Ting suggests that Justin Martyr's *Logos spermatikos*, the presence of seeds of the Logos in all human beings, has been warmly received by Chinese Christians, as has Thomas Aquinas' view of grace perfecting and not supplanting nature. Chen Zemin in 1957 had written in a similar vein:

It was not humanity's utter depravity that caused God to seek us, but that humanity is the crown of creation, created in the image of God to help God oversee this world. It is only because of this that we are worthy of God's redemption.[23]

How close to the generous and world-affirming spirit of Irenaeus is all this! In an appreciation of the theology of Teilhard de Chardin Ting has pointed to the importance of Teilhard's linking of the process of creation to that of salvation and sanctification, and he attacks the dispensational interpretation that divides history into three periods, that of the Father, that of the Son and that of the Spirit. Probably Ting has the teaching of Watchman Nee very much in mind, and his reply is on the basis of a re-assertion of the central tenets of Trinitarian belief. He is critical of the so-called social gospel, with its inadequate Christology, and affirms the centrality of the Cosmic Christ for faith. Ting is attracted by Teilhard because Teilhard's view is able to see "all truth, goodness and beauty and affirms that this is of Christ, is of God".[24]

This positive affirmation of the worth of creation leads to a deep appreciation of the world of culture and history. Shen Yifan has said that "the incarnation affirms all just, honest and self-sacrificing efforts in human life and opens up the way for their acceptance by God".[25] Ting can go so far as to say that, "there is not only the historic but also the ultimate importance and value of what one does with nature and in the world, and what one makes of oneself".[26] The denial of culture and the separation of humanity into the "saved" and the "reprobate", so characteristic of the message of the majority of missionaries, is here replaced by an insight drawing upon the heart of Chinese tradition – a profound concern with the human world and with the conduct of human life. In the history of Chinese theological reflection one can find examples of people who have allowed their theology to be overwhelmed by this ethical concern – either expressed in the 1920s through Confucian categories or in the 1950s through Marxist ones. Christian "ultra-leftism" has been the most damaging result of this tendency, and in their evaluation of liberation theology contemporary Chinese theologians show how much they are aware of this danger. Bishop Ting, in welcoming the insights of liberation theology, warns that while liberation is extremely important "it does not engage, let alone solve, the question of reconciliation with God".[27] Ting clearly believes that socialism is an attempt to embody love in human society even though it has not been very effectively implemented so far. Where this belief differs from the "leftist" identification of socialism with the Kingdom is in its affirmation of the supremacy of God's grace – human effort, however important, depends upon the work of Christ who alone "can correct and complete the relationship between God and the rest of revealed existence and bring it to its pinnacle".[28]

Bishop Ting has been accused of selling out the Gospel. There has been a public and a private campaign to discredit him, and it seems appropriate therefore to stress at this point that K.H. Ting is making one of the most important contributions to the reformulation of Chinese theology in the present period, and that he is doing so within the parameters of what we may term the "catholic" tradition. Out of the Chinese experience, and bringing an awareness of Chinese culture and tradition, as well as a deep appreciation of what is positive within Marxism, Ting and other thoughtful Chinese Christians are articulating insights that move beyond the former horizons of Chinese theology, either Protestant or Catholic, liberal or conservative. Theirs is no partisan approach, rather they are able and willing to draw on the insights of Protestant, Catholic and Orthodox theologies as they seek to express a new theological understanding appropriate for China. It might indeed be more appropriate to say that this new Chinese theology has uncovered the partial nature of Protestant theology and its inadequacy in the face of the questions posed by Chinese culture. But equally, it affirms the freedom of the Christian person that was so central to the Reformation protest against the medieval Church, and in this has a powerful word to speak to society. The concerns of the democracy movement are implicit within the "patriotic" stance of this theology. So it is that both liberal and conservative Protestant theologies are transcended and replaced by a theology that, while only partially articulated as yet, is full of potential for the creative engagement of Christian faith with Chinese culture.

Balthasar says of the great Russian philosopher and theologian, Soloviev, that his thought takes as its starting point the work of Maximus the Confessor, who makes the Chalcedonian dogma of the synthesis between God and man in Christ the foundation upon which the entire structure of the natural and supernatural reality is erected, and adds to this static world picture the dynamic element of German idealism – the evolution of nature towards man, of history towards Christ, and of the Church towards the Kingdom of God in its completeness. In this way he transcends the limitations of the form of medieval and Eastern Christian thought without succumbing to the dangers of the Hegelian, and ultimately Protestant, dialectic, which "relentlessly transcends all things to finds its term in the absolute Spirit". "The Kingdom of God does not break in 'unilaterally' from above and from outside; it must necessarily grow to maturity just as much from within."[29] Chinese theology, in stressing the person of Christ and a Logos theology, is also faithful to Chalcedon, and by adopting a dynamic view of the process of sanctification it rejects dialectical theology in favour of an integrationist approach.

This development in Chinese theological thinking has been one result of the encounter with Marxism. It would be wrong to suggest that the thinking of all, or even the majority, of Chinese Protestants has shifted in this way. Old perspectives persist and even threaten the new forms. The struggle between a Gospel open to the future and that which seeks to preserve the narrow perspectives of the past is by no means over in China, just as in the West. Insensitive handling by government or church officials could result in the perpetuation of the old forms. The emphasis on "mutual respect" and "seeking the common ground while reserving differences" is essential to the evolution of Christian attitudes in China.

Marxism, at least in the form in which it has found expression in China for the greater part of our period, must itself face the challenge presented by the newly emerging understanding of a non-reductionist science. Reductionist, monistic materialism is no longer scientifically admissible, at least if the insights of modern theoretical physics are to be taken seriously. The old Cartesian-Newtonian mechanistic paradigm is being replaced by a holistic and dynamic conception of the universe where matter can only be described in terms of dynamic balance. As Fritjof Capra has said:

> Relativity theory has made the cosmic web come alive, so to speak, by revealing its intrinsically dynamic character; by showing that its activity is the very essence of its being. In modern physics, the image of the universe has been transcended by a view of it as one indivisible, dynamic whole whose parts are essentially interrelated and can be understood only as patterns of a cosmic process.[30]

There is, he says, "no absolute truth in science".[31] In his book *The Tao of Physics*,[32] Capra has himself pointed to some of the analogies of this "post modern" view of science with Eastern thought, and notably with Buddhist and Taoist views on the unity and dynamism of the natural world. The "intuitive" mode of Chinese thinking, which Li Zehou has drawn recent attention to in his discussion of Chan Buddhism and Zhuang Zi, is indeed a corrective to the Western stress on analysis and reason, and fits better with the perspectives of sub-atomic physics. Thus Marxism, as well as Western Christianity, needs to reformulate its understanding of matter. The historical materialism of classical Marxism, with its acceptance of the primacy of economics over the superstructure, based as Barth has rightly argued on an acceptance of the "soulless" man of pseudo-scientific materialism, must be overcome and replaced by a non-reductionist view of reality. Here, Chinese Marxism needs to enter into dialogue with its own cultural tradition in a way that so far it has revealed little interest in or has denounced as heretical. Li Zehou's article may be unrepresentative but it is, nevertheless, a significant indication that such a dialogue is not now impossible. If such a discussion develops then Christian thinkers will themselves have much to contribute in so far as their own thinking is being modified in the light of Chinese tradition and the contemporary realities.

Here one must draw attention to the need for an extension of ecumenism in China to cover relationships between Catholics and Protestants, which up to now have been limited to discussions about issues of mutual concern within the context of State United Front policy. A major obstacle to this is that Catholic theology has revealed little of the development apparent in Protestant circles. It appears not to have moved beyond the neo-Scholastic forms of Tridentine thought, with its tendency to claim exclusive possession of truth. The Catholic Church in China has yet to free itself from the monarchical understanding of authority, despite the fact that this is a central issue dividing the CCPA and the Vatican. The strength of the Catholic tradition may be seen in its ability to hold disparate forces together, in comparison with the Protestant tendency towards ever greater fragmentation. The two traditions in China have much to teach each other. There is considerable evidence that former overt hostility between Catholics and Protestants has disappeared, and there are reports of friendly contact and even co-operation over practical matters. Thus in Beihai City in Guangxi local Catholics helped the Protestants to obtain land and to build a church.[33] It will no doubt be many years before matters of belief are discussed together. Yet, remembering that not so long ago in the West it was unheard of for Roman Catholics to pray in public with non-Catholics, the situation could well change sooner than appears possible at present.

There remains, then, an immense task of moving further along the Three Self road. There is no longer any question that the Church in China is indigenous. The need now is to tackle the outstanding issue of "inculturation". The seed has been sown but it could take a century or more to come to maturity. In terms of Chinese history this will be as nothing. Part of this process may well be the development of an appropriate discussion over theological concepts in relation to other aspects

of Chinese thought – Marxist, Buddhist, Taoist and Confucian –
but to be a genuine encounter it must engage at other levels of
experience. Thus while Bishop Ting has shown himself aware
of the importance of the teaching of the *Dao De Jing*, in his
discussion of Teilhard de Chardin he draws attention to
another dimension of experience. He refers to Teilhard's visit
to the Jade Buddha Temple in Shanghai, quoting him as
saying, "I love the Buddha of Jade because it tells me of something that Christianity must annex. I feel more and more
strongly the need to free our religion from everything that is
specifically Mediterranean." Ting's comment is interesting:

> What I understand here is that the Jade Buddha is a thing
> of beauty which has accumulated within it the sweat and
> blood of countless people seeking after goodness and
> truth, and nothing of beauty is outside Christ. Therefore,
> Christianity ought to annex it.[34]

For "annex" one perhaps ought to read "find a place for it", for
neither comment is probably intended to imply an annexation
of Buddhism by Christianity.

So we return once more to the Chinese experience of the
spiritual within art and nature, to the "analogy of beauty" and
the intuitive vision of the depth of material reality which lies
always open to the flow of the creative spirit. At the heart of
Chinese painting at its best there has always been a profound awareness of the flow of the life-force *qi* through the
strokes of the brush. As Gong Yanshi explains:

> . . . to draw trees or rocks the solid stroke is used; to
> draw clouds and mists the vacant stroke is used. Through
> that which is vacant the solid is moved and that which is
> solid becomes vacant. Thus the entire picture will be full
> of the life-rhythm.[35]

Surely, it is within the splendour of forms that the beauty of
the divine shines forth? Is that not a gift from the East to the
West, and is it not in the unity of prayer and life, of contemplation and action, that we are faithful to the One who

transcends all our knowing, all our human theologies and philosophies?

> There is in God (some say)
> A deep, but dazzling darkness; As men here
> Say it is late and dusky, because they
> See not all clear
> O for that night! where I in him
> Might live invisible and dim.

Henry Vaughan: "The Night"

There can, of course, be no simplistic synthesis within an authentic encounter between cultures. The Christian believes in a transcendent God to whom the most fitting attribute is "Love". To traditional Chinese thought, the *Dao* is impersonal. And yet, do not both traditions express something of supreme importance? As we await with anticipation the next stage in the unfinished encounter it is fitting to allow the last word to come from China:

> The splendour of Spring slowly, slowly departs – but whither?
> Once more I face the flowers, and raise my cup.
> All day I ask of the flowers, but the flowers make no reply:
> For whom do you fade and fall?
> For whom do you blossom?

Yan Yun (Ninth century)[36]

REFERENCES

1. Wickeri, Philip L., "Theological Reorientation in Chinese Protestantism 1949-84, Part I", p. 41, *Ching Feng*, Vol. 28, No. 1, March 1985.
2. Ecclestone, Alan, *The Night Sky of the Lord*, Darton, Longman and Todd, London 1980, p. 9.
3. Leech, Kenneth, *Spirituality and Pastoral Care*, Sheldon Press, London 1986, p. 35.
4. Robinson, John. A.T., *Truth Is Two-Eyed*, SCM Press, London 1979, p. 131.
5. Lao Tzu, *Tao Te Ching*, translated with Introduction by D.C. Lau, Penguin Classics, 1963.
6. Balthasar, Hans Urs von, *The Glory of the Lord: A Theological Aesthetics II: Studies in Theological Style: Clerical Styles*, T. & T. Clark, Edinburgh 1984, p. 148.
7. ibid., p. 205.

8. *The Cloud of Unknowing*, ed., Phyllis Hodgson, Early English Text Society, Oxford 1944, p. 26 (my translation). For a modern translation see Walters, Clifton, Penguin Classics, 1961.
9. Julian of Norwich, *Showings*, translated with Introduction, Colledge, Edmund, O.S.A., and Walsh, James, S.J., The Classics of Western Spirituality, Paulist Press, New York 1978.
10. Küng, Hans, *Christianity and the World Religions: Paths of Dialogue with Islam, Hinduism and Buddhism*, Collins and Fount Paperbacks, London 1987.
11. ibid., pp. 395-6.
12. ibid., p. 396.
13. Balthasar, op. cit., p. 64.
14. ibid., p. 184.
15. Baggley, John, *Doors of Perception – icons and their spiritual significance*, Mowbray, London and Oxford 1987, p. 81.
16. Julian of Norwich, op. cit., p. 186.
17. Barth, Karl, *Church Dogmatics, Vol. III, The Doctrine of Creation, Part 2*, T. & T. Clark, Edinburgh 1960, p. 382.
18. ibid., p. 387.
19. ibid., p. 390.
20. ibid.
21. Paton, David M., *Christian Missions and the Judgement of God*, SCM Press, London 1953, p. 51.
22. Ting, K.H., "Theological Mass Movements in China", *Chinese Theological Review* 1985, p. 68.
23. Chen Zemin, "The Task of Theological Construction in the Chinese Church (II)", *Nanjing Theological Review*, No. 7, August 1957, p. 6, quoted in Wickeri, op. cit., p. 60.
24. Ting, K.H., "Inspirations from Liberation Theology, Process Theology and Teilhard de Chardin", *Chinese Theological Review* 1986, p. 60.
25. Shen Yifan, "Chinese Christianity in Theological Reflections", *Chinese Theological Review* 1985, p. 64.
26. Ting, K.H., "Theological Mass Movements", op. cit., p. 74.
27. Ting, K.H., "Inspirations", op. cit., p. 52.
28. ibid., p. 66.
29. Balthasar, Hans Urs von, *The Glory of the Lord: A Theological Aesthetics III, Studies in Theological Styles: Lay Styles*, p. 284.
30. Capra, Fritjof, *The Turning Point: Science, Society and the Rising Culture*, Wildwood House, London 1982, p. 83.
31. op. cit., p. 42.
32. Capra, Fritjof, *The Tao of Physics*, Fontana, London 1976.
33. *Bridge*, No. 9, January 1985.
34. Ting, K.H., "Inspirations", op. cit., p. 60.
35. Quoted in Chang Chung-yuan, *Creativity and Taoism: A Study in Chinese Philosophy, Art and Poetry*, Wildwood House, London 1975.
36. Yan Yun, "The Fall of the Flowers", translated Kotewall, Robert, and Smith, Norman L., *The Penguin Book of Chinese Verse*, ed., Davis, A.R., London 1962, p. 26.

Appendices

APPENDIX ONE

Time Line

Period	Dynasties	Chinese Context	Outside China
1500 B.C.	PREHISTORIC	Painted Pottery Black Pottery cultures	Stonehenge
1300	SHANG	Bronzes, Silkworms Ancestor Worship	c1230 The Exodus
1027	WESTERN ZHOU	Writing	King David
770	EASTERN ZHOU Spring & Autumn Period	Book of Odes	Rome Founded
551		Confucius Lao Zi (?)	560 Buddha
475	Warring States	Iron Age Irrigation works Mo Zi	500 Zoroaster Parthenon built
372		Mencius Book of Rites 300 Dao De Jing ?240	Plato, Aristotle First Punic War
221-210	QIN Emperor Qinshihuangdi	Building Great Wall Standardization, script coinage, cart axles weights and measures	Bible into Greek

A.D. 206-9	WESTERN HAN	Triumph of Confucianism	
		Silk Road (100)	Julius Ceasar
		Rivival of Literature	
A.D. 9-23	XIN		27 B.C.-A.D. 14 Augustus Emperor
		(A.D. 2) Est. pop. 60 million	?4 B.C. Birth of Jesus Christ
23-220	EASTERN HAN	58 Buddhism introduced	c130-c200 Irenaeus
		Invention of paper	
		165 Translation Buddhist sutras into Chinese	
		33-156 Taoism develops into organized religion	c150-c215 Clement of Alexandria
220-589	SIX DYNASTIES Three Kingdoms	Feudal warfare colonization S. China compass invented	
			285 Partition Roman Empire
		Growth of Buddhism	312 Conversion of Constantine
		334-416 Hui-yuan founds Pure Land School of Buddhism	325 Council of Nicea
			339 persecution of Persian Christians
			354-430 Augustine
			410 Sack of Rome Council of Seleucia
			431 Council of
500		Golden Age of Buddhism Chan Buddhism develops	Ephesus
			527-65 Justinian Emperor of Byzantium
			563 Columba founds Iona
581-618	SUI	Rebuilding Great Wall Grand Canal Built	597 Augustine of Canterbury lands in Kent

618-907	TANG		
618-26	Gao Zu		
626-49	Tai Zong	630 Confuciansim regains central position	632 Death of Muhammad
		635 Aloben arrives from Persia	
649-83	Gao Zong		
683-705	Empress Wu	Age of Poetry	642 Fall of Persia to
		701-62 Li Bo	Muslims
712-56	Xuan Zong	712-70 Du Fu	735-804 Alcuin
		755 An Lushan Rebellion	
		772-846 Bo Juyi	771 Charlemagne
		781 Nestorian Tablet	
840-6	Wu Zong	845 dissolution Buddhist monasteries & end Nestorians	
		(742) Est. population: 52 million	865 Vikings invade England

907-60	FIVE DYNASTIES	Foot binding Printing of Buddhist & Confucian Classics begins	

960-1275	SONG		
960-76	Tai Zu		
976-97	Tai Zong	Ocean-going junks	1033 St Anselm
1022-64	Ren Zong	1045 first movable type	1066 Battle of
1067-85	Shen Zong	Great Age of Painting	Hastings
1100-25	Hui Zong	Development mathematics and botany	
	Southern	1130-1200 Zhu Xi	
	Song	Neo-Confucianism	
1212	Mongol invasion		1210 Francis of Assisi
			1215 Magna Carta
			Dominicans founded
1215	Beijing captured		
		1260 Khubilai Khan Great Khan (early 13th c.) Est. pop. 130 million	

1279-1368 YUAN		Second Nestorian period	
1271-94	Khubilai Khan	1275-92 Marco Polo in China	
1294-1307 Timur		1294 Arrival of John of Montecorvino in Beijing	1295 Model Parliament
		1307 John Archbishop of Beijing	1314 Bannockburn
1368-1644 MING		Est. pop. 70 million	
			1340-1400 Chaucer
1368-98	Hongwu Emperor	Restoration of civil service	1381 Peasants Revolt
1403-24	Yongle Emperor		
1420		Beijing reconstruction as national capital	1415 Agincourt
1405-33		Zheng He's maritime expeditions	
1465-87	Chenghua Emperor		
1472-1529		Wang Yangming	1455-85 Wars of Roses
			1492 Columbus first voyage
1506-21	Zhengde Emperor		1517 Martin Luther
1514		Portuguese in China	
1522-67	Jiajing Emperor		1534 Jesuits Founded
1557		Portuguese settlement in Macao	1545-63 Council of Trent
		General prosperity	1549 First Prayer Book
			1558-1603 Elizabeth I
1573-1620 Wanli Emperor			
1573-82		Grand Secretary Zhang Juzheng	
1582		Beginning of Ming decline	
1583		Matteo Ricci enters China	
1604		Donglin Academy Restored	
1610		Death of Ricci	
1620-27	Tianqi Emperor	Eunuch Wei Zhongxian dominates court	1620 Mayflower arrives at Cape Cod

toward end Ming

in China

1628-44	Chongzhen Emperor		
1644		Li Zicheng Rebellion Foundation of Qing (1664) Est. pop. 108 million	1642 English Civil War 1644 Battle of Marston Moor

---

1644-1912 QING

1644-61	Shunzhi Emperor		
1659		Yang Guangxian Memorial	
1661-1722 Kangxi Emperor			
1666		Death of Adam Schall	1666 Great Fire of London
1669		Verbiest Chief Astronomer	
1692		→ Edict of Toleration	
1710		→ Rites Controversy	
1721		→ Edict bans Christianity	
1722-36	Yongzheng Emperor		
1736-96	Qianlong Emperor		1783 End American War of Independence 1789 French Revolution
1796-1820 Jiaqing Emperor			
1796-1805		White Lotus Rebellion	1805 Battle of Trafalgar
1807		Morrison arrives in China	
1821-50	Daoguang Emperor		
1839-42		→ First Opium War	1848 Year of Revolutions in Europe
1851-62		→ Taiping Rebellion	
1854		Hudson Taylor arrives (1851) Est. pop. 430 million	

1856-60		Arrow War	1854-56 Crimean War
1862-74	Tongzhi Emperor	Tongzhi Restoration Self-Strengthening Movement	
1870		Tianjin Massacre	1869-70 First Vatican Council
1875-1908 Guangxu Emperor			
1894-95		Sino-Japanese War	

1898		Reform Movement	
1900		Boxer Uprising	
1908-12	Xuantong Emperor (Puyi)		
1911		Wuchang Uprising	

1912-49	Republic of China		
1912-13		Sun Yat-sen President	
1913-16		Yuan Shikai President	1914-18 First World War
1919		May Fourth Movement	
		"21 Demands"	1917 Russian Revolution
1921		Foundation Chinese Communist Party	1922 Mussolini Italian Prime Minister
1924	Sun Yat-sen establishes Guomindang Government		1926 General Strike
1927		Northern Expedition	
1927-49	Chiang Kai-shek head of Guomingdang		
1931		Japanese occupy Manchuria	
1934		Long March	1933 Hitler German Chancellor
1937		Japanese Invasion	1936-39 Spanish Civil War
1946-49		Civil War	1939-45 Second World War
		(1953) Est. pop. 573 million	
			1948 First Assembly WCC

1949-	People's Republic of China		1950-53 Korean War
			1956 Hungarian Uprising
1957		Hundred Flowers	
1958		Great Leap Forward	
1960		Russians withdraw aid	1960 Kennedy US President
1966-76		Cultural Revolution	

		1963 Kennedy Assassinated
		1965 US troops in Vietnam
1971	Death of Lin Biao	1968 Prague Spring
1975	Death of Zhou Enlai	1974 Watergate
1976	Death of Mao Zedong	Scandal
1978	Return of Deng Xiaoping	1978 USA and China
	CCP Third Plenum	establish relations
	Democracy Movement	
1979	Churches reopen	1979 Thatcher British P.M.

1980	Hua Guofeng Resigns	
	Hu Yaobang & Zhao Ziyang appointed	1981 Reagan US President
1982	New Constitution	
	1982: Pop. 1000 million	
1983	Spiritual Pollution Campaign	
1984	Hong Kong Agreement	
1987	Hu Yaobang Dismissed	
	Autumn 1987: Thirteenth CCP Congress Zhao Ziyong appointed CCP General Secretary	

Major Meetings of the Chinese Communist Party (CCP) and National People's Congress (NPC)

1947-1986

CCP MEETINGS

Seventh Congress	23 April – 11 June 1945

(Seven Plenums)

Eighth Congress	15-27 September 1956
Second Session Eighth Congress	5-23 May 1958

(Twelve Plenums)

Ninth Congress	1-24 August 1969

(Two Plenums)

Tenth Congress	24-28 August 1973

(Three Plenums)

Eleventh Congress	12-18 August 1977
Third Plenum	December 1978

(Seven Plenums)

Twelfth Congress	1-11 September 1982

(Six Plenums up to September 1986)

MEETINGS OF THE NATIONAL PEOPLE'S CONGRESS AND NATIONAL CPPCC

First Chinese People's Political Consultative Conference	21-30 September 1949

First NPC (and Second CPPCC)   15-28 September 1954

(Five Sessions)

Second NPC (and Third CPPCC)   17-28 April
                                                                      1959

(Four Sessions)

Third NPC (and Fourth CPPCC)   21 December
                                             1964 to 4 January 1965
Fourth NPC   13-17 January 1975
Fifth NPC (and Fifth CPPCC)   26 February to 1
                                                       March 1978

(Five Sessions)

Sixth NPC (and Sixth CPPCC)   6-21 June 1983

(Four Sessions to April 1986)

Note: The CPPCC meetings usually preceded the meetings of the NPC.

APPENDIX THREE

Important National Christian Meetings
1950-1986

PROTESTANT MEETINGS

Conversations with Zhou Enlai	2-13 May 1950
Conference on Finances from U.S.A.	16-21 April 1951
First Plenum Preparatory Committee Three Self Reform Movement	25 April 1951
First National Christian Conference	22 July-6 August 1954
Second National Christian Conference	12 November 1960-14 January 1961
Enlarged Meeting Standing Committee TSPM	25 February-1 March 1980
Third National Christian Conference	6-13 October 1980
Second (Enlarged) Plenum Third TSPM Committee and First China Christian Council	19-24 September 1982
Fourth National Christian Conference	16-23 August 1986

CATHOLIC MEETINGS

Meeting with Zhou Enlai	17 January 1951
Preparatory Committee Catholic Patriotic Assocation	19-26 July 1956
Second Preparatory Committee	12-16 February 1957
First National Catholic Conference	17 June-2 August 1957
Second National Catholic Conference	5-19 January 1962
Third National Catholic Conference and First All China Representative Meeting	22-30 May 1980
Enlarged National Delegates Conference	early 1983
Fourth National Catholic Conference	18-29 November 1986

APPENDIX FOUR

Protestant Leaders in 1986

THREE SELF PATRIOTIC MOVEMENT

Chairperson:
Ding Guangzun (K.H. Ting), Bishop, Principal, Nanjing Theological Seminary.

Vice-Chairpersons:
Deng Yuzhi (Cora), General Secretary, National YWCA.
Li Shoubao, General Secretary, National YMCA.
Luo Guanzong, Chairperson, Shanghai TSPM
Qi Qingcai, Senior Pastor of Huai En Church, Shanghai
Ren Zhongxiang, Shanghai
Shen Derong, Vice-President, Shanghai Christian Council
Wang Shenyin (Stephen), Bishop, Chairperson, Shandong TSPM
Xiong Zhenpei, Chairperson, Guangdong TSPM
Zhao Fusan, Deputy Director, National Academy of Social Sciences

Advisers: Liu Liangmo, Tang Shoulin and Sun Pengxi

Secretary General: Shen Derong

Associate Secretary General: Shen Cheng'en (Editor *Tian Feng*)

CHINA CHRISTIAN COUNCIL

President:
Ding Guangxun (K.H. Ting)

Vice-Presidents:
Cai Wenhao (Peter), Pastor, President, Zhejiang Christian Council
Han Wenzao, Chairperson, Jiangsu TSPM

Jiang Peifen (Ms), Old Testament teacher, Nanjing Seminary, President Jiangsu Christian Council

Shen Yifan, Senior Pastor, Shanghai Community Church

Shi Ruzhang (Phoebe), Associate General Secretary, National YWCA

Wu Gaozi (George), former General Secretary, National Christian Council

Yan Jiale, former Little Flock leader, Beijing

Zheng Jianye, Bishop, General Secretary, China Christian Council

Zeng Youshan (Francis), Bishop, Chairperson, Henan TSPM

Advisers: Liu Liangmo, Tang Shoulin and Sun Pengxi

General Secretary: Zheng Jianye

Associate General Secretary: Cao Shengjie (Ms)

APPENDIX FIVE

Chinese Catholic Bishops

Diocese	Name	Year consecrated
Beijing Diocese:	Fu Tieshan	1979
Shanghai Diocese:	Gong Pinmei	1949
	Zhang Jiashu	1960
	Jin Luxian	1985
	Li Side	1985
Anhui Province:		
Bengbu Diocese	Zhu Huayu	1986
Fujian Province:		
Fuzhou Diocese	Lin Quan	
Xiamen Diocese	Huang Ziyu	1986
Mindong Diocese	Zhang Shizhi	1986
Gansu Province:		
Tianshui Diocese	Zhao Jingnong	1981
Guangdong Province:		
Guangzhou Diocese	Ye Yinyun	
Jiangmen Diocese	Li Panshi	1981
Shantou Diocese	Cai Tiyuan	1981
Hebei Province:		
Hengshui Diocese	Fan Wenxing	1981
Tangshan Diocese	Liu Jinghe	1981
Xianxian Diocese	Liu Dinghan	1982
Heilongjiang Province:		
Harbin Diocese	Wang Ruihuan	1959
Henan Province:		
Kaifeng Diocese	He Chunming	1962
Hubei Province:		
Wuhan Diocese	Dong Guangqing	1958

Hunan Province:
    Changsha Diocese   Li Shuren
    Changde Diocese   Yang Gaojian   1958

Province / Diocese	Bishop	Year
Hunan Province:		
Changsha Diocese	Li Shuren	
Changde Diocese	Yang Gaojian	1958
Inner Mongolia:		
Hohhot Diocese	Wang Xueming	1952
Jiangsu Province:		
Nanjing Diocese	Qian Huimin	1981
Suzhou Diocese	Ma Longlin	1981
Xuzhou Diocese	Qian Yurong	
Jiangxi Province:		
Nanchang Diocese	Chen Duqing	
Jilin Province:		
Jilin Diocese	Li Xuesong	1986
Liaoning Province:		
Shenyang Diocese	Zhao Youmin	1984
Shaanxi Province:		
Xi'an Diocese	Ji Huairang	1981
Dali Diocese	Zhang Wenbing	1981
Hanzhong Diocese	Yu Renshen	1986
Shandong Province:		
Jinan Diocese	Zong Huaide	1962
Shanxi Province:		
Taiyuan Diocese	Zhang Xin	1981
Sichuan Province:		
Chengdu Diocese	Li Xiting	1958
Leshan Diocese	Deng Jizhou	
Chongqing Diocese	Liu Zongyu	1981
Wanxian Diocese	Duan Yinming	1949
Yibin Diocese	Chen Shizhong	1985
Yunnan Province:		
Kunming Diocese	Kong Linzhong	1958
Zhejiang Province:		
Hangzhou Diocese	Wu Guohuan	
National Seminary:	Tu Shihua	1962

Total Number of Bishops: 41

Theological Seminaries in China
Protestant Seminaries

National Seminary

Nanjing (Jinling) Union Theological Seminary, 13, Da Jian Yin Xiang, Nanjing, Jiangsu.

Provincial and Regional Seminaries

Anhui Seminary, 68, Suzhou Lu, Hefei.
Fujian Seminary, 71-1, Chuang Xiazhou, Taijiang Qu, Cangxiazhou, Fuzhou.
Guangdong Seminary, Dongshan Church, 9, Shi Bei Tong Jin Lu, Dongshan, Guangzhou.
Huadong Seminary, 316, Xi Zang Zhong Lu, Shanghai.
Shenyang Seminary, 5 Er Li, San Duan, Yijing Jie, Shenhe, Shenyang, Liaoning.
Sichuan Seminary, Shang Xiang Jie, Chengdu.
Yanjing Seminary, 21, Beida Jie, Dongdan, Beijing.
Zhejiang Seminary, 104 Jiefang Lu, Hangzhou.
Zhongnan Seminary, 185, Minzhu Lu, Wuchang, Wuhan, Hubei.

Catholic Seminaries

National Seminary

China Catholic Institute of Philosophy and Theology, 14, Liu Yin Jie, Xicheng District, Beijing.

Major Seminaries

Beijing Major Seminary, Xibeiwang Village, Dongbeiwang, Beijing.

Hohhot Major Seminary, Hohhot, Inner Mongolia.
Shanghai Major Seminary, Sheshan, Songjiang District, Shanghai.
Shenyang Major Seminary, 2, Hua Guang Lane, 1st Section, Xiao
  Nan Jie, Shenyang, Liaoning.
Sichuan Major Seminary, 29, Ping Qiao Jie, Chengdu.
Wuchang Major Seminary, Hua Yuan Shan, Wuhan City, Hubei.
Xi'an Major Seminary, Tang Fang Jie, Xi'an City, Shaanxi.

Minor Seminaries

Jinan Minor Seminary, Jiang Jun Miao Jie, Jinan City, Shandong.
Shijiazhuang Minor Seminary, Shijiazhuang City, Hebei.
Taiyuan Minor Seminary, Ge Liao Kou, Taiyuan City, Shanxi.
Xi'an Minor Seminary, Xi'an, Shaanxi.
Guangzhou Minor Seminary: due to open 1986/7.

Number of Protestant Christians*

How many Protestants are there in China? This is a question often asked by Christians overseas. The China Christian Council recently released the following statistics:

1. Churches   **4,044**
    (1,067 newly built)
2. Family meeting
    points: **16,868**
3. Christians
    (Protestants):   **3,386,611**
4. Baptisms in 1986:   **151,062**
5. Church workers: **4,575**
    (including those in
    family meeting points)
6. New church workers
    in 1986:
    Ministers ordained: **69**
       (including 8 women)
    Elders ordained: **172**
    Evangelists appointed: **376**
7. Lay church workers: **26,336**
8. Theological students
    in training: **594**
9. Lay workers training
    programmes in 1986:   **401**
    Participants in these
    programmes: **14,891**
10. Church workers and
    Christians known to
    have been awarded in
    their work units in
    1986:   **7,713**

* Quoted in *Bridge* No. 25, September-October 1987

These statistics were compiled by Christian Councils and Three-Self organizations at various levels. Some clarification, however, may be in order.

As far as the number of churches and meeting points is concerned, some churches are simply counted as meeting points in certain places. Furthermore, many home worship gatherings, when they are small and unorganized, may not be counted. Thus the number of churches and family meeting points may be under-estimated.

The figure of over three million Protestants is a good estimate, although again it may be conservative. Our reasons for saying this are: (1) Church authorities in China are understaffed, and it is difficult for them to cover all areas for a complete survey, especially rural and mountainous areas. (2) Some Christians, although this number is dwindling, do not register as such, out of a lingering fear, and some give only one or two names per family, even if all members of the family may be believers. (3) Many claim to believe in Jesus, some saying that their families have been believers for several generations, but lack of facilities for proper catechetical classes and baptism makes them ineligible for church membership. (4) Some officials in the Religious Affairs Bureau, especially at the local level.

Bibliography

SELECT BIBLIOGRAPHY

Adeney, David H., *China: The Church's Long March*, Regal Books,
  Venura, California and OMF, Singapore, 1985.
Allen, Roland, *The Spontaneous Expansion of the Church*, World
  Dominion Press, 1927.
Attwater, Rachel, *Adam Schall: A Jesuit at the Court of China, 1592-1666*,
  Geoffrey Chapman, London 1963.

Baggley, John, *Doors of Perception – icons and their spiritual significance*,
  Mowbray, London and Oxford 1987.
Balthasar, Han Urs von, *The Glory of the Lord: A Theological Aesthetics, I:
  Seeing the Form*, T. & T. Clark, Edinburgh 1982.
  *The Glory of the Lord, A Theological Aesthetics: II, Studies in Theological
    Style: Clerical Styles*, ibid., 1984.
  A Theological Aesthetics III, Studies in Theological Styles: Lay Styles,
    ibid., 1986.
Barnett, Suzanne Wilson, and Fairbank, John K., ed., *Christianity in
  China, Early Protestant Missionary Writings*, Harvard University
  Press, 1985.
Barth, Karl, *Church Dogmatics, Vol. III, The Doctrine of Creation, Part 2*,
  T. & T. Clark, Edinburgh 1960.
Bates, M. Searle, *Gleanings from the Manuscripts: The Protestant
  Endeavour in Chinese Society 1890-1950*, National Council of
  Churches of Christ, U.S.A., 1984.
Baum, Richard, *Prelude to Revolution, Mao, the Party, and the Peasant
  Question, 1962-66*, Columbia, New York 1975.
Bianco, Lucien, *Origins of the Chinese Revolution 1915-1949*, Stanford
  University Press, California and Oxford University Press,
  London 1971.
Blunden, Caroline, and Elvin, Mark, *Cultural Atlas of China*, Phaidon
  Press, Oxford 1983.
Bohr, Paul Richard, *Famine in China and the Missionary: Timothy Richard
  as Relief Administrator and Advocate of National Reform, 1876-84*,
  Harvard East Asian Monographs No. 48, Harvard, 1972.

Unfinished Encounter

Bonavia, David, *The Chinese: A Portrait*, Allen Lane, Penguin Books, London 1981.

Breslin, Thomas A., *China, American Catholicism and the Missionary*, Pennsylvania State University Press, 1980.

Broomhall, A.J., *Hudson Taylor – China's Open Century*, Parts 1-5 so far published, Hodder & Stoughton and Overseas Missionary Fellowship, 1981-85.

Brown, Thompson G., *Christianity in the People's Republic of China*, Revised Edition, John Knox Press, Atlanta 1986.

Bush, Richard C. Jr., *Religion in Communist China*, Abingdon Press, New York 1970.

Capra, Fritjof, *The Tao of Physics*, Fontana, London 1975.
The Turning Point: Science, Society and the Rising Culture, Wildwood House, London 1982.

Cary-Elwes, Columba, *China and the Cross: Studies in Missionary History*, Longmans, Green and Co., London 1957.

Chan, Wing-tsit, *Religious Trends in Modern China*, Octagon Books, New York 1978.

Chao, Jonathan ed., *The Spirit of God at Work in China*, China Graduate School of Theology, Hong Kong 1975.
A Glimpse of Christian Community Life in a Chinese Village, China Graduate School of Theology, Hong Kong 1974.

Ch'en, Kenneth, *Buddhism in China: A Historical Survey*, Princeton, 1964.

Chen Zemin, "The Task of Theological Construction in the Chinese Church (II)", *Nanjing Theological Review*, August 1957.
"Self-Propagation in the Light of the History of Christian Thought", *Nanjing Theological Review*, June 1985, reproduced in *Chinese Theological Review* 1986.

Chesneaux, Jean; Le Barbier, Françoise; Bergère, Marie-Claire, *China from the 1911 Revolution to Liberation*, The Harvester Press, 1977.

Ching, Julia, *Confucianism and Christianity: A Comparative Study*, Kodansha International, Tokyo, in co-operation with the Institute of Oriental Religions, Sophia University, Tokyo 1977.
Christianity and the New China. Vol. 1: *Theological Implications of the New China*. Vol. 2: *Christian Faith and the Chinese Experience*, Lutheran World Federation and Pro Mundi Vita, Ecclesia Publications, William Carey Library, South Pasadena, California 1976.

Chu, Michael, S.J., ed., *The New China: A Catholic Response*, Paulist Press, New York 1977.

Chu, Sister Theresa and Lind, Christopher, eds., *A New Beginning: An International Dialogue with the Chinese Church*, Canada China Programme, 1983.

The Cloud of Unknowing, Phyllis Hodgson, ed., Early English Text Society, Oxford 1944. For a modern translation see Walters, Clifton, Penguin Classics, 1961.

Cohen, Paul A., *China and Christianity, the Missionary Movement and The Growth of Anti-foreignism 1860-70*, Harvard University Press, 1963.

Cronin, Vincent, *The Wise Man from the West*, Rupert Hart-Davis, London 1956. Re-published Fount Paperbacks, 1986.

Dai, Houying, *Stones in the Wall*, translated by Frances Wood, Michael Joseph, London 1985.

Dawson, Christopher, ed., *The Mongol Mission: Narratives and Letters of the Franciscan Missionaries in Mongolia and China in the 13th and 14th Centuries*, Sheed & Ward, London 1955.

Digan, Parig, *China and the Churches in the Making of One World*, Pro Mundi Vita, Brussels 1975.

Document No. 19, (classified), "The Basic Viewpoint and Policy on the Question of Religion during Our Country's Socialist Period", CCP Central Committee, March 1982. Reproduced in full in Wickeri, *Seeking the Common Ground*, pp. 549-64.

Documents of the Three Self Movement, National Council of Churches, U.S.A., New York 1963.

Dunne, George H., S.J., *Generation of Giants: The First Jesuits in China*, Burns and Oates, London 1962.

Ecclestone, Alan, *The Night Sky of the Lord*, Darton Longman and Todd, London 1980.

Endicott, Stephen, *James G. Endicott, Rebel Out of China*, University of Toronto Press, 1980.

Fairbank, John K., ed., *The Missionary Enterprise in China and America*, Harvard University Press, 1974.

Fitzgerald, C.P., *The Birth of Communist China*, Penguin, London 1964.

Foster, John, *The Church of the Tang Dynasty*, SPCK, London 1939.

Fung, Raymond ed., *Households of God on China's Soil*, WCC, Geneva 1982.

Garrett, Shirley, *Social Reformers in Urban China: The Chinese YMCA*

1895-1926, Harvard University Press, 1970.

Garside, Roger, *Coming Alive: China after Mao*, Andre Deutsch, London 1981.

Gernet, Jacques, *China and the Christian Impact*, Cambridge University Press, 1985.

Glüer, Dr Winfried, *Christliche Theologie in China T.C. Chao 1918-56*, Missionswissenschaftliche Forschungen, V 13, Gutersloher Verlagshaus Gerd Mohn, Gutersloh 1979.
"T.C. Chao and the Quest for Life and Meaning", *China Notes*, Vol. 18, No. 4, NCCC U.S.A., Fall 1980.

Granet, Marcel, *The Religion of the Chinese People*, Basil Blackwell, Oxford 1975.

Guglieminetti, Pierfilippo, S.J., "The Catholic Church in China: One Church, Two Testimonies", Tripod No. 37, 1987.

Guide To the Catholic Church in China, China Catholic Communication, A Queen Street, Singapore 0718, 1985.

Guillemaz, Jacques, *The Chinese Communist Party in Power 1949-76*, Westview Press, Boulder, Colorado 1976.

Hall, R.O., *A Missionary Artist Looks at His Job*, International Missionary Council, New York 1942.

Hayward, V., *Christians and China*, Christian Journals, Belfast 1974.

Hensman, C.R., *China: Yellow Peril? Red Hope?*, SCM Press, London 1968.

Hickley, Dennis, *The First Christians of China: An Outline History and Some Considerations Concerning the Nestorians in China during the Tang Dynasty*, China Study Project, London 1980.

Hockin, Katharine, *Servants of God in People's China*, SCM Press, London 1964.

Hood, George A., *Mission Accomplished? The English Presbyterian Mission in Lingtung, South China*, Verlag Peter Lang, Frankfurt 1986.
"The Planting of a Mission", *CSP Journal* No. 1, April 1986.
"Establishing the Church", *CSP Journal* No. 2, August 1986.
"A Question of Identity", *CSP Journal* No. 3, November 1986.

Hook, Brian, General Ed., *The Cambridge Encyclopedia of China*, Cambridge University Press, 1982.

Hunter, Edward, *The Story of Mary Liu*, Hodder & Stoughton, London 1956.

Jiang Ping, "Study Conscientiously Marxist Theory on Religion and the Party Policy on Religion", *Hong Qi (Red Flag)*, 1 May 1986, *CSP Journal* No. 2, 1986.

Jin Luxian, "The Church in China Past and Present", *Tripod* No. 6, 1986.

Jones, Francis P., *The Church in Communist China: A Protestant Appraisal*, Friendship Press, New York 1962.

Joseph, William A., *The Critique of Ultra-Leftism in China, 1958-81*, Stanford University Press, 1984.

Julian of Norwich, *Showings*, translated with Introduction, Colledge, Edmund, O.S.A., and Walsh, James, S.J., The Classics of Western Spirituality, Paulist Press, New York 1978.

Kinnear, Angus I., *Against the Tide: The Story of Watchman Nee*, Victory Press, Eastbourne 1973.

Küng, Hans, *Christianity and the World Religions: Paths of Dialogue with Islam, Hinduism and Buddhism*, Collins and Fount Paperbacks, London 1987.

Lao Tzu, *Tao Te Ching*, translated with Introduction by D.C. Lau, Penguin Classics, London 1963.

Lancashire, Douglas, translator and ed., *Chinese Essays on Religion and Faith*, Chinese Materials Center, San Francisco 1981.

Latourette, Kenneth Scott, *A History of Christian Missions in China*, SPCK, London 1929.

Lazzarotto, Angelo S., *The Catholic Church in Post-Mao China*, Holy Spirit Study Centre, Hong Kong 1982.

Lee, Hong Yung, *The Politics of the Chinese Cultural Revolution: A Case Study*, University of California Press, 1978.

Lee Shiu Keung, *The Cross and The Lotus*, Christian Study Centre, Hong Kong 1971.

Leech, Kenneth, *Spirituality and Pastoral Care*, Sheldon Press, London 1986.

Li Zehou, "Zhuang Zi and Chan Buddhism", *Social Sciences in China*, No. 1, 1987.

Liu, Kwang-Ching, ed., *American Missionaries in China, Papers from the Harvard Seminars*, Harvard East Asian Monographs, 1966.

Liu Qingfen, "Three Self in Tianjin", *Tian Feng* March 1985, *CSP Bulletin* No. 28, November 1985.

Lochman, Jan Milic, *Church in a Marxist Society: A Czechoslovak View*, SCM Press, London 1970.

Lotz, Denton, ed., *Spring Has Returned . . . Listening to the Church in China*, Baptist World Alliance, McLean, Virgina 1986.

Lutz, Jessie Gregory, *China and the Christian Colleges 1850-1950*, Cornell University Press, 1971.

Lyall, Leslie, *Three of China's Mighty Men*, Overseas Missionary
  Fellowship, 1973.
  New Spring In China, A Christian Appraisal, Hodder &
  Stoughton, London 1979.
  God Reigns In China, Hodder & Stoughton, London 1985.

MacFarquhar, Roderick, *The Origins of the Cultural Revolution, Part I:
  Contradictions Among the People 1956-57*, Oxford University Press,
  1974.
  *The Origins of the Cultural Revolution, Part II: The Great Leap
  Forward, 1958-60*, Oxford, 1983.
MacInnis, Donald E., *Religious Policy and Practice in Communist China:
  A Documentary History*, Hodder & Stoughton, London 1972.
Mao Zedong, *Report on an Investigation of the Peasant Movement in
  Hunan, Selected Works, Volume 1*, Foreign Languages Press, Peking,
  1965.
  *Some Questions on the Methods of Leadership, 1 June 1943, Selected
  Works, Vol. 3*, Peking 1967.
  On the People's Democratic Dictatorship, Selected Works, Volume 4,
  Peking 1969.
  Preface to Socialist Upsurge in China's Countryside, Foreign Languages
  Press, Peking, 1966, and *Selected Works Vol. 5*, 1977.
  Speech at the CCP Conference on Propaganda Work, Foreign
  Languages Press, Peking, 1966, and *Selected Works Vol. 5*, 1977.
Merwin, Wallace C., *Adventure in Unity: The Church of Christ in China*,
  William B. Eerdmans, Grand Rapids, Michigan 1974.
Miao, Chester, ed., *Christian Voices in China*, Friendship Press, New
  York 1948.
Minjung Theology: People as the Subjects of History, ed., Commission on
  Theological Concerns of the Christian Conference of Asia, Orbis
  Books, Maryknoll, New York 1983.
Moule, A.C., *Christians in China Before The Year 1550*, SPCK, London
  1930.
Munro, Donald J., *The Concept of Man in Contemporary China*,
  University of Michigan Press, Ann Arbor, 1977.

"Nanjing '86: Ecumenical Sharing: A New Agenda, An Ecumenical
  Conference, 14-20 May 1986", Report 10 August 1986.
Ng Lee Ming, "A Study of Y.T. Wu", *Ching Feng*, Vol. 15, No. 1, 1972.
  "Wang Ming-tao – An Evaluation of His Thought and Action",
  Ching Feng, Vol. 16, No. 2, 1973.

"A Bibliography of T.C. Chao and Y.T. Wu", *Ching Feng*, Vol. 16, Nos. 3 and 4, 1973.
"The Promise and Limitations of Chinese Protestant Theologians, 1920-50", *Ching Feng* Vol 21, No. 4, 1978.

Orr, Robert G., *Religion in China*, Friendship Press, New York 1980.
Overmeyer, Daniel L., *Folk Buddhist Religion: Dissenting Sects in late Traditional China*, Harvard University Press, 1976.

Parish, William L. and Whyte, Martin King, *Village and Family in Contemporary China*, University of Chicago Press, 1978.
Urban Life in Contemporary China, University of Chicago Press, 1984.
Paton, David M., *Christian Missions and the Judgement of God*, SCM Press, London 1953.
"R.O.": The Life and Times of Bishop Ronald Hall of Hong Kong, Diocese of Hong Kong and Macao and the Hong Kong Diocesan Association, Alan Sutton Publishing Ltd, Gloucester 1985.

Rees, Dr D. Vaughan, *The Jesus Family in Communist China*, The Paternoster Press, London 1959.
Ren Jiyu, "Investigate Religion and Criticize Theology", *Guangming Ribao* 27.9.1977, translated in *Ching Feng*, Vol. 20, No. 3, 1977.
"The Struggle to Develop a Marxist Science of Religion", *Zhexueyanjiu* No. 4, 1979, translated, *Ching Feng*, Vol. 22, No. 2, 1979.
Ricci, Matteo, S.J., *The True Meaning of the Lord of Heaven*, Translated with Introduction and Notes by Douglas Lancashire and Peter Hu Kuo-chen, S.J.: A Chinese-English Edition ed. Edward J. Malatesta, S.J. The Institute of Jesuit Sources, St Louis 1985.
Robinson, John A.T., *Truth Is Two-Eyed*, SCM Press, London 1979.
Robinson, Lewis Stewart, *Double-Edged Sword: Christianity and 20th-Century Chinese Fiction*, Tao Fong Shan Ecumenical Centre, Hong Kong 1986.

Schurmann, Franz, *Ideology and Organization in Communist China*, California, 1971.
Shen Yifan, "Chinese Christianity in Theological Reflections", *Chinese Theological Review* 1985.
Song, Choan-Seng, *The Compassionate God: An Exercise in the Theology of Transposition*, SCM Press, London 1982.
Soothill, W.E., *The Three Religions of China*, Oxford 1929. Reprinted Curzon Press Ltd, London 1973.

Spae, Joseph J., *Church and China: Towards Reconciliation?*, The Chicago Institute of Theology and Culture, Chicago and Leuven 1980.

ed., "Catholic Life in a Chinese Village", privately circulated paper, December 1981.

"The Catholic Church in China", *Religion in Communist Lands*, Vol. 15, No. 1, Spring 1987.

Spence, Jonathan, D., *The China Helpers: Western Advisers in China 1620-1960*, The Bodley Head, London 1969.

The Memory Palace of Matteo Ricci, Faber & Faber, London 1984.

Su Deci, "Three Tasks in Chinese Theological Work Today", *Nanjing Theological Review*, June 1985, reproduced in *Chinese Theological Review* 1986.

Takenaka, Masao, *God Is Rice: Asian Culture and Christian Faith*, WCC Geneva, 1986.

Thomson, James C., Jr., *While China Faced West: American Reformers in Nationalist China 1928-37*, Harvard University Press, 1969.

Thompson, Laurence G., *The Chinese Way in Religion*, Dickenson Publishing Company Inc., California 1973.

Ting, K.H., "On Christian Theism", 1957, in *Documents TSPM*.

"Religious Policy and Theological Re-orientation in China", address at Toronto School of Theology, October 1979. Reproduced in *CSP Bulletin* No. 13, July 1980.

"How To Study The Bible", *Tian Feng* No. 1, 10 October 1980. Translation Tao Fong Shan Ecumenical Centre, Hong Kong 1981.

"A Call for Clarity: Fourteen Points from Christians in China to Christians Abroad", *Ching Feng*, Vol. 24, No. 1, March 1981.

"The Church in China", Lecture at School of Oriental and African Studies, 14 October 1982, British Council of Churches, London 1982.

"Evangelism as a Chinese Christian Sees It", Lecture at Uppsala University, Sweden, 2 November 1982, *Missiology*, Vol. 11, No. 3, July 1983.

"Another Look at Three Self", translated in *Ching Feng* Vol. 25, No. 4, December 1982.

"A Rationale for Three Self", September 1984, reproduced *CSP Bulletin*, No. 28, November 1985.

And Others: *Chinese Christians Speak Out – Addresses and Sermons*, New World Press, Beijing 1984.

"Theological Mass Movements in China", Lecture at Rikkyo

University, Tokyo, 23 September 1984, *Chinese Theological Review* 1985.

"Inspirations from Liberation Theology, Process Theology and Teilhard de Chardin", *Chinese Theological Review* 1986.

Towery, Britt E., Jr., *The Churches of China: Taking Root Downward, Bearing Fruit Upward*, Long Dragon Books, Hong Kong, Houston and Waco, Second Revised Edition, 1987.

Treadgold, Donald W., *The West in Russia and China, Vo. 2: China 1582-1949*, Cambridge University Press, 1973.

Twitchett, Denis, and Fairbank, John K., General Eds., *Cambridge History of China Vol. 10 Part 1: Late Ch'ing 1800-1911*, Cambridge University Press, 1978.

Weber, Max, *The Religion of China*, The Free Press, Macmillan, New York 1968.

Welch, Holmes, *Buddhism Under Mao*, Harvard University Press, 1972.

West, Charles C. ("Barnabas"), *Christian Witness in Communist China*, SCM Press, London 1951.

Wickeri, Philip L., *Seeking the Common Ground: Protestant Christianity, The Three Self Movement and China's United Front*, PH.D. Dissertation, Princeton, New Jersey 1984. (Forthcoming, Orbis Books, Maryknoll).

"Theological Reorientation in Chinese Protesantism 1949-84, Part I", *Ching Feng*, Vol. 28, No. 1, March 1985.

"Theological Reorientation in Chinese Protestantism 1949-84, Part II", *Ching Feng*, Vol. 28, Nos. 2 and 3, August 1985.

Wu Yaozong, "The Present Day Tragedy of Christianity", *Tian Feng*, April 10 1948, translated in *Documents TSPM*.

"The Significance of Christian Faith in These Critical times", translated by Janice Wickeri in *Ching Feng* Vol. 28, No. 1, March 1985.

Xiao Zhitian, "Some Opinions on Recent Religious Phenomena, Collected Essays on Research in Religion", Shanghai, September 1982, translated by Janice Wickeri, *Ching Feng*, Vol. 26, No. 4, 1983.

Yao Dao Wen Da (Chinese Catechism), translation in *Chinese Theological Review* 1985.

Yang, C.K., *Religion in Chinese Society*, University of California, 1967.

Young, John D., *Confucianism and Christianity: The First Encounter*, Hong Kong University Press, 1983.

Zhao Fusan, "Penitence and Renewal in China", Paton David M.,
    ed., *Essays in Anglican Self-Criticism*, SCM Press, London 1958.
    "A Reconsideration of Religion", *Zhongguo Shehui Kexue*, No. 3,
    1986, translated by Feng Shize in *Social Sciences in China*, Autumn
    1986.
    "The Past Forty Years in Christianity in China", Carino,
    Theresa C., ed., *Three Lectures by Zhao Fusan*, China Studies
    Program, De La Salle University, Manila 1986.
Zheng Jianye, "On the Question of a Church Affairs Organization",
    October 1980, *CSP Documentation*, No. 5, May 1981.
Zhou Enlai, "Selected Writings on the United Front", People's
    Publishing House, Beijing, 1984, pp. 180-7, translated with
    commentary by Philip Wickeri in *CSP Journal*, Vol. 2, No. 1, April
    1987.

The following two books were received too late for consideration in
the text:

Chan, Kim-kwong, *Towards a Contextual Ecclesiology, the Catholic
    Church in the PRC (1979-83). Its Life and Theological Implications*,
    Chinese Church Research Centre, Hong Kong 1987.
Covell, Ralph R., *Confucius, the Buddha and Christ: A History of the Gospel
    in China*, Orbis Books, Maryknoll 1986.

Index

Index

Abahai, 67
Abeel, David, 102
accommodation, mission policy of Jesuits, 58
age (18) of permitted belief, 382
Age of Discovery, 54
Agrarian Reform Law, 196
Ai Niansan, 216
Ai Tian, 62
Alan embassy to Rome, 46
Alan people, 44
alchemy, 54
Alcock, Rutherford, 115
Aleni, Giulio, 64
Allen, Roland, 122, 126
Aloben, 35-6
American Board of Commissioners for Foreign Missions, 102, 126
Amherst, Lord, 96
Amity Foundation, 420-1
    printing press, 422,435
anarchism, 142, 148
ancestor rites, 58, 81,90-1, 171, 323
Anderson, Rufus, 126
Anderson, W.A., 169
Andrew Li, Father, 81
Andrew of Perugia, 43, 45
Anglicanism, 181-2
Anglicans in China, 98, 118
    Zhong Hua Sheng Gong Hui, 118, 127, 133, 147, 182, 200, 234
    Pastoral Letter 1950, 218
Anglo-Chinese College, Malacca, 101
Anhui Province, 236, 428, 447
An Lushan Rebellion, 37

anti-Christian activity, 66, 69, 124, 79-82, 128-9, 164
Anti-Christian Student Federation, 152
anti-Communism, 472
Anti-Confucius campaign, 309
Anti-Rightist Movement, 258-60, 265-6, 326
Aquinas, Thomas, 476
Arnold of Cologne, 45
arrests of Christians, 225, 230, 244, 248-50, 350, 406, 440-1, 443
astrology, 54
Astronomical Bureau, 68-9
astronomy, 54
atheism, 273, 380
Atheism, Chinese Association of, 355
Aurora University, Shanghai, 134
Austin-Sparks, T., 175
Australian Free Churchmen, delegation to China, 271

Bagou City, Rehe (Inner Mongolia), 116
Balthasar, Hans Urs von, 85, 275, 336, 465, 468, 479
Boading City, Hebei, 63, 265
Baoma, Shaanxi, 236
Baotou, Inner Mongolia, 429
baptism, 118, 128, 174, 382, 399, 451
baptism of dying children, 82, 129
    Holy Infancy Movement, 116
Baptist Missionary Society, 135
Baptists, 130, 147, 157, 200, 234
Barber, Margaret, 174

Barcata, Louis, 295
Barnett, Doak, 309
Barth, Karl, 145-6, 473, 475, 480
Bartoli, Daniello, 63
Basel Mission Society, 100
Båstad Ecumenical Seminar (1974), 310
Beifang Army, 140
Beihai City, Guangxi, 481
Beijing, 41, 60, 63, 79, 133, 139, 146, 201, 239, 248-9, 267, 429, 450
Beijing Diocese, 107; *see also* Xiwanzi
Beijing University, 133
belief, statements of, 125, 238
Benedict XV, Pope, 161
Bereczky, Bishop, 227
Bible, 96-7, 296, 377, 435, 465
    Catholic version, 452
    Scofield Bible, 175
Bible smuggling, 376-7
Bible societies, 118, 422
Bible Union (1920), 158
Biblical criticism, 121
"big character poster" (Mao Zedong, 1966), 289
bishops, Chinese Catholic, 161, 190, 278-81, 346, 444, 451
Bishops' College, 347, 451
Bixiejishi (A Record of Facts to Ward off Heterodoxy), 129
Board of Rites, 66
Boxer Uprising, 117, 137-9
Brethren Movement, 174-5
Bridgeman, Elijah C., 102
British Council of Churches Delegation (1983), 383, 423
Buck, John Lossing, 168
Buddhism, 32, 37-8, 89-90, 94, 233, 465-6, 469
    Christianity and, 466-7
Buddhism, Chan School, 89, 180, 334-6, 480
Buddhism, Pure Land School, 32, 94, 467
Buddhist Association, Chinese, 308
Budeyi (I Could Not Do Otherwise), 129; *see also* Yang Guangxian
Buglio, Ludovico, 64

Burns, William Chalmers, 106, 120, 123
Butterfield, Kenyon L., 166

Caihui (vegetarian sect), 130
Cao Shengjie, 352, 436
Capra, Fritjof, 480
Casaroli, Cardinal Agostino, 439
Catechism, Catholic, 451
Catechism, Protestant, 436
Catholic Conference
    First National (17 June-2 August 1957), 250, 277-8
    Second National (5-19 January 1962), 282
    Third National (31 May-2 June 1980), 347
    Fourth National (19-29 November 1986), 451
Catholic Council of the Church of China, First Plenary (May 1924), 161
Catholic Intellectuals, Association of, 452
Catholic National Administrative Commission, 347
Catholic Patriotic Association (CCPA), 249-50, 276, 279, 341, 347-9, 388, 437-9, 443, 445, 449-51, 481
    international contacts, 441-2
Catholic resistance to CCP, 247-9, 276, 443
Catholics and Protestant relations, 110-11, 296, 481
Cattaneo, Lazzaro, 62-3
Centre for Religious Studies, Nanjing, 357
Chalcedon Ecumenical Council, 479
Chang'an (Xi'an), Shaanxi, 34, 39
Changsha City, Hunan, 150, 452
Chao, Jonathan, 319
Chao, T.C. (Zhao Zichen), 179-86, 196, 204, 214, 227, 230, 272, 337, 345, 355, 462
Chaozhou City, Shantou, Guangdong, 123

Chapdelaine, Auguste, 103
Chefoo (Yantai) Convention, 120
Chen Boda, 289, 299, 305
Chen Chonggui (Marcus Cheng),
    232, 263
Chen Duxiu, 149-50
Cheng Jingyi, 156
Chen Guangzu, Father, 280
Cheng Zhiming, Shanghai RAB, 263
Chengdu City, Sichuan, 432, 450
Chen Jianzhen, Bishop Robin, 229,
    272
Chen Mengnan (Zhaoqing
    Evangelization Society), 127
Chen Shizhong, Bishop of Yibin, 447
Chen Sisheng, 214
Chen, Stephen, Father, 441
Chen Wenyuan, Methodist Bishop,
    229-30
Chen Zemin, 273, 353, 396, 425, 462,
    476
Chen Zhimei, 294
Chiang Kai-shek, 154, 164, 167,
    170-2, 224, 472
Chiang, Madame (Song Meiling),
    167
Chifeng City, Inner Mongolia, 447
Children of God, 407
China Christian Council, 350-2,
    394-9, 403, 422-3, 425, 436
China Evangelization Society, 119,
    127
China, founding of People's
    Republic, 187
China Inland Mission, 101, 119-23,
    132, 134, 147, 158, 200, 232
Chinese dress, adoption by
    missionaries, 60, 121
Chinese Jesus Indepedent Church,
    127, 196, 200, 234, 240
Chinese nationalism and
    Christianity, 205, 470
Chinese Repository, 102
Chinese Union, 99-100, 117, 123;
    see also Gutzlaff, Charles
Chongqing City, Sichuan, 173, 232,
    245
Chongzhen Emperor (1628-44), 53

Christian Conference
    First 1954, 232, 239, 243
    Second 1961, 271-2
    Third 1980, 350
    Fourth 1986, 394-6, 436
Christian Conference (Shanghai
    1922), 153, 156, 165
Christian Council of Higher
    Education, 172
Christian Literature Society, 229
"Christian Movement", 153, 181,
    189, 196, 203, 214, 472
Christian Occupation of China, 103, 156
Christian Peace Conference, 425
Christianity and Communism,
    187-91, 274, 331-3, 462-3, 470-6
Chu Chin-ih, 168
Chu, Father Michael, 346
Church Missionary Society, 126-7,
    174
Church of Christ in China, 157, 196,
    200, 234
Church of the East, 34, 40, 47
church order, 117-18, 125, 395
    episcopacy, 399
churches
    closure of, 235, 291
    return of, 344-5, 391
    registration of, 402
Civil War, Chinese, 186-8
Cixi, Empress Dowager, 114, 137-8,
    140
clan councils, Catholic, 108-9
class struggle, 208, 284
Clavius, Christopher Klau, 59
Clement of Alexandria, 463
Clement V, Pope, 45
Clement XI, Pope, 70
Clement XIV, Pope, 80
clergy, Protestant, 128
clocks, European and Chinese, 61
Cloud of Unknowing, 466
Columbus, Christopher, 54
Comintern, 150
"comity" arrangements, 118
Common Programme, The
    (CPPCC), 208, 218, 238
Communion, Holy, 118, 399

Communist Party, Chinese (CCP), 50, 150-1, 154, 165, 186-8, 196-7, 255-8, 261-2, 298-300, 323, 330, 378
Communist Party meetings
CCP Party Congresses: **Eighth**, 256; Third Plenum September 1957, 259; Lushan Plenum August 1959, 262; Ninth Plenum January 1961, 282; Tenth Plenum September 1962, 283; Twelfth Plenum October 1968, 298
Ninth, 290, 298, 305
Tenth, August 1973, 309; Third Plenum July 1977, 325
Eleventh, 325; Third Plenum December 1978, 327; Sixth Plenum June 1981, 380
Community Church, Shanghai, 231, 296, 412
concubinage, 132
Confuciansim, 32, 71-7, 87-8, 148, 179-81, 286, 461, 465
Confucius, 32
Congregatio Immaculati Cordis Mariae (CICM), 116
Congregationalists, 132, 147, 157
Constantini, Archbishop Celso, Apostolic Delegate, 161, 171
Constitution, Chinese (1954), 208; (1978 and 1982), 342-3
control, CCP system of, 212
conversion, Christian, 50, 130
Correct Handling of Contradictions Among the People (Mao Zedong), 210
Cotta, Father Antony, 160
Council of Ephesus (A.D. 431), 34
Council of Seleucia (A.D. 410), 34
Counter-Reformation, The, 57
counter-revolutionaries, suppression of, 223
Cowman, Mrs Charles E., 273
Criminal Law, 342
Criticizing theology and studying religion (1963 Directive), 285
Crusades, The, 54
Cultural Revolution, 49, 118, 163, 211, 282, 284, 288-98, 439

Cultural Revolution Small Group, 289, 298
culture, Chinese, 36
Christianity and, 83-92, 121, 158, 203-4, 333-7, 461-3, 467-70, 481-3

da Gama, Vasco, 55
Dali, Yunnan, 267
Dalian, Liaoning, 418
Damazhan House Meeting, Guangzhou, 409
Dao De Jing, 465, 482
Darby, John Nelson, 175-6
Darwinism, 87, 148
de Besi, Louis-Marie, 108
Declaration of Principles, The Church in China (February 1951), 245
Decree of Nanjing (7 February 1707), 70
Deism, 84
Democracy Movement 1978-79, 327-31, 478
1986, 378
Democracy Wall, 326
Democratic parties, 257
de Morales, Juan Baptista, 64
Deng, Cora (Deng Yuzhi), 214, 236, 272
Deng Pufang, 294, 442
Dengshikou Church, Beijing, 266
Deng Xiaoping, 258-60, 294, 310, 313, 315-16, 325, 327, 376, 378
Deng Yiming (Bishop Dominic Tang), 278, 339, 348, 439-40
Deng Yingchao (Madame Zhou Enlai), 173, 383
Deng Zhaoming, 390
Den, Kimber, Anglican Bishop, 230
denominational divisions, 346
Denunciation Movement, 223-6, 229-30, 243
de Salazar, Bishop of Manila, Domingo, 56
destroy religion, Campaign in Cultural Revolution, 295
de Tournon, Charles, 70
Dewey, John, 152

Dialogues Between Two Friends (tract by Milne), 96
Dingxian, Hebei (literacy project), 165-6
Ding Xiancheng, Dr James, 294
Ding Yuzhang, 272
diocesan restructuring in Catholic Church, 446-7
discrimination against Christians in society, 393
dispensational interpretation of Bible, 175, 477
divination, 90
Document Nineteen (CCP Statement on Religion, March 1982), 384-8, 402
Dominicans, 43, 64, 91, 106
Dong Guangqing, Bishop of Hankou (Wuhan City), 280, 442, 446
Dong Hongwen, 264
Dongsi Mosque, Beijing, 306
Dong Wenlong, Vicar-General Jinan, 276
Dongyang and Yiwu Incident (1982), 408
Dorgon, 67-8
Dou (Du), Simeon, Orthodox Bishop, 201
Double Tenth (Wuchang Uprising), 140
dualism, 32, 73-4, 467-8
Duan Yinming, Bishop of Wanxian, 447
Dufresse, Bishop, 82
Dunhuang, Gansu, 35, 38
Dyer, Maria, 120

East India Company, 96, 102
Eastern Grove (Donglin) Academy, 52, 60
Ecclestone, Alan, 462
Ecumenical Sharing: A New Agenda (Nanjing Conference May 1986), 424
Eddy, Sherwood, 144, 147, 471
Edkins, Joseph, 119
education
    missionary contribution to, 101, 125, 132-4, 152-3, 200, 221
    western style, 133, 142-3
    agricultural, 167-8
    Christian universities, 133-4, 154, 200
    women's, 133
    foreign teachers with Amity, 422
Educational Association of China, 132
"Eight Bans", 381-2
"Eight Diagrams" sect (White Lotus Branch), 130
Eight-Point Internal Policy on Religion, 382
encirclement campaigns (against CCP), 167
Encyclicals: Ad Apostolorum Principis (Pius XII, June 1958), 280
    Ad Sinarum Gentes (Pius XII, October 1954), 249
    Ex Illa die, 70
    Maximum Illud (Benedict XV, November 1919), 161
    Pascendi Gregis (Pius X, 1907), 136
    Rerum Ecclesiae (Pius XI, 1926), 161
Endicott, James G., 188, 309, 311
Engels, Frederick, 286
Enlightenment, The, 55, 87, 464
Enxian County, Shandong, 127
Episcopalians, American, 127
Erasmus, 57
Erastianism, 84
Etchegaray, Cardinal Roger, 347
European expansion, 43, 56
Evangelical Revival, 84, 121
evangelism, 62, 122-3, 131, 134, 143, 169, 174-5, 406, 416
evangelism by migration, 176
excommunication, threat by Vatican, 280
exorcism, 91, 318, 343, 411-12
extra-territorial rights, 86, 102-3, 124

faith healing, 241, 265, 318, 339, 343, 411-15
family cult, 90

family planning, 449
famine
  1849-1850, 104
  1876, 135
  1888-89, 135
  relief, 167
Fan Aishi, Ningbo pastor, 264
Fan Daojiang, Bishop of Nanchong, 447
Fan Wenlan, 288
Fan Wenxing, Bishop of Hengshui, 443
Fan Xueyan, Bishop of Baoding, 441
Fangcheng county, Henan, 406
Fascism, 472
female infanticide, 132
Feng Yunshan, Taiping leader, 104
Feng Yuxiang, the "Christian General", 147
feudal superstitions, 287, 417
Fèvre, Etienne le, 64
filial piety, 74, 81
Five-Anti Campaign, 223, 241
"five characteristics of religion", 262, 379
Fleming, Dr John, 308, 312
foot binding, 131
Ford, Bishop Francis Xavier, 225
Forum on the Study of Religion (1978), 285
Forward Movement (NCC December 1946), 187
Four Basic Principles of CCP, 329
Four Books, 32, 60
Four Clean-ups Movement, 284, 287
Four Modernizations, 310, 326, 421
Four Olds, 289, 295
France, 102-3
Francis, St, 43
Franciscans, 43, 64, 91, 107, 161
Franco, General, 279
Fraser, J.O., 123
"Free China", 173
French protectorate of missions, 115, 159, 161
French Revolution, 84
Friends of the Church in China, 423
friendship, art of, 97, 469

Fu Hezhou, S.J., 441
Fujian Province, 43, 56, 64, 70, 106, 128, 130, 177, 198, 231, 320, 338, 399, 408, 410, 422, 426, 434
fundamentalism, 97, 117, 136, 146, 150, 158, 202, 464, 471
Fu Ren University, Beijing, 134
Fu Tieshan, Bishop of Beijing, 280, 346-7, 442, 449
Fung, Raymond, 270, 337
Fuzhou City, Fujian, 102, 133, 174, 198, 225, 242, 294, 320-1, 432

"Gang of Four", 315
Gansu Province, 430
Ganzhou Nestorian Monastery, Gansu, 41
Ganzhou vicariate, Jiangxi, 166
Gao Gang, 224
Gao Zong, Emperor (649-83), 37
Gao Zu, Emperor (618-26), 35
Garside, Roger, 315
Ge Jingqing, 415
Genghis Khan, 40-1
George (Kerguz), Prince, 44
Gerald, Bishop, 45
Germany, 164
Gernet, Jacques, 74
Gibson, John Campbell, 124-5, 169
Gibson, Tom, 169
Gleyo, Father, 82
Glüer, Winfried, 180, 184
"God's Call to a New Beginning" (Montreal Conference 1981), 423
"God-Worshipping Society" (1847), 104
Gong Pinmei, Bishop of Shanghai, 204, 247, 282, 438, 444, 462
Gong, Prince, 114
Gong Yanshi, 482
Good Words to Admonish The Age (Liang A-fa), 98, 103
Gordon, Major Charles, 105
Great Leap Forward, 260, 282
Gregory of Nyssa, 469
Gu Ren'en, evangelist, 230
Guangdong Province, 99, 128, 162, 323, 427

Guangxi Province, 94, 103, 128, 392, 394
Guangxu, Emperor (1875-1908), 114
Guangyuan, Sichuan, 245
Guangzhou Benevolence Social Service Centre, 418
Guangzhou City (Canton), Guangdong, 39, 95, 102, 127, 133, 146, 173, 321, 409, 420, 432, 451
Guébriant, Vicar-Apostolic of Guangzhou, 161
Guglieminetti S.J., Pierfilippo, 438
Guizhou Province, 431
Guling, Jiangxi, 167
Guo Moruo, 222, 257
Guo Xiumei (Kuo Siu-may), 228
Guomindang (Chinese Nationalist Party), 139, 146, 150, 154, 164-5, 170, 186-7, 189, 207
Guotan, Henan, 236
Gutian District, Fujian, 130
Gutzlaff, Charles, 99-101, 110, 113, 117, 119, 121, 123

Hai Rui, Dismissal From Office of, 283
Haifeng county, Guangdong, 123, 166
Hakka people, 94, 104
Hall, Bishop R.O. of Hong Kong, 89, 145, 181, 228, 301, 468
Hall, Charles Cuthbert, 143
Han Hua, RAB official, 366
Han Wenzao, 352-3, 425, 436
Handan City, Hebei, 429
Hangzhou City, Zhejiang, 42, 120, 339, 344, 392, 432
Hanson, Eric, 250
Harbin City, Heilongjiang, 429
Hardoon Road Assembly, Shanghai, 175
Heaven and Hell, doctrine of, 73
Hebei Province, 165, 249, 429, 443
He Daguan, Catholic woman leader in Nanjing, 108
Hefei City, Anhui, 432
Heilongjiang Province, 391, 429
Henan Province, 322, 381-2, 405, 407, 411

Henry the Navigator, 55
heretical beliefs, 338, 406
Heshen, Minister under Qianlong, 93
heterodoxy, Christianity as, 82, 92, 103, 105, 129-31
Hezheng county, Gansu, 383
Hideyoshi, General, 52
Hohhot City, Inner Mongolia, 429, 451
Holiness Movement, 176
home meetings, 237, 317-19, 322, 352, 386, 392, 400-4
Hong Kong, 101-2, 138-9, 420
Hong Xiuquan (Taiping leader), 103, 130
Honolulu, 139
Honor Oak Fellowship, 175
Hood, George, 100, 123, 157
Hooker, Richard, 182
Hopkins, Gerard Manley, 468
Hu, Joseph, Bishop of Taizhou, 250
Hu Fuming, 326
Hu Shi (Hu Shih), 149
Hu Wenyao, CCPA leader in Shanghai, 247, 282
Hu Yaobang, CCP General Secretary to 1987, 327, 329, 331, 367, 378
Hua Guofeng, 315, 325
Huanan College, Fuzhou, 133
Huang Daozhou, 73
Hubbard, Hugh, 187
Hubei Province, 127, 427
Hui-yuan, 32
humanism and alienation in socialist society, 374, 377
humanism, Catholic, 84
Hunan Province, 120, 128-9, 163, 241, 265, 392, 427
Hundred Flowers Movement, 257-8, 263, 274, 276
Hungarian Church delegation, 425
Hungarian Revolt (1956), 257
Hungary, visit by Protestant Group from China (1958), 271
Hunter, George, 123
Huoqiu county, Anhui, 236

Huxley, Thomas, 148
Huzhou City, Zhejiang, 120
hymnal, Chinese, 400
Hymn to the Holy Trinity, 38

iconoclasm, 91
"inculturation" of the Church, 373, 416, 445, 453, 481-2
Independent Chinese Church (Shangdong), 127-8
India, China Christian Council visit, 425
indigenization, 122, 127, 161-2, 179, 182, 201, 340, 400, 415
indigenous Christian sects, 174-8, 240-4
industrial workers, 151
industry and commerce, reforms, 377
Inner Mongolia, 107, 429, 447
  Catholic Church in, 116
Innocent IV, Pope, 43
Institute for World Religions, Beijing, 263, 285, 354-7
Institute of Christian Virgins, 82
Institute of Religious Studies, Shanghai, 359
international contacts, China Christian Council/TSPM, 227-8, 285, 310-13, 352-4, 420-6
International Missionary Council, 155
Irenaeus, 275, 468
Islam, 34, 55, 87, 233
Islamic Association of China, 306
Italy, fascist influence, 164
Izzard, Ethel, 224

Jade Buddha Temple, Shanghai, 482
James, F.H., 130
James of Florence, Friar, 46
Jansenism, 82, 84-5
January Storm (1967), 289
Japan, 139, 142, 148
  Japanese militarism, 172, 187
Jardine, Dr, 113
Jesuits, 36, 49ff., 58-9, 63, 80, 90, 107-8, 110, 134, 170

Jesus Family, The, 177, 200, 240-1
Jews, Chinese, 62
Ji He, Bishop from Church of the East, 37
Jia Yuming, Principal Spiritual Cultivation Seminary, 265, 271
Jiang Changchuan, Bishop (Z.T. Kuang), 216, 229
Jiang Ping, deputy Director United Front Work Dept., 363
Jiang Qing (Madame Mao), 288, 306, 310, 315
Jiang Wenhan, 172, 355
Jiang Yizhen (Newton Chiang), 266
Jiangmen, Guangdong, 162
Jiangnan area, 107, 128
Jiangning county, Jiangsu, 168, *see* Shunhuazhen
Jiangsu Province, 421-2, 428, 448
Jiangxi Christian Rural Service Union, 167
Jiangxi Province, 162, 393, 422, 427
Jiangxi-Fujian border area, 166
Jiaqing Emperor (1522-67), 93
Jiayu county, Hubei, 265
Jilin Province, 429
Jin Luxian, Assistant Bishop of Shanghai, 442, 450
Jinan City, Shandong, 127, 130, 428, 451
Jing Dianying, founder Jesus Family, 177, 240
Jinggangshen Red Base, 166
Jingpo people, 436
Jinling Women's College, 133, 173
John XXIII, Pope, 281
John of Marignolli, 44
John of Montecorvino, 33, 44
John of Plano Campini, 43
John Paul II, Pope, 346, 439
Johnson, Dr E.H., 312
Johnson, Hewlett (the Red Dean of Canterbury), 228
Johnson, William, 167
Julian of Norwich, 466, 469
Justin Martyr, 476

Kaifeng, Jewish community in, 62

Kaifeng City, Henan, 225
Kan Xueqing, Beijing pastor, 307
Kang Sheng, 289, 299
Kang Xi Emperor (1661-1722), 49, 67, 69, 75, 79, 91, 469
Kang Youwei, 137, 207
Kanzo, Uchimura, 273
Kerait tribe, 41
Khanbaliq (Beijing), 41
Khrushchev, Nikita, 257
Khubilai Khan, 41, 44
Kierkegaard, Søren, 145
kinship relations, 212
Köenig, Cardinal, 347
Korea, 60
   North Korea, 425
   churches in, 429
Korean War, 223, 255
Kumarajiva, 38
Küng, Hans, 466
Kunming City, Yunnan, 431

Lacy, Gene Carleton, 225
Lahu people, 431, 436
Laimbeckhoven, Bishop of Nanjing, 80, 108
Lambeth Preparatory Conference, 228
land ownership, Catholic, 162-3
land reform, 163, 235, 237
   land reform law June 1950, 223
Lanxi county, Zhejiang, 390
Lanzhou City, Gansu, 430
Lapwood, Professor Ralph, 285
Lazarists (Vincentians), 65, 80, 106, 109, 116, 160
Lebbe, Father Vincent, 160, 170, 472
Lechler, Rudolf, 100, 123
Leech, Kenneth, 463
"Leftism", 261, 264, 306, 385, 392, 405, 427
Legge, James, 88, 97, 473
Legion of Mary, 245
Lenin, 364
Leo X, Pope, 56
Letter to Christians Throughout China (issued 1954 Conference), 233
Lew T.T. (Liu Tingfeng), 180

Liang A-fa (Liang Fa), 98, 103, 130, 181, 462
Liang Hao, 287
Liang Qichao (Liang Ch'i Ch'ao), 50
Liangcheng, Inner Mongolia, 447
Liaoning Province, 339, 429
Liberal Christianity, 202
liberal theology, 84, 145, 184, 403, 465, 471; *see* Modernism
Liberation of 1949, 187, 197
Liberation Theology, 452, 478
Li Bo, 80
Li Boyu, Bishop of Zhouzhi, 277, 280
Li Changshu, Hunan TSPM leader, 265
Li Changshou (Witness Lee), 176, 242, 408
Li Daonan, Bishop of Puqi, 280
Li Dazhao (Li Ta-chao), 149
Li Hongzhang, 114
Li Panshi, Bishop of the Jiangmen Diocese, 449
Li Shoubao, General Secretary YMCA, 353
Li Weiguang, Vicar-General, Nanjing, 246, 249
Li Weihan, Director United Front Work Dept., 262, 291, 379
Li Xiannian, President PRC to 1987, 388
Li Yanlin, Shanhaiguan Hebei, TSPM leader, 265
Li Zehou, 334-6, 480
Li Zhicao, one of the "Three Pillars of the Early Catholic Church", 62, 67
Li Zicheng, rebel leader, 53, 67
Lichuan project, Jiangxi, 167
Lijiacan, village, Pucheng, Shaanxi, 430
Lin Biao, 262, 290, 299, 305
Lin Jinshui, 50
Lin Xiangao, meeting point leader in Guangzhou, 409, 412, 414
Lin Xianyang, Bishop Timothy (Anglican Bishop of Beijing), 301
Lingdong Synod, Shantou, Guangdong, 123, 235, 296

Lingwu Nestorian monastery, 37
Linqu county, Shandong, 418
Lisu people, 431, 435
literacy work, *see* Dingxian
literature, distribution of, 99. *See also*
    Bibles; tracts
Little Flock, 128, 174-6, 196, 199,
    202, 240-3, 268, 396, 398, 410, 426-7
Liu Dinghan, Bishop of Cangzhou,
    443
Liu Hede, Father Odoric, 279
Liu Jinghe, Bishop of Tangshan, 443
Liu Junwang, 286
Liu Liangmo, 216, 229-30, 309, 341,
    436
Liu Lingqiu, Editor *The Christian
    Farmer*, 264
Liu Qingfen, Tianjin pastor, 285,
    404, 410
Liu Shaoqi, 211, 258, 260, 294
Liu Yucang, Bishop, 294
Liupanshui, Guizhou, 431
Lobenstine, E.C., 156
Local Church, 176; *see also* Li
    Changshou *and* "Yellers"
London Missionary Society (LMS),
    96, 119, 177
Long March, The, 167
Longjiang county, Yanbian, Jilin,
    418
Longobardo, Nicolo, 63, 65
Longquan county, Zhejiang, 418
Louvain Colloquium (September
    1974), 310
Loyola, Ignatius St, 58, 73
Lu Dingyi, 223
Lu Xun, 142
Lugouqiao (Marco Polo Bridge),
    Incident, 173
Luo Guangzong, 341
Luo Ruiqing, 249
Luo Zhenfang, 185
Luoranggou Seminary, 81
Luoyang City, Henan, 37
Luquan county, Yunnan, 431
Lushan Plenum (August 1959), 262
Luther, Martin, 57, 85
Lutheran Church, American, 220

Lutherans, 147, 200
Lyall, Leslie, 177, 240

Ma Xiangbo (1840-1939), 134
Ma Xingge, Baoding City TSPM
    leader, 265
Macao, 55, 61, 65
MacArthur, General, 221
Mackenzie, Hur, 86
Macquarrie, John, 145
Maigrot, Charles, Vicar-Apostolic,
    Fujian, 70
Maitreya, Buddha, 95
Manichaean Religion, 38, 95
Manifesto, Christian, 215-19, 240,
    242
manual labour, 292
Manzhouguo, puppet regime of, 172
Mao Zedong (Mao Tse-tung), 150,
    166, 181, 187, 206, 210, 255-6, 260,
    263, 283, 287, 290, 299, 305-6, 315
Mao, cult of, 328
Mar Sargis, 42
Mark and Sauma, Nestorian monks,
    47
Martin, W.A.P., 133
Marxism, 87, 150, 170, 190, 194, 328,
    330, 333, 356-7, 373, 462, 473, 475,
    479
Marxism, Society for the Study of,
    149
Mary, cult of, 339
Maryknoll Fathers, 162
"mass line" policy, 209-10
Mateer, Calvin W., 132
materialsm, 473-4, 480
Maurice, Frederick Denison, 145,
    464
Mawei Port, Fuzhou City, Fujian,
    459
Maximus the Confessor, 479
May 16 Circular (1966), 289
May 30 Incident (Shanghai 1925),
    154
May Fourth Movement, 133, 148,
    152, 179, 330, 333, 471
Mazhuang village, Shandong, 177,
    240

Medhurst, Walter, 99
Medical Association of China, 135
Medical Missionary Society, 101
medical missionary work, 101,
    134-5, 226
Medical schools, 135
medicine, holistic, 411; *see also* faith
    healing
Meixian, District, Guangdong, 413
Melanchthon, 273
*Memoir on the Catholic Mission to
    China* (Vincent Lebbe), 161
Mencius, 75
*Message from Chinese Christians to
    Mission Boards Abroad* (1950), 220
Methodists, 132-3, 147, 157, 200, 216
Mi Fei (1051-1107), 89
Miao people, 94, 237, 431, 435
Miao (Miao Qiusheng), Chester, 228
Millennial Kingdom, 55
Milne, William, 96, 98, 101
Ming dynasty, 42, 51-3
Misner, Monsignor, 162
mission stations, 117, 120, 124
missionaries, exodus, 219-26
missionaries, numbers of, 110, 117,
    120, 128, 155, 190, 226
Missionary Conference (1877), 132
Missionary Conference (1907),
    Centenary, 125, 155
missionary doctors, 134
missionary societies, number of,
    117, 155
model workers, Christian, 418
Modernism, 136, 139, 150, 157-9,
    183, 243, 472; *see* liberal theology
modernization, 114, 170; *see also* Four
    Modernizations
Moody, Dwight L., 143
More, Thomas, 57
Morrison Education Society, 101,
    132
Morrison, Robert, 96-7, 101, 110, 132
Möser, Bishop Georg, 346
Mott, John R., 143-4, 155
Mouly C.M., Monsignor, 107
Möye, Jean-Martin, 82
Muhammad, 34

Muslims, *see* Islam
Muslim Rebellions, 106
mutual respect, 233, 269, 345, 397-9

Najran, Nestorian monk, 39
Nanchang City, Jiangxi, 60
Nanchong Diocese, Sichuan, 447
Nanjing City, Jiangsu, 60, 66, 105,
    108, 120, 133, 173, 285, 312
Nanjing Union Theological
    Seminary, 168, 238, 272, 284, 312,
    358, 430-1, 467
Nanjing University, 133
    College of Agriculture, 167
Nantang (Southern Cathedral),
    Beijing, 307
National Council of Churches of
    China, 156, 167, 173, 187, 203, 214,
    218, 228-9
National People's Congress **First**,
    208
    Second, 276
    Fourth, 310, 313
    Fifth, 341; (Fifth Session Fifth
    NPC, 342
nationalism, Chinese, 146
Neo-Confucianism, 33, 52, 71-2, 87,
    114, 469
Nestorian mission, 33ff
    relationship to Chinese culture,
    83
Nestorian texts, 38
Nestorius, 34
Netherlands Missionary Society, 99
New Life Movement, 170-1, 179
New Testament, Delegates Version
    of the, 97
Ng Lee-ming, 182-3
Ni Zan (1301-74), 89
Nian rebels, 105
Nicholas IV, Pope, 44
Nicholas of Cusa, 466
Niebuhr, Reinhold, 146, 473
Nietzsche, 145
Ningbo City, Zhejiang, 102, 120,
    264, 284, 317, 412
Ningdu county, Jiangxi, 166
Ningguo county, Anhui, 428

Ningxia Hui Autonomous Region, 430, 435
Nirvana, 32
Nixon, Richard, 306
Northern Expedition (1925), 154
numbers of Christians, 147, 199-201, 340, 410
Nurhachi (1559-1626), 67

Oboi, Regent, 69
opium of the people (religion), 274, 359, 363, 400
opium trade, 100, 113, 131
Opium Wars, 86, 95, 99, 102-3, 113
ordination, 118, 433-4
Organic Law (passed CPPCC September 1949), 208
Origen, 463
orphanages, Catholic, 116, 129
Ortelius, Abraham, 61
Orthodox Church, Russian in China, 200, 429-30
Orthodoxy, Eastern, 182, 275, 469
Greek Fathers, 464
Otto, Rudolf, 87

Padroado (granted Pope Leo X, 1515), 56
Pan Xiao, 331-2
Parker, Dr Peter, 101
Party members beliving in religion, 387
Passionists, 163
Paton, David M., 145, 153, 196, 204, 226, 294, 311, 453, 475
David and Alison, 219-20
"Patriotic Pledge", 269, 392
patriotism, Chinese, 152, 203, 232-3, 417-20
Paul VI, Pope, 281
Pearl Harbour, 173
Peng Dehuai, 262, 283
Peng Pai, leader Haifeng Soviet, 166
Peng Shengyong, pastor, Community Church Shanghai, 412
Peng Zhen, 288-9
People's Communes, 260

People's Democratic Dictatorship, On (Mao Zedong), 207
People's Liberation Army (PLA), 198
Peregrine of Castello, 45
Philip II of Spain, 56
Philippines, 56
Pi Shushi, Archbishop of Shenyang, 276, 280, 341
Pingquan City, Rehe (Inner Mongolia), 131
Pingyang county, Wenzhou, Zhejiang, 318
Pius XI, Pope, 161
Pius XII, Pope, 190, 249, 279
Political Consultative Conference (CPPCC), 207, 214, 257
Fifth CPPCC, 341-2, 352, 361, 392
Pollio, Monsignor Gaetan, 225
Polo, Maffeo and Nicolo, 44
Polo, Marco, 43
Popular religion, Chinese, 89-92, 98, 411-14
Portugal, 55
Pottier, François, 81
Practice, On (Mao Zedong), 181
Presbyterians, 110, 123-7, 132, 147, 157, 200
Presentadines (Association of the Presentation of the BVM), 108
Prester John, 45
Price, Frank Wilson, 168-9, 223-4, 236
priests, attitudes towards CCPA, 348-9
priests, Chinese, 65, 117, 160, 190, 199
Propaganda Work Conference (12 March 1957), 257
Providence, Sisters of, 162
Pseudo-Dionysius (Denys), 465, 468
Pu Yi (Xuantong Emperor 1908-12), 140, 172
publications, Christian
tracts, 97
other, 234, 435-6; *see* Bible; Hymn Book
Puyang county, Anhui, 236

Qahar Right Wing Front Banner,
Inner Mongolia, 447
Qiang people, 431
Qianlong Emperor (1736-96), 79, 93
Qiao Liansheng, 388-9
Qingdao City, Shandong, 127, 428
Qinghai Province, 430
Quanzhou City (Zaitun), Fujian, 43,
46, 321, 427

railway workers, massacre of, 151
"rectification" campaign (1942 and
1957), 257
Red Guards, 289-91, 293, 299, 318
Red Turban revolt, 94
Red Turbans, 42
Rees, Dr Vaughan, 240
Reform Movement (1898), 137, 142
Reformation, The, 54, 57
English, 281
*Regulations Governing All Organizations
Subsidized with Foreign Funds*
(December 1950), 221
Rehe (Jehol), 131
Reid, Gilbert, 135, 148
relief work of NCC in Second World
War, 173
religion, Marxism's critique of,
see opium, religion
Religion Group, CPPCC, 341
Religious Affairs Bureau (RAB), 213,
263, 292, 296, 307, 344, 366, 388-9,
440
religious policy of CCP, 206, 208,
262, 375, 388
religious sisters, Chinese, 108, 162
convents, 451
Renaissance, The, 54
Ren Jiyu, 285, 343, 354-5, 358
Ren Wuzhi, Director RAB, 389
re-opening of churches, 345
Research on World Religions Journal,
356, 360
Restore Educational Rights
Movement (1924), 154
Riberi, Antonio, Apostolic Nuncio,
245-6
Ricci, Father Matteo, 33, 49-50, 53,

56, 59, 61, 65-6, 72, 76, 87-8, 92, 97,
139, 159-60, 170, 291, 461, 467, 469
Rice Market Street Church, Beijing,
307, 315
Richard, Timothy, 135-6, 148
Rites Controversy, 64, 171, 444, 470
Ritschl, Albrecht, 136
Roberts, Issachar J., 104
Robinson, John, 463
Roman Empire, 86
Rublev, Andrei, 468
Ruggieri, Michele, 59-60
Ruijin county, Jiangxi, 166
Runcie, Dr Robert, Archbishop of
Canterbury, 423
rural policies of CCP, 256, 260-2, 376
rural Protestant communities, 169
rural reconstruction work,
Christian, 165-9
Rural Service Union, North China,
166
rural society, 135, 151
Catholic Church within, 162-3,
206
role of religion, 324-5
Russell, Bertrand, 152
Russell, Maud, 309
Russian Revolution, 148-9
Russo-Japanese War (1904-5), 139

Sailer, Randolph, 146
Salvation Army, 200, 268
Sanmenxia, Henan, 412
Sanshijiazi village, Jianchang
county, Rehe (Inner Mongolia),
131
Sanz, Petrus, 80
Schall, Adam von Bell, 49, 68-9, 139
Scholasticism, 54, 71
science, 51, 136, 334, 480
Searle Bates, M., 121, 146
secret societies, Chinese, 94
sectarian religion, role in Chinese
society, 91, 138
sectarian revolt, 93, 130, 138
sectarianism, Christian, 174-8,
240-4, 375, 398
"seeking the common ground", 210,

Unfinished Encounter

405; *see* mutual respect
Self-strengthening Movement, 114, 137
Semedo, Alvaro, 66
seminaries, Catholic, 450
  illegal seminary, 443
  survey of seminaries 1986, 450-1
seminaries, Protestant (conservative seminary Shandong), 158
  survey of seminaries, 238-9, 431-4
Separation Act, French, 160
Seventh Day Adventists, 200, 234, 268, 398, 427
Shaanxi Province, 64, 187, 236, 430
Shandong Province, 127, 130, 135, 138, 148, 177, 322, 422, 428, 448
Shandong Assembly (Independent Chinese Church), 127
Shanghai, 62-3, 119, 127, 154, 175-6, 201, 231, 239, 247, 264-7, 282, 295, 321, 344, 392, 427, 432, 452-3
Shanghai Commune (1967), 289
Shangquan Island (Xiaquan, Sancian), Guangxi, 59, 163
Shanhaiguan, Hebei, 265
Shantou City (Swatow), Guangdong, 86, 100, 120, 123-4, 126, 169, 296, 427
Shanxi, Province, 64, 135, 176, 429
Shaoyang City, Hunan, 427
Shaozhou City, Guangdong, 60, 65-6
Shen Baishun, Father, 441
Shen Chengen, Editor *Tian Feng*, 352, 436
Shen Derong, 352, 425, 436
Shen Que, 66, 129, 205
Shen, Father Stanislaus, 350
Shen T.K. (Shen Zigao), Anglican Bishop, 231
Shen Tilan, 214
Shen Yifan, Senior pastor Community Church, Shanghai, 231, 477
Sheng Hua Drug Manufacturing Factory, 242
Shenyang City, Liaoning, 432, 450
Sheshan Catholic Centre, Shanghai, 349, 448, 450

Shijia Hutong, Beijing (location Wang Mingdao's church), 177
Shijiazhuang City, Hebei, 429, 443, 451
Shouan, Bishop Basil (Orthodox), 201, 233
Shouguang county, Shandong, 428
Shunan, Anhui, 236
Shunhuazhen village, Nanjing, 168, 236
Shunzhi Emperor (1644-61), 67
Sichan Province, 65, 80, 140, 157, 245, 265, 309, 431, 446
Silk Road, 34
Simao Prefecture, Yunnan, 431
Simeon the New Theologian, 459
sin, concept of, 73, 274, 476
Sin, Cardinal Jaime, Archbishop of Manila, 442
Sino-Japanese War, 115, 137
Sixian county, Anhui, 428
Six-Point External Policy on Religion, 382
Siziwang, Inner Mongolia, 447
Smedley, Agnes, 188
Smith, Arthur H., 87
Smith, George, 123
social and economic problems of China, 376
Social Gospel, 136, 143-4, 181, 183, 471
Socialist Education Movement (1964-66), 283-4, 287
Socialist Upsurge in the Countryside, 256
Société des Missions Étrangères of Paris, 65, 80-1, 107
society, Christian attitudes towards, 121, 135-6, 325, 416-20, 449
Society for the Diffusion of Christian and General Knowledge (SDK), 132, 137
Society for the Diffusion of Useful Knowledge (1834), 102
Society for the Revival of China (1894), 139; *see also* Sun Yat-sen
Society for the Study of Religion (1979), 355

Society of the Divine Word (SVD), 130
Soghdiana, 34
Soloviev, Vladimir, 479
Sorocan (mother of Khubilai Khan), 41
Soviet aid, withdrawal of, 261
Soviet Union, 149-50
Soviets, Chinese, 123, 166, 196
Spain, 55
Spiritual and Theological Institute, Shanghai (1956), 239
"spiritual civilization", 329, 365-7
Spiritual Cultivation Seminary, 265
spiritual dances, 236
Spiritual Exercises (Ignatius Loyola), 73
Spiritual Food Quarterly, 178
spirituality, 86-9, 176, 460, 462-7, 482-3
spiritual pollution, 376-7, 388
Stalin, 257
St John's College, Shanghai, 133
Stockwell, Eugene, 312
Streams in the Desert, 273; *see also* Cowman
Strong, John, 308
Student Christian Movement, 143
Student Volunteer Movement (SVM), 143-4
Su Deci, 395-6
Sun Jingxuan, 328-33
Sun Pengxi, 264, 436
Sun Yat-sen (Sun Zhongshan), 134, 139-40, 146, 148, 150, 208
superstition, 87, 89-90, 261, 330, 358-61, 413, 417
Suzhou City, Jiangsu, 80, 269, 448
syncretism, 38, 411

Taiping Heavenly Kingdom, 94, 99, 104-5, 109, 120, 202, 207, 411
Taiwan, 56, 224, 281, 330, 347
Taiyuan City, Shanxi, 176, 267, 429, 451
Tai Zong, Emperor (626-49), 35-6
Tang Dynasty, 33-40
Tang, Edmond, 339

Tang Shoulin, 242, 436
Tangshan City, Hebei, 429
Tao Qian (373-427), 89
Tao Yuanming (365-427), 180, 185
Tao Zhu, 294
Taoism, 32, 38, 89-90, 95, 180, 334-7, 465, 469, 480, 482
Tawney, R.H., 168
Taylor, Hudson, 101, 106, 110, 119-22
Teilhard de Chardin, 477, 482
Temple of Heaven, 88, 301
"Ten Don'ts", 381-2, 406
Ten Great Relationships (Mao Zedong), 257
Tengzhou, Shandong, 132
Teresa, Mother, visit to China, 442
terms controversy, 63, 97-8
theism and Christian doctrine, 272-6, 459, 463-7
Theological Education Committee (May 1987), 433
theological training (part-time), 434
theology, Chinese, 84-5, 174, 178, 185
  contextual, 415, 476-83
Thomas, St, 31
Thought-reform, 212
  study classes, 231
Three-Anti Campaign against corruption (August 1951), 223
"Three Pillars of the Early Catholic Church", 62
Three Self Patriotic Movement, 127, 153, 203, 217-18, 222, 228-34, 243, 264, 374, 395, 400, 403, 425-6
Three Selfs
  origins, 122, 125-7, 169, 196
  understanding of, 320
TSPM
  Second Plenum March 1956, 234
  Tenth Plenum December 1957, 264
TSPM, *Open Letter to all Christians of China* (March 1980), 350
Tian, Cardinal, Thomas, 190
Tian Feng (Heavenly Wind), 188, 284
Tian Jia (Christian Farmer), 166

Tian Weiyun, Father, 447
Tiananmen Incident, 314-15, 325
Tianjin Municipality, 129, 139, 160, 190, 201, 285, 404, 429, 432
Tianjin, Treaty of, 103, 123
Tianqi Emperor (1620-27), 52
Tibet, 291
Tibetan Buddhism, Society for the Study of, 355
Timur, Emperor, 44
Ting, Bishop K.H. (Ding Guangxun), Anglican Bishop, 85, 158, 189, 228, 244, 270, 274, 285, 297, 300, 308, 341, 351-2, 355, 357, 359, 383, 392, 423, 425, 436, 462, 476, 478
tolerance of China in religious matters, 76
Tongchuan City, Shaanxi, 430
Tongmenghui (United League, founded 1905), 139
Tongwenguan School, Beijing, 133
Tongzhi Emperor (1862-74), 114
Tongzhi Restoration, 137
Tongzhou College, Beijing, 133
Treaty Ports, 102, 106, 119, 123
Trent, Council of, 57, 71
Triad Secret Society, 94, 105, 151
Trigault, Nicholas, 62
Trinity College, Fuzhou, 174
True Jesus Church, 128, 174, 177, 196, 200, 240-1, 265, 320, 398
True Meaning of the Lord of Heaven (Matteo Ricci), 72
Truman, President, 222
Tsu Y.Y. (Zhou Youyu), Anglican Bishop, 229
Ts'ui H.H. (Cui Xianxiang), 216, 231
Tu Shihua, Bishop, 442
Tu Y.C. (Tu Yujing), 216, 230
Tumd Right Banner, Inner Mongolia, 429
Tung, Barnabas, 177
Tutu, Bishop Desmond, 425
Twelve Year Programme for Agriculture, 260
Twenty-one Demands, 148
"Two Whatevers", 326

Uighur people, 39
Unequal Treaties, 102, 124, 131, 179
United Front, 173, 187-8, 255, 261, 341
United Front
    First, 154
    Second, 172, 206
United Front policy, 206-14, 262, 286, 288, 341-3, 360, 367, 379, 416, 438, 481
United Front Work Department, 209, 291
    Seventh National Conference on UFW, 262
United Nations force in Korea, 221
United States of America, 186, 307, 353
unity, church, 232, 267, 345, 350-1, 395, 481
Urad Front Banner, Inner Mongolia, 429
Urumqi City, Xinjiang, 422, 430

Va people, 431, 436
Vagnoni, Alfonso, 64, 66
Valignano, Alessandro, 59
van Melckebecke, Bishop of Ningxia, 281
Vatican, China and, 115, 160, 189, 245-9, 277-81, 439-45, 453
Vatican, Second Council, 281, 445, 452
Vaughan, Henry, 483
Venn, Henry, 126
Verbiest, Ferdinand, 49, 69-70, 139
Verbiest, Theofiel, 116
vicariates apostolic, 115, 161
Virgins, Holy, 82, 108

Walsh, Bishop James E., 282, 307
Wang Dongxing, 326
Wang Hongkui, Shanghai RAB, 389, 392
Wang Hongwen, 289, 310, 315
Wang Jiting, Thomas, Vicar-General Beijing, 307
Wang Liangzuo, Father, 245
Wang Mingdao, 177, 204, 240, 243-4,

256, 374-5, 462
Wang Ruoshui, 377
Wang Shenyin, Anglican Bishop of
    Shandong, 406, 428
Wang Xueming, Bishop of Hohhot,
    280, 447
Wang Yangming, philosopher, 52,
    71, 181
Wang Yuhua, Ms, Beijing TSPM, 307
Wanli Emperor (1573-1620), 52, 61
Wanxian, Sichuan, 446
warlords, 146-7, 164
Watchman Nee (Ni Duosheng), 174,
    176, 178, 241, 374, 400, 477
Way, The (*Dao*), 32, 483
Wei, Isaac, 241, 266
Wei Jingsheng, 328
Wei, Paul, 241
Wei Zhongxian, 52
Wei Zhuomin, Francis, 264
Weijia Village, Jinan, Shandong,
    448-9
Weir, Dr A.J., 197, 402
Weixian county, Shandong, 127
Wenchuan county, Sichuan, 431
Wenling county, Zhejiang, 236, 418
Wenzhou City, Zhejiang, 236, 317,
    392, 408
White Lotus Sect, 82, 93-4, 105,
    130-1, 138, 151, 202, 411
Wickeri, Philip, 127, 242, 359
William of Rubruck, 43
Williams, Samuel Wells, 102
Williams, W.P.W., 226
witness, Christian, 416
Witness Lee, *see* Li Changshou
Wolfe, John R., 226
women, attitudes towards, 81
women's education, 133
World Conference on Religion and
    Peace (1979), 353
World Council of Churches, 196,
    227, 424
world map, Ricci's, 62
World Missionary Conference
    Edinburgh 1910, 155
    Tambaram 1938, 196
World Peace Council, 227

World Student Christian Federation,
    143, 152
World War, First, 144
worship, Catholic, 452
worship, Protestant forms of,
    399-400
Wu, Bishop of Hong Kong, 442
Wu, Empress (683-705), 37
Wu De, 325-6
Wu Gaozi, George, 352
Wu Leiquan, 179
Wu Li, Father, 65
Wu Peifu, 151
Wu Yaozong (Y.T. Wu), 153, 188-9,
    191, 203-5, 214, 229-32, 234, 236,
    242, 263, 272, 294, 309, 341, 345,
    375, 462, 472
Wu Yifang, Ms, 173, 214, 272, 308,
    341, 351
Wu Zong, Emperor (840-46), 38
Wuchang Uprising (Double Tenth,
    10 October 1911), 140
Wuding county, Sichuan, 237, 431
Wuhan City, Hubei, 161, 265, 280,
    283, 288, 427, 446, 450

Xavier, Francis, St, 58-61, 163
xenophobia, 76
Xi Zhongxun, 366
Xiamen (Amoy), Fujian, 102, 123,
    127, 264, 321
Xi'an City (Chang'an), Shaanxi,
    35-6, 430, 451
Xi'an Incident, 172
Xianfeng Emperor (1850), 107
Xianbo Catholic School, Beijing, 418
Xiangchun Street Church,
    Changsha, Hunan, 390
Xiangxiang county, Hunan, 417
Xiao Xianfa, 295, 307, 379, 389
Xiao Zhitian, 332
Xie Fuzhi, 295, 360
Xie Yongjin, 272
Xie Yongqin, 127, 240
Xinfeng Town, Jiangxi, 116
Xining City, Qinghai Province, 431
Xinjiang Autonomous Region, 291,
    355, 361, 422, 430

Xin Qingnian (New Youth Magazine), 149

Xiwanzi Village, Catholic centre in Inner Mongolia, 107, 116; *see* Beijing Diocese

Xu, Bishop Simon, 161

Xu Changzhi, author *Poxieji*, 66

Xu Guangqi, one of "Three Pillars of Early Catholic Church", 62-3, 67, 71, 75-6, 108, 161, 247, 461

Xue Pingxi (Moses Hsiek), Anglican Bishop of Fuzhou, 294, 338

Xuan Zang, Buddhist monk translator, 38

Xuan Zong Emperor (712-56), 37

Xujiahui Catholic Church, Shanghai, 63, 109, 247

Ya Hanzhang, 286-7, 358, 379

Yan, James, 165; *see also* Dingxian

Yan Jiale, Little Flock leader, 341

Yan Yun, 483

Yanan, Shaanxi, 172

Yanbian Korean Autonomous Prefecture, Jilin, 429

Yang Geojian, Bishop of Changde, Hunan, 341, 344, 348, 440

Yang Guangxian, author of *Budeyi*, 68-9, 92, 129

Yang Tingyun, one of "Three Pillars of Early Catholic Church", 62

Yang Weizhong, 294

Yang Xianzhen, 284

Yang Zhen, 287, 356

Yangzhou City, Jiangsu, 120

Yanjing Theological Seminary, 432

Yanjing Union Theological Seminary, 239, 432

Yanling county, Henan, 413

Yantai (Chefoo), Shandong, 127, 176

Yao Guangyu, Joseph, Bishop of Beijing, 346

Yao Wenyuan, 288-9, 310, 314-15

Ye Jianying, 329

"Yellers" (Local Church), 176, 406-8

Yi people, 431

Yi Xuanhua, Bishop of Xiangyang, 280

Yibin Diocese, Sichuan, 447

Yin Jizeng, Beijing pastor, 307

Ying Lianzhi, founder Fu Ren University, 134

Yingshang county, Anhui, 428

Yiyang city, Hunan, 427

Yiyang county, Jiangxi, 427

YMCA, 143-4, 152, 171, 216, 229, 268, 290, 392, 418

Yongjia county, Wenzhou, Zhejiang, 318

Yongzheng Emperor (1722-36), 79

You Ruilin, Fuzhou pastor, 294

Young China Society, 152

Yu Bin, Cardinal, 171, 189, 278

Yu Guozhen, founder Chinese Jesus Independent Church, 127

Yu Peizang, of Zhengzhou, 264

Yü Xian, Governor of Shandong, 138

Yu Xiang, 286

Yüan (Mongol) dynasty, 40-8

Yuan Shikai, 140, 146

Yuan Wenhua, Bishop of Wuchang (Wuhan), 280

Yui (Ru Jikun), David Z.T., 156

Yujiang mission, Jiangxi, 162

Yukinaga, Konishi, 65

Yunnan Province, 431

YWCA, 143-4, 171, 229, 418

Zaili sect, 117, 131

Zeng Guofan, 105, 114, 129

Zhang, Beda, Father, 248

Zhang Chunting, RAB official, 366

Zhang Fuliang, NCC Rural Secretary, 165, 168

Zhang Guangxu, Bishop Michael (Michael Chang), 226, 294

Zhang Haisong, Anglican Bishop in Wuhan, 265

Zhang Jiashu, Bishop of Shanghai, 248, 278, 282, 341, 348

Zhang Jinglong, 433

Zhang Juzheng, Chief Grand Secretary, 52

Zhang Qunqiao, 289, 310, 315

Zhang Shilang, Father, 248, 277

Zhang Xueyan, editor *Christian Forum*, 214

Zhang Zhidong, nineteenth-century reformer, 50

Zhao Fusan, 185, 292, 297, 353, 356, 360-1, 363, 367, 463

Zhao Puchu, President Chinese Buddhist Association, 308, 353, 355

Zhao Ziyang, Premier, 327, 441

Zhaoqing City, Guangdong, 60

Zhaoxian county, Hebei, 429

Zhejiang Province, 128, 231, 234, 317-18, 338, 381, 391, 398, 410, 422, 426, 434

Zhen Wentang, S.J., 441

Zheng He, Ming Admiral, 55

Zheng Jianye, Anglican Bishop, 230, 351, 436

Zheng Shaohuai (Sheffield Cheng), 338

Zheng Weixin, S.J., 65

Zhengde Emperor (1506-21), 51

Zhengzhou City, Henan, 390

Zhenjiang City, Jiangsu, 42

Zhili Clique, 146

Zhong Hua Sheng Gong Hui, 118

Zhongguo Tianzhujiao (Catholic Journal), 446

Zhongshan, Guangdong, 139

Zhou Enlai, Premier, 173, 211, 214, 220, 245, 257-8, 276, 291, 299, 306, 309, 313-14, 360

Zhou Fuqing, pastor in Shanghai, 264

Zhou Qingze, pastor in Xiamen, 264

Zhou Yang, 354, 377

Zhu Hongsheng S.J., 441

Zhu Huayu, Bishop of Bengbu, 447

Zhu Shipu, Orthodox priest in Harbin, 430

Zhu Xi, Neo-Confucian philosopher, 52, 71-2

Zhu Yuanzhang, Red Turban leader, 42

Zhuang Zi, 334-5, 480

Zong Huaide, Bishop of Jinan, 347, 451

Zongli Yamen, 115

Zoroastrian religion, 34

BOOKS BY WILLIAM JOHNSTON

Silent Music

A brilliant synthesis which joins traditional religious insights with the discoveries of modern science to provide a complete picture of mysticism – its techniques and stages, its mental and physical aspects, its dangers, and its consequences.

The Inner Eye of Love

"This is a lucid comparison and exposition of eastern and western mysticism, from Zen to the Cloud of Unknowing, which can do nothing but good all round."

Gerald Priestland, The Universe

The Mirror Mind

"William Johnston continues his first-hand studies of Zen meditation and Christian prayer . . . At his disposal he has had a twofold large and demanding literature. His use of it can be startlingly luminous."

Bernard Lonegan

The Wounded Stag

This book examines the Old and New Testaments, the Christian mystical tradition, the Eucharist and mystical prayer, and explains how these can lead to the resolution of the conflict within men's hearts. A book with a message for today.

Also *available in Fount Paperbacks*

BIOGRAPHIES

Bonhoeffer
Eberhard Bethge

"Will surely stand as the definitive and authoritative work on the subject . . . more than just a fascinating exploration of a hero of our time. It is, as well, a spiritual experience."
Malcolm Muggeridge, The Observer

A Backdoor to Heaven
Lionel Blue

". . . an extraordinary man . . . an extraordinary auto-biography . . . not to be missed."
The Tablet

Audacity to Believe
Sheila Cassidy

A "humorous, warm, moving, terrifying and enormously readable . . . account of one woman's struggle to understand what Christian obedience demands . . ." in South America.
The Baptist Times

Thomas More
Richard Marius

"A biography as good as this one – uncluttered, brightly written, yet scrupulous in its use of sources – brings a complex man out of romantic legend and puts him squarely in the clear light of history."
Times Educational Supplement

Fount Paperbacks

Fount is one of the leading paperback publishers of religious books and below are some of its recent titles.

- ☐ GETHSEMANE Martin Israel £2.50
- ☐ HIS HEALING TOUCH Michael Buckley £2.50
- ☐ YES TO LIFE David Clarke £2.95
- ☐ THE DIVORCED CATHOLIC Edmund Flood £1.95
- ☐ THE WORLD WALKS BY Sue Masham £2.95
- ☐ C. S. LEWIS: THE MAN AND HIS GOD
  Richard Harries £1.75
- ☐ BEING FRIENDS Peter Levin £2.95
- ☐ DON'T BE AFRAID TO SAY YOU'RE LONELY
  Christopher Martin £2.50
- ☐ BASIL HUME: A PORTRAIT Tony Castle (ed.) £3.50
- ☐ TERRY WAITE: MAN WITH A MISSION
  Trevor Barnes £2.95
- ☐ PRAYING THROUGH PARADOX Charles Elliott £2.50
- ☐ TIMELESS AT HEART C. S. Lewis £2.50
- ☐ THE POLITICS OF PARADISE Frank Field £3.50
- ☐ THE WOUNDED CITY Trevor Barnes £2.50
- ☐ THE SACRAMENT OF THE WORD Donald Coggan £2.95
- ☐ IS THERE ANYONE THERE? Richard MacKenna £1.95

All Fount paperbacks are available through your bookshop or newsagent, or they can be ordered by post from Fount Paperbacks, Cash Sales Department, G.P.O. Box 29, Douglas, Isle of Man. Please send purchase price plus 22p per book, maximum postage £3. Customers outside the UK send purchase price, plus 22p per book. Cheque, postal order or money order. No currency.

NAME (Block letters)_____

ADDRESS _____

_____

_____